MEDICAL ETHICS AND THE LAW

MEDICAL ETHICS AND THE LAW
Implications for Public Policy

MARC D. HILLER

University of New Hampshire
School of Health Studies

BALLINGER PUBLISHING COMPANY
Cambridge, Massachusetts
A Subsidiary of Harper & Row, Publishers, Inc.

International Standard Book Number: 0-88410-707-8

Library of Congress Catalog Card Number: 81-3890

Printed in the United States of America

Library of Congress Cataloging in Publication Data

Main entry under title:

Medical ethics and the law.

  Bibliography: p.
  Includes index.
  Contents: Medical ethics and public policy / Marc D. Hiller—
Ethical aspects of the right to health care / Robert M. Veatch—
Ethics and health planning / Michael J. O'Sullivan, Marc D.
Hiller— [etc.]
  1. Medical ethics. 2. Medical policy—United States.
3. Medical laws and legislation—United States.
I. Hiller, Marc D.
R724.M293   174'2   81-3890
ISBN 0-88410-707-8 (cloth)   AACR2
ISBN 0-88410-935-6 (paperback)

In Memory

Rosamond and Meyer Hiller

CONTENTS

LIST OF FIGURES

LIST OF TABLES

FOREWORD

At no time in the development of our health care system has it been more important for clinicians, administrators, educators, and government officials to consider the ethical implications of their decisions. The astonishing power of modern medicine and the complex institutional settings in which it is practiced raise in new and complex ways questions of what is just, what is good, and what is right about the behavior of individuals and institutions. Whether to have continued the life support system that kept Karen Quinlan alive in a seemingly irreversible coma or to have required the parents of the leukemia-stricken child Chad Green to place their son, against their will, in the hands of physicians at the Massachusetts General Hospital are dramatic examples of such questions—fundamentally questions not only of who shall live but of who shall decide who shall live.

Moreover, no longer are the ethical values underlying health care decisions just questions of individual choice—as, for example, the obligations of physicians in prolonging life. They have also become questions of institutional and governmental policy, as health care delivery has become organized in formal organizations, such as in hospitals, and as it has become a public good, as reflected in federal programs such as Medicare and Medicaid. The Congress of the United States, with the concurrence of former President Richard M. Nixon, by enacting the Social Security Amendments (PL 92-603),[1] which pay for their care, has even decided that the victims of a particular disease (namely, chronic renal disease) would be kept alive through hemodialysis.

The exalted study of ethics, once limited to the interest of philosophers and academicians, has left the halls of academia and become an unavoidable concern of most, if not all, who work in the field of health care. Human conduct has always had ethical consequences, but never before have physicians, administrators, policymakers, and other members of the health world had to face so explicitly the ethical implications of their decisions and behavior.

This book is, therefore, especially timely, and it is well suited to the needs of the day. It is addressed to a wide audience of clinical practitioners, administrators, and policymakers in public and private institutions as well as to undergraduate and graduate students. In exposing readers to a broad perspective of theories, analytical tools, and actual life situations, and attempting to promote a basic understanding of the ethical issues involved, little technical or professional jargon is used.

The book, consisting of twenty-one separate essays written by a range of authors from professional and academic fields, takes an inter- and multidisciplinary approach to its subject. Much of the literature on medical ethics focuses upon the ethical issues surrounding medical practice and draws predominantly from philosophical sources. In *Medical Ethics and the Law*, the reader hears from a wide range of writers, including economists, political scientists, health administrators, theologians, physicians, and lawyers, in addition to philosophers. The book also approaches its subject with a broad definition of ethics. Yet each essay deals with a specific topic and in the aggregate provide readers a comprehensive, if not complete, sampling of the spectrum of ethical issues. In addition, the authors' contributions vary from considerations of individual choice to ethical questions at a societal level embedded in matters of public policy and thus present a macro as well as a micro approach to their respective subjects. The book's consideration of questions of public policy is unique. Heretofore, little has been done in this area, except for the examination of research policies involving the use of human subjects and the examination of approaches to principles of justice in plans for the distribution of health care, as in the analysis of alternative proposals for national health insurance.

Unlike most books of essays, its authors' contributions to medical ethics and public policy are almost all original essays, written for and integrated into the five sections of the book. For this, the editor is to be congratulated.

As with most human matters, ethical questions are rarely solved: They are lived with. It is how we do so that makes the difference. Few comfortable answers are, therefore, to be found in books or experience. This in no way diminishes the need for inquiry, for the ethical issues we increasingly face as members of the health care community are inescapable. Raising and subsequently analyzing the serious ethical questions associated with modern health care are essential steps in making the hard choices that confront us in the decades ahead. As Sissela Bok wisely observes, "The need for ethical inquiry is great. And, the choices made—individually and socially— in the biomedical areas are moral choices at bottom. But the recognition that this is so only sharpens the question of what tools exist for making such choices wisely."[2]

To be a moral person, or a moral institution, or a moral government is not necessarily to be right, or good, or fair, but to consider thoughtfully the ethical implications of the choices before us and to try to act accordingly.

Basil J.F. Mott

Durham, New Hampshire
August 1981

NOTES

1.   Social Security Amendments of 1972, Public Law 92–603, §299I, 42 USC 401 (October 30, 1972).
2.   Sissela Bok, "The Tools of Bioethics," in Stanley Joel Reiser, Arthur J. Dyck, and William J. Curran, *Ethics in Medicine: Historical Perspectives and Contemporary Concerns* (Cambridge, MA: The MIT Press, 1977), p. 138.

ACKNOWLEDGMENTS

Like other published works, particularly those dependent on a wide range of collaborators, this book has a history; like most authors, this one is deeply indebted to countless friends and colleagues for helping this book to become a reality. The original idea for this work arose from a series of related, although somewhat disparate, events.

In the early 1970s, while working on a variety of health policy issues, I realized the need for a greater integration of ethics and human values in health care. While at the University of Pittsburgh (Pitt) Graduate School of Public Health, I was afforded the opportunity to pursue study in the area and to develop professional educational seminars on ethics and health policy for long-term care professionals from throughout the Commonwealth of Pennsylvania. These activities stimulated further discussion of ethical issues and decision-making among health professionals, students, and interested consumers–patients. Being at a major university medical center, the rich mixture of academia and practicing health professionals in a stimulating urban environment contributed untold wealth to the exploration and elaboration of ideas.

Concurrently, I attended several national and regional conferences and workshops relating to general and specific bioethical issues and concepts. Coming from an interdisciplinary field such as public health, I somewhat naturally developed strong linkages with colleagues who, while sharing similar interests and health care concerns, were grounded in a wide range of disciplines, including medicine and nursing, economics, political science, philosophy, and law. In addition, while participating in various conferences and workshops I met and exchanged ideas with some of the early leaders in the field. As my appreciation and comprehension of ethics developed, my awareness of a deficiency in applying basic ethical principles and human values to many health policy and individual medical (clinical) care decisions affecting life and death increased.

In 1977, as chairperson of the Western Pennsylvania Public Health Council, Inc. (WPPHC), I was responsible for planning the organization's annual meeting. From that effort evolved the Fifteenth Annual WPPHC Seminar, **Medical Ethics and the Law**. Rather than editing its *Proceedings*, I chose to collect a series of essays that would analyze many of the ethical implications of the medical, social, and legal decisions affecting the health care system in the final decade of the twentieth century.

Among the earliest and most significant supporters of this undertaking was Annabelle L. Kleppick, director of the Long Term Care Unit at Pitt's Graduate School of Public Health. For the opportunity, the challenge, and above all else her relentless encouragement, I will always be grateful. Admittedly, however, my full appreciation did not come until the delivery of the final manuscript to the publisher! Additional colleagues at Pitt provided the incentive, constructive criticism, and breadth of experience and expertise without which I might never have undertaken this task. For this, deep appreciation is extended to M. Allen Pond, acting dean of the graduate school; Rabinder K. Sharma, assistant professor of health services administration at the school; and Joseph C. Morreale, associate professor of economics at Bard College.

Following my move to the University of New Hampshire (UNH), even before all the contributing authors were confirmed, new support for this endeavor emerged from colleagues in the Health Administration and Planning Program in the School of Health Studies. For their special efforts and support, I am deeply indebted to Basil J. F. Mott, dean of the School of Health Studies; and Lee F. Seidel, chairperson of the program. In addition, for their continual scholarly stimulation, optimism, and jokes during trying times, my colleagues and friends—John W. Seavey, Michael J. O'Sullivan, David E. Berry (now at the University of Kentucky)—are thanked.

Obviously, as in any undertaking that is so dependent on the commitment of others for their talents, knowledge, time, and patience, I extend my heartiest appreciation to the contributing authors. Without their acceptance of the challenge to collaborate and overcome many traditional barriers associated with such an interdisciplinary endeavor, this work could never have become a reality.

Furthermore, I owe significant gratitude to a group of people whose contributions in many ways made possible the actual completion of this book. Maureen E. Molloy assisted in many ways, serving as a sounding board for ideas, professional colleague, and friend. Carol Franco at Ballinger Publishing Company remained supportive at times when even I had doubts whether there would be any light at the end of the tunnel. In addition, I remain indebted to those who offered invaluable technical assistance, including Michaele L. Canfield, Patricia T. Hartzell, Noreen Brophy-Gaetjens, Cheri Guerrero, Kristine J. Bachinski, Donna Labrie, and the fine staff at Ballinger.

Finally, for the countless others who in many special ways helped assure the completion of this book, I extend my sincerest appreciation. And for the many who for the past two years continually asked me, "Well, is it done yet?" hopefully, the product proves to be worth the waiting. Obviously, for the strengths identified in the work, all those who gave of themselves are to be congratulated; for the weaknesses, I assume responsibility.

                                              Marc D. Hiller

Durham, New Hampshire
August 1981

NOTE TO READERS

On May 4, 1980, the educational responsibilities and functions of the U.S. Department of Health, Education, and Welfare (DHEW) were removed from this department and a new cabinet-level department was created, the U.S. Department of Education. With the elimination of Education from DHEW, it was renamed the U.S. Department of Health and Human Services (DHHS). Hence, during the editing of this volume, reference is made to DHHS except in cases of those DHEW activities dated before the reorganization. For example, when talking about current federal regulations, most references are to DHHS regulations even though they may have been promulgated initially by DHEW (i.e., enforcement of current health and welfare regulations regardless of the date they became effective is now the responsibility of DHHS).

INTRODUCTION

1 MEDICAL ETHICS AND PUBLIC POLICY

Marc D. Hiller, Dr.P.H.

As the twenty-first century approaches, difficult choices and critical decisions confront all people. No area demands more attention than the state of health and health care. Never before has the health care system in the United States been challenged by so many forces both from the external environment and from within. Traditionally, many of the externalities have guided the changes through incremental shifts, largely precipitated by the nation's economic condition. However, during the last decade, increases in public demands and expectations, tremendous advances in medical technology, spiraling health care costs, scarce resources, and shifting values have prompted public questioning of the future of the system. The unique set of conditions, coupled with recent dramatic changes in political leadership and governance, pose challenges for policymakers and health professionals. As the alternative options are clarified, it is likely that the patching of weaknesses or deficiencies may no longer suffice: Bold, innovative, and sensitive choices are going to have to be made. The nature of these decisions will require actions at both societal and individual levels.

But regardless of level or specific action, the major unanswered questions remain: At what costs—economic, social, ethical—will the decisions of the 1980s and 1990s be entertained? These issues require transcending many of the domains that traditionally have remained untouched by public intervention, not the least of which

3

are the delivery of personal health care services, the practice of medicine and the nature of the physician–patient relationship, and the use of human subjects in biomedical and behavioral research. There is no longer opportunity to ask whether change ought to occur: The question now is how forthcoming policies and programs affecting health care will be made and developed.

With the multitude of complex issues confronting the health care system, there is a need to examine the ethical theories and values employed in the evolution and the later evaluation of health policies. Furthermore, it is increasingly important to maximize the use of ethical analysis in making hard choices and limiting the confusion that arises over ethical decisions on a societal and individual level. The purpose of this chapter is to suggest, and then further to examine, the application of ethics to health care decisionmaking in light of many related disciplines. In pursuing this objective, the discussion is divided into three major sections.

The first part investigates the field of medical ethics, including its derivations and major concepts and the related disciplines that also demand value considerations. In light of the relationships shared by ethics and related disciplines, this section concludes with an examination of the contribution of ethics and related disciplines in the evolution of policy outcomes. The second section focuses on possible models for analyzing health policy from an ethical perspective and proposes a series of guides for ethical decisionmaking. The chapter concludes by highlighting five broad health policy areas in which key ethical issues confront U.S. health policy in the 1980s.

MEDICAL ETHICS AS A FIELD OF STUDY

What Is Medical Ethics?

Largely due to the sudden surge of interest in ethics and health care and the plethora of public materials on related issues over recent years, many definitions of medical ethics have evolved. Terms such as bioethics, health ethics, and research ethics, among others, are commonly interchanged with the oldest of terms, medical ethics. While some authors circumscribe specific differences of one term versus another, little can be gained by an entrapment in a debate over semantics, particularly among health policymakers and practitioners.

However, on review of the literature, it is important for those engaged in the field, albeit for primarily academic and historical purposes, to understand the basis for much of the differentiation. Bioethics constitutes the broadest, most encompassing approach to the entire "branch of applied ethics which studies practices and developments in the biomedical fields."[1] Embodied within this relatively new schema are other popular terms, including medical ethics, health ethics, and research ethics.

The oldest and most popular component of bioethics is medical ethics. Since the time of Hippocrates, medical ethics has provided the fundamental ethical standards governing the practice of medicine, at least with respect to the clinical treatment of patients. From such hallmarks as the Hippocratic Oath[2] and the original Code of Ethics of the American Medical Association[3] in the mid–1800s, codes of ethical conduct have evolved for most of the health professions. More recently, patients and the institutions in which they are treated have begun to develop their own lists of expectations.

Some of the more popular issues commonly assigned under the rubric of medical ethics and reflecting the traditional orientation to individual clinical issues are (1) the physician–patient relationship in general, (2) patient confidentiality and privacy, (3) informed consent, and (4) truth telling. Largely as a result of the failure of health professionals to uphold many of these ethical norms, the 1960s and 1970s saw the emergence of patient rights as an issue. The first and most notable patients' bill of rights was promulgated by the American Hospital Association (AHA) in 1972[4] and was followed not long thereafter by the publication of the American Civil Liberties Union's handbook, *The Rights of Hospital Patients*.[5] More recent use of the term medical ethics reflects the inclusion of broader policy issues related to health care in addition to the more standard, traditional interpretation of the term focusing on individual clinical issues.

The term health ethics has come into vogue primarily in an effort to broaden the interpretation of medical ethics. Since medical care may be defined as a subset of health care, which encompasses social, economic, and political dimensions, some suggest that use of the term medical ethics constitutes an inappropriate reference to a more distinct and limited area of applied ethics. Once again, differentiation between medical ethics and health ethics is mostly dependent on individual interpretation. Some argue that health ethics more aptly reflects such public interest topics as policymaking related to the allocation of scarce medical resources and the social implications of medical practices and research at a societal level. For this reason, the distinction of health ethics from medical ethics might allow the differentiation of two levels of ethical analysis—the micro level associated with what has been defined as medical ethics or those associated with individual patient care issues and the macro level concerned with broader health (and public) policy issues affecting the public at large.

One of the newest divisions of bioethics is research ethics. Due to the advent of major technological advances, research ethics created a need to establish codes for the protection of human subjects. The first major code was developed in the late 1940s as a result of objectionable research practices conducted by Nazi scientists during World War II. Since the formulation of the Nuremberg Code,[6] as it has become known, other significant international proclamations[7] and sets of federal regulations[8] have ensued. Research ethics also can be discussed at two broad levels—the micro, or individual level, that deals with practices of individual researchers and their use of human subjects; and the macro, or societal level, that focuses on the development of sound public policies to govern all research practices and investigates the long-range consequences of biomedical research and technology.

Even from this discussion of the various terms, it is clear that at best, considerable overlap exists. For example, in decisions regarding the allocation of scarce resources, which usually falls under the rubric of health ethics, do not such considerations impinge on the individual choice of medical treatments (e.g., organ transplants, renal dialysis, advanced life support systems) that would be considered under the more traditional rubric of medical ethics. Furthermore, when does the administering of a new experimental drug to an individual with a particular disease (e.g., angina, leukemia, diabetes) constitute therapeutic treatment (i.e., a medical ethics decision) rather than research in need of human subjects (i.e., research ethics consideration).

Hence, due to its being both the oldest and most widely accepted of the terms, particularly among health professionals, and the fact that it can be defined very broadly in the context of twentieth century developments, this author chooses to use the term medical ethics over the others. Whether one accepts this reasoning or adopts another term is not overly significant so long as meanings are understood. With the magnitude of the issues of life and death before the public today and the need for their discussion and analysis, these terms should be considered close enough in meaning so as not to warrant misdirected attention in semantical debates.

For purposes of this study, medical ethics is defined as that branch of applied ethics involved with the application of values in the formulation of judgments concerning problems in the practice of medicine; the planning for and delivery of health care; and the conduct of medical, behavioral, and biological research. More simply, it constitutes the application of a branch of the discipline of philosophy, known as ethics, to health and medical care issues. It provides an opportunity for health care professionals, in concert with philosophers, legal scholars, policymakers, clergy, and others (not the least of which should be the public at large), to examine the critical choices that lie before mankind. Fruitful discussions of the issues ought to help resolve differences and explore new alternatives for confronting the challenges of tomorrow's medical sciences. Furthermore, the debates engendered by discussions of many of the controversial ethical dilemmas in health care are not meant to be knockdown arguments; rather, they are designed to provide a forum for rational objective analysis—a systematic examination of the issues leading to sound decisionmaking. Where choices are not immediately forthcoming, these discussions should at least offer further illumination of what ought to be done under given circumstances and conditions.

Due to the variety of principles, rights and obligations, and values analyzed or appealed to in discussions of such issues, there is little likelihood that intricate arguments will always lead to the identification of basic common denominators. However, three dominant theories—justice, beneficence, and self-determination—precipitate most discussions.[9] However, seldom do difficult questions involving them ever reach unanimous resolution due to the varying priorities assigned to opposing theories in specific situations by different actors. Each of these themes and their respective incongruities are examined later in this chapter.

Basic Ethical Principles and Concepts

Macro-Micro Orientation. Before attempting to illustrate the application of ethics to policy analysis, it is important to understand several basic ethical concepts and principles used in analyzing health policy. First, ethical issues related to health care can be divided among those that address problems at a societal level (i.e., macro orientation) and those directed at concerns on the individual level (i.e., micro orientation). Issues considered societal are those that represent broad social policies, usually involving governmental action predicated on public demand or need. In contrast, at the micro level, the issues are those that people commonly encounter at a personal level during the course of a lifetime, frequently relating to professional–patient relationships and decisions regarding medical treatment. Although areas often overlap and many philosophical principles can be applied at both the macro and micro levels, these issues by nature lend themselves to such a differentiation for analytical purposes. Table 1–1 shows some of the major principles and issues that are addressed in health care discussions.

Justice and the Right to Health Care.   The concept of justice evolves almost inevitably in the discussion of medical ethics, particularly in light of an increasing scarcity of medical resources. Justice can be defined as fairness and is closely associated with need. Hence, discussions of alternative means for the macroallocation and microallocation of limited resources generally are grounded in a theory of justice.

Distributive justice involves the distribution of social benefits and burdens. Thus, payments of taxes or health insurance premiums represent burdens, whereas the receipt of welfare checks or Medicare payments constitutes benefits. In a macro sense, the development and implementation of health planning and other systemwide endeavors help assure equity in the health care system. Two major dimensions arise in these efforts: (1) an economic component that suggests how scarce resources can be allocated most efficiently to satisfy human wants and needs; and (2) several different ethical positions designed to ensure distributive justice in the distribution of these resources. In many ways, these two dimensions are more or less inseparable.

Although ethicists suggest several theories of justice, little consensus exists as how to distribute the benefits. According to Beauchamp and Childress, "Recent literature on distributive justice has tended to focus on considerations of fair *economic* distribution, especially unjust distributions in the form of inequalities of income

Table 1-1. Principles and Issues in Medical Ethics.

	Micro Level	Macro Level
Target Level	Individual (professional, institutional, or patient)	Societal (public policy)
Major Philosophical Themes and Principles	Distributive Justice (principles governing the allocation of limited, costly patient care technology and treatment) Beneficence (principle governing the goals of medical practice) Self-determination; Autonomy (principle governing the rights of personhood)	Distributive Justice (principles governing the allocation of scarce public resources in the best interest of society as a whole)
Examples of Applicable Health Issues	Patient rights Informed consent Confidentiality and privacy Truth telling Respect for persons Right to die Use of extraordinary means of life support Paternalism	Public financing of health care (e.g., national health insurance) Policy governing research involving human subjects Health planning and regionalization of resources Definition of life and death (i.e., medical standards)

between different classes of persons and unfair tax burdens on certain classes."[10]

Deeply embedded in almost all discussions of justice is the question of whether (and to what degree) there is or should be a right to health care. Barring the existence of limited legal rights, the ethical concept of a right to health care is central to any discussion about justice. If no right exists from an ethical standpoint, then there are no justifications for guaranteeing health care to ensure justice. Hence, arguments about alternative theories of justice must be predicated on the acceptance of certain degrees of rights to the benefit of health care.

Veatch presents four different principles of justice related to the question of an individual's right to a certain level of health care—the entitlement principle, the utilitarian principle, the Rawlsian (maximin) principle, and the egalitarian principle—and illustrates how each would apply to establishing a national health policy for the distribution of health care.[11] Fried proposes a fifth intermediary, one that draws upon several of the others and is called the decent minimum principle.[12]

More recently, Veatch[13] and others[14] have expanded the discussion of opposing theories of justice and equity rights in public policy issues related to the macroallocation of resources. Undoubtedly, as public resources become more scarce, the problems are going to become even more acute. In that light, caution is recommended to assure a continued ethical dimension in the deliberations as opposed to depending solely on an economic one.

Theories of justice are also important in analyzing problems of microallocation of scarce resources. At this level, the demands for certain costly medical equipment and treatments are greater than existing supplies. Hence, competitive environments are created in which decisionmakers, usually other than the patients involved, must allocate life-saving resources to some and thereby allow others to die. Although a variety of means on which to base such decisions exist—for example, complex criteria systems,[15] random selection models,[16] and refraining from treatment—problems in assuring justice remain. Should every patient in need have an equal right? Obviously, due to immediate needs and limited resources (e.g., kidney dialysis machines, organ transplants), choices must be made. Many of the theories associated with macroallocation are useful in cases requiring microallocation decisions, particularly justice. For example, should certain individuals on the basis of given characteristics be awarded treatment as opposed to others (i.e., are some more entitled than others)? Should everyone have an equal chance (i.e., be selected randomly)?

Since questions associated with microallocation usually fall closer to home, personal factors make decisionmaking more difficult. Hence, it becomes even more problematic to address Childress' question: "Who Shall Live, When Not All Can Live?"[17] In an effort to answer many of these questions on an individual level, there is a growing popularity among hospitals to establish special bioethics committees to address more ethically certain life and death issues.

Beneficence and Nonmaleficence. The principle of beneficence serves as the ethical foundation of the profession of medicine and the other health professions. Embodied in numerous professional codes, historically dating back to the Hippocratic Oath (1857), it places the duty "to do good" on members of the health care team. Translated into everyday language, this means that the priority goal of the health professions is to actively pursue the positive state of health among their patients.

Closely related to beneficence is the duty of nonmaleficence, which means above all, "do no harm." In addressing the responsibilities of physicians, it reflects the minimum expectation of providing no harm (or risk of it) to patients, whereas the principle of beneficence constitutes the more ideal, and difficult, responsibility of actually benefiting patients.

Possibly, the area of discourse most often associated with nonmaleficence revolves around the issue of killing and letting die. In clarifying the distinction between the two terms, it becomes clear that in medical practice, the former is prohibited while the latter is both authorized and becoming more common. Many terminally ill and/ or suffering patients seek death with dignity and not to be maintained indefinitely through extravagant life support techniques and machines. While such patients may in the context of confronting unbearable pain and poor prognosis ask to be allowed to die, they should not expect assistance in the active process of being killed. A complex and widely disparate literature has emerged over recent years addressing this topic.[18] Suffice it to say in the context of introducing the principle of nonmaleficence that although opinions differ, health professionals generally are not expected to cross the line between active (i.e., killing) and passive (i.e., allowing to die) euthanasia.

In dealing with the subject of death and dying other complicating issues emerge, including what constitutes extraordinary means of life support. The differences between ordinary and extraordinary treatment remains quite vague and is receiving attention in both the medical and the legal (and judicial) communities.

Finally, possibly the most controversial question in cases of terminal conditions is, Who should decide? Obviously, the principle of autonomy requires that any competent person be allowed to make this type of decision. In the absence of competence, there are various proposed alternatives—the family, the courts, the clinicians involved, hospital bioethics committees. In the end, however, the principles of nonmaleficence and beneficence demand that the patient's physician uphold that which is in the best interest of the patient—particularly should there be conflicting opinions or possible evidence of abuse.

With respect to beneficence, the health professional is obligated to do more than refrain from the noninfliction of harm—that is, there is a duty to do good. As might be expected, fulfillment of this directive requires a careful weighing of potential risks and harms against the possible benefits to be gained from certain therapies. Since many treatments require certain risks and costs, the physician must weigh all costs, benefits, and alternatives carefully to determine the most suitable therapy. Then, the principle of autonomy dictates their explanation to the patient in a comprehensible manner.

The principle of beneficence is particularly important when considering any form of biomedical or behavioral research involving human subjects. In addition to the rights of such subjects to informed consent and privacy, this principle mandates a careful evaluation of potential benefits, risks, and costs to the research subject. If there is no therapeutic benefit for the subject, then analysis should also reveal minimal risk and the potential for social gain as a result of the research.

Furthermore, the principle of beneficence requires that except in special well-defined types of situations, physicans are not to engage in paternalism. In summation, careful and strict adherence to the tenets of beneficence and nonmaleficence—whether viewed independently or as two ends of the same continuum—helps assure high quality standards of medical care and limits potential legal liabilities from arising.

Autonomy. Autonomy, or the right to self-determination, constitutes one of the most essential ethical principles. As a form of personal liberty, autonomy is grounded in the tradition of human rights
and serves as the central element from which most of the so-called
patient rights evolve.

From a medical ethics perspective, autonomy serves as the foundation for both the ethical command and the legal doctrine of
informed consent. Historically, it emanates largely from established
standards of medical practice based in case law and standards for
research derived from the Nuremberg Code and the Declaration of
Helsinki. Informed consent has become one of the most critical elements in professional (medical and research) codes of ethics, and
failure to assure it has contributed to a series of legal proceedings.
Furthermore, a growing number of states are adopting informed
consent statutes. In recent years, these actions have fostered an environment in which physicians are ethically expected and legally mandated to gain the informed consent of patients and subjects prior to
initiating therapeutic or research procedures.

Informed consent consists of five major elements that may be
divided among three main variables (i.e., provision of information,
competency, and understanding), one precondition (i.e., voluntariness), and one consequence (i.e., consent or refusal). Although assurance of informed consent is mandatory and the provisions for
autonomous decisionmaking by patients are well-proscribed, major
difficulties may remain, largely due to problems in defining and
in judging competency. In Chapter 9, Alan Meisel presents a clear
model for assuring consent and discusses what practices are recommended if and when patients are judged to be less than competent.

From a clinical perspective, Shaw reports of special dilemmas of
informed consent when parents assume the right to deny treatment
of their minor children that results in their death.[19] Instances involving the withholding of consent for treatment of the critically ill
create serious ethical and legal questions about the rights and obligations of physicians, nurses, hospital administrators, parents, and
society.

Further problems are confronted in respecting the rights of adults
who elect to refuse treatment. If informed consent is accepted as a
valid concept, then refusal of treatment constitutes its alternative and
should be subject to the same five elements in the consent process.
Beyond the ethical dimension of this question, most judicial deci-

sions have upheld this stance except in cases of extenuating circumstances such as when a patient's refusal of life-saving therapy imposes overwhelming consequences on others.[20]

Thus, it appears that the principle of autonomy influences many patient care issues. It accords patients the right of final decisionmaking in most cases and either directly or indirectly extends additional obligations and responsibilities to health professionals. Most notable among the other rights derived from the principle of autonomy are those of privacy and confidentiality. Both patients and subjects of biomedical and behavioral research hold reasonably well-defined rights in this area. Mounting case law and statutes, in addition to broadly defined interpretations of the Constitution, support, albeit to varying degrees, the ethical obligation placed on health professionals to assure confidentiality and privacy. However, many limitations and other problems are apparent with respect to the legal dimension of this issue, particularly associated with the disclosure of medical records and the handling of sensitive, confidential information.[21]

Related Disciplines and Ethics

Who should be discussing medical ethics—physicians, lawyers, policymakers, economists? Possibly in dealing with subjects related to ethical issues confronting medicine and health care there is more of a need than in any other field for these, among others, to engage in serious discussions.

Ethics, as a branch of philosophy, provides a set of general value principles that are applicable to many other disciplines. In turn, individual disciplines commonly govern themselves through their respective ethical codes and standards that embody many of these general value principles in a more specific and applied sense.

More specifically, as medicine and biomedical technology become more complex, and thereby in many cases less humanistic, there is a growing need for the application of ethical analysis in decisionmaking affecting health care. Medical ethics affords the opportunity for those engaged in this process, whether at individual (i.e., practitioner–patient), organizational (i.e., institutional policy), or societal (i.e., governmental or public policy) levels, to apply the value dimensions embodied in broad philosophical principles and those espoused by specific related disciplines.

In an effort to illustrate the many disciplines that are called upon in making ethical decisions pertaining to health policy and medical care, it is useful to visualize them by the three major academic groupings—namely the humanities, the natural sciences, and the social sciences. In Figure 1-1, these groups that serve as inputs to ethical decisionmaking are so divided.

The humanistic values associated with medical ethics largely arise from concepts and principles grounded in religion (or theology) and philosophy (or more specifically, ethics). In turn, the appropriate natural sciences (including medicine), related research activities, and resulting technological advances are influenced by these ethics and value considerations. The third group of elements that enters into any discussion of medical ethics is the social sciences, particularly political science and economics. When humanistic values are applied to medicine or health care and the social implications are examined, the product is the evolution of sound ethical decisionmaking. This decisionmaking may be observed in a variety of outcomes, including social behavior and attitudes, public policies, professional codes of ethics, and individual decisions.

The field of ethics, as well as medical ethics, is closely intertwined with commands emanating from theology and issues raised therefrom. Throughout Judeo-Christian teachings, ethical concepts predominate, particularly questions of right and wrong human actions (i.e., the Ten Commandments, the Bible, etc.). Furthermore, the general concept of values is inextricably predicated on one's personal religious and humanistic beliefs. Hence, many of the more fundamental ethical questions are resolved by deference to theological principles and religious values. It is not uncommon, therefore, for many to turn to members of the clergy for guidance when confronting ominous situations and having to make difficult decisions (e.g., those involving sanctity of life versus quality of life issues, the right to die with dignity). Most theological leaders are generally more prepared to provide assistance at such trying times, in part due to their study of religion and philosophy, than the lay public.

The historical connection between ethics and medicine is clear. In every medical decision, regardless of the expertise and skills employed, some value judgment is made. Obviously, there are many factors that influence the value component of each medical decision—it may be the adherence to professional codes, it may reflect personal religious or moral convictions, it may be in response to the

Figure 1–1. Disciplines Contributing to Medical Ethics Decisionmaking.

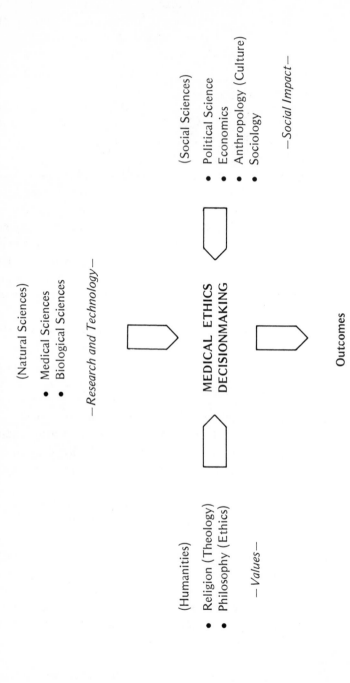

(Natural Sciences)

• Medical Sciences
• Biological Sciences

—Research and Technology—

(Social Sciences)

• Political Science
• Economics
• Anthropology (Culture)
• Sociology

—Social Impact—

MEDICAL ETHICS
DECISIONMAKING

(Humanities)

• Religion (Theology)
• Philosophy (Ethics)

—Values—

Outcomes

• Individual Decisions
• Professional Group Decisions
• Institutional Policies
• Public Policy Decisions

patient's wishes, it may be a product of societal or cultural demands or expectations, or in some cases it may be dictated by law. Regardless of the reason, there is a value element in the decisionmaking process.

While the therapeutic treatment associated with medical practice may engender humanistic patient concern, such may not be the case in solely research-dominated pursuits. Many of the natural sciences, particularly those of a biological nature that are largely or totally directed toward research and technological objectives, precipitate major ethical dilemmas. Researchers commonly contend that there is no scientific answer to every problem, to every unknown. Many argue that there should be no limits to scientific inquiry or to technological advancement. Furthermore, some claim that it is their individual right (or academic freedom) to engage in research, presumably for the benefit of humanity.

Obviously, scientists place high priority or value on the freedom to conduct research. Such a perspective is somewhat narrow, for it largely excludes concerns associated with the social and ethical implications of such research. Furthermore, it tends to minimize and subjugate potential risks (or costs) associated with the research and the rights of human subjects (e.g., informed consent, privacy, benefits). Finally, researchers frequently fail to look at the potential long-range implications of their actions, choosing to focus on the more immediate projected results of their work.

Amid the ongoing technological revolution, there is a growing need coupled with an increasing public demand that researchers include a more significant value dimension in their work. This suggests that there are certain levels of risks and costs to the public that cannot be ignored or discounted, even at the price of denying the freedom of inquiry to some scientific investigators or of postponing technological advances.

Inescapable influences are exerted on ethical decisionmaking from many social sciences. While the interrelationship between the humanities and the natural sciences (including medicine and research) fosters ethical decisionmaking at the individual (patient or human subject) level, imposition of social considerations directs attention toward the societal implications. Hence the need for discussing the public policy domain.

First and foremost in this arena is the critical appreciation of the longstanding interaction between values generated through the humanities and their authoritative allocation facilitated by political science. While the questions posed by modern medicine may be resolved through the application of a wide range of scientific and technological as well as humanistic concerns, it is inevitable that most of the change—regardless of direction—will occur in the political arena. Not disregarding the fundamental importance of values and technology in shaping change, the process of governing that change is embodied in the formulation of public policy.

Hence, regardless of the particular issue—be it the allocation of scarce medical technology, the decision regarding public financing of abortion, or embarkation on a mass genetic-screening program— the linkage between ethical and political decisionmaking remains. Furthermore, the environment for all such decisionmaking may be described as predominantly political in nature.

The relationship between ethics and political science can scarcely be considered accidental, of recent origin, or inappropriate. Accordingly, Seavey, Hiller, and O'Sullivan report:

> The relationship between ethics and politics is as old as both disciplines. It is not by accident that both political scientists and philosophers have common ancient sources in Plato and Aristotle. Political theory and the "larger questions" involving such concepts as justice, individual rights, and the nature of man have been fundamental themes in political science. The tie between ethics and politics is evident in the current thinking of political science.[22]

Eastman defines politics as "the authoritative allocation of values" for a society.[23] An equally fashionable definition is the allocation of decisionmaking. Hence, the value dimension and the decisionmaking responsibility illustrate the major linkage between ethics and political science. With the disparity of values found in most societies, the political system functions to sort them, to balance them, to take action to reflect each of them to some degree, and then to defend them.

Conflict and power in decisionmaking are dominant within the heterogeneous political system. The values of society further complicate matters since they never appear to be absolute, due in part to circumstances changing with time, conflicting values, and limiting capacities to attain goals. Circumstances such as historical events, technological innovations, and demographic shifts in society contribute to change. Values are continually coming into conflict, fostering compromise and sacrifice. For example, when should an individual's right to privacy (such as in the treatment of venereal disease) be sacrificed for the sake of maintaining the public's health. Furthermore, there are always factors that impose on the attainment of goals. All societies have limits on their resources, their capacities for growth, and their financial condition.

Hence, according to Braybrooke and Lindblom, "Policy making is not simply a pursuit of objectives but is rather an expenditure of some values in order to achieve others."[24] Again, politics enters into the decisionmaking process, for while compromise may occur, usually individuals who are in a position to wield power are making the decisions. Whether these are elected officials, health professionals, or those able to buy power with their wealth, they are the ones most likely to affect the decisionmaking process. Most likely, their values—regardless of the principles on which they are based—will take precedence over the weak and less affluent. The fact that the process of allocating values is authoritative does not justify or imply its rightness, rationality, or morality. It only means that the state is empowered to implement and enforce the political decisions or policies enacted.

Advocacy and constituency building play important roles in American politics. On controversial ethical issues such as abortion, political decisions are often predicated on the success or failure of certain political groups. Due to the nature of the American political system, groups that steadfastly hold to a given position and are able to orchestrate their opinion (albeit while representing a minority of the actual population) increasingly are able to impose it and their values on the majority.

Another increasingly important discipline affecting critical ethical choices to be made at both the individual and societal levels is economics. Economics may be defined as the social science that investigates problems arising from the scarcity of resources available to satisfy human wants. In turn, health economics is concerned chiefly with determining the optimum means for allocating scarce—and increasingly very costly—resources. Amid escalating costs, increasing public expectations, and limited resources, economics provides valuable tools for examining some of the difficult ethical choices that lie ahead.

Although this discipline influences decisionmaking, it alone cannot provide solutions. For as Fuchs states in *Who Shall Live: Health, Economics, and Social Choice*, there is a

> necessity of choice at both the individual and social levels. We cannot have all the health or all the medical care that we would like to have. "Highest quality care for all" is "pie in the sky." We have to choose. Furthermore, while economics can help us to make choices more rationally and to use resources more efficiently, it cannot provide the ethics and the value judgments that must guide our decisions. In particular, economics cannot tell us how much equality or inequality we should have in our society.[25]

Hence, when considering policy alternatives, it is important that adequate attention be given to the appropriate ethical implications of the decisions being made. These implications should be viewed as both long-range and short-term and should be judged at both the societal (or macro) and individual (or micro) levels. Moreover, responsibility dictates that any appropriate discipline that offers inputs to the decisionmaking process be called upon. To this end, the ethical principles embodied in the fields of philosophy and theology and the social sciences facilitate means of analysis and should be used in decisionmaking pertaining to medical and health care practices and policies. The products of this dynamic process, defined as medical ethics decisionmaking, include the evolution of multiple forms of policies and social expectations at the four levels depicted in Table 1–2. These outcomes represent the judgments or actions about what *ought* (or *ought not*) to be done.

The outcomes may be grouped in two large categories according to their nature—those that have been formalized, or codified, into a form of legal (or quasi-legal) document and those of a less formal nature. Included in the more formal category are policies that are the product of some form of legal action (e.g., laws, legally binding documents and agreements) or voluntarily imposed professional mandates (e.g., professional codes of ethics). Less formal outcomes are more in the line of social expectations. These are less definitive in detail and carry less risk of liability or sanctionable offense. In many cases, social expectations create and legitimize the establishment of more formal policy.

One of the most complicated situations associated with showing how multiple disciplines are used in an ethical analysis is the dynamic relationship between law and ethics—and to a lesser extent, political

Table 1-2. Outcomes of Ethical Decisionmaking Regarding Health and Medical Care.

	Formal Policy	Social Expectations
Individual Decisions	Physician's treatment plan	Attitudes and behaviors
	Patient's consent	Choice of providers
	Guardian or parent consent for minors	Autonomy (self-determination)
Professional Group Decisions	Professional codes of ethics (e.g., AMA, ANA, AMRA, AICP)	Beneficence
	Professional licensure, certification, accreditation	
Institutional Policies	Institutional licensure and accreditation (e.g., JCAH, state)	Etiquette
	Hospital policies, standards manuals	Community responsibility
	Clinical protocols	
Public Policy Decisions	Legislative enactments (e.g., public laws)	Social consensus, norms
	Executive orders (e.g., presidential orders)	Equity, justice
	Regulations (e.g., DHHS regulations)	
	Judicial opinions, common law	

science—in the evolution of health policy. Whether it is through legislative enactment, judicial interpretation based on precedence or common law, the Constitution, or quasi-judicial regulatory bodies, most law is based on sound ethical reasoning and values. Moreover, some suggest that law, in essence, represents a codification of ethical principles. Once again, it is important to reiterate that despite the use of ethical analysis as a basis for legal decisionmaking, this does not mean that all decisions reached through the legal process are subject to public approval or satisfaction. Furthermore, just the opposite produces the plethora of legal challenges in the courts and the restrictive policies enacted by legislative and executive bodies.

Although laws represent one of the major formal outcomes of the ethical decisionmaking process, they also are related closely to many ethical principles (e.g., justice, autonomy) that serve to govern the evolution of sound decisions. They commonly limit practices prescribed by certain ethical principles, particularly when both coexist with respect to the same issue (e.g., privacy, informed consent, the right to health care, abortion). Often it is difficult, particularly for nonlegal clinical practitioners, to understand fully where legal mandates or restrictions end and ethical stances commence, especially those circumscribed by one's profession. This problem is due to a large degree to the vicissitudes associated with the codification of ethical values. For example, practices related to ensuring informed consent and privacy for patients are engrained in the ethical codes of health professionals. However, these ethical values have been encased in law to varying degrees.

In the case of privacy, despite specified constitutional protections and legislative enactments, significant room exists for expansion based on ethical values. With respect to a patient's right to health care, some laws exist for special cases such as in emergency situations and under certain conditions.[26] However, the right to health care remains largely a matter of ethical values, a sense of human rights, and political debate as opposed to being a legal right. Another controversial area in which growing political pressure, evolving judicial interpretation predicated by litigation, and the ethical concept of an individual's right to self-determination undoubtedly will merge in the 1980s is the right to die with dignity—that is, not to be kept alive through the use of extraordinary means of life support. This is only one example of an area where conflict may arise due to the generally indistinct relationship between ethics and law.

Finally, although laws may be repealed, their existence commonly serves to guide the application of ethical values and the promulgation of additional laws that may be in conflict. This, by the nature of the American judicial system, is often seen when the U.S. Supreme Court rules on a controversial issue. In most cases, states not specifically identified in the decision will accept it and, if necessary, assure their compliance. However, on heavily debated issues, such as abortion, a Supreme Court decision that conflicts with the values or social expectations of a segment of society may be challenged through the enactment of subsequent state statutes that are knowingly in conflict with the Court's ruling.

PARADIGMS FOR THE ETHICAL ANALYSIS OF HEALTH POLICY AND MEDICAL PRACTICES

A background of medical ethics—a description of the field, several key principles and concepts, and an orientation to the relationship between ethics and other disciplines in decisionmaking—provides a reasonable basis from which further analytical frameworks can be established. However, none of the alternative paradigms offer conflict-free solutions. Due to the multiple theories and principles involved (most of which have more than a single interpretation) and the individual priorities assigned to them, use of ethical analysis in the development of health policy will by its very nature produce a range of outcomes. In the end, the responsibility of selecting the best policy or patient care decision falls upon those delegated to make the choice from among the various alternatives. The models used in an ethical analysis provide the mechanism through which policymakers learn not only of the variety of choices before them but, more importantly, of the potential short-term and long-range implications of their decisions. In turn, both the individual patients and the public at large are better able to understand the justification that has led to certain treatment plans or public policy proposals. But as Bok warns, "there are a great many ethical conflicts where there is no such agreement even in principle, let alone in practice."[27] However, she further concludes, "The need for ethical inquiry is great. And, the choices made—individually and socially—in the biomedical areas are moral choices at bottom. But the recognition that this is so only sharpens the question of what tools exist for making such choices wisely."[28]

Several alternative paradigms are applicable, individually or jointly, to an ethical analysis of health policies, medical practices, and biomedical research protocols. These theoretical models are grounded in ethical theory or religious principles and are not limited in applicability to issues related to health and medicine.[29]

One model, illustrated in Figure 1-2, identifies the dominant dimensions of argumentation in ethical analyses: (A) right versus wrong, (B) good versus evil (or bad), and (C) just (or fit) versus unjust (or unfit).[30] The overlapping circles provide a diagramatic representation of three normative value sets, or categories, that often may be used—explicitly or implicitly—in the ethical justification of particular decisions or actions. Decisionmaking may be based on an appeal to one, two, or three of the dimensions. Obviously, arguments supporting positions that are right, good, and fit usually lead to an optimal decision. Within each dimension, there is a wide degree of flexibility.

Figure 1-2. Dimensions of Ethical Analyses.

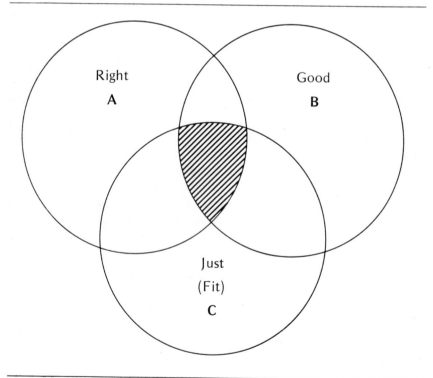

Initially, it is possible to examine a proposed or given health policy or medical decision in the context of dimension **A**—that is, based on the concept of right (and wrong). From this perspective, one attempts to discern in an objective manner whether or not an action complies with universally accepted positions circumscribed by absolute principles, laws, or doctrines (e.g., the Ten Commandments). In a more technical sense, adherence to such fundamental rules illustrates a deontological approach to medical ethics.

Although prima facie duties such as being fair, telling the truth, and not committing murder are "right," it is critically important that decisions also reflect the other dimensions as well. For as Stackhouse argues, without such flexibility:

> . . . mere clarification of the kinds of acts that are required, forbidden or permitted without simultaneous attention to other dimensions of more moral experiences, this mode of ethical reflection can end in oppressive legalism, vast systems of rational rules that box in every area of life.[31]

For example, "thou shalt not kill" represents a principle with which most societies agree, because it is clearly not right (i.e., it is wrong) to kill. Although particular conditions do not change the rightness or the wrongness of certain acts (such as killing in war, self-defense, or capital punishment) some situations require their justification using a second set of values, namely an appeal to good versus evil (i.e., dimension **B**).

Positions predicated on good and evil evoke a second dimension of ethical analysis. Dimension **B** primarily focuses on purposes or the ends of making a particular decision. It usually attempts to envision or create a "desirable state of affairs."[32] In assuming this perspective, one's goals are directed to that which achieves "the greatest good for the greatest number" regardless of the means required to achieve it. Hence, in some situations, upholding that which is right (or discounting that which is wrong) might be sacrificed in an effort to do good.

Returning to the example of killing, an act that most would agree is wrong, some kinds of killing might be tolerated by those interpreting a slight variance between justifiable killing and premeditated murder. In situations such as war, self-defense, or capital punishment, killing might be viewed as a tolerable means, regardless of its being wrong, to a good end.

In the debates over abortion, most acknowledge that abortion is an act of killing and is therefore wrong. However, most also agree that at least in certain defined situations (e.g., in cases of rape, incest, fetal deformity, or the endangered life of the mother) such an act produces a good end and is not evil. Similar reasoning may be applied in ethical arguments supporting some forms of euthanasia in cases of severely suffering, terminally ill patients.

In terms of ethical theory, these arguments are illustrative of utilitarianism. Dating back to Hume, Bentham, and Mill, utilitarianism urges that the worth of actions be gauged by their ends and consequences.[33] Therefore in some cases it may be acceptable to do something that generally is viewed as wrong, if it produces a good (or desired) consequence. Hence, it would support the above kinds of killing.

In contrast, the deontological theories, more often used to describe right and wrong (i.e., dimension A), have wider, more diverse classical origins. Deontologists maintain that acts are separate from the results they produce and that certain acts in and of themselves are good while others are evil. For example, some deontologists appeal solely to divine commands or religious principles of a particular faith. Hence, some religious deontologists hold that abortion is absolutely a wrong act that should not be performed under any circumstances. They argue that its performance is an evil that should not be allowed regardless of the consequences.

A third dimension of ethical analyses assists in decisionmaking about what ought to be done on the basis of what is just or fit. This dimension, represented by circle C in Figure 1-2, is clearly the most complex and "sustains the whole context of life as a human enterprise."[34] When examining issues in this dimension, one may be somewhat more concrete and specific, based on the individual situation at hand and all the facts comprising its surroundings. Yet, decisions are guided by interpretations of more general models. For example, the young adolescent (i.e., aged 12-14) is not expected to follow the same patterns of right and good that are expected of adults. Hence, should such a girl beget an unplanned pregnancy, it may be just and fitting for her to be allowed to have an abortion performed. Indeed, noting the risks and implications of her carrying the pregnancy to term, refusal of the abortion option might be very unjust and unfitting.

Included in analyses in C are considerations of a more personal or subjective nature. According to Stackhouse:

> Here [in dimension C], a sense of proportion and balance, of richness and flexibility as aesthetic or interpretive ethical ingredients must be acknowledged. The concern for the "fitting" puts the round cork in the round bottle; it tells the story that evokes the appropriate sensibilities; it captures the dilemmas of the everyday tissue of life by humor, irony, analogy, or hermeneutical model.[35]

Hence, this dimension does not have the restrictiveness or limitations found in A and B. It requires the consideration of policies and practices in light of given surrounding conditions (e.g., poverty, racism, sexism), which may at times generate a greater lack of consensus or confusion. From some deliberations, however, more sensitive, humane, and caring outcomes may emerge as opposed to those limited solely to what is right and/or good. Just as the utilitarian view of what constitutes good is particularly valuable in dimension B, an assessment in C frequently calls upon multiple views of what constitutes justice under given circumstances. Clearly, analysis at this level is the most dynamic, as it is predicated on individual changing situations and must attempt to preassess the consequences of doing or not doing a particular act (without necessarily knowing what is good or evil).

In sum, it is essential that sound ethical analyses address these three critical dimensions—that is, the questions of right, good, and fit—and not see them in isolation. While others may use other terms, and while this model is not void of error at certain points, it renders a realistic ethical vision "that links together the duties and privileges of 'right', the concern for intentions and consequences of 'good', and the contextual–interpretive dimensions of 'fit'."[36]

Using a second comparable paradigm, Beauchamp and Childress diagram their approach to ethical reasoning in the form of hierarchical levels of justification (see Figure 1–3):

> Although our diagram may be oversimplified, it is designed to indicate that in the process of moral reasoning we appeal to different reasons of varying degrees of abstraction and systematization. Let us start with the lowest level and move upwards. A *judgment* is a decision, verdict, or conclusion about a particular action. Although the precise nature of the distinction between rules and principles is somewhat controversial, *rules* state that actions of a certain kind ought (or ought not) to be done because they are right (or wrong). A simple example is, "It is wrong to lie to a patient." *Principles* are more gen-

Figure 1-3.   Hierarchical Levels of Moral Justification.

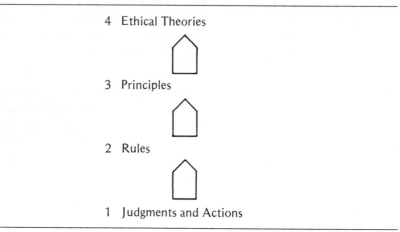

4   Ethical Theories

3   Principles

2   Rules

1   Judgments and Actions

Source: Tom L. Beauchamp and James F. Childress, *Principles of Biomedical Ethics* (New York: Oxford University Press, 1979), p. 5.

eral and fundamental than moral rules and serve as their foundation. The principle of respect for persons, for example, may ground several moral rules of the "it is wrong to lie" sort. Finally, *theories* are bodies of principles and rules, more or less systematically related. They include second-order principles and rules about what to do when there are conflicts.[37]

In analyzing a particular health issue, it is important to remember that while the models presented in Figures 1-2 and 1-3 provide an analytical framework, not all dimensions or levels carry equal weights, and therefore, not all ethical dilemmas can be assessed equally at each level. In conducting some analyses, for example, primary consideration may be placed on the level of good and evil to facilitate maximum analysis of the potential positive or negative impact of implementing a particular program or policy—in other words, suggesting that a particular program ought or ought not to be implemented. Even in cases in which reference to all dimensions or levels is made, it is likely that depending on the issue, one clearly will predominate over the others in decisionmaking. In addition, it is very common for them to be in competition and in conflict with each other. It is particularly important that beyond acceptance of certain degrees of flexibility within each (although this flexibility may vary), specific ethical theories should be applied to assist in resolving arguments.

Once again, in analyzing the abortion issue, almost all would agree that since abortion is a form of killing, it is wrong. However, depending on the specific circumstances surrounding the situation, it may or may not be the least evil or the most fitting (just) thing to do at a given time for a particular person. These factors may individually or collectively override the objection on the principle that it is wrong. With a basic understanding of how complex ethical dilemmas may be resolved through the application of an analytical model (i.e., such as one of the two presented here), one has the tools to examine more soundly many critical health policy and medical care questions confronting society in the 1980s.

ETHICAL ISSUES IN HEALTH POLICY DEVELOPMENT

Some suggest that the surge in interest in medical ethics is simply a passing fad. They argue that the issues being addressed by ethicists and humanists in the health field today constitute a rehash of the same health care concerns identified by the Committee on the Costs of Medical Care in the early 1930s.[38] Others argue that while some of the underlying problems related to economics may be similar, many more recent technological developments and the growth of the health care system in general are responsible for most of the increasing concerns. They further argue that possible resolutions of problems confronting the system will require seeking answers at a different level—raising some very basic ethical questions and forcing an examination of societal and personal values regarding health and health care. Although debate may subdue, existing underlying factors generating significant social and ethical concerns are here to stay. Ethical analysis can help in making difficult choices regarding public policy. However, resolution of many issues may not be imminent due to the lack of clearly acceptable options. For purposes of briefly examining these issues, they are categorized in five broad areas:

1. Unreasonable demand and government intervention,
2. Problems in allocating scarce resources,
3. Biomedical and behavioral research and technology,
4. Establishing a quality of life ethics, and
5. Balancing individual and social rights

Unreasonable Demand and Government Intervention

Never before in American history have public demands and expectations for availability, accessibility, and quality of health care resources been greater. Never before have the high costs for care generated such consumer behavior, public reaction, and demand for relief. With little evidence of solutions emerging from the private sector (at least to the degree perceived necessary), these factors increasingly have dominated the political agenda demanding government intervention.

The first major public intervention arose with the passage of the Social Security Act in 1935; in health care, it came largely as a product of the enactment of public financing programs (e.g., Medicare and Medicaid) and strengthened federal health planning efforts in the mid-1960s. Since that time, government has pushed for a greater public voice in health care issues, with many additional health and social programs, including major expansions in the arena of federal control of health policy through the enactment and implementation of strong legislation and the promulgation of many regulations. At least through the 1970s, this trend continued. What are the implications of such action?

Once government intervenes, at least through such a formal mechanism as legislating public policy, on issues so private as an individual's personal health care, ethical debate and power struggles become inevitable. Regardless of the legitimacy of its decision, government intervention in itself precipitates a major ethical conflict among those who argue that such action constitutes a violation of the laissez-faire philosophy and tips the balance of fate (that presumably would be resolved by time or a supernatural force, i.e., God). Some argue that government involvement disregards individual autonomy and, furthermore, that it creates a conflict between its role and that of religion or personal values.

More specifically, ethical debate flares when particular government actions to support or not to support a particular type of health policy or program offend a given group in society that declares them to be unethical or immoral positions. For example, to alleviate the accessibility issue, some proposals call for the development of alternative health care delivery systems. Many such proposals meet strenuous organized opposition on the grounds that consumers might lose autonomy in selecting their physicians and that, in turn, physicians might lose certain freedoms in their practice of medicine. Other ensuing ethical arguments emerge when federal funding programs are proposed to support controversial research (e.g., using human subjects, recombinant DNA) or to finance certain services (e.g., abortion, genetic screening) for the poor.

Arguments in behalf of federal intervention to alleviate the demand for health care commonly stem from both economics and ethical theories of justice[39] and can be lodged on individual equity or public health grounds. While the clamoring over skyrocketing health care costs continues and claims for a right to health care grow, the issue of public demand and government intervention simmers. Regardless of the cause, costs for health care are reaching historical highs, and control and containment through some mechanism is sought by nearly all. Yet, the proposed solution that government can or ought to guarantee a right to health care is grounded more in an ethical belief than in law or economic feasibility; it does little to satisfy public demands for greater access, availability, and quality of medical care.

Although much need can be legitimized, particularly in medically underserved areas such as urban ghettos and rural towns, the demand remains insatiable, in spite of significant increases in the manpower supply. Health care, as a commodity, violates the traditional rules of the marketplace economy: It does not adhere solely to the economic theory of supply versus demand, largely due to its complexity.[40] The demand for health care always surpasses its availability. Furthermore, as Wildavsky concludes, the demand for and subsequent use of medical services will always extend to the limits of the available supply.[41] For a variety of related reasons, costs of health care alone do not serve as much of a barrier function as they do for other commodities. Since only a small proportion of Americans pay for their own health care due to major dependence on third party reimbursement programs,[a] many remain personally ignorant of the costs. Moreover, if they had to bear the costs individually, most would find them prohibitive. Thus, despite government intervention, it remains questionable as to whether the growing demands for health care can ever be assured. Even if accessibility were increased through greater

---

a. The sources of third party reimbursement are both public (e.g., Medicare and Medicaid) and private (e.g., Blue Cross–Blue Shield plans or commercial insurance companies).

government or private expenditure, evidence strongly suggests that this would have little if any impact on the health status of the population.[42]

In addition to the continually growing supply demands on the system, in part due to the lack of public understanding and one's theory of justice, the public also holds expectations beyond the capabilities of the health care establishment. Growing demands for increased quality of care assurances are voiced around the nation. Once again, government responds by imposing regulations designed to ensure quality standards. These moves further fuel the ethical debates over the right of government to regulate the industry and the costs, benefits, and effectiveness of this mode of intervention.

Finally, unrealistic expectations exist about medicine's capabilities. The public stands more convinced than ever that major, far-reaching medical advances will create a magic bullet to cure every disease, discomfort, or undesired condition. In part, the news reports of medical advances and pharmaceutical cures and prolific advertising campaigns successfully generate heightened, unwarranted public expectations that are commonly far beyond the limits of modern medicine. Frequently, this creates additional strain on physician-patient relationships as patients erroneously insist that they know the appropriate cures. For example, it is not unusual for individuals suffering from viral conditions (e.g., the common cold) to demand penicillin, which is an inappropriate treatment for conditions not of a bacterial origin. Some physicians argue that if they fail to follow patient demands, they will lose the patient to the doctor down the road.

How can the public be educated and sensitized to the unrealistic demands being placed on the system, on the one hand; and on the other, how can the system operate in a more just and fitting manner? While there are tremendously difficult choices to be made, there is little evidence to suggest that decisions are forthcoming in the near future that will ease the problem of demand or satisfy competitive arguments based on different ethical values.

Problems in Allocating Scarce Resources

Within the health care system, there is an inescapable need to allocate scarce resources. In turn, decisions attempting to address this need are responsible for a wide range of ethical and economic dilemmas. From an economic perspective, problems arise in trying to devise the most efficient means for allocating the available resources to relieve human wants. From an ethical standpoint, differences arise due to various theories of justice governing the distribution of resources. Obviously, these problems are interrelated: Adoption of an acceptable policy requires inputs from multiple disciplines.

Initially, decisions at the highest policy levels must be made about what proportion of the total budget will go toward health care. Then, more allocation decisions must be made to determine which health projects should receive funds from the total amount allocated to health care and how much each should receive. Undertaking such a task requires the consideration of both the competing health care needs of the society and the competing non-health care needs. Ethical principles and values must be considered in these allocation decisions at every level.

As health care costs associated with medical care and research and technology grow, and as available resources decrease, the choices become more difficult. In acknowledging the limited health care resources, the public is beginning to recognize that it is not possible to have all the health or all the health care that might be desired. However, major debates erupt when efforts are made to prioritize and to allocate resources.

Several critical issues arise from resource allocation endeavors, and conflicts do not appear to precipitate resolutions. On one hand, arguments center on principles of justice, which Beauchamp and Walters summarize in five different ways:

(1) To each person an equal share;
(2) To each person according to individual needs;
(3) To each person according to individual effort;
(4) To each person according to societal contribution;
(5) To each person according to merit (individual ability).[43]

Another issue on which little agreement appears to be forthcoming is the degree of quality for which society should strive. Achievement of the highest level of quality may require investments beyond what society should—or is prepared to—strive to reach. Will the acceptance of lower standards of quality facilitate a more rational means of allocation? Are there certain standards that do not bear sacrifice?

Another set of questions surrounds issues of priority for certain types of programs. Over the past twenty years, major investments have gone into highly skilled, tertiary level care. More recently, particularly in the area of health manpower development, there appears to be an increased emphasis on primary care. Does this constitute a shift in priorities to care for the more deprived or poor, who are in greater need of such care? In addition, a critical area of choice surrounds the decision to allocate scarce resources to preventive medicine as opposed to the more traditional curative medicine.[44] On dividing the available resources, should a greater percentage be allocated to further research and technological developments that are known to be costly, or should more be focused on public health concerns and better distribution of basic primary care?

From a health-planning perspective, should more dollars be allocated on a regional basis, or should individual local institutions simply compete for limited resources? Should regulations (such as certificate of need laws) exist to assist in regional allocation of resources, or should such decisions remain at the individual level? This issue must be addressed by Congress again in the near future, and its political outcome is uncertain.

Whereas the policy issues cited above reflect macroallocation decisions, other debates center on microallocation of resources. A wide range of controversial social and ethical values are associated with the provision of scarce life-saving technology and the treatment of individuals with costly terminal conditions. On what grounds will life and death decisions be made? Furthermore, should more resources be allocated to provide greater accessibility and more availability of life-saving technologies at the expense of others?

Should some cost be associated with a life? In other words, should human life be prolonged and/or repaired regardless of cost or circumstance? Should society bear the responsibility for absorbing extraordinary costs to sustain dying patients for indefinite periods of time?

In sum, difficult and possibly unanswerable questions remain in attempting to determine a just means of allocating a limited amount of resources. Providing answers for such questions requires careful ethical analysis using ingredients—or tools—from multiple disciplines as shown in Figure 1-1. Particularly important in analyses of both microallocation and macroallocation issues is the identification of the long-range social and personal implications of the alternatives—before finalizing a policy or treatment decision.

Biomedical and Behavioral Research and Technology

With the coming of the scientific revolution and the ensuing explosion of medical technology, many advances have occurred as a result of biomedical research. Coupled with many of the significant breakthroughs have been substantial social benefits and the reduction of considerable human suffering. However, despite the positive implications for and the impact on health care delivery in the United States, human experimentation and the expansion of high level technology pose many difficult ethical questions that remain unresolved by health professionals, researchers, and public policymakers.

Public concern about the ethical dilemmas created through the use of human subjects as the final test site has grown quite rapidly since the conclusion of World War II. Largely precipitated by reported abuses of concentration camp prisoners by physicians and scientists engaged in human experimentation at that time, the Nuremberg Code (1947) was promulgated as a set of standards for judgments during the Nuremberg War Crimes Trials. The Code became the prototype of many later efforts to further assure the protection of human research subjects. Among the best known and probably most widely accepted others are the Helsinki Declaration of 1964 (revised in 1975) and the 1971 guidelines and subsequent sets of federal regulations (1974, 1978, 1981) issued by the U.S. Department of Health, Education, and Welfare (now the Department of Health and Human Services, DHHS).

In addition, private professional organizations have contributed to better understanding and practices through their own respective sets of professional ethical codes and standards. However, due to the range of scientific and biomedical investigations, the matrix of rules is not always adequate to cover complex situations, to resolve conflicts, or to simply interpret, apply, and adhere.

At this point, even the clearest understanding of the ethical principles presented earlier in this chapter may be jeopardized due to the inherent differences in the primary goals of the research or of those conducting it. In the case of patients suffering from some condition for which medical science has no known effective treatment, a physician may suggest the use of an experimental treatment (i.e., an experimental drug, procedure, or technique) solely for therapeutic purposes. Obviously, the monitoring of the progress or the results of such usage provides the basis for reporting aggregate findings. Alternatively, a researcher may search for patients having a certain pathology to test a given experimental therapy primarily for purposes of gathering data. In this case, the research may serve a therapeutic purpose; however, the major goal is to run an experimental trial to prove or disprove a particular hypothesis. Regardless, there is a potential benefit, from a health perspective, for the subject and much research could be judged sound from an ethical perspective.

The third use of human subjects is the most controversial and ethically the most troublesome—namely, the use of experimental drugs, procedures, or techniques on perfectly healthy individuals. Hence, due to the lack of definitively known therapeutic benefits, the risks to the subject are much more open to criticism. Support for the use of human subjects in nontherapeutic research has evolved from the utilitarian argument that the public benefits from engaging in such research are generally positive. Thus, since the end product is good, conducting human experimentation toward such an end is justified. Additional support is based on a theory of justice that claims that society has survived because prior generations submitted themselves to experimentation. Therefore, as beneficiaries of past human experimentation, it is unfair for present generations not to make their reciprocal contributions to future generations.

Despite these supportive arguments, serious questions remain. The degree of potential risk associated with modern biomedical research is often greater than for earlier research. Furthermore, with increasing quantities of research either being sponsored or conducted by government, even broader questions of public policy arise. The magnitude and social impacts of current research pose increasing ethical dilemmas. In many cases, the area of research itself raises public controversy before even considering the actual protocol. Recombinant DNA research, cloning, in vitro fertilization, fetal research, and psychosurgery are but a few examples of research controversial enough to demand special policy decisions.

Research involving human subjects or having major social implications requires exploration of a wide range of ethical principles and human values. Among the critical issues, are those relating to autonomy (including informed consent), confidentiality and privacy, and compensation for harm. Heightened concern often arises in situations where subtle coercion exists—for example, when there is the slightest hint that conditions may improve for those who "volunteer." Certain population groups, particularly the institutionalized (e.g., prisoners, nursing home residents, mental hospital patients) risk such coercion to participate in human subject research. At bottom, coercion destroys autonomy.

In addition, coercion among specific population groups raises concerns of justice. Selection of research subjects due to their easy availability, compromised position, or manipulability rather than for reasons directly related to the problem being studied is unjust. In addition, persons should be treated in an ethical manner not only by respecting their decisions and protecting them from harm, but also by making efforts to secure their well-being. Such treatment falls under the principle of beneficence.

Hence, during the 1980s society undoubtedly will confront complex, possibly unresolvable dilemmas involving research with human subjects. Although legal regulations may restrict certain forms of research and establish some standardization of protocol review (i.e., through mandating institutional review boards, IRBs) to protect subjects from unreasonable risks and attempt to guard against fraudulent research practices, to what degree can—or ought—the government intervene? As may be observed from the recently promulgated final DHHS regulations (January 1981)[45] addressing this subject, much of the responsibility is being returned to the local community level (e.g., university or hospital IRBs). At bottom, apart and beyond any definable legal responsibility, the ethical principles heretofore discussed and social and personal values must guide the research decisions and practices involving the use and the protection of human subjects as the demand for technological advances continues.

Establishing a Quality of Life Ethic

Is there such a thing as a life that is not worth living? How does society address such a question—a question dependent on individual personal values, religious preferences, and lifestyles. As a fourth area, issues associated with the quality of life ethic raise other difficult, if not unresolvable, sets of public policy concerns.

In part, some of these issues are precipitated by the enormous costs associated with maintaining or sustaining life for certain individuals, who at best confront coma, unbearable pain, irreparable brain damage, or imminent death. However, beyond the economic

and social costs to individuals and families—and often to society—
there are issues involving the degree to which medical science is (or
is not) obligated to maintain a basic biological function, often sustained only through extensive life support technology. Furthermore,
decisions are complicated by the ongoing debate as to what constitutes death and by conflicting values associated with death and
dying.

Two competitive ethical theories—the sanctity of life versus the
quality of life—are embedded in most arguments. Advocates of the
former base their position on deontological beliefs that life is sacred
regardless of its quality or state and that medicine is obligated to
preserve it whatever the cost. This stance often reflects the theological belief that only God can—or has the right—to terminate a life
and that human action in this regard constitutes the greatest wrong—
killing. In contrast, there is a growing recognition among many that
not all "life" is worth sustaining and that an individual (or his or her
guardian) has a right to choose death with dignity. Those holding this
belief argue that life without a sense of quality is not worth living.
They claim that to prolong and/or to repair life regardless of costs
and circumstances (or consequences) does not constitute an ethical action. Furthermore, they claim accordingly, that such action
represents a lack of sensitivity, humanistic values, and respect for
autonomy.

Obviously, in debating this issue one cannot escape the ethical
principles of nonmaleficence and beneficence. Those supporting a
right to life argue that not sustaining life—regardless of its quality—
constitutes doing harm or at least not doing good for the patient.
Advocates of basing decisions on the quality of life contend the
opposite—namely, that decisions not based on a determination of
the quality of life constitute a violation of patient autonomy and/or
the imposition of the physician's values (i.e., paternalism) on the
patient.

Issues closely aligned to this dilemma are questions relating to who
should decide in life and death situations and on what criteria or
basis such decisions should be made. Based on the principle of autonomy, informed consent affords the right of self-determination to the
individual. However, what happens if the patient is judged to be
incompetent? Society generally allocates decisions in such cases to
the patient's family, since they usually bear the ultimate financial
and psychological hardships. However, in some situations, particu-

larly those involving children and adults having estates, leaving the decision to the patient's family may not be in the best interests of the legally or medically incompetent. As mentioned earlier, leaving the decision with the patient's physician contributes to paternalistic practices in medicine and fears of possible medical malpractice. Despite this, some argue that patients or their families can never fully appreciate the vast array of facts, the psychological stress they are under, and the short period of time in which critical decisions frequently must be made. Thus, they defend the position that the physician is best prepared and most able to assume the decisionmaking role.

Due to the resource questions and the potential economic burden on society (i.e., public support for long-term institutional care), social pressure often presents an intervening factor affecting decisionmaking. In some cases, the court may intervene, due to the state's mandate to protect the welfare of all citizens.

In addition to ethical concerns relating to decisionmaking in these cases, politics usually plays a role as well. For example, if the only available institutional care setting is in a public facility (i.e., one run by the local, state, or federal government) for which adequate funding was never appropriated to maintain acceptable standards, then one may decide that the extension of life of a loved one forced to live under very poor conditions is worse than allowing the patient to die. In essence, this decision, in part, represents a condemnation of the existing political system's failure to support a major component of the health care system. If the opportunity to receive quality care was available, this decision, which placed a high value on a quality of life ethic, might have been different. Hence, a complex subset of issues surrounding who should decide what constitutes a quality of life ethic exists at both individual and societal levels.

It is relatively obvious that achieving a quality of life ethic that defines a society's values in this critical area is an arduous task, one that may defy public policy solutions or remedies. Some argue that it should never be attempted; others that it simply is impossible to gain a consensus. Some continue to try. Clearly, however, as modern technology advances in finding the means to sustain life, such decisions and hard choices about what constitutes a quality or meaningful life must be made. But, even then, the question still remains, who should decide?

Balancing Individual and Social Rights

Current trends in the formulation of health policy commonly revolve around the protection of individual rights. Arguments fostering this perspective are found in both traditionally conservative and liberal camps. Conservative thinking, which follows a laissez-faire theory, suggests that policies are ethically right only if government does not intrude on the property rights of individual citizens. In philosophical terms, this ideology has been circumscribed as adhering to the entitlement theory of justice. Traditionally, health policies cautiously have avoided any impingement on private individuals—be they physicians in the private practice of medicine or consumers who maintain the freedom to choose their private doctors.

Albeit for an entirely separate set of reasons, so-called liberal-thinking advocates also defend the need to maintain individual personal rights. These proponents of civil liberties generally support the individual's right to privacy, right to refuse treatment, or right to choose whether to bear or beget a child. Public policy reflecting this philosophy appeared strong throughout the 1970s, as patient rights issues were addressed by Congress, the U.S. Supreme Court, several state legislatures, and many professional associations and other groups.

The alternative perspective in developing health policies, however, assumes more of a public health orientation, which engenders appreciation for what Jonsen and Butler label public ethics.[46] This approach recognizes that pursuit of an improvement in health status may in certain instances require giving priority to the social good at the risk of sacrificing individual rights or liberties. In adopting this philosophy, there is a realization that maximizing the health and welfare of the majority may require sacrifices by or infringements on some who may be in better socioeconomic conditions than others.

Thus, in undertaking an ethical analysis of health policies, there is an inherent, if not inescapable, clash of two strongly held values. In the promotion of social benefits or the assumption of a social ethics stand, individual autonomy represented by one's exercising the right to self-determination may be diminished. The two cannot coexist without a mediated outcome; although compromise may occur, extremes are impossible.

Figure 1-4. Social Ethics versus Individual Rights in Health Policy Development.

Domain of Social Ethics (social good/public health)			Domain of Individual Rights (civil libertarian/private ownership)	
Utilitarian	Rawlsian	Equity	Egalitarian	Entitlement
•	•	•	•	•
Theory	Theory	Theory	Theory	Theory

Source: John W. Seavey, Marc D. Hiller, and Michael J. O'Sullivan, "Ethical Issues in the Evolution of Health Policy." Presented at the 108th Annual Meeting of the American Public Health Association, Detroit, MI, October 21, 1980.

Moreover, when the various theories of social justice are examined in conjunction with the dichotomy represented in the societal versus individual rights paradigm, they can be illustrated on a continuum, as shown in Figure 1-4. Both the most conservative ideology, the entitlement theory, and the most liberal one, the egalitarian theory, support one's claim for individual rights—that is, the protection of personal freedoms despite the inherent risks in the aggregate social status. Although their supportive arguments in this direction differ strongly, both reflect an unyielding stance to uphold individual autonomy—be it for purposes of assuring the security of the more affluent or guaranteeing their respective life styles, or be it for purposes of assuring equal treatment for all individuals.

In contrast, the utilitarian theory, in arguing that the means would justify the ends, purports that that action should be taken that produces the most significant improvement in the health outcome of the population. For example, in light of Blum's conceptual model of the four major determinants of health (i.e., heredity, health care services, individual and social behaviors, and the environment),[47] utilitarians would support major inputs being directed at environmental determinants for the improvement of the nation's health status. Such efforts ought to be launched even if some individuals might stand to lose some of their autonomous rights. In essence, one could argue that only with this approach to health policy would further improvement in health status be achieved. Thus, if public policy is to more often reflect the public good (i.e., the public's health), then certain individual rights (i.e., autonomy) must be sacrificed to assure such ends.

CONCLUSION

For public policy purposes, the directive is clear. Specific public policies can be proposed to address many of the nation's health care problems, but more is needed. Clearly, an ethical framework for analyzing and justifying the alternatives is both desirable and becoming increasingly necessary. Without such an analytical approach utilizing ethical principles and values, proposed solutions may overcome some technical questions, but the long-range ethical and social implications would remain unknown, unstudied, and potentially very dangerous. At best, they would not ensure reasonable degrees of justice, autonomy, or beneficence and nonmaleficence.

Few engaged in public affairs, clinical practice, or biomedical research can doubt the importance of the issues raised or the task that remains before us as a society and as individuals. Neither this chapter nor the book that it serves to introduce is meant to exhaustively explore the ethical and legal implications of evolving health policies or to suggest answers for the problems with which society has wrestled for centuries. However, this chapter is designed to provide an overview of the field of medical ethics and its application to the policymaking process. It has highlighted several ways in which ethical values and reasoning can be introduced into decisionmaking at both the societal and the individual level concluding with five health policy areas in which ethical considerations are critical, and noting the persistent difficulties inherent in resolving controversial matters based on competing value systems.

NOTES TO CHAPTER 1

1. Tom L. Beauchamp and Le Roy Walters, *Contemporary Issues in Bioethics* (Belmont, CA: Wadsworth Publishing Company, Inc., 1978), p. 49.
2. Hippocrates, *Oath of Hippocrates*, trans. by W.H.S. Jones, in *The Loeb Classical Library* (Cambridge, MA: Harvard University Press, 1923), vol. 1, pp. 164–165.
3. American Medical Association, *Principles of Medical Ethics* (Chicago, 1957).
4. American Hospital Association, "Statement on a Patient's Bill of Rights," *Hospitals*, Vol. 4, February 16, 1973.

5. George J. Annas, *The Rights of Hospital Patients* (New York: Avon Books, 1975).

6. "The Nuremberg Code," in *Trials of War Criminals before the Nurenberg Military Tribunals under Control Council Law No. 10* (Washington, D.C.: U.S. Government Printing Office, 1949), vol. 2, pp. 181–182.

7. World Medical Association, *Declaration of Helsinki* (Helsinki: World Medical Assembly, 1964). Revised in 1975.

8. Protection of Human Subjects, 45 C.F.R. § 46 (January 11, 1978); revised, see: U.S. Department of Health and Human Services, "Public Health Service Human Research Subjects," *Federal Register* 46: 8366–8392 (January 26, 1981).

9. Beauchamp and Walters, p. 50.

10. Tom L. Beauchamp and James F. Childress, *Principles of Biomedical Ethics* (New York: Oxford University Press, 1970), p. 169.

11. Robert M. Veatch, "What Is a 'Just' Health Care Delivery?" in Robert M. Veatch and Roy Branson, *Ethics and Health Policy* (Cambridge, MA: Ballinger Publishing Company, 1976).

12. Charles Fried, "Equality and Rights in Medical Care," *Hastings Center Report* 6: 29–34 (February 1976).

13. Robert M. Veatch, "Voluntary Risks to Health: The Ethical Issues," *Journal of the American Medical Association* 243: 50–55 (1980); and Chapter 2 of this volume.

14. John W. Seavey, Marc D. Hiller, Michael J. O'Sullivan, "Ethical Issues in the Evolution of Health Policy." (Presented at the 108th Annual Meeting of the American Public Health Association, Health Administration Section, Detroit, Michigan, October 21, 1980); Sherry I. Brandt–Rauf and Paul W. Brandt-Rauf, "Occupational Health Ethics: OSHA and the Courts," *Journal of Health Politics, Policy, and Law* 5: 523–534 (Fall 1980); and James F. Smurl, "Distributing the Burden Fairly: Ethics and National Health Policy," *Man and Medicine: The Journal of Values and Ethics in Health Care* 5: 97–137 (1980).

15. Nicholas Rescher, "The Allocation of Exotic Medical Lifesaving Therapy," *Ethics* 79: 173–186 (April 1969); and Renee C. Fox and Judith P. Swazey, "Patient Selection and the Right to Die: Problems Facing Seattle's Kidney Center," in Howard D. Schwartz and Cary S. Schwartz, *Dominant Issues in Medical Sociology* (Reading, MA: Addison-Wesley Publishing Company, 1978), pp. 527–535.

16. James F. Childress, "Who Shall Live, When Not All Can Live?" *Soundings* 53: 339–355 (Winter 1970).

17. Ibid.

18. James Rachels, "Active and Passive Euthanasia," *The New England Journal of Medicine* 292: 78–80 (January 9, 1975); Paul Ramsey, *Ethics at*

the Edge of Life (New Haven: Yale University Press, 1978); Robert M. Veatch, *Death, Dying, and the Biological Revolution* (New Haven: Yale University Press, 1976); James Childress, "To Kill or Let Die," in Elsie Bandman and Bertram Bandman, *Bioethics and Human Rights* (Boston: Little, Brown, and Company, 1978); and George J. Annas, "The Incompetent's Right to Die: The Case of Joseph Saikewicz," *The Hastings Center Report* 8: 21–23 (February 1978).

19. Anthony Shaw, "Dilemmas of 'Informed Consent' in Children," *The New England Journal of Medicine* 289: 885–890 (October 25, 1973).

20. Robert M. Byrn, "Compulsory Life Saving Treatment for the Competent Adult," *Fordham Law Review* 44: 1–36 (1975); and Norman Cantor, "A Patient's Decision to Decline Life-Saving Medical Treatment: Bodily Integrity Versus the Preservation of Life," *Rutgers Law Review* 26: 228–254 (1973).

21. Readers are referred to Chapter 7 of this volume and Alan F. Westin, *Computers, Health Records, and Citizen Rights* (Washington, D.C.: U.S. Government Printing Office, 1976).

22. Seavey, Hiller, and O'Sullivan, p. 1.

23. David Eastman, *The Political System* (New York: Alfred A. Knopf, 1953).

24. David Braybrooke and Charles Lindblom, *A Strategy of Decision: Policy Evaluation as a Social Process* (New York: The Free Press of Glencoe, 1963), p. 24.

25. Victor R. Fuchs, *Who Shall Live: Health, Economics, and Social Choice?* (New York: Basic Books, Inc., 1974), p. 7.

26. Edward V. Sparer, "The Legal Right to Health Care: Public Policy and Equal Access," *Hastings Center Report* 6: 39–47 (October 1976).

27. Sissela Bok, "The Tools of Bioethics," in Stanley Joel Reiser, Arthur J. Dyck, and William J. Curran, *Ethics in Medicine: Historical Perspectives and Contemporary Concerns* (Cambridge, MA: The MIT Press, 1977), p. 140.

28. Ibid., p. 138.

29. For a more comprehensive review of the philosophical theories addressed here, readers are referred to: Beauchamp and Childress, p. 3–55.

30. Max L. Stackhouse, "Ethics: Social and Christian," *Andover Newton Quarterly* 13: 173–191 (January 1973).

31. Ibid., p. 176.

32. Ibid., p. 177.

33. Beauchamp and Childress, p. 20.

34. Stackhouse, p. 178.

35. Ibid.

36. Ibid., p. 179.

37. Beauchamp and Childress, p. 5.

38. Committee on the Costs of Medical Care, *Medical Care for the American People — The Final Report of the Committee on the Costs of Medical Care* (Washington, D.C.: U.S. Government Printing Office, October 31, 1932), pp. 32–34.

39. A brief discussion of these appears earlier in this chapter. For a more detailed discussion of several theories of justice, readers are referred to Chapter 2 of this volume.

40. Herbert E. Klarman, *The Economics of Health* (New York: Columbia University Press, 1965), pp. 11–19; and William C. Richardson, "Financing Health Services," in Stephen J. Williams and Paul R. Torrens, *Introduction to Health Services* (New York: John Wiley and Sons, 1980), pp. 287–321.

41. Aaron Wildavsky, "Doing Better and Feeling Worse: The Political Pathology of Health Policy," in John H. Knowles, *Doing Better and Feeling Worse: Health in the United States* (New York: W.W. Norton and Company, Inc., 1977), pp. 105–123.

42. Ibid.; in addition, readers are referred to Chapter 4 of this volume.

43. Beauchamp and Walters, p. 348.

44. H. Tristram Engelhardt, Jr., "Personal Health Care or Preventive Care: Distributing Scarce Medical Resources," *Soundings* 63: 234–256 (Fall 1980).

45. U.S. Department of Health and Human Services, "Public Health Service Human Research Subjects."

46. Albert R. Jonsen and Lewis H. Butler, "Public Ethics and Policy Making," *Hastings Center Report* 5: 19–31 (August 1975).

47. Henrik L. Blum, *Expanding Health Care Horizons: From a General Systems Concept of Health to a National Health Policy* (Oakland, CA: Third Party Associates, Inc., 1976).

FUTURE DIMENSIONS OF THE HEALTH CARE SYSTEM

Most analyses of the health care delivery system reveal similar major trends during the development of health policy in the United States. In addition, critical problem areas can be identified and grouped into four general categories—those that deal with issues of accessibility, availability, costs, and quality of care. Hence, policymakers, and society as a whole, must wrestle with those questions that embody any planning effort: Where are we now with respect to current health policy? Where do we want to go with it in the future? And, how do we get there?

Without engaging in an indepth analysis of the overall health care system, it is not difficult to observe the successive shifts in health policy since World War II. Between 1946 and 1963, the United States saw major investments in the system and a massive development of resources—specifically, biomedical knowledge brought about through research, expansion of health care facilities and equipment, and increased emphasis on health manpower development. To some, there appeared to be the belief that such tremendous investments in resources would automatically bring about the desired services for the general population.

During the mid-1960s (1963-1966), it was realized that simply having a wealth of resources would have little effect on the goal of equitably providing health care to meet the needs of the American people. Thus, during this period the trend in health policy (not un-

47

related to the explosion of other social concerns of the 1960s such as the civil rights movement, the antiwar effort, and the like) focused on issues of organization and delivery of health care services. With the objective to improve the accessibility and availability of care, we saw the birth of Medicare, Medicaid, the Community Mental Health program, and Office of Economic Opportunity health programs such as neighborhood health centers, among others. Also during this period, government increased its commitment to—and thereby its role in developing—a comprehensive, regionalized health-planning approach.

Between the late 1960s and the present, a third major period shifted policy trends toward increasing government involvement on health care. This era marked the major beginning of the concept of health care as a right within the population at large. However, the issue that soon gathered most attention was, At what cost? Both government and consumers became much more deeply involved in organizing, monitoring, and planning health care. Government increasingly began to regulate health care in an effort to assure higher quality and more accessibility. The major problem to evolve was financing. We had the resources, we had various models of delivery, but we failed to have the means to control the escalating costs. This led to many proposals for mandatory and voluntary cost-containment. Also during this period was the growing acknowledgment that simply providing more medical care (regardless of the costs) did not guarantee better health or increased health status. Concurrently, since the late 1950s, the country continued to experience a further expansion—what might be called an explosion—in the growth of medical research and advances. Some go so far as to conclude that technology has captured the health care system. So, what does the future hold?

It appears that the final decades of the twentieth century suggest several trends, but also hold many mysteries. Among the most demonstrable trends, we appear to have little concern and have no desire to restrain technological growth, although some efforts are underway in an attempt to repersonalize it. Opinion is divided as to whether the push toward centralization—whereby government will increase its responsibility and control—will continue or whether there may be a period of retrenchment. It appears that at least for the short-term future, the latter appears more imminent. Federal health policy now appears to be focusing on deregulation, greater competition in the private sector, and the growth of individual, private enterprises. At minimum, whether government increases or decreases its involvement, it appears that the overwhelming concern will be the allocation of scarce resources and the prioritization of determined areas of need.

Clearly, this means that social and ethical concerns are going to become more prominent and justified in shaping future health policy, either openly or behind closed doors. With the issues of macro-allocation before us, issues of distributive (social) justice are unavoidable. Furthermore, decisions and critical choices pertaining to the direction of policy toward a more preventive approach versus the more traditional curative-crisis approach, a primary care focus versus a tertiary care thrust, regional planning versus institutional and strategic planning require examination of the ethical and social implications of the alternative routes.

In Chapter 1, Hiller outlined many critical issues confronting the health care system that warrant ethical analysis. His focus on both national health policy and individual medical practice decisionmaking allowed a thorough review of problems using analytical tools from multiple disciplines. With the background and framework provided by this comprehensive overview, he set the stage for the first five chapters, which discuss several broad ethical and social implications of critical health policies. Representing a wide range of professional expertise, the authors critically examine questions of social justice, equity, and general trends of federal intervention in the planning and delivery of health care in the United States. In addition, they openly challenge widely accepted views concerning existing public policies and offer an intuitive look at what certain changes could bring about. The essays offer a penetrating study of the relationships between health, health care, and ethical theories of social justice.

In Chapter 2, Veatch examines the prevailing models for promoting justice in the delivery of health care. He further critically analyzes the implications of holding any of these theories of justice in developing a national health policy. He concludes by advocating why it is important that justice be identified as a conscious goal in health planning in order to provide a basis for legislating at least a limited right to health care.

In Chapter 3, O'Sullivan and Hiller pursue the issue raised by Veatch in their examination of a rational basis for health planning with respect to social justice. In addition, they examine major ethical principles and professional codes governing the practice of health planning. Although health planners use alternative approaches to planning, the authors conclude that due to the lack of ethics in most health-planning program curricula, many planners are neither prepared nor able to undertake an ethical analysis in making their decisions. The authors contend that with the critical choices that health planners must make regarding the macroallocation of health resources, it is imperative that they understand and be able to apply ethical principles and human values.

As an economist, Morreale (Chapter 4) assumes somewhat of an economic perspective on issues of justice. Clearly noting the distinct differences between health care and levels of health (or health status), he sharply criticizes current approaches to assuring equity and rights in the delivery of health care in the United States. Morreale's major thesis is that causes of injustices in both the health status of Americans and the health care system are based on fundamental ethical values that are fostered by the economic system. He contends that analysis of the health care system in the absence of a thorough understanding of the economic system in which it operates is nonproductive and does not contribute to health. He concludes by constructing a case for an egalitarian model in which there is a need to fundamentally change the present economic, social, and political systems of society.

In recent efforts to assure more justice in the health care system, the government has engaged in a wide range of regulation. In Chapter 5, Andreano and Wilde examine many of the regulations that have been imposed by government on the health industry. While they acknowledge that there are risks involved with overregulation, their economic and social analysis of the system concludes that something is needed to "pierce through the professional mystique that surrounds the nation's health provider institutions and the veil of reimbursement mechanisms" that prevent consumers from seeing clearly the true costs of the system and the causes of those costs. They argue that some mix of regulations is necessary to guard against the inefficiencies that are documentable in the industry and to promote a more equitable system.

With the increasing awareness of the need to limit scarce resources, there is a plethora of alternative health policy decisions that must be made. One of these is whether or not the United States should invest more of its resources in a national health promotion and disease prevention strategy. In the final chapter of Part I, Green poses an interesting alternative. As an approach that may contribute to solving some of the problems confronting the system, Green analyzes the implications and the potential impact of moving in such a direction. He warns that it is critical for all parties concerned to appreciate the limits of government, and in turn, he looks at potential involvement from the private sector and at consumer participation in his preventive strategy. He concludes by charging health professionals with the responsibility of overseeing government's intervention into the health promotion arena.

2 ETHICAL ASPECTS OF THE RIGHT TO HEALTH CARE

Robert M. Veatch, Ph. D.

INTRODUCTION

The legal right to health in contemporary America is at most tenuous and problematic. Although there have been recent attempts to suggest a constitutional right to health care, there can hardly be any such right to health. Even the right to health care as a constitutional claim seems implausible or, at least, very limited. The Fourteenth Amendment provides that no state shall deprive a person of life, liberty, or property without due process of law; but virtually no one, at least until recently, has suggested that this protection of life implies an obligation on the part of the state to provide health care. The Fourteenth Amendment also prohibits the denial of equal protection of the laws. As some legal rights related to health care are granted to certain citizens through Medicare, Medicaid, and the Veterans' Administration, other citizens may begin to claim the same rights under the equal protection clause.

The legal right to health care is only somewhat greater in statutory law.[1] One may safely say only that Medicare and Medicaid patients have the right to have certain procedures partially paid for provided they can find medical personnel willing to deliver services.

This chapter constitutes an expanded revision of "Legislative Prerogatives and the Right to Health Care," in Paul Andreini and Madeline Nevins, *Policy Making and Health Resources Allocation* (Gaithersburg, MD: Information Planning Associates, Inc., forthcoming).

Actually the present legal right to health care is apparently somewhat broader. Under common law there may be a right to be treated in an unmistakable emergency when the ill person relies upon a well-established custom of the hospital to render aid in such cases.[2] Some states, including New York, have imposed by statute a duty on the general hospital to provide aid in an emergency. The Hill–Burton law requires that "a reasonable volume of services" be provided for persons unable to pay for them, but until recently this was never enforced. At most, it required that some persons be given medical care; never was a generalized right of access implied. The Internal Revenue Service policy used to be that hospitals qualified for tax exempt status only if providing free or below cost care for those unable to pay, but recently even that requirement has come into question.[3] Particular groups, such as veterans and residents in communities that have public hospitals, may have a more extensive right to care; but many people do not have such access, and the care rendered is often of questionable quality.[4] In short, the statutory right to health care seems to be almost as limited as the constitutional right.

As a result, it appears as if those with legalistic inclinations have been wasting their energies trying to establish that statutory and constitutional rights of health care presently exist. It appears that a far more fruitful question is whether such rights ought to exist. Ought there to be legislated a general right to health or health care? If not, ought there to be legislated a right of access to certain kinds of health care? The author is convinced that the answer to the first question must be no, but to the second question the answer is yes.

Certainly a right to be healthy should not be legislated. To do so would be foolish. It would appear to grant a right to something that cannot be delivered. Neither should even a general right to health care be legislated, because it is no more possible to provide all the health care that any individual may desire than it is to provide health to all citizens. Platitudinous and idealized slogans about the right to health care can at best raise false hopes; at worst, they can divert efforts from the more significant task of normative reflection about what kinds of health care society should feel obligated to provide. At the same time, everyone agrees that some health care ought to be provided at public expense, at least where public contract has been made to existing veterans and public employees injured in the line of duty. Therefore, the real questions that exist are how much and what kinds of health care should society provide and what is the normative basis for providing that care?

FOUR PRINCIPLES FOR DISTRIBUTING
HEALTH CARE

Some of the first possible principles of distributing health care are not very plausible. If it is foolish to try to provide all the health resources for everyone to be healthy, then we might consider a policy of providing equal health resources to everyone. In one sense this treats people equally, but it ignores the obvious fact that people have very different needs for health care. In fact, if the principle of equality means that everyone should get the same amount of health resources, either the very sick will go without needed care or the well will have unneeded care forced upon them.

A modification of such a policy might be to provide an equal maximum amount of care to everyone. Such a family health insurance plan introduced into Congress would have provided $50,000 worth of lifetime care for each individual with an additional $2,000 per year restoration. This would, however, permit the very healthy to expend their allotted resources on trivial marginal care while the sickly might quickly consume their allotment and be turned away at the hospital door. It would mean that the senile, semicomatose patient rapidly and inevitably dying of cancer, who had experienced a healthy youth, would have a greater claim to health care than the young, vigorous person who happened to have a sickly childhood. Current developments in philosophical debate over the theories of justice suggest four possible principles for a right to health care.

The Entitlement Theory

The first is the most limited in providing a basis for claiming a right to health care at public expense. Robert Nozick in his important book, *Anarchy, State, and Utopia*,[5] has developed the so-called entitlement theory. Nozick claims that individuals are entitled to what they possess, provided it was acquired justly—from appropriation of goods not previously possessed, by gift, or by exchange. The state's role is to protect against unjust appropriation. This is really a nontheory of justice or a theory of nonjustice. It is really a theory of individual rights of possession.

This strong theory of individual rights seems closely akin to the ideology of mainstream medicine in the United States. It is compatible with the individualistic bias of the Hippocratic Oath. Robert Sade, a Boston physician, articulated this in self-righteous, almost indignant tones in his 1971 essay in the *New England Journal of Medicine*.[6] His claim is roughly that the life and training of physicians are their own. Therefore, the choice of how, when, and if they will practice medicine belongs to them alone "as a consequence of his right to support his own life."[7] Ayn Rand is cited as his authority.

However Nozick, from his much more sophisticated position, recognizes that this libertarian conservative principle does not grant as much freedom as one might expect at first. For one thing, economic, intellectual, and status possessions that now are held by physicians may not have been appropriated justly. To the extent that these possessions were derived from coerced labor or deceptive or fraudulent economic practices by physicians or their ancestors, even Nozick's principle would find that they did not justly belong to physicians. Furthermore, many of the physicians' possessions are received essentially by gift or exchange—by federal support for medical education, by the privilege granted by society in the licensing of the medical profession, and by the funds that are provided by governmental support of physician-rendered services. While some of those gifts may have been given by society to physicians in the past, the linking of them in the future to services rendered to society seems in order. Sade's image of physicians as rugged individualists is, in fact, far from the truth. In our highly integrated, complex society it is fair to say that physicians simply could not practice their profession were it not for the support and good grace of the society. Even under the principles of private contract, society has the right to impose requirements on the physicians that it sanctions and supports.

In the end, the most decisive case against the libertarian entitlement theory is its implausibility. Most people simply do not find plausible the view that people are entitled to hoard resources and skills desperately needed by others simply because of a desire not to share them. Thus, the entitlement theory of an individual's relationship with others is terribly implausible, even if it is coherent.

The Utilitarian Principle

A second principle for distributing health care and therefore acknowledging a right to health care at the expense of society is derived from

ETHICAL ASPECTS OF THE RIGHT TO HEALTH CARE

classical utilitarian theory compatible with much of contemporary economic theory. Advocates of the utilitarian view might hold that morality requires the distribution of resources so that they produce the greatest good for the greatest number.

For medicine this might mean that our national health policy objective should be to maximize aggregate health indicators, such as average life expectancy, or to minimize the average number of missed workdays or days of hospitalization. Of course, there can be disagreements about what produces the most good health. However, the more basic question is why some want (or feel obligated) to maximize aggregate health indicators in the first place. It is quite possible to maximize the average healthiness of the population while maintaining great differentials in health status among individuals. Letting the most sickly individuals, with chronic, multiple illnesses and low education potential, die certainly would decrease morbidity. If the medical resources presently expended on such individuals were used more efficiently, then many other lives could be saved. Average mortality might even decrease.

The utilitarian approach to health care does not address whose health is being promoted, but focuses on the public at large. This approach might be viewed simply as the ethic of public health. Thus, while the individual physician must be concerned with the individual, a national health policy must be concerned with aggregate health. Accordingly, if some individuals must suffer for the good of the society, so be it. Further, the defender might argue that often the best way to increase average health status is to improve the condition of the least healthy. Using such an argument, one could suggest that the Appalachian infant, who is sickly through life due to the lack of adequate pre- and postnatal care, could have a dramatically improved health status through the provision of simple, inexpensive services. Although it is probably true that in some cases average health status could be improved most efficiently by devoting disproportionate resources to the least healthy, such is not likely always to be the case.

Once one grants that there are moral claims on society beyond the protection of individual rights to possess what one has acquired, it is not obvious why we should then select the utilitarian principle of the greatest good for the greatest number as the basis for social distribution. Anyone who recognizes the moral duties of justice, promise keeping, and honesty as independent moral claims must reject the aggregate utility goal as the only basis for allocating resources. In the final analysis, attempting to maximize only aggregate utility appears to be as implausible as the policy of only protecting the individual's right to continue to possess what has been acquired.

The defense of cost–benefit analysis as a method of health planning is rooted in the principle of utilitarianism—that the most appropriate course is the one that would maximize total net benefit in comparison with harm. Thus, frequently when policy alternatives get complicated, more sophisticated calculating tools, such as cost–benefit analysis, are deemed the necessary remedy.

There are two possible objections to cost–benefit analysis. The first, which often receives the most attention, is the issue of quantification. It is argued that many more subjective benefits and harms are not easily quantifiable and therefore tend to be omitted. For example, we recognize that life has more value than the economic worth of future labor and that retired people are not worthless. Yet there may be a strong bias to work with hard numbers, while hoping or assuming that the more subjective, intuitive benefits and harms shall be superimposed at a later time. This can be a real problem, albeit not necessarily an insurmountable one.

The second problem associated with cost–benefit analysis is what is done with the numbers once they are generated. Utilitarians say, without any defense, that they should be aggregated and that the aggregate should be maximized. For example, if one wanted to know whether to develop an artificial heart, this method would call for the calculation of the individual benefits and harms, their summation, and subsequently their comparison with net benefits from alternative courses. Yet one must ask why anyone should be interested solely in net aggregate benefits and harms? Although one could understand a psychological egoism that advocated a maximization of an individual person's net benefits, with the abandonment of an entirely egocentric perspective, why maximize aggregates? Furthermore, there is strong concern as to how the benefits and harms are distributed.

The potential risk to third parties from the nuclear-powered artificial heart presents another interesting case on which to expand. According to the cost–benefit theorist, the risk of exposure to radiation counts as a harm, but the question of who is at risk (i.e., the one in which the device is implanted or the one sitting next to that person at any given time) logically counts for nothing. In other words, a risk is simply a risk. With the summation of harms, more specific information about who is harmed is lost (except insofar as the quantity of harm changes as the one harmed changes).

The amount and distribution of benefits and harms are relevant to social policy. The same estimates of individual benefits and harms could be used to calculate the standard deviation rather than, or in addition to, the total aggregated net benefit. However, such is not the approach taken by government; the public constantly hears about the gross national product, but never hears about the gross national standard deviation of product.

In the case of the artificial heart, for example, use of such an approach may have important implications. In contrast to the utilitarians, the Artificial Heart Panel[a] assumed that risks to third parties are not comparable to those of individuals in need of receiving artificial hearts. The panel's concern seemed to be more with the difference between a risk to someone who stands to benefit and someone who has nothing to gain. On the other hand, if distribution of welfare is critical, then policy options may differ. If the innocent third party exposed to radiation is relatively well off in comparison with the one needing the artificial heart, then possibly we can minimize inequalities in individual welfare by using the nuclear-powered heart rather than those using alternative power sources.

In summation of this approach, the utilitarians count risks, but not who suffers the risk. However, one need not abandon the sophisticated techniques of cost–benefit analysis in order to take distribution into account. Simply programming the computer to calculate measures of distribution would address the problem in principle. Whether it deals with the problem of quantifiability is another matter. Furthermore, it is not adequate simply to indicate the rarity of conflicts between maximizing aggregate utility and maximizing equality of distribution. That is an empirical matter. Whether they are as rare as utilitarians suggest is not the issue. Rather, if one is seeking a principle to govern the allocation of resources, then the utilitarian forms of cost–benefit analysis cannot be adopted on the grounds that it provides the right principle of distributive justice.

a. This panel was established by the National Institutes of Health to investigate and report on the ethical implications of the development of an artificial heart.

The Rawlsian Maximin[b] Principle

A third possible answer to the question of how much health care society ought to provide to individuals can be derived from a theory of justice based, in part, on need. The work of John Rawls, *A Theory of Justice*,[8] provides the theoretical underpinning for this position. It is based on two principles.[c] The first is that every person is to have an equal right to the most extensive total system of equal liberties compatible with a similar system of liberty for all. At first, this would appear to justify the individualistic private rights position assumed by Nozick and Sade, but upon reflection, it clearly does not. The liberty to withhold medical services is clearly not compatible with the maintenance of liberty of one who will die if medical care is not rendered. The second principle is that social and economic inequalities should be arranged so that they are both to the greatest benefit of the least advantaged and open to all under conditions of fair equality of opportunity.[9]

The application of Rawlsian theory to health policy raises complex problems. First, Rawls clearly articulates that his principles are for the basic social institutions of society and not for making day-to-day decisions. Second, Rawls appears to consider health a natural good rather than a social one; thus, his principles are less relevant to the question of how health care ought to be distributed. A strong case can be made, however, that health is in reality a social phenomenon rather than a natural one. If so, the Rawlsian principles become much more relevant to the questions of distributing health care.

---

b. Editor's Note: A *maximin* strategy or principle may be defined as one which *maxi*mizes the *min*imum payoff (i.e., the amount of health care) to be received by any interested party.

c. They are derived from the Rawlsian method of the *original position*. It is one of many more or less similar methods of attempting to determine what would be a reasonable social practice from an impartial or disinterested perspective. Provided one continues to realize that no one can, in fact, become blind to one's own interests and biases, the author has no real problem with the metaphor of the contractors in the original position as a way of asking what would be reasonable. Some of the more zealous advocates of the method tend to believe that principles or practices are correct simply because such unbiased people would agree to them. However, it should be viewed much more as an epistemological tool — as a way of getting a good estimate of what is right rather than as a definition of what is right. Nevertheless, the method seems to be useful.

This Rawlsian theory of justice whereby social policies are designed to maximize the least well off would, for health policy, mean distributing health care on the basis of improving the health of the most needy. According to Rawls, this would be the fair thing to do even if it might lower the overall average health status of the population. The fair and reasonable position to assume, that which reasonable people would choose if their decisions were not biased by their present egocentric perspective, would be to permit certain inefficiencies that would improve the health of the least well off.

However, what if one of the ways of improving the health of the least healthy is to pay extremely unequal economic incentives to a small group of talented people in order to bribe them to help the least healthy by pursuing important research and development work or by spending longer hours than desired in the delivery of health care to the needy? For Rawlsian theorists, such inequalities are justified. The benefits given to the unusually talented or skilled will trickle down to the most sickly who will be helped in the long run. The fact that inequalities are increased in the process is morally irrelevant. In fact, such inequalities are not only justified, they are fair.

It is possible that some inequalities would be permitted in a capitalist society in which high rewards are expected in order to provide incentives to the elite. Some, however, will find it difficult to defend the position that such inequalities are fair or just. At least in those cases in which the least well off are willing to waive their claim to equality in order to improve their health, probably such inequalities should be tolerated, but that is no reason to conclude that they are just.

The Egalitarian Principle

In the opinion of this author, it is more reasonable to take the position that the fair approach is to distribute health care resources on the basis of the principle that everyone has a claim to the health care needed to provide an opportunity for a level of health equal, insofar as possible, to other persons' health. With certain qualifications, health care should be distributed on the basis of need, if it is to be fairly distributed. If 1,000 employees of an automobile manufacturer could have their annual incomes increase by $800 each, provided that the president of the corporation was paid $1 million a year more than he presently receives, it is not obvious that it would be a fair thing to do. Rawlsian principles suggest it would be.

With respect to health care, does the improvement of the health of the least healthy justify increasing the gap between the unhealthy and the healthy or providing uniquely high economic incentives to skilled providers? For example, with a national health insurance, the wealthy and healthy may actually get more benefits from some health programs than the poor. But if the poor would get some benefits, the program would be justified according to the maximin principle (provided there is no more efficient way to improve the health of the poor). Under the egalitarian principle, it may be efficient—or even right—to produce inequalities in order to improve the condition of the least well off, but it should not be considered fair or just.[10]

POSSIBLE LIMITS TO THE EGALITARIAN NEED PRINCIPLE

There are both theoretical and practical objections to the egalitarian principle. The first set of questions raises the issue of giving public policy priority to medical need. Why should distribution be based on medical need rather than on more general needs? And if priority is to be given to medical need, is it really possible to separate needs from desires?

Why Improve Health Rather Than Well-being?

Regardless of whether one accepts a utilitarian, maximin, or egalitarian principle, one must ask why the policy focus should be on medical care in isolation rather than on improvement of well-being more generally. Why does the sick, rich person get priority over the healthy poor person? If the goal is, for instance, to improve conditions of the least well off, would it not be more practical to distribute some generalized medium like money to the least well off, letting people buy whatever they believe would improve their condition? This is the argument of the laissez-faire welfare planner. Since no one knows as well as individuals what will make them happier, giving them the more general resource will allow them to maximize their respective positions.

In principle there may be more to this argument than defenders of centralized social planning are willing to accept. In theory, there may be a strong case for this policy. In practice, however, withholding money from the sickest will not guarantee that it will be given to the poorest or the more generally least well off, regardless of the criterion. If the condition of some may be improved by reallocating resources to those who are medically least well off, there is a good chance that this will tend to improve the status of the least well off. If this can be achieved politically, this course should be taken.

Can Health Needs Really be Distinguished from Desires?

A second line of attack has been posed in the form of the question, Is it really possible to distinguish health care needs from desires? The argument is that it is impossible as part of the policy-planning process to separate needed care and desired care and that therefore goods should be distributed more evenly on the grounds that claims are not distinguishable. Whether it is a general medium like money or a health resource, all individuals should get the same amount to spend in the manner that will maximize their health or welfare as the case may be.

However, is it really that difficult to separate needs and desires? If some spend a large portion of their allotted health care on rhinoplasty for a somewhat enlarged nose, while others spend it on blood transfusions for an incurable genetic disease, is there any real doubt who are more needy? While there is no absolute and objective difference between a health care need and a mere desire, such an absolute distinction is unnecessary. All that is necessary is an ability to make a rough separation reflecting the amount of resources available for health care. If one listed all possible medical interventions, there would be relatively little disagreement about the classification of most. An unproved, expensive surgical intervention to overcome an infertility problem in a woman who has had six children sounds less compelling than penicillin for the young boy who has contracted a simple, curable case of pneumonia. All that is needed is a rough rank ordering with special attention going to that small group of interventions near the borderline, given the limited resources and choices devoted to health care. A sustained policy debate, using mechanisms described below, will be necessary only for a few marginal interventions. In relative terms, making the distinction between needed and merely desired care may not be a terribly difficult task, even if there is no way that an absolute dichotomy between the two is possible.

Despite acceptance of such a policy in principle, its application to health care in isolation from other welfare measures will still produce objections. The remaining objections constitute competing moral claims and may lead to the conclusion that the right to health care should be limited by considerations other than the egalitarian principle.

Efficiency

The most apparent of the competing claims is efficiency. The futility of the egalitarian principle as a sole sufficient criterion for allocating health care may be observed through the realization that the most equal health care possible would be no health care to anyone. All equally sick or dead would be very egalitarian. There may be times when in order to produce basic and essential goods for some people, others will not be able to have the same right of access to these goods. At some point society must be willing to sacrifice equity for efficiency.

Critics of the egalitarian argument say that the egalitarian principle creates a demand that is impossible to satisfy. The suggestion that there are not enough resources to meet the claims cannot logically be an acceptable answer. Neither can an appeal to a most comprehensive, discerning, and impartial cost–benefit analysis. What is at stake is not how comprehensive, how discerning, and how impartial the data are, but what is done with them after they are gathered. Aggregating costs and benefits is neither more impartial nor more rigorous than calculating standard deviations. However, it may be less fair. It is no more plausible to totally sacrifice efficiency for equity than it is to surrender equity for efficiency. No readily available formula permits a balancing of the two, but both goals—maximizing the mean and minimizing the standard deviation—must be maintained.

Freedom and Justice

Another set of competing claims is made in the name of freedom or autonomy. These are really a series of separate problems. First, does one really have a claim to health care at public expense for a medical need resulting from a health risk voluntarily taken? Do we really believe that the mountain climber who has fallen off a cliff, the professional automobile racer, the smoker, the individual who has previously refused a standard therapy, or the professional wrestler have a claim to be patched up at public expense? As the causes of illness and accidents become more identified and the lifestyle correlates of medical conditions become more recognized, health care needs will increasingly be seen as a result of voluntary choices.

Turning such patients away at the hospital door is not desirable. Doing so would be too uncomfortable. However, it does seem reasonable that such individuals be expected to pay into a national health insurance pool an amount calculated to equal the cost of the marginal medical care needed for voluntarily engaging in health-risky behavior. A tax on cigarettes to reimburse the government for such costs is appropriate not as a paternalistic deterrent to smoking nor as a luxury tax to raise general revenues, but as a source of the funds predictably needed to pay for future care.[11] Claims for health care for culpable illness or injury when the risk is not run for a public good are not comparable to claims for nonculpable conditions. That is why the principle calls for an opportunity for health. If one has previously declined recommended care and then needs more expensive intervention to solve what has developed into a more serious health problem, it is difficult to understand why a principle of equity would require public support of the more costly treatment.

A second dimension of the potential conflict between justice and freedom is introduced in acknowledging that equity, and efficiency as well, might be increased by placing certain constraints on the freedom of citizens and medical professionals. The naive image of individual physicians responsible only to themselves for their current skills, experience, and status has already been considered. If physicians are in their present positions because society has granted them and their ancestors certain privileges, then imposition of certain correlative obligations seems reasonable. Constraints on income, geographical area of service, and area of specialization seem fitting if such constraints will promote health and/or other fundamental values such as equity. At the same time, freedom is a fundamental value, too. Unless there are strong reasons to place such constraints (as there often will be), physicians, like other citizens, should be entitled to as much freedom as possible.

Likewise, constraints on individual citizen's private contracting for medical care might be necessary in the name of efficiency and equity. At least compulsory participation in a social security tax for national health insurance seems plausible. The battle over the compulsory participation issue was fought and won decades ago for the social security tax itself. Its defense was not so much on the grounds of paternalism as due to the benefits that would accrue to society of not having to cope with those who are in need but banned from the system because they had not paid their share. At present, it is necessary to carefully watch how equitable the funding of the various national health insurance proposals is.

The increase of the percentage of the social security tax deduction is probably the least equitable. Paying for health care from general revenues would be preferable in this regard, especially if the income tax were more equitable. Perhaps the most egalitarian way to fund national health insurance would be by removing the ceiling on social security deductions and, if necessary, raising additional funds by additional tax on larger incomes.

The question of citizen freedom raises a more radical question. It may be that equity and efficiency could be increased not only by compulsory participation in the funding of national health insurance but also by compulsory participation in the delivery system. For some time, Britain has had a parallel national health service and private delivery system and is currently debating the acceptability of certain parts of the private care system. It might be that certain restraints on the privilege of buying one's way out of the community's system of care would improve the quality of care for those now receiving poor care. This could come not only from economies of scale but, more importantly, from the social effect of having those of high status and political power receive care through the same drab, overcrowded emergency rooms that the poor now use.

Health care may be the institution in which both equity and benefits to others will require certain compromises of freedom. As with efficiency, neither freedom nor equity can totally dominate the nation's health policy. Some discretion certainly must be retained—at least to select physicians within a common delivery system—but there may be necessary limits on individual freedoms necessitated by other competing moral claims.

Other Prima Facie Duties and Rights

There may be other obligations and rights that conflict with equitable provision of health care. Charles Fried has argued that other rights are at stake in health care beyond the claims of equity and efficiency.[12] In the opinion of this author, however, there are other moral duties at stake that generate correlative claims of rights. A physician may have made a promise to a patient to offer continued care. This implied promise or contract may generate obligations for the physician that would easily resolve the dilemma of who should be cared for if both this patient and another who had no previous contact with the physician were in equal need of immediate attention. However, the duty to keep contracts may conflict with claims of equity—as when a person in much poorer condition needs care at the same time as an ongoing patient with only marginal needs.

The obligations of truth telling, consent and the right to refuse treatment, gratitude, reparation for previous harm, and possibly other more specific duties such as not killing may often conflict with the duties derived from the principle of equity. The arbitration of these conflicts will not be an easy task and will not reduce to a simple formula. Equity is a significant moral claim in health care policy that does indeed conflict with the rights, duties, claims, and interests more traditionally emphasized in medical ethics. The arbitration of these conflicts will require sophisticated policy-planning mechanisms and a full understanding of the nature of the conflicts.

MECHANISMS FOR ARBITRATING CLAIMS AND DECIDING NEEDS

Indeed, many competing moral duties and rights are at stake in deciding what health care is sufficiently needed to warrant its support at public expense. If this claim is correct, at least two tiers of policy planning will be necessary. The first issues are more global policy questions. How much of the nation's resources should be devoted to health care as opposed to other social problems, such as transportation, housing, education, defense, and so forth? Certainly that is a question that must be answered by federal and state legislatures at the most general policy levels. It would be as irrational to permit medical professionals to decide the level of resources that should be devoted to health care as to let military leaders decide the defense budget. Each can be expected to have a unique perspective and special professional commitment to the cause for which they have given their lives.

At this same level of legislative prerogative, some basic policy decisions within the health sphere should be made. The question of the proportion of medical resources devoted to basic research, technological development of delivery systems, and actual delivery involves basic value choices, such as one's sense of obligation to future generations and one's confidence in man's ability to plan rationally. Basic budget questions of this sort should also be dealt with legislatively.

The legislatures will want, however, to delegate some of the more specific evaluations to agencies capable of dealing with smaller scale problems. The ranking of diseases, treatments, and patient groups to facilitate giving the highest priority to those who are medically least well off will have to be done by such agencies. In the end, there will be constant interplay between the legislature and these administrative agencies, with the agencies deciding that a particular intervention—orthodontics, for instance—does or does not meet a need of a group sufficiently poorly off to be included in a national health insurance plan at the present time. The legislature might respond by mandating that a marginal intervention is sufficiently important to replace something covered. Alternatively, it might choose to increase the funds allocated to the medical care sphere to permit the inclusion of marginal intervention without cutting anything else out.

In each case, the first question ought to be, What can be done to give people opportunities for health equal, insofar as possible, to the health of others, and then, Are there competing claims based on efficiency, responsibility for taking health risks, and other rights and responsibilities that militate against providing resources to provide those opportunities for health for the least well off? Certainly there must be an accumulation of the data on the benefits and harms from alternative courses of action, but those data can never directly lead to policy. In particular, these essentially political decisions should never be reduced to calculations of maximum aggregate benefit and harm. While the data should be processed, measures of distribution also need to be calculated—measures of equity, as well as measures of aggregate benefit. The final ethical choice involves the determination of what constitutes a reasonable mix of these competing claims, among which efficient maximizing of aggregate utility is but one. As long as only efficiency and equity are under consideration, the objective should be to maximize the ratio of a standardized measure of net aggregate benefits divided by a distribution measure such as standard deviation.

The policy dilemma of the artificial heart should be handled in this way. It is a provocative case not only because it is so expensive, but also because it is on the margin of needed care that possibly should be provided at public expense.[13] A planning agency would begin by applying its norm. Given the costs of the device and the potential benefits at any point in its technological development, will it provide an opportunity for health for the group that is medically least well off? If so, are there other values, rights, and interests radically jeopardized by a policy of developing and supplying the heart to those who are in need?

For a policy as basic as this one, regardless of the decision of the planning agency, the question should be returned to the legislature. Recognizing that the costs are so enormous and that all citizens in need might justifiably make a claim on the device developed at public expense, the legislature might well decide that its resources should be expended elsewhere in an effort to better meet the needs of others who are perhaps in a worse condition than artificial heart recipients. The burden of supplying the artificial heart for some but not others is tolerable only if the inequities that would be involved are acceptable and if the benefits to others that will have to be foregone are not considered.[14]

The newly established agencies for controlling medical costs—Professional Standards Review Organizations (PSROs), Health Systems Agencies (HSAs), and Health Maintenance Organizations (HMOs)—appear to be taking on some of the functions of the local and regional bodies. Most of the planning that led to the creation of these agencies, however, failed to recognize the essentially evaluative nature of the tasks they must perform. Often the problem has been seen as a technical one of ferreting out useless or detrimental care and banning it rather than of making priority choices based on one or more of the principles of efficiency, equity, and freedom. Decisions as to which kinds of intervention are worthy of being supported at the present time have not always been made on the basis of commonly shared value systems.

The PSRO is especially misconceived in this regard. By law, with a rare potential technical exception, the PSRO must be made up entirely of physicians. However, physicians have no special expertise in making ethical choices on behalf of the American public, and in all likelihood, they are committed to a unique set of values. The Hippocratic ethic is uniquely poor in giving guidance on questions of equity and freedom and provides no guidance or assistance in deciding how the American public should spend its scarce resources. An agency such as a PSRO might have to decide whether national health insurance should provide a fifth or sixth day of hospitalization for normal childbirth. The problem is one of marginal benefits at a high price (at least if one assumes that the additional day of hospitalization provides benefit on balance). The physician is in no position to decide whether marginal benefits in controlling infection and giving the mother an additional day's rest outweigh the benefits of reuniting the family in their home and spending the resources saved on a housing program; yet now, physicians are being asked to make such decisions. They might even be asked whether a national health insurance program should pay for midwives for home delivery. If one recognizes the ideological conflicts that such proposals generate, it seems unreasonable to permit a group of physicians (including obstetricians) to make that policy choice.

There is a need for local and regional groups such as the HSA and the PSRO. However, if the legislature is going to delegate its responsibility for the fine tuning of health policy to such local groups, then it should insist that the makeup of the group reflects the values of the general population it represents and not the special, idiosyncratic values of a single professional group.[15] Although the group will have to have competent technical advice that also will be tinged with the value perspective of the experts, it is far safer than granting complete authority for value choices in health policy planning to the expert group.

SUMMARY

The crucial policy question is not whether there presently exists a constitutional right—or even a statutory right—to health care, but rather, whether such a right should be legislated. Such realization thrusts the debate into the arena of normative thinking. Currently, society is running the risk of deciding health policy solely on the basis of the norm of efficiency, choosing those policies that will maximize the number of added years of life per dollar invested or those policies that will most greatly decrease average morbidity.

The health of Americans is in a sorry state. You have heard the figures. The United States ranks ninth in life expectancy at birth. Infant mortality in the United States is 60 percent higher than in Sweden. What is not recognized is that the continual recitation of aggregate social indicators such as life expectancy, infant mortality, or gross national product implies that maximizing aggregates is a morally legitimate goal. When is the last time that the press emphasized a government report of the gross national distribution of life expectancy or infant mortality? Ninety percent of those earning over $10,000 in 1970 were covered by health insurance. For those earning less than $5,000, the figure was 49.9 percent; for blacks earning less than $5,000, 38.8 percent. Infant mortality goes down as income increases. An infant born to a woman with less than eight years of schooling is twice as likely to die as one born to a woman with twelve years of schooling or more. Black infant mortality in New York is two-thirds greater than white infant mortality in Arkansas, despite similar income and schooling levels. Black death rates are from 50 to 300 percent higher than the rates for whites for all age groups. This is true for heart disease and cancer as well as accidental and violent deaths.

We live in a tradition committed to the pursuit of health, happiness, and efficiency, but we also live in a tradition committed to more than that. It is the tradition of an Amos who pleaded, "Let justice roll down like waters and righteousness like an overflowing stream."[16] It is the tradition of a Declaration of Independence committed to the proposition that all men were created equal, as well as to life, liberty, and the pursuit of happiness.

In summary, the United States is trapped between two dominant ethics—the hyperindividualism of the Hippocratic Oath and emphasis on individual rights on the one hand and the utilitarian ethic of maximizing social indicators on the other. Either might by accident also promote justice, but it will be only by accident. The time has come to include justice as a conscious goal in our health policy planning. That will give us a basis for legislating a right to health care without at the same time writing a blank check implying that all citizens have a right to every imaginable kind of desired medical intervention at government expense.

NOTES TO CHAPTER 2

1. Edward V. Sparer, "The Legal Right to Health Care: Public Policy and Equal Access," *Hastings Center Report* 6: 39–47 (October 1976).
2. Wilmington General Hospital v. Manlove, 54 Del. 15, 174 A.2d 135 (1961).
3. EKWRO v. Simon, 370 F. Supp. 326 (1973), rev'd. 506 F.2d 1278 (1974); EKWRO v. Simon, 44 U.S.L.W. 4724 (May 1976).
4. Sparer.
5. Robert Nozick, *Anarchy, State, and Utopia* (New York: Basic Books, Inc., 1974).
6. Robert M. Sade, "Medical Care as a Right: A Refutation," *New England Journal of Medicine* 285: 1288–1292 (December 1971).
7. Ibid.
8. John Rawls, *A Theory of Justice* (Cambridge, MA: Harvard University Press, 1971).
9. Ibid., p. 302.
10. Robert M. Veatch, "What Is a 'Just' Health Care Delivery?" in Robert M. Veatch and Roy Branson, *Ethics and Health Policy* (Cambridge, MA: Ballinger Publishing Company, 1976), pp. 127–153.
11. Robert M. Veatch, "Who Should Pay for Smokers' Medical Care?" *Hastings Center Report* 4: 8–9 (November 1974).
12. Charles Fried, "Rights and Health Care—Beyond Equity and Efficiency," *New England Journal of Medicine* 923: 241–245 (July 1975).
13. Artificial Heart Assessment Panel, *The Totally Implantable Artificial Heart*, DHEW Publication No. (NIH) 74–191 (Washington, D.C.: U.S. Government Printing Office, 1973).
14. Charles Fried, "Equality and Rights in Medical Care," *Hastings Center Report* 6: 29–34 (February 1976).
15. Clark C. Havighurst and James F. Blumstein, "Coping with Quality/Cost Trade-Offs in Medical Care: The Role of PSROs," *Northwestern University Law Review* 70: 6–68 (March–April 1975).
16. Amos, 5: 24.

3 ETHICS AND HEALTH PLANNING

Michael J. O'Sullivan, Dr.P.H.
Marc D. Hiller, Dr.P.H.

During the past decade, an interest in the application of ethics to various aspects of public life has emerged as a national issue with significant practical implications. The reasons for this concern are no doubt manifold. However, it appears to be rooted in a widespread uneasiness in which questions of morals and values are swept aside by the demands of rampant technology, by professionals acting out of self-centered interest rather than the welfare of the public, by politicians becoming the captives rather than the captains of government. More simply, there is a widespread belief that people in public office or with a public trust are not behaving the way they should or living up to society's expectations.

The concern for ethics is nowhere more evident than in the field of medicine. Numerous publications, conferences, and courses have been developed for both practicing physicians and medical students. However, medical ethics remains circumscribed to professional questions, examining the nature of the physician–patient relationship in such areas as truth telling on the part of physicians, the right of individuals to death with dignity, and women's right to legal abortions. Each of these issues has significant factual, value, and emotional dimensions that require systematic and sober analysis. A closely related area of ethical analysis known as bioethics also has grown in prominence. Bioethics tends to encompass a wider range of topics than does medical ethics. Genetic engineering, population control, and the allocation of very expensive, and hence relatively scarce, exotic medical devices represent only a small sample of issues addressed under the rubric of bioethics. However, the boundaries between the two are very permeable and no hard and fast distinctions can be made, nor is one necessary.[1] However, interestingly, ethical issues in health planning, particularly those related to the construction of health care facilities and the development of resources, areas that have grown immensely since World War II and are currently practiced under the National Health Planning and Resources Development Act, (PL 93-641)[2] have not been targets of extensive or critical ethical analysis by medical ethicists, bioethicists, or health planners themselves.

However, earlier work in the ethics of health policy development draws attention to the ethical nature of problems confronting health planning. For example, in 1973 the proceedings of a national Conference on Health Care and Changing Values was published under the title of *Ethics of Health Care*.[3] This volume emphasizes that a significant amount of health care decisionmaking has shifted from a highly individual perspective to more of a social one; consequently, qualitatively different ethical problems are emerging. Tancredi summarizes the situation by stating that:

> Few decisions are being made by individuals, and more are being made by the collective action of public officials, consumers and health professionals . . . there is little precedent in our medical-ethical tradition for the way in which these important social contributions should be considered in defining medical responsibility and in resolving such questions as what care should be available to which segments of the population.[4]

These are central questions to health planning, where collective decisions regarding the location of health facilities and the need for various health services commonly are made.

In 1976, Veatch and Branson applied ethical analysis to various aspects of health policy planning.[5] Their book, *Ethics and Health Policy*, responds to consumer and public interest in the issues of how and to whom health care is delivered, the increasing use of cost-benefit analysis in health policy development, the growing societal interest in human rights and social justice, and the growth of systematic health planning. According to the authors:

> The questions now being asked are more health policy questions, questions of distribution and priority. They are fundamentally questions of social

and political ethics, not those of the individual patient–physician relationship, and they are more and more being asked by patients, citizens, and governmental officials who have never shared the values of the Hippocratic tradition.[6]

While these two volumes span a wide range of issues fundamental to health care policymaking and planning, both omit specific reference to health planning under PL 93–641.

While concern is growing for the ethical issues surrounding health planning among providers, consumers, and governmental officials, it is by no means clear how this concern should be pursued, discussed, or analyzed or how health-planning students should be educated about potential ethical implications of planning decisions. Hence, the purpose of this chapter is to explore some of the more important ethical questions confronting health planning. The working hypothesis is that health planners are not prepared adequately either through their education or their socialization to deal with the complex ethical issues that are embedded in the resource allocation decisions required in health planning. Furthermore, the authors contend that health-planning practice could be improved significantly with the addition of ethical analysis to the array of planning techniques employed by health planners.

The questions of ethics and health planning are probed at four levels: (1) ethical problems confronted by individual health planners; (2) ethical dilemmas of the health-planning profession; (3) ethical assumptions embedded in the various modes of health planning; and (4) ethical criteria used in evaluating the consequences and the outcomes of the health-planning process. Although each level is treated separately for purposes of analysis, each is interdependent with the others.

ETHICS AND THE INDIVIDUAL
HEALTH PLANNER

When individual ethics in health care are addressed, the discussion is usually limited to an analysis of the relationship between physicians or other clinical health care providers and their patients. Ramsey develops ethical principles relevant to the question of "what ought the doctor to do" within the confines of the patient–practitioner relationship when facing an ethical dilemma.[7] Serious issues also arise for health planners at the individual level, and the question of what the health planner ought to do in a variety of situations and under varying conditions has not received much attention. This may be due in part to the complexity of the situation, since within health planning, no clearly delineated framework exists such as the physician-patient relationship. One might ask who are the clients of the health planner and get a variety of answers. Is it the public at large, the board of directors of the planning agency, or some other special group? The lack of a clear client–practitioner relationship raises a series of problems.

For example, suppose that a health planner, recently employed by a planning agency, conducts a detailed technical analysis and concludes that the plan adopted by the agency's board of directors contains policies that over time will favor the construction of health facilities and the expansion of health services into the outlying suburban neighborhoods of the designated planning region. These policies will decrease accessibility to the new health care services for the poor and minority groups living in the center city. Should the planner, as part of regular job activities, confront the board, knowing that the board will not respond to a highly technical analysis by a neophyte employee? Perhaps the planner should funnel this information to a local health activist group? Successful application of political pressure on the board might force a change of its plan and instead emphasize health services development in the center city. Should the planner simply refrain from assuming a proactive stance? Which role constitutes the most ethical behavior?

These are but three of the wide range of ethical propositions involved in this situation that are in conflict with each other. On the one hand, there is the planner's concern for the public interest represented by the poor center city dwellers. On the other, there is the board's expectation that staff will carry out the goals and objectives established for the organization. Which of these prescriptions is the health planner to follow? Which criteria or standards should serve as guides? How should these guidelines be developed—and by whom?

There are no simple answers to such questions; and no approach, ethical or otherwise, will ever be fully adequate to deal with the myriad of individual dilemmas that will arise in such situations. These are existential problems that will be confronted again and again by the individuals involved. However, both health planners and the public should be aware that ethical issues are at stake in these types of situations. Ethical thinking and analysis certainly would be an improvement over present practice, which appears to be little more than a melange of personal ideas, beliefs, and opinions. This assumption raises the question of how health planners acquire their beliefs about what is correct or incorrect in their individual behavior.

One may presume that the ethical principles and criteria used by health planners arise in much the same manner as the ethics of members of other professions—namely, as a consequence of the manner in which individuals are selected, educated, and socialized by those who already dominate their respective professions. An examination of the early era of health planning sheds some light on where and how health-planning professionals have acquired the standards that guide their behavior.

When the Hill–Burton Hospital Construction and Survey Act (PL 79–725), the nation's first national health planning law, was passed in 1946, a small number of health-planning agencies were established. Most of the original staff members of these agencies wandered into the health-planning field and more or less developed the practice of areawide health planning as the agencies themselves evolved. Those who entered the health-planning field came from a wide range of backgrounds, including hospital administration, health education, public health, law, city planning, and social welfare. The wide diversity of backgrounds and perspectives brought varying norms, rules, and standards about how to govern individual behavior. A broad range of ideas, beliefs, and attitudes guiding ethical behavior emerged that continues to the present day.

Although some may argue that such a range of values represents the pluralistic nature of the health care system and is therefore beneficial, health-planning activities cannot be effective and ethical dilemmas cannot be resolved satisfactorily by simply relying on a diverse set of ideas and notions about what is right or wrong. Health planners must develop a sound understanding of various ethical theories and an ability in ethical reasoning. The Comprehensive Health Planning Act of 1966 (PL 89–749) established formal educational programs for health planners. Although most of these programs remain operational today, courses, case study materials, or textbooks that address ethical issues in health planning are still lacking.

The development of ethical analysis skills in health planners can be improved if changes are made in the current approach to the topic in undergraduate, graduate, and continuing education for health planners. Exposing health-planning students to the writings of prominent ethical thinkers would constitute a logical first step and should be encouraged, but it would scarcely be enough. Students need more: They need exposure to those pressing problems of health planning that have both significant ethical aspects and practical implications.

The case study approach in teaching ethical analysis is one means of satisfying these requirements and offers several advantages over other types of educational methods. Foremost is that this approach avoids the pretentiousness of simply preaching morality or indoctrinating students with the instructor's ethical perspective. Moreover, it offers students the opportunity to develop and test their own ethical principles against those of early and contemporary philosophers, their peers, and field practitioners. In addition, it allows for the comparison of ethical reasoning with a variety of other rationales, such as cost–benefit analysis and political approaches commonly used in health planning.

Health-planning educators do not have to become experts in ethics to adopt the case study approach; they could integrate ethical thinking with the usual types of analysis taught in health-planning courses. Since health-planning education and practice tend to be eclectic, this should not pose any significant problem to educators who are accustomed to incorporating materials from a variety of sources. Furthermore, they could adopt a wide range of resources from other fields.

Case studies already are used in many settings for teaching ethics.[8] As used in medical education, the case study approach parallels that employed in legal education. However, this method is not without pitfalls. Ramsey argues that there are distinct differences between legal education and the teaching of medical ethics.[9] While law students have precedential concepts of justice and fairness to which they can refer, medical students have few if any of these resources. In legal education, theoretical notions of rightness or wrongness are examined within a context established by precedents developed in similar kinds of cases and then further refined by continued study and criticism. In medical ethics, usually the bare case is examined without referring to historical precedents for guidance as to the rightness and wrongness of the medical behavior being studied. In Ramsey's opinion, the situation in medical ethics needs to be changed— "unless we deem pouring the concepts of one empty mind into another to be the discussion of a medical ethical problem."[10] The situation in health planning is even bleaker; only a handful of developed cases exist, and they are hardly seasoned by past precedents or in conceptual frameworks,[11] beyond narrowly construed attempts at cost–benefit analysis. However, the previously cited works of Tancredi and of Veatch and Branson, as well as experience from city planning and public policy, offer sound guidance to health planning.

Another means for resolving the problem, which requires a longer time, would be for academicians and health services researchers to conduct substantive investigations into the decisionmaking processes employed by health-planning agencies and individual planners. The reasons for the planning decisions could be documented; the majority and dissenting opinions and the arguments supporting them could be recorded. The research could reveal whether decisions are based on principles that governed past cases, are subscribed to by other planning bodies and individuals, or represent a new line of reasoning.

With both approaches, a body of precedent knowledge would develop and could be linked closely to the concrete concerns and experiences of the health planners. If neither approach is adopted, then health planning will continue with an ad hoc decisionmaking system in which alternative proposals are approved or denied without the decisionmakers benefiting from the larger body of ethical reasoning. If adopted, however, valuable materials would exist to which health-planning students and practitioners could refer in guiding their decisions and behaviors.

ETHICAL DILEMMAS OF THE HEALTH-PLANNING PROFESSION

The professions in society derive a large degree of autonomy from at least three sources. First, they control the number of professionals entering the field by influencing and to varying degrees limiting the entry of students to professional schools. Second, in a tort case, the conduct of professionals is typically evaluated by reference to the standards of customary practice of the local community. The result is that the standards of law used to judge professionals are generated by the professionals themselves. Third, the professions are allegedly self-policing with respect to ethical issues, and many have ethics committees that censure or rescind the licenses or certificates of practitioners who violate the profession's tenets.[12]

These mechanisms of self-regulation are not particularly powerful in the health-planning profession due to its relatively young age. Health planners lack significant control over the admissions or curricula in the planning schools; the standards of customary practice to which professional health planners commonly ascribe are not clearly delineated; and means of censure, outside of formal legal recourse, are virtually nonexistent. However, the health-planning profession can be expected to gain greater prominence in each of these areas as time passes, and a code of ethics will probably emerge as the profession matures. Therefore, an examination of code ethics and health planning appears timely.

A code of professional conduct is a formal statement of commonly accepted standards and norms. Many such codes govern the practices of various health professions. The most well-known in the health field is probably the Ethical Principles of the American Medical Association. The professional society of health planners, the American Health Planning Association (AHPA), could look to a number of sources for guidance in the development of ethical codes for health planning. The Code of the American College of Hospital Administrators, the Code of the American Association for Hospital Consultants, and the Code of Professional Responsibility of the American Institute of Certified Planners (AICP) were developed by their respective professional organizations. The members of these professional bodies engage in practices that are somewhat similar, although not identical, to the practice of health planning.

In general, these codes address topics such as the relationship of professional planners and administrators to their clients or the client community, their relationship with other professionals, the appropriate manner in which to charge fees and expenses, and the proper forms of business solicitations to be made by those who function primarily as consultants. Although some subjects are emphasized to a greater or lesser degree in one set of codes than in another, generally the same concerns are addressed in each of them.

The Code of Professional Responsibility of the AICP,[13] a professional planning code to which many architects and city planners ascribe, governs an area of practice very similar in process, if not content, to that of the health planner. It is divided into four parts; the first two are—the Canons and the Rules of Discipline. The Canons are strongly worded statements that express in general terms the expected standards of professional conduct. They represent exhortations to appropriate and proper behaviors considered essential for professional planners. The authors of the Code refer to them as axiomatic, well-established principles. Examples of the Canons include:

(1) A planner primarily serves the public interest and shall accept or continue employment only when the planner can insure accommodation of the client's or employee's interest with the public interest . . .

(2) A planner shall preserve the secrets and confidences of a client or employee . . .

(3) A planner shall avoid even the appearance of improper professional conduct.[14]

While in theory, at least, these virtues may be considered self-evident, in practice they present a number of problems due to their potential of being interpreted and acted out in a countless variety of behaviors.[15] One would have to question their usefulness to the hypothetical ethical dilemma of the health planner described earlier, due to their generality and, in some instances, contradicting guidance.

The AICP Code is much more explicit in its Rules of Discipline. These statements provide guidance for the more common social and economic transactions that occur between the planners, between the planners and their clients, and between the planners and the public. The Rules of Discipline express the minimum level of conduct below which no member may fall without being subject to disciplinary action. According to the Rules, for example:

(1) A planner shall not engage in conduct involving dishonesty, fraud, deceit or misrepresentation . . .

(2) A planner shall not accept employment to perform planning services which the planner is not competent to perform . . .

(3) A planner shall not give, lend, or promise anything of value to a public official in order to influence or attempt to influence the official's judgments or actions.[16]

Any AICP member found in violation of the Rules of Discipline is subject to either expulsion, suspension, or censure, depending upon the character of the offense and the circumstances surrounding it. However, due to the difficulty of enforcement and vagueness, at least in certain parts of the Code, serious questions arise as to the effectiveness of the Rules in influencing planners who are members. The problem is not unique to the AICP; it is common to all the professions with written codes.

Often code ethics are criticized as being pretentious and empty, since they may offer little practical guidance for behavior, and violations often go undetected or, if detected, unenforced. However, the

Canons, the Rules, and the calls to appropriate behavior contained in AICP Code and others like it express a certain set of ideals that individuals believe they ought to observe and see actualized by their profession. These "ought" statements constitute the crux of the codes and represent the substance that qualifies them as ethical precepts rather than simply harsh rules and regulations or benign platitudes or etiquettes that govern polite, but not necessarily ethical, behavior.[17]

The development of a code by the AHPA or another representative group of professional health planners could be a valuable·experience for the profession. It would require serious thought and reflection on the appropriate attributes and behaviors of health planners and existing barriers blocking their realization in our society. Such a code will likely be developed as the profession matures and as more concerns arise regarding those qualified to become health-planning practitioners. A code for health planners would establish standards of appropriate behavior and would therefore be a valuable mechanism for the acquisition and transfer of ethical precepts needed in health planning.

A theory of ethical behavior codified into a set of standards of practice would be another valuable step in the development of health-planning ethics, as would a body of case material. However, for several reasons, neither is sufficient to ensure the actual ethical behavior of planners or to provide a satisfactory foundation for ethically evaluating health planning. First, there will always be cases of individual misconduct that a code will never be able to prevent. Second, areawide health planning entails considerably more than individual decisionmaking and professional judgment. Any explanation or analysis of the ethics of health planning must examine that which it proposes to do and how it will go about achieving its results. Therefore, one must look far beyond the morals of individual actors and the codes of the profession and conduct an ethical assessment of the substance and consequences of health planning.

ETHICAL ASSUMPTIONS OF VARIOUS MODES OF HEALTH PLANNING

A review of the planning literature reveals that a general consensus on what constitutes an adequate theory of planning currently does not exist.[18] Furthermore, no single dominant mode of health-planning methodology or practice is favored consistently over another.

Health planning in the United States has evolved and been shaped largely by two very important traditions.[19] The most obvious tradition is the widespread Western belief in the rationality of science, in which planning is viewed as the institutionalized application of the methods and findings of science to social affairs. One branch of health planning, based largely on this tradition, has developed an extensive body of literature based on this perspective. However, of equal importance is the tradition of the social reform and public health movement that flourished at about the turn of the century. This branch tends to view social action, often consisting of partisan political activity, as a means for improving the health status of a community. It does not concentrate on the development of purely scientific approaches involving medical care for realizing an improvement in health status. Rather, it often encourages social and political actions advocating specific improvements that taken together are expected to benefit the society as a whole.[20] Better housing, improved sanitation, and better education and working conditions, as well as opportunities for recreation, are viewed as effective ways to promote better health status.

Since these two traditions suggest somewhat conflicting roles and since neither deals directly with ethical questions, they create problems for health-planning practice and theory. Scientific tradition suggests that health planners should be applied scientists committed to objective methods and careful data collection and rigorous adherents to techniques and procedures of scientific methodology. Thus, the scientific planner should avoid questions of values and ethics. In contrast, the reform tradition suggests that health planners should work toward fundamental social change, often promoting the best interests of specific clients in efforts to benefit the population at large. Furthermore, the reform tradition requires that the clients to be affected by the change must actively participate in bringing it about. This perspective is manifested in the maximum feasible participation concept of the poverty programs and the partnership for health notion, which requires citizen participation in health planning.

In the reform tradition, ethical and value questions are not avoided. Rather, health-planning behavior and decisions are justified as being proper, if not ethical, if they advance the causes of a specific segment of the community. This approach suggests a belief in some sort of political hidden hand, somewhat analogous to economic free market assumptions. In a free market, the community expects to derive the optimal economic benefit because the various subsegments of the community advocate their individual causes. The best ones, those that allocate resources most efficiently and effectively, are advanced. It is critical, however, to realize that most segments of the community do not have advocates, economic or otherwise. Thus, the reform approach relies on a process model and a belief that everything works out for the best if each segment of a complex community works for its own betterment and improvement. Accordingly, no one need pay attention to the overall picture; no one need apply rational analysis to the outcomes of the entire process.

With these two traditions, health planners confront the dilemma of which of the two planning options should be adopted—the scientific approach that abjures ethical issues or the reform approach that relies on process. Klosterman describes the problem as follows:

> Thus, perhaps inevitably, practicing and academic planners are left with a feeling that ethical positions are mere relative matters of individual taste and preference (such as the preference for one color over another) and that planners' views can only compete with many conflicting and equally valid political opinions. Motivated by this belief, contemporary planners have generally adopted two conflicting perspectives on the ethical issues of public policy planning. Some, emphasizing planning's scientific nature and adopting the perspective of the positive social sciences, attempt to avoid all ethical questions by collecting and providing decision makers with factual information on the probable effects of alternative policies. The implicit belief here is simply that better information will lead to better public policy decisions. Others, emphasizing planning's political nature and downgrading policy analysis, just assume their political positions to be "correct" and engage in pragmatic politics in order to, perhaps, promote the interests of underrepresented groups or, more generally, improve their political effectiveness. The implicit belief here is that, by acting politically, planners can improve the political process and its representativeness and, thus, public policy decisions.[21]

Unfortunately, neither approach is particularly suited to attempting to produce desirable social change—a commonly avowed and stated purpose underlying most planning efforts. If health planning is to fulfill this purpose, this dilemma requires resolution. However, prior to attempting such, one must first examine the degree to which the nature of planning is truly scientific and the relationship of politics to planning. Regardless of which tradition is followed, these two questions continually plague health planning.

As stated earlier, a powerful theme embodied in scientific planning is that planners can and should avoid serious ethical questions. It appears that early efforts at organized health planning, from the mid-1940s to the late 1960s, followed this dictum. This era of health planning, often referred to as the Hill–Burton era, was a time dominated by hospital construction, adding many thousands of hospitals beds. The central questions were, How many beds should be built and where should they be located? A hospital bed allocation model[a] was adopted by the Hill–Burton planners and became the dominant health-planning rationale. It had all the appearances of a scientific approach to health planning. However, this approach avoided substantive analysis and violated the most basic tenets of epidemiologic and social research in that it failed to consider illness patterns, population, and socioeconomic dynamics. It restricted the role of health planners to the identification of the optimal—or the most effective—configuration of hospital beds for a given area. However, it avoided the questions of who benefited or who had to bear the burden of such an allocation. Furthermore, the results were shrouded in such technical language that the input of a variety of groups was excluded—most notably, labor, consumers, and low income groups.[22]

The Hill–Burton approach, however, did have its political side. The Hill–Burton formula was somewhat scientific in the sense that it employed quantification; it was equally political in that health planners had to convince public officials to accept and to act on their technical determinations. To the extent that health planners were successful in influencing the policies and actions of individual and corporate health providers, they were acting in the most fundamental of political processes—they determined who got what and when, where, and how they got it.

This account demonstrates that health planners have affected and will probably continue to affect society both positively and negatively. Furthermore, it shows that the decisions and actions of health planners require their consideration of ethical issues. It is absurd, if not impossible, to limit health planning solely to the quantitative appraisal of means, while ignoring its ends and consequences. In addition, some health-planning theorists and practitioners argue that technical, and hence value-free, planning is impossible because of the essential allocative and political nature of the planning process.[23]

---

a. The Hill–Burton model was relatively simple. It called for the allocation of hospital beds to a health-planning area (geographically determined) by applying a current use rate to a predicted future population base.

In light of these developments, Friedman[24] and Blum[25] call for normative planning, in which planners subject not only the means but also the outcomes of health planning to rational consideration. These proposals are important because they suggest that health planning can combine scientific analysis with reform and can integrate both its intellectual roots. However, advocates of normative health planning do not specify procedures whereby planners are able to ethically evaluate planning actions. At a more basic level, they have not developed the logical foundations for a rational consideration of ethical issues in health planning.

SCIENTIFIC AND ETHICAL REASONING

Philosophers now recognize that sound ethical reasoning is more similar to sound scientific reasoning than has been widely accepted. Generally, it is accepted that empirical evidence alone cannot completely justify an ethical belief. However, a similar situation exists for scientific laws and theories, since they too cannot be supported conclusively on observational evidence alone. The important work by Kuhn on the process of scientific advances shows that more than one theoretical explanation for any set of observational data always exists and that personal choice on the part of scientists has played an important role in the selection of one theory or paradigm over another.[26] However, the choice between competing theories is not wholly arbitrary or purely individualistic. In practice, the choice is regulated by the norms and procedural requirements of the scientific method. Furthermore—and most important—reliance on the criteria of choice employed in the scientific method can itself be justified, but not by scientific means. The scientific method must rely on the rules of logic on inductive and deductive reasoning for justification.

For example, two different explanations may be offered for an observed social phenomenon, such as the behavior of individuals who are ill. The procedural norms of the scientific method suggest several criteria for choosing among competing explanations of observed behaviors. Which explanation accounts for the greater amount of available empirical data? Which is more parsimonious and thus elegant? The reliance on such criteria can be defended, not on personal preference, but by assuming that nature is simple rather than complex and that parsimonious explanations should be favored over

more complex ones. However, the assumption that science constitutes an entirely cognitive and rational process and that ethics does
not fails to recognize that the norms and criteria of the scientific
method are not justified by scientific observation alone, but by logical and rational argumentation.

The pattern of reasoning in which the criteria themselves must
be justified underlies not only scientific reasoning but all rational
discourse. For example, consider the purely empirical claim that
an injection of Salk vaccine will prevent polio in individuals. This
statement can never be proven conclusively. However, considerable
support can be given by an inductive argument that most persons
who received immunizations have not contracted polio and it is
highly unlikely that they will contract the disease. However, complete justification of the original claim requires the inclusion of a
justification for reliance on the rules of inductive logic.

Similarly, the ultimate justification for nonempirical knowledge,
such as that found in mathematics and formal logic, is embodied in
the rules of inference and substitution of deductive logic. Rational
argument, whether inductive or deductive, presupposes the reference
to one or both sets of principles. Although knowledge claims of
either type can be supported by demonstrating that their derivation
is in accordance with the relevant set of principles, a complete justification for the claims must include a justification for reliance on
those principles themselves.

Hence, scientific reasoning, as well as all other forms of rational
discourse, ethics included, must ultimately be supported by criteria
that can be justified rationally. This suggests that ethical questions
can be examined to see whether defensible criteria exist for validat-
ing or invalidating ethical principles and decisions. In other words, a
scientific discovery is viewed as valid only because it conforms to
widely accepted and defensible criteria for the evaluation of scientific observations and theories. If sets of criteria for evaluating ethical principles and values are developed and rationally justified, then
ethical positions could be accepted or rejected because they meet
grounds that are more substantial than personal taste or preference.
Using this approach, Klosterman defines ethics as "an attempt to
formulate rationally defensible principles and criteria which match
our considered moral judgments, just as the philosophy of science
attempts to develop systematic principles which agree with accepted
scientific practice."[27] The development of ethical approaches that

are embodied in this definition is well underway. The criteria and logical foundations that compose the various theories of social justice can be adapted to evaluate the normative aspects of health planning. It is readily apparent that concerns for social justice are directly related to the objectives and outcomes of health planning.

HEALTH PLANNING AND SOCIAL JUSTICE

While health planning is relatively new in the United States, its activities have come to be pervasive throughout the health care system. Planning decisions and actions are required constantly for the maintenance of the system, for the allocation of resources, and for the development of the structural changes necessary for the continued adaptation and development of the system. A crucial aspect of planning, with respect to ethical questions, is the ability of the planning method to indicate which segments of the population will reap the benefits of planning decisions and resulting actions and which segments will bear the burdens.

When benefits and burdens can be distributed through decisions such as those made in health planning, the problem of justice arises. Except for a very limited set of circumstances, some individuals who will reap the benefits will not bear the costs; some who will bear costs will not benefit. Jonsen and Hellegers[28] conclude that when a situation depends on planned and conscious decisions rather than on chance or accident, it is necessary to raise certain questions. What justifies the imposition of a burden, cost, or risk on an individual or an identifable group? Who should realize certain benefits at apparent cost to others? These are fundamental questions, as much at the core of health-planning decisions as of justice. Although much is written that addresses the common good in health-planning theory, very little addresses the notion of justice.[29] Nonetheless, there is a contention on the part of many health care providers and consumers that the current methods of health care delivery involve significant social injustices. Questions of justice, or a just society, are always central to the study of ethics. Health planners often do not view their activities and functions as having a significant effect on social justice and therefore often ignore, or perhaps simply overlook, the ethical evaluation of their work.

In his book *A Theory of Justice*,[30] Rawls develops the concept of justice as fairness that is particularly relevant to ethics and health planning. His theory is very complex and only broadly outlined in this study. He provides a set of principles and criteria that deal with the allocation of scarce resources within a just society. These are rationally developed and can be evaluated on their own merits, without recourse or appeals to personal taste, preference, or pragmatic political belief. In his system of justice, the essential criteria is that the expectations of those who are well off are just only if they improve the expectations of the least well off members of society. Two principles of distribution are required of the social, economic, and political institutions of society to meet this criteria.

Rawls' first principle requires that each person in society has an equal right to the most extensive system of liberties compatible with a system of equal liberty for all. The second principle states that social and economic inequalities should be arranged to facilitate the greatest benefit to the least advantaged individuals in society in a manner that is consistent with the equal liberty principle and that the benefits should be available under conditions of fair equality of opportunity. Hence, Rawls suggests that health-planning policies with distributive, redistributive, or regulatory functions that benefit the least advantaged are just and fair if they conform to these principles and criteria. This is not because they distribute benefits according to some a priori notion that is right, but rather because they are the attributes of a just society. Thus, health planners can rely on Rawlsian principles and arguments of justice as fairness in support of decisions that may, at times, benefit the poor more than the rich. The ethical positions of health planners using Rawlsian principles would not reflect merely personal preferences or tastes, but would be based upon rational and defensible concepts.

Others in disagreement with Rawls' theory of justice could pursue alternative objectives. However, under the Rawlsian approach to normative planning, they must justify their conflicting position and allow its rational evaluation. For example, Veatch strongly argues for an egalitarian foundation for a just health care system (see Chapter 2). Veatch's principles, even though different, can be evaluated in the same manner as Rawls'. Since planners can choose among numerous theories of social justice, this approach does not eliminate the inevitable conflicts surrounding health-planning outcomes and the groups they tend to favor. However, it provides a framework within which normative conflicts can be considered and rationally evaluated.

The adoption of a normative planning approach based on principles of social justice would integrate the reform and scientific roles of health planners. It provides a sound basis for evaluating the goals, plans, and outcomes of the health-planning process. Health planners would no longer be dependent solely on personal preferences, codes of professional ethics, or pragmatic political positions. At bottom, health-planning positions and their outcomes would be defendable on well-reasoned, logical grounds.

In conclusion, the implication of viewing health planning as linked to social justice requires the development of new planning techniques and the clarification and evaluation of older ones. This perspective fundamentally changes the way in which health planners view their role in the health system. It provides opportunity for health planners to combine their dual commitments to social reform and scientific analysis in the rational evaluation of the difficult and important normative questions of health planning. Joining the ethical evaluation of health-planning ends with the technical analysis of health-planning means as a guiding principle of the profession suggests that social justice considerations would take precedence and give guidance for resolving individual, professional, or methodological issues.

NOTES TO CHAPTER 3

1. See Chapter 1, pages 4-7, of this volume.
2. For a review of health planning, readers are referred to Daniel I. Zwick, "Health Planning: Past, Present, and Future," *Health and Medical Services Review* 2: 2-15 (1979); and James F. Blumstein and Frank A. Sloan, "Health Planning and Regulation Through Certificate of Need: An Overview," *Utah Law Review* 1: 3-37 (1978).
3. Laurence R. Tancredi, *Ethics of Health Care* (Washington, D.C.: National Academy of Sciences, 1974).
4. Ibid., p. iv.
5. Robert M. Veatch and Roy Branson, *Ethics and Health Policy* (Cambridge, MA: Ballinger Publishing Company, 1976).
6. Ibid., p. xx.
7. Paul Ramsey, *The Patient as Person* (New Haven: Yale University Press, 1970), p. xi.

8. Joel L. Fleishman and Bruce L. Payne, *Ethical Dilemmas and the Education of Policymakers* (Hastings-on-Hudson, NY: The Institute of Society, Ethics and the Life Sciences, 1980).

9. Paul Ramsey, "The Nature of Medical Ethics," in Robert M. Veatch, Willard Gaylin, and Councilman Morgan, *The Teaching of Medical Ethics* (Hastings-on-Hudson, NY: The Institute of Society, Ethics, and the Life Sciences, 1971), pp. 14–28; reprinted in Stanley Joel Reiser, Arthur J. Dyck, and William J. Curran, *Ethics in Medicine: Historical Perspectives and Contemporary Concerns* (Cambridge, MA: The MIT Press, 1977), pp. 123–129.

10. Ibid., p. 124.

11. Alan A. Altshuler, "The Anker Hospital Case Study," in Alan A. Altshuler, *The City Planning Process* (Ithaca, NY: Cornell University Press, 1965); and Leda R. Judd and Robert J. McEwen, *A Handbook for Consumer Participation in Health Care Planning* (Chicago: Blue Cross Association, 1977).

12. Peter G. Brown, "Ethics and Public Policy: A Preliminary Agenda," *Policy Studies Journal* 7: 132–137 (1978).

13. American Institute of Certified Planners, "Code of Professional Responsibility," *AICP Bylaws, Amended* (Washington, D.C., April 1980), pp. 13–15.

14. Ibid., p. 1.

15. Gunther S. Stent, "The Poverty of Scientism and the Promise of Structuralistic Ethics," *The Hastings Center Report* 6: 32–40 (December 1976).

16. American Institute of Certified Planners, pp. 15–17.

17. Albert R. Jonsen and Andre R. Hellegers, "Conceptual Foundations for an Ethics of Medical Care," in Laurence R. Tancredi, *Ethics of Health Care* (Washington, D.C.: National Academy of Sciences, 1974), pp. 3–20.

18. Richard S. Bolen, "Emerging Views of Planning," *Journal of the American Institute of Planners* 33: 233–245 (July 1967); and John Friedman, "A Conceptual Foundation for the Analysis of Planning Behavior," *Administrative Science Quarterly* 12: 225–252 (September 1967). For a further discussion of the issues described in this section and the one that follows, readers are referred to Richard E. Klosterman, "Foundations for Normative Planning," *Journal of the American Institute of Planners* 44: 37–46 (January 1978).

19. Klosterman, pp. 37–46.

20. Paul Davidoff, "Advocacy and Pluralism in Planning," *Journal of the American Institute of Planners* 27: 103–115 (1965).

21. Klosterman, p. 40.

22. Dan Freshback, "What's Inside the Black Box: A Case Study of the Allocative Policies of the Hill–Burton Program," *International Journal of Health Services* 9: 313–339 (1979).

23. Basil J.F. Mott, "The Myth of Planning Without Politics," *American Journal of Public Health* 59: 797–802 (1969).
24. John Friedman, *Retracking America* (Garden City, NY: Doubleday Anchor, 1973).
25. Henrik Blum, *Planning for Health* (New York: Human Sciences Press, 1974).
26. Thomas S. Kuhn, *The Structure of Scientific Revolutions* (Chicago: University of Chicago Press, 1970).
27. Klosterman, p. 43.
28. Jonsen and Hellegers, p. 135.
29. Dan E. Beauchamp, "Public Health as Social Justice," in E. Gartley Jaco, *Patients, Physicians and Illness* (New York: Free Press, 1979), pp. 443–457.
30. John Rawls, *A Theory of Justice* (Cambridge, MA: Harvard University Press, 1971).

4 TOWARD SOCIAL JUSTICE
Political-Economic Issues in Health and Health Care

Joseph C. Morreale, Ph.D.

This chapter presents a variety of political-economic issues related to health care and health status in the United States. Its basic thesis is that the causes of inequities in health status and health care are based on fundamental ethical values that are fostered by the economic system. Hence, in order to address the issues of equity in health and health care, we cannot simply change the health care system but need to alter these values and the economic system intertwined with them. Furthermore, it is necessary to understand and analyze the general economic framework within which the health care system operates and in which health status is affected for at least four reasons:

1. The allocation and distribution mechanisms of the overall economic system will largely determine the allocation and distribution of resources in specific subsectors such as health care.

2. The role of government and therefore public policy in any one subsector is dependent on and colored by the overall role of government in the economic system.

3. The economic system is a major determinant of the health status of the overall population and has different impacts on the health status of various groups within a society.

4. The basic goals of society and the fundamental priorities of its institutions are set forth in the economic base.

Therefore, it is necessary to proceed by outlining the economic system as it exists in the United States and then analyzing the health care system within this context.

The first part of the chapter analyzes the relationship between health status and health care. The second part focuses on five key social determinants of health status. Part three presents the conservative and liberal viewpoints on the relationship of social justice to equity in health and health care. The fourth segment critiques the conservative and liberal perspectives with respect to the evidence cited in the first two parts. The chapter concludes with a discussion of some egalitarian principles related to health.

HEALTH CARE AND HEALTH STATUS

Policymakers and health professionals commonly assume that improvements in access to and quality of health care result in increases in health status of populations. A corollary of this assumption is that increasing expenditures for health care generate positive effects on mortality rates and life expectancy. These theses have become so prominent that two researchers assert that it is modern heresy to question—much less to refute—this assumption.[1] However, recently accumulated evidence casts doubt on both of these assumptions.

Leveson reports on the impact of various factors on mortality rates between 1930 and 1975 in the United States.[2] In reviewing health expenditures versus mortality rates, he finds a rapid decline in mortality rates from the late 1930s to the early 1950s, yet only a slow growth in health care expenditures. Then, as the rate of expenditures rapidly accelerated in the 1950s, the rate of health improvement slowed. Substantial evidence suggests that health spending has a much more significant effect on infant and child mortality than on the general population. Since 1973, a renewed decline in mortality has occurred amidst a reduction in expenditures for health care. Thus, Leveson concludes, "the corollary to the dominance of environment in accounting for health differences among population groups is that medical care has an influence which is decidedly more modest."[3]

The McKinlays analyze the decline in mortality between 1900 and 1974.[4] Like Leveson, they find little relationship between accelerating expenditures and declines in mortality rates. Generally, they conclude that medical measures have contributed little to the overall decline in mortality in the United States during the twentieth century. Moreover, they show that the sharp rise in expenditures began after nearly 92 percent of the modern decline in mortality during this century had already occurred. Furthermore, Newhouse and Friedlander report that variations in the amount of health resources available across thirty-nine metropolitan areas of the United States had no systematic effect on any of six indicators of ill health.[5]

In *The Role of Medicine: Dream, Mirage, or Nemesis?*, McKeown analyzes mortality changes in England and Wales between 1851 and 1971. He identifies four causes of declining mortality trends: (1) changes in the character of diseases, (2) developments in immunization and therapy, (3) reduction in exposure to infection, and (4) improvements in nutrition.[6] Moreover, the main determinant of mortality declines was improved nutrition. Decreases in mortality from water-borne and food-borne diseases related to various improvements in hygiene. Advances in immunization and therapy had little impact on the continuing downward trends in mortality, with the exception of streptomycin therapy for tuberculosis and the poliomyelitis vaccine.

Finally, after reviewing the health economics literature, Fuchs concludes: "When the state of medical science and other health determining variables are held constant, the marginal contribution of medical care to health is very small in modern nations."[7]

This mounting evidence raises disturbing questions about the direction of future health policy and the allocation and distribution of health resources. Is too much money being invested in medical and health care? Is the correct model being used in formulating health policy? What is needed in considering the equitable distribution of health services?

POLITICAL-ECONOMIC DETERMINANTS OF HEALTH STATUS

Simultaneously with the increasing questioning of the relationship of health care to improving health status, there is an increase in research concerning various social, economic, political, and environmental determinants of health status. Attention focuses on five key factors that have significant effects on health status: (1) economic instability, (2) economic inequality, (3) class structure, (4) education, and (5) environmental pollution. The interrelationship between these factors and the economic system warrants further analysis.

Economic Instability

The instability of the capitalist system is the subject of considerable debate. The familiar boom-bust business cycle is well documented, and many theories attempt to explain economic fluctuations. Key factors causing fluctuations are the volatile nature of investment, the inventory cycle, government spending and taxation, and the monetary factors of changing interest rates, changes in the money supply, and the availability of credit.

Historically, the business cycle has been viewed as a natural and relatively predictable characteristic of capitalism. However, only in the last twenty years have economists generally regarded the cycle as more controllable by government macropolicy. More specifically, Keynes' basic departure from classical economic theory was his argument that the capitalist economy is inherently unstable and therefore requires government regulation to stabilize it. He then developed tools of macropolicy analysis through government spending and taxation that permitted greater government control of the economy. During the past twenty years, government has used fiscal and monetary policy to help stabilize the economy, but at the price of increased government intervention in the capitalist system. The government now has the power to create booms and recessions almost at will. Some economists contend that this intervention is only a stopgap measure and that the underlying laws of motion of advanced capitalism are working toward ever-increasing destabilization and worsening economic crises. Of interest here is the relationship between economic fluctuations and changes in the health status of a population.

Historical evidence shows the relationship between economic development in Western Europe and the increase in the life expectancy of the European population in the eighteenth and nineteenth centuries. More importantly, international comparisons suggest that the most significant source of life expectancy differentials is the level of economic development. More recently, studies by Brenner on the interrelationship of changes in economic activities and changes in health status in industrialized countries show that recessions in such nations result in adverse effects on the health status of their populations. Using key indicators of aggregate economic activity (e.g., unemployment rates, rates of employment and per capita personal income) in the United States, he finds that:

1. Economic downturns are associated with increased mortality from heart disease and that mortality due to heart disease decreases during economic upturns;[8]

2. There is an inverse relationship between national economic changes and infant mortality and nonwhites appear to carry a greater risk of fetal mortality than whites during economic downturns;[9]

3. Consumption of distilled spirits is inversely related to the state of the national economy on a cyclical basis and that mortality from cirrhosis of the liver increases substantially following national economic recessions;[10]

4. There is an inverse relationship between economic changes and mental disorders; cyclical changes in the economy are the single most important factor in trends of mental hospital admissions, and recessions are associated with substantial increases in both first admissions and readmissions to mental hospitals.[11]

Many of these findings are corroborated by studies in other Western European countries. In a recent, more comprehensive study, the unemployment rate is related directly to overall mortality rates, cardiovascular-renal mortality rates, suicide rates, homocide rates, and imprisonment rates.[12] These studies build a strong case linking declines in a population's health status to economic recessions. Hence, acknowledging the government's ability to manipulate the economy, such findings raise serious ethical questions about the economists' policy prescription of creating a recession to fight inflation.

Economic Inequality

The capitalist economy also generates inequality in income and wealth. Analyzing the distribution of aggregate money income in the United States reveals that the richest 20 percent receive about

40 percent of the income; the poorest 20 percent receive about 5 percent of the income.[13] This distribution of earnings has remained constant over the past thirty years. Moreover, the wealth distribution is even more unequal. Estimates suggest that the wealthiest 20 percent control 76 percent of the total wealth and 96 percent of the corporate stock.

The primary theoretical justification for income inequality is the marginal productivity of distribution that asserts that all resources (including labor) should be rewarded in proportion to their contribution to output. The resulting pattern of income distribution is viewed as both just and efficient. It is just because workers receive all of the income they produce; it is efficient because entrepreneurs use resources in a way that maximizes their contribution to output. In this way, the resources obtain the largest possible reward, and society gains the greatest overall output.

In addition, economic growth and economic incentive are two other grounds for the justification of inequality. The former argument asserts that income inequality produces sizeable amounts of private savings, especially by the wealthy, that are invested in the economy. This investment provides increased capital goods, thereby spurring economic growth and eventually improving the lot of the poor. The latter justification—economic incentive—asserts that income inequality furnishes incentives for people to work, produce, and innovate; these incentives are the driving forces of the economy. Hence, an unequal distribution of income is an essential and desirable consequence of the price system in allocating resources in terms of their productivity.

What are the consequences of this income and wealth inequality on the allocation and distribution of health care resources and health status? If resources generally flow to where they obtain the highest payoff, then they will go to the most profitable sectors and be distributed to those persons with the greatest ability to pay. Thus, in the health care market, resources are allocated to the more profitable sectors of the health care industry and distributed to the higher income areas of the United States. For example, in the last ten years, health care resources have been increasingly allocated to the profit-seeking institutions of the health care market—namely, for profit hospitals and nursing homes—and away from the nonprofit or less profitable institutions—for example, public hospitals and charitable agencies.

In addition, there is an unequal distribution of health care resources according to income differentials across the country. This is particularly true in the distribution of health personnel across states, with the higher per capita income states having a much greater proportion of health personnel per capita. Also, health personnel migrate considerably more to affluent urban and metropolitan areas as opposed to poorer rural and ghetto areas.

In addition to the resulting unequal distribution of health care resources due to the inequitable distribution of income and wealth, there is an even more important unequal distribution of health status. A large volume of literature on this subject documents an inverse relationship between socioeconomic status and mental and physical disabilities. There is a direct correlation between higher rates of morbidity due to physical disorders and a shorter life expectancy among lower socioeconomic groups. There is a similarly consistent inverse relationship between socioeconomic status and mental disorders. Brenner reports that three factors largely account for these inverse relationships:

1. Comparatively low levels of nutrition among low socioeconomic status groups increase their vulnerability to acute and chronic infectious diseases;

2. Higher levels of social–psychological stress in lower socioeconomic groups expose them much more to a variety of mental disorders;

3. Lower utilization of health care services and facilities among lower socioeconomic groups increases their chances of death or long-term disability from disease.[14]

Salkever has analyzed access to medical care in five countries (Canada, England, Finland, Poland, and the United States) with considerably different health care systems.[15] Following the subdivision of each population into three income classes, he finds that higher family income is associated with greater access to medical care among children at all levels of need. The relationship between income class and access to care among adults is much more variable.

Moreover, racial discrimination compounds the relationship between income inequality and health status. For the period between 1950 and 1975, Leveson shows that the mortality of nonwhite males appears to retain its relation to mortality of white males,[16] but the death rate for black females is dropping faster relative to white females. A substantial part of the shift occurred before 1966 and thus is not attributable to Medicaid. Furthermore, no reason exists to suspect that health-financing programs would have an effect on black females but not on black males.

A much more likely explanation is that the improvement is the result of income changes. Over the entire period of the shift, incomes of black females rose rapidly compared to white females and reached the level of whites with comparable education before 1920. At the same time, the ratio of incomes of black males to white males remained relatively constant so that no relative improvement in health status could have been expected.

Thus, the economic inequality generated by the economic system creates an unequal allocation and distribution of health care resources and is directly related to unequal health status outcomes. This is observable in terms of physical and mental disorders, supply and utilization of services, and differences by race and by health care system. However, this basic inequality has additional influence on the health care system.

Class Structure

The income inequality inherent in the capitalist system leads to class structure in the economy and therefore in the health care system. Analysis of the distribution of wealth reveals that it is more unequally distributed than income. Moreover, the pattern of distribution of wealth and income has remained remarkably constant over the last thirty years. With this unequal distribution of wealth comes unequal distribution of political power. The wealthiest members of the community, through their ownership of the means of production, wield the greatest amount of power in political institutions and largely determine the social relations of production. Furthermore, these social classes feel a class consciousness, whether motivated internally or imposed externally.

Navarro argues that there are five distinct social classes in the United States:

1. The upper (corporate) class constitutes a relatively small group of people (1.3 percent of the population) that controls the owner-

ship of a disproportionate share of personal wealth and/or controls its use.

2. The upper middle class consists of professionals (14 percent), including physicians, lawyers, middle rank executives, academicians (characterized by their intellectual work, requiring professional training), and businessmen (6 percent) associated with small and medium-sized enterprises.

3. The lower middle class consists of self-employed shopkeepers, craftsmen, and artisans (7 percent); and office and sales workers (23 percent).

4. The working class (49 percent) includes primarily industrial or blue collar workers, service workers, and agricultural wage earners.

5. The poor class contains persons outside the mainstream of the economy, many of whom are unemployed and on welfare.[17]

This class difference is manifested in the control of health care institutions. In analyzing the boards of trustees of foundations, private and state medical teaching institutions, and voluntary community hospitals, there is a predominance of representatives of financial and corporate capital and to some extent of the upper middle class (primarily physicians and representatives of the business middle class). The similarity of the predominance of the same social classes for each of these types of institutions is evident.

Foundations constitute important sources of grant support for health research and experiments in the delivery of health services. Given the social class bias of their decisionmaking boards, one finds that they tend to support only those projects and programs that maintain their interests. The medical teaching institutions are the key educators and socializers of future health professionals. Again, given the social class bias on their respective boards, these institutions perpetuate the same class structure of the health work force and the same values of traditional medical practice. Finally, community hospitals comprise the largest component of health care delivery institutions. So the priorities set in, and the organization and delivery of services to their communities would be biased by decisionmaking bodies dominated by a certain social class representing a minority of that community. In all of these cases, it should be clear that the community's or the nation's health needs and priorities will coincide only accidentally with the interests represented on the decisionmaking bodies.[18]

In addition to control of the allocation of health care resources by the upper class, the existence of class structure is mirrored in differences in the health status of the various classes. Navarro finds higher rates of mortality and morbidity among the working class than among the corporate and upper middle class.[19] He also cites a Baltimore study[20] that shows a higher age-standardized mortality among working class communities than among upper class communities. Furthermore, the study reveals that this difference in mortality is increasing. In addition, Conover reports that nationally, working class individuals have proportionally more chronic conditions than members of the upper classes.[21] Compounding the problem are the recent findings of increased cancer risk to workers in workplaces having dangerous substances such as asbestos, vinyl chloride, arsenic, and lead. More importantly, evidence shows that these substances commonly infiltrate the workers' homes and communities and thereby affect the health of the families of workers.

Finally, there is a growing problem of alienation among the majority of workers,[22] stemming from three principal factors:

1. Work is not a means of creativity and self-expression; rather, acquiring the income necessary to participate in the consumer-oriented society is the main realization and fulfillment for most workers.

2. Workers have no control over what is produced and how it is used, since such decisions remain with the owners of capital.

3. Workers have little influence over the process of production and what they must do during their work time. These are determined by corporate executives and managers.

Worker alienation often has serious health consequences. Tedious and unrewarding work threatens both the physical and mental health of workers. Alcoholism and drug addiction are not uncommon responses to working conditions in American factories. A noted government report, *Work in America*,[23] concludes that on the basis of "an impressive 15-year study of aging, the strongest predictor of longevity was work satisfaction. The second best predictor was overall happiness."[24]

Finally, with respect to the relationship of class structure to health care and health, Fuchs reports that:

In Great Britain . . . the National Health Service (NHS) has undoubtedly served to sharply reduce differences in access to medical care, but the traditionally large class differentials in infant mortality and life expectancy are no smaller after three decades of NHS. Also, despite free access to medical care, time lost from work because of sickness has actually increased greatly in Britain in recent decades.[25]

Education

The correlation between educational level and good health is a subject of considerable debate. Some argue that increased educational levels are needed to improve health. One such correlation, reported by the National Bureau of Economic Research, shows that education is a key variable in explaining interstate variations in mortality rates and that the return on expenditures for additional education is far greater than on additional expenditures for health care.[26]

In a more recent study examining in greater detail the relationship between health and education, Grossman shows that with past health and other variables held constant, schooling has a positive and statistically significant impact on current health.[27] He interprets this relationship as evidence that schooling increases an individual's efficiency in producing health. He then speculates that persons with more education might choose healthier diets, be more aware of health risks, obtain healthier occupations, and use medical care more wisely. In considering these results, Fuchs suggests that both schooling and health may be manifestations of differences among individuals in their willingness and/or ability to invest in human capital.[28]

The use of education to improve health status is particularly appealing to liberal reformers. In part, this attitude stems from a broader view of education as a mechanism for upward mobility in a capitalistic system. Capitalism in the United States, characterized by a high degree of income and wealth inequality, translates into unequal social classes. Defenders of capitalism accept that the distribution of income will be unequal, but they contend that equality of opportunity is achievable through educational attainment. Hence, the intelligent and ambitious rise on the income ladder through their higher educational achievements.

However, there are two important sources of unequal opportunity under capitalism. One source is transmission of inherited wealth. As long as income-producing property is inheritable by the children of wealthy parents, the children of the rich will have a significantly better chance of economic success than the children of the poor. The second source is the transmission of inherited talents. Parents from high socioeconomic classes generally pass on to their children certain personality traits, values, and expectations that play a crucial role in determining an individual's success in gaining a high income or prestigious occupation vis-à-vis a lower income person. According to Bowles: "The arguments that our 'egalitarian' education compensates for inequalities generated elsewhere in the capitalist system is potentially fallacious."[29] For education to compensate for class difference, poor children require not equal but more than equal benefits from education.

Moreover, two mechanisms are at work linking educational inequality to economic equality. First, the principle of rewarding academic excellence serves to "legitimize the process by which the social division of labor is reproduced . . . [and] . . . socializes young people to work for external rewards."[30] Second, the principle of financing elementary and secondary schools mainly from local revenues produces an unequal distribution of school resources among children of different classes.

Thus, one could argue that the differences between educational status and health status in U.S. capitalism are probably due to the fact that educational attainment is directly related to social class. Therefore, improvement in health status through a strategy of increasing educational attainment will be limited by the inherent nature of the educational class structure.

Environmental Pollution

In addition to the economic, social, and political aspects of health under capitalism, there is also increasing awareness of the interrelationship of the economic system and environmental hazards. Capitalism is generating increased levels of pollution, much of which is proving harmful to the public's health. With the continued growth of the United States, a greater amount of pollution is spewed into the environment. Yet capitalism requires material economic growth for its survival. In an advanced capitalist system, the ability of the economy to produce products tends to outstrip its ability to consume these products. This creates a surplus, causing firms to curtail production and reduce employment and thereby creating a recession. The solution is to apply monetary and fiscal policies to stimulate aggregate demand to absorb the surplus and thereby keep the economy growing. According to England and Bluestone, "the private market economy is caught on a treadmill: to forestall mass unemployment, even higher levels of consumption must be stimulated and even higher levels of investment must be forthcoming."[31] The environmental problem is that the presently required future increases in GNP certainly will result in the more rapid depletion of exhaustible resources and will tend to generate more pollution.

In addition, ecological irrationalities are apparent in the advanced capitalist system. Planned obsolescence and emphasis on frequent changes in packaging and style exacerbate the use of resources. This not only increases inputs into the production process but also increases wastes after consumption. Furthermore, production of individual, rather than social, consumption stimulates the use of resources and contributes to pollution. It causes overconsumption of underutilized capital goods and prevents the realization of economies of scale. Finally, increased growth requires greater energy production and utilization. These latter two activities help deplete the resource base and increase environmental pollution.

However, it also should be clear that adopting Soviet style socialism does not necessarily guarantee increased environmental concern. It appears that the levels of environmental pollution in the Soviet Union (USSR) are as high as in the United States. Many incentives to pollute exist in the USSR due to emphasis on economic growth, stress on increased material production, treatment of raw materials as free goods, lack of social cost accounting, and pervasive powers of the state. Furthermore, following his study of environmental pollution in the USSR, Goldman concludes: "Not private enterprise but industrialization is the primary cause of environmental disruption. This suggests that state ownership of all the productive resources is not a cure at all."[32] The causes of pollution in the Soviet Union are very similar to those in the United States.

Considerable recent research has focused on the effects of air pollution on human health.[33] Strong evidence now links air pollution of levels prevailing in many cities to heightened incidence of a variety of respiratory diseases including asthma, chronic bronchitis, emphysema, pneumonia, and colds. Further data suggest that air pollution boosts the frequency with which people, especially children, contract short-term respiratory ailments; compounds problems of heart attacks; and is related to lung and stomach cancers.

Lave and Seskin have completed a comprehensive and detailed analysis of the effects of air pollution on human health across seventeen SMSAs (Standard Metropolitan Statistical Areas) in the United States for the years 1960, 1961, and 1969.[34] Their findings indicate that measures of air pollution (i.e., sulfates and suspended particulates) are significant factors in explaining variations in the total death rate across areas of the nation. Moreover, measures of air pollution appear more closely associated with mortality among nonwhites than among whites and among the older age groups than among younger ones. Additional time series analyses and consideration of alternative hypotheses lead to the conclusion that "air pollution does not simply 'harvest' deaths of susceptible individuals, but seems to reduce life expectancy in general."[35] Moreover, a 58 percent reduction in particulates and an 88 percent reduction in sulfur oxides would lead to a 7 percent reduction in total mortality.

The unequal distribution of income, wealth, and power mirrors the unequal incidence of social costs and benefits that flow from the production of pollution. Economic necessity forces many of the poor and near poor to live in harmful environments while many of the rich enjoy better environmental conditions. Similarly, blue collar workers suffer more than professional workers since they are more likely to work and live near polluting plants and factories. Proposed pollution control policies, like pollution taxes and effluent charges, are apt to be based on regressive systems of financing, causing the poor and working classes to bear more of the burden of cleaning the environment.

In their analysis of the distributional impacts of a fully implemented national air pollution policy (Clean Air Act of 1970), Gianessi, Peskin, and Wolf analyze the effects of implementing stationary sources, mobile sources, and total pollution control.[36] Their results show that those who gain the most are in low income groups. Their analyses of net benefits (i.e., the differences between gross benefits of control and costs of control) by income class and race demonstrate that for stationary sources, net benefits accrue to all income classes except the highest class and are two to five times higher for nonwhites than whites. For mobile sources the net benefits are negative to all income classes, and for the total air pollution policy nonwhites are the only gainers. Furthermore, the incidence of net benefits on households (as a fraction of family income) is progressive for the stationary sources policy, regressive for the mobile sources policy, and with the exception of the lowest income class, slightly regressive for the total policy.

Taken as a whole, the results of these studies on environmental pollution suggest (1) that industrialized countries that stress material economic growth will continue to accelerate environmental pollution, (2) that environmental health hazards are taking on increased importance, and (3) that these health hazards and public policy aimed at reducing environmental pollution are regressive in nature. Such results compound the health differentials brought forth by previously discussed income, social class, and educational inequalities.

SOCIAL JUSTICE AND HEALTH

The studies examined thus far show how the distribution of health care resources and health status are affected by the U.S. economic system and illustrate that the correlation between the increased amount of health care and the health status of a population is at best very weak. It appears that factors such as economic stability, environmental pollution, economic development, and improved nutrition are considerably more relevant to the improved health status of a population, while great inequities exist in health status levels that relate largely to economic inequality, education, class structure, and environmental hazards.

Collectively, these conclusions suggest a need to reconsider appropriate health policy and to reanalyze questions surrounding social justice in health and health care. Thus, a review of the two fundamental philosophical positions that underly both the science of economics and recent health policy analysis is in order. Furthermore, in light of the empirical findings previously reported, these positions warrant critical examination.

The Conservative Viewpoint

Orthodox neoclassical economics rests on the eighteenth century libertarian philosophy as developed by Adam Smith, Jeremy Bentham, and David Ricardo and refined by William Stanley Jevons, Leon Walras, and, in the twentieth century, Milton Friedman. The cornerstone of their thinking is that an economic system run by unfettered market forces, in which producers and consumers seek their own respective self-interests, achieves the optimal allocation and distribution of resources and products. The key regulating device in this system is competition among both buyers and sellers. Furthermore, orthodox economics increasingly uses mathematical techniques and marginal analyses to further refine these basic tenets and to make them objective. Embodied within this neoclassical ideology is a very limited role of government.

Nozick is the most recent spokesperson for this philosophical viewpoint, with the basis of his theory of justice being the principle of individual rights.[37] He contends that the minimal state, limited to restricted functions such as protection against force, theft, fraud, and enforcement of contract, is the only state compatible with the protection of individual rights. According to his view, a distribution is just if everyone is entitled to the holdings they possess under the distribution, and a person is entitled to a holding if it is acquired justly (e.g., through a voluntary exchange or a gift). Individuals possess the right to acquire and dispose of their holdings in accordance with their desire and without interference from anybody. Therefore, the free market system, ruled by an invisible hand, is the only system that can protect individual liberty.

With respect to health care, Illich represents contemporary conservative thinking.[38] His ideological view of health care emphasizes the individual's control of his/her own health. In his book *Medical Nemesis* he asserts: "Better health care will depend . . . on the level of willingness and competence to engage in self-care."[39] He insists on the acceptance of a new ethical imperative for the improvement of health: "Act so that the effect of your action is compatible with the permanence of genuine human life."[40] Advocates of personal lifestyle changes for improvements in health adopt the same individualistic view of health. For example, Fuchs argues that "the greatest potential for improving health lies in what we do and don't do for and to ourselves. The choice is ours."[41]

Illich argues that the key issues in the debate surrounding the health of a population should be medical nemesis (i.e., clinical, social, and cultural iatrogenesis), the recovery of personal responsibility for health care, and limitation of professional medical monopolies.

He recommends three basic solutions to the present health care dilemma: (1) the deprofessionalization and debureaucratization of the medical profession, (2) maximum emphasis on individual responsibility for health and health care, and (3) the decentralization of industry and return to the market model. Two well-known conservative economists, Milton Friedman and Reuben Kessel, support these same positions.[42] Illich calls for new legislation that would

> tax medical technology and professional activity until those means that can be handled by laymen were truly available to anyone wanting access to them . . . guarantee the right of people to drop out and to organize for a less destructive way of life . . . [with] . . . more control of their environment . . . shift the full burden of the responsible use [of drugs] onto the sick person and his next of kin . . . recognize each man's right to define his own health — subject only to limitations imposed by respect for his neighbor's rights . . . give the public a voice in the election of healers to tax-supported health jobs . . . have [health professionals] evaluated by the community they serve.[43]

The Liberal Viewpoint

The liberal position evolves from a modification of neoclassical orthodox economics. It concurs with the writings of John Maynard Keynes and was refined by such contemporary thinkers as Paul Samuelson, John Kenneth Galbraith, and Wassily Leontief. Keynes' major contribution to orthodox theory was the recognition that capitalism is inherently unstable because it requires increasing expansion of aggregate demand for further capital investment and that the government has an important role to play in helping to stabilize the market system at high levels of employment.

Samuelson offers an integration of Keynesian with neoclassical economics. The Keynesian theory provides the knowledge necessary to maintain a full-employment economy, and the market system could operate within this Keynesian framework to allocate resources according to the principles of the neoclassical ideology. As with Keynes' view of the need for state intervention in the capitalist system, the liberal position is for a considerably more active role for the state in general.

In the liberal view, the state in a modern democracy adequately reflects individual wishes through group representatives. The government is justified in acting essentially because it incorporates the preferences of all individuals and because it seeks to advance the public interest. There are three basic rationales for government intervention in the life of the citizenry and in the economic system. First, since the economic system generates income inequality, causing some to live at or below subsistence levels, the government should redistribute income. Second, since the capitalist system fails to act correctly when certain imperfections are evident in the market, the government should act to correct the market to more effectively reflect consumer preferences. Third, since the capitalist system fails to provide certain goods (called public goods), the government should act to provide such goods (e.g., national defense).

Rawls is the most recent spokesman of the liberal philosophical position. The basis of his theory of justice is that "all social primary goods—liberty and opportunity, income and wealth, and the bases of self-respect—are to be distributed equally unless an unequal distribution of any or all of these goods is to the advantage of the least favored."[44] He elaborates on this basic tenet with two fundamental principles of justice. The first says that each person is to have an equal right to the most extensive total system of equal basic liberties compatible with a similar system of liberty for all. The second requires that social and economic inequalities meet two conditions: They must (1) be to the greatest expected benefit of the worst off members of society and (2) be attached to offices and positions open to all under conditions of fair equality of opportunity. Furthermore, according to Canterbery and Johnson, "A Rawlsian social contract would include the principle that those who have been favored by nature with talent, wealth, or other social advantages may gain in their good fortune only on terms that improve the situation of those who have otherwise lost out."[45]

Bryant[46] and Rosenthal[47] suggest similar arguments for creating a more equitable distribution of health care. Bryant argues that Rawls' concept of justice, as it relates to health care, can be stated as: "Whatever health services are available should be equally available to all unless an unequal distribution would be to the advantage of the least favored."[48] From this primary principle, four more basic ones follow: (1) there should be a floor or minimum amount of health care for all; (2) health care resources above the floor should be distributed according to need (i.e., used to serve those in greatest need); (3) in those instances in which health care resources are nondivisible or necessarily uneven, their distribution should be of advantage to the least favored; and (4) the population actually or potentially receiving health care should participate in the decisionmaking about the distribution and use of those resources.

The rationale for the establishment of such a floor is to "identify the *public* interest in personal health services"[49] and to describe "the least that will meet the public obligation."[50] Furthermore, Rosenthal argues that such a policy has three guiding premises: (1) if government defines the minimum entitlement that the public will support, private allocation above the minimum would permit a wide variety of personal preferences; (2) a floor would provide the psychological and economic security for everyone; and (3) people would press for higher standards, as has occurred historically with other minimum standards. For an advanced nation, a floor would involve a basic health network organized around community health workers and health centers providing primary care, maternal and child care, environmental control, and specific disease control.[51]

A CRITIQUE OF THE CONSERVATIVE
AND LIBERAL POSITIONS

The preceding section describes the philosophical positions of the conservatives and liberals and their resulting policy descriptions for the health of the population and the health care sector. Each view has some elements of the changes needed to improve the health of the population. However, both fail to address the underlying causes of the inequities in health and health care.

Critique of the Conservative Position

The conservative position emphasizes individual self-care and health care as a private good. Though there is some merit to this argument, it fails to recognize the social nature of health and disease and the social determinants analyzed earlier in this chapter. It is true that an important gain in personal independence can result from people learning more self-care, having much more medical knowledge, and living healthier lifestyles. However, such an emphasis ignores two important facts: (1) that many of the factors affecting illness and health are determined externally (i.e., of a social nature and not controllable by the individual) and (2) that lifestyles are influenced, if not determined, by the social milieu in which they exist. For example, consider a patient's desire to reduce the risk of developing cancer. People can control where they live, what they eat, what occupation they choose, but their efforts can be easily thwarted by private business or by a government decision to build a nationwide system of nuclear power plants or to allow continued air and water pollution.

The conservative view places great trust in the market system. However, this system is geared to profit making and commoditization of health care. The market system emphasizes the purchase of health through individual consumption of health care: "An intrinsically social, cooperative process has been transformed under capitalist medicine into a commodity exchange process."[52] Thus, production of health care becomes a commodity offered for a price on the market, and the provider reaps the profit. As long as the market system remains intact, even an informed public cannot avoid the problems that such a system creates.

Illich's emphasis on deprofessionalization and debureaucratization of medicine is a valuable point. Either would allow informed consumers greater choice of the type of health care they want. In addition, consumers would gain more control over their own health care. Deindustrialization is also a good idea. Many environmental and occupational health problems stem from the growth of large-scale industrialization. As illustrated earlier, industrialization entwined with an emphasis on material growth and increased production leads to similar health hazards in the United States and the Soviet Union. In addition, deindustrialization would most likely lead to a decrease in monopolies and oligopolies, increased employment, and increased control of industry at the local level. However, if it did not lead to control by local communities, then the inequality in power and wealth still would remain.

The most fundamental problem in the conservative position is its failure to acknowledge the interaction of economic inequality and economic fluctuations on health status. A laissez-faire capitalist system would generate income and wealth inequality and would suffer from the boom-bust business cycle, both of which have a detrimental effect on health status. The former leads to class-differentiated health status; the latter results in sharp declines in health status of the population during recessions. Clearly, social justice is not being served if such inequality and instability remain.

Critique of the Liberal Position

The liberal position does recognize the social aspects of health and disease and the need for public action. Presumably, this is why it calls for a redistribution of health care services. However, its solution is for government action to correct the maldistribution of health care services. This position assumes that government is independent of specific interest groups and functions in the public interest. Since this position does nothing to diffuse the political power of the medical establishment, government most likely would be influenced strongly by the interests of the health professions and health care institutions. Given the present emphasis on maldistribution of health care services and an orientation of the health establishment toward providing such services in the most profitable markets, it is difficult to believe that these groups would favor the redistribution proposed by the liberals.

The liberal position advocates the establishment of a floor on some basic set of health care services. Although it might contribute to some redistribution of services, this proposal is inadequate for a few reasons. Upon defining the floor as the public role to be played in the health care market, there is a very real possibility that the floor becomes the maximum public effort. For example, when viewed collectively, welfare programs have attempted to set some floor under the poor, yet they have "not been growing relative to the rest of the economy and in many cases have suffered declines."[53] Second, the floor set in other markets, such as public education, reveals that undisturbed income inequality still creates inequality in that market. Third, establishing a floor for any vital service usually results in a two class system of delivery of that service. The government's role becomes simply to appear to offer some solution to a public problem without disturbing the basic class structure of the economic system. Medicaid provides a good example of this outcome.

Additionally, the liberal position calls for some type of public participation in the distribution and utilization of health care resources. However, it fails to foster the independence of the individual from the health establishment. Basically, the liberal proposal is to maintain high technology and scientific medicine and simply to bring more of these health care services to the most needy. This, of course, means that the population remains dependent upon the professional health practitioner, subject to the mystification of the medical miracle and imbued with the concept of buying health care.

Finally, the liberal position does attempt to replace the allocation of health care resources by way of the profit motive with allocation according to need. While this is commendable, nothing is done to address the problem of maintaining an overall economic system that stresses profits as its allocative mechanism. Since the health care system is related to the economic system and since it is a highly profitable sector, one wonders how the United States could decide to reallocate health care resources on the basis of need without changing or at least questioning the underlying profit-oriented allocative mechanism.

SOCIAL PRINCIPLES FOR AN EGALITARIAN SOCIETY

In concluding that neither the liberal nor the conservative position offers a viable solution to social justice in health, it becomes necessary to examine the principles that a society should follow to ensure an egalitarian health system. From the outset, it should be clear that health status is a function of a complex set of variables, has characteristics that are both public and private in nature, and can never be guaranteed by anyone. Hence, it is impossible to assert that health will become a publicly determined right. However, it is possible to go much further in reducing the risk to disease and in fostering positive health concepts and policies.

Hence, the underlying principle that should be established in fostering an egalitarian system of health is that the economic, social, and political systems should hold the preservation of life as their number one goal—the life of humans, subhumans, and future generations. From this initial principle, two subprinciples flow: (1) Society should not willfully establish any institution or enact any program that will increase the risk of disease to the population; rather, it should use all means to foster a reduction in any factor that leads to general health hazards and health differences among people. (2) Society should promote a positive health attitude in all its citizenry and the recognition of the interdependence of human life on the preservation of the environment.

Based on all available evidence to date, the adoption of such principles would require several structural changes in society. Hence, there is a need to begin emphasizing the quality of life and material sufficiency.[54] At this point in history, advanced industrialized countries are enamored with economic growth as the determinant of human happiness. Unfortunately, such a view converts people into insatiable pleasure seekers and leads to continual destruction of the life-supporting environment. In this author's view, these characteristics are antihealth. Material sufficiency means obtaining the maximum of well-being with the minimum of consumption. As Daly says, "The goal of life becomes wisdom, enjoyment, cultivation of the mind and soul and community."[55]

Associated with this first change is the need to adopt a more humane, environment-preserving technology. As of this date, an insistence on consuming nonrenewable resources as rapidly as possible for the sake of stimulating economic growth continues. In fact, it is generally accepted that increasing the use of energy and natural resources is related directly to growing affluence and improved well-being. In addition, the increased air, water, and land pollution that results clearly leads to reduced health status for much of the population. Society is now on the verge of adopting potentially the most dangerous energy technology in history—nuclear power. What is needed is a turning to what Lovins calls soft energy paths through the use of direct solar energy, wind, and biomass conversion.[56] In addition, greater stress and reliance on more labor-intensive, as opposed to capital-intensive, production processes would foster this effort. Such changes would greatly reduce the health hazards of environmental pollution and simultaneously stimulate employment.

A third change is the need for increased emphasis on the independence of the individual and the cooperativeness of the community. Advanced contemporary society has made people dependent on professionals for very basic services, individuals are much less likely to provide care for themselves than they were at one time. Yet, simultaneously, the sense of community needed when individuals have to work together has been destroyed.

As stated before, health has both public and private aspects. Basic health maintenance is an individual or family function. Hence, there is the need for public education on self-care and to restore the individual's ability to heal oneself. At the same time, there is a need for a community-controlled network of health service activities to provide the necessary health care to support private efforts. Such community health service facilities should (1) educate the local community on those factors that increase disease risks and promote health; and (2) monitor and stimulate community awareness of key environmental, social, and economic factors affecting health status.

Related to these changes is the need to decentralize control of industry. To help foster the goals of community and self-reliance, much more decisionmaking power would have to be allocated to the people. This could be accomplished by instituting a limit on corporate size or encouraging community ownership of economic enterprises. In either case, more people would be involved directly in setting the priorities of the economic institutions. Furthermore, with greater emphasis on personal control, creativity and self-expression of work could be reinstituted.

Intertwined with these changes is a requirement for a much more equitable distribution of income and wealth and a reduction in social class differences. The evidence demonstrating the effect of inequality in income and wealth, and of the maintenance of social classes on the health of different groups is clear. Moreover, to insure political rights and democracy, a much more egalitarian distribution of economic resources is necessary. In paraphrasing John Stuart Mill on this point, Daly argues that "[p]rivate property, when some own a great deal of it and others have very little, becomes the very instrument of exploitation rather than the guarantee against it."[57] Hence, some maximum and minimum limit on income and wealth should be established through the system of taxation.[58] Since there would be no incentive to go beyond the maximum limit, greater opportunities for economic pursuit would exist for the not so wealthy (and therefore for a considerably larger proportion of the population). Since a family could not fall below the minimum lower limit, significantly greater economic security would be provided, and a higher level of health status would be guaranteed.

In conclusion, social justice in health requires major comprehensive changes in the economic, social, and political systems of society. An egalitarian system of health requires the material sufficiency ethic; a humane, environment-preserving technology; greatly reduced limits on income and wealth inequalities; decentralization of decisionmaking; and independence and self-reliance. Anything less than these fundamental changes will, at best, only temper the existing injustices in the present economic, social, and political systems and their effects on health status and, at worst, lead to greater health problems, increased mortality rates, and perhaps the eventual destruction of human life.

NOTES TO CHAPTER 4

1. John B. McKinlay and Sonja N. McKinlay, "The Questionable Contribution of Medical Measures to the Decline of Mortality in the United States in the Twentieth Century," *Milbank Memorial Fund Quarterly/Health and Society* 55: 405–428 (Summer 1977).

2. Irving Leveson, "Some Policy Implications of the Relationship Between Health Services and Health," *Inquiry* 16: 9–21 (Spring 1979).

3. Ibid., p. 9.

4. McKinlay and McKinlay, p. 414.

5. J.P. Newhouse and M.J. Friedlander, *The Relationship between Medical Resources and Measures of Health: Some Additional Evidence.* (Santa Monica, CA: The Rand Corporation, 1977).

6. Thomas McKeown, *The Role of Medicine: Dream, Mirage, or Nemesis?* (London: The Nuffield Provincial Hospital Trust, 1976).

7. Victor Fuchs, "Economics, Health, and Post-Industrial Society," *Milbank Memorial Fund Quarterly/Health and Society* 57: 156 (Spring 1979).

8. M. Harvey Brenner, "Economic Changes and Heart Disease Mortality," *American Journal of Public Health* 61: 606–611 (March 1971).

9. M. Harvey Brenner, "Fetal, Infant, and Maternal Mortality during Periods of Economic Instability," *International Journal of Health Services* 3: 145–159 (1973).

10. M. Harvey Brenner, "Trends in Alcohol Consumption and Associated Illnesses: Some Effects of Economic Changes," *American Journal of Public Health* 65: 1279–1292 (December 1975).

11. M. Harvey Brenner, "Effects of Adverse Changes in the National Economy on Health" (Presented at the 103rd meeting of the American Public Health Association, Chicago, November 18, 1975).

12. M. Harvey Brenner, "Health Costs and Benefits of Economic Policy," *International Journal of Health Services* 7: 581–623 (1977).

13. Frank Ackerman and Andrew Zimbalist, "Capitalism and Inequality in the United States," in Richard Edwards, Michael Reich, and Thomas Weisskopf, *The Capitalist System, 2nd Ed.* (Englewood Cliffs, NJ: Prentice-Hall, 1978), pp. 293–307.

118   FUTURE DIMENSIONS OF THE HEALTH CARE SYSTEM

14. Brenner, "Effects of Adverse Changes," p. 2.
15. David Salkever, "Economic Class and Differential Access to Care: Comparisons among Health Care Systems," *International Journal of Health Services* 5: 373–395 (1975).
16. Leveson, p. 15.
17. Vincent Navarro, *Medicine under Capitalism* (New York: Prodist, 1976), pp. 82–85.
18. Ibid., pp. 148–156.
19. Ibid., pp. 84–87.
20. M. Lerner and R.N. Stutz, "Mortality Differentials among Socioeconomic Strata in Baltimore, 1960 and 1973," in American Statistical Association, *Proceedings of the American Statistical Association* (Washington, D.C., 1975), pp. 517–522.
21. P.W. Conover, "Social Class and Chronic Illness," *International Journal of Health Services* 3: 357–368 (1973).
22. For a review of alienation in the American work force, readers are referred to Chapter 7 in Richard Edwards, Michael Reich, and Thomas Weisskopf, *The Capitalist System, 2nd Ed.* (Englewood Cliffs, N.J.: Prentice–Hall, 1978).
23. "Report of the Special Task Force to the Secretary of Health, Education, and Welfare," *Work in America.* (Cambridge, MA: The MIT Press, 1973), pp. 76–92.
24. Howard S. Berliner, "Emerging Ideologies in Medicine," *The Review of Radical Political Economics* 9: 119 (Spring 1977).
25. Fuchs, p. 156.
26. Richard Auster, Irving Leveson, and Deborah Sarachek, "The Production of Health, an Exploratory Study," in Victor Fuchs, *Essays in the Economics of Health and Medical Care* (New York: National Bureau of Economic Research, Columbia University Press, 1972), pp. 135–158.
27. Michael Grossman, "The Correlation between Health and Schooling," in Nester Terleckyj, *Household Production and Consumption* (New York: National Bureau of Economic Research, Columbia University Press, 1975), pp. 147–211.
28. Fuchs, p. 159.
29. Samuel Bowles, "Schooling and the Reproduction of Inequality," in Edwards, Reich and Weisskopf, *The Capitalist System*, p. 324. For a more extensive treatment of these ideas, readers are referred to Samuel Bowles and Herbert Gintis, *Schooling in Capitalist America* (New York: Basic Books, Inc., 1976).
30. Ibid., p. 328.
31. Richard England and Barry Bluestone, "Ecology and Social Conflict," in Herman Daly, *Toward a Steady-State Economy* (San Francisco: W.H. Freeman and Company, 1973), p. 199.

32. Marshall Goldman, "The Convergence of Environmental Disruption," *Science* 170: 42 (October 2, 1970).
33. For an extensive review of the literature on this subject, readers are referred to Appendix A in Lester Lave and Eugene Seskin, *Air Pollution and Human Health* (Baltimore: The Johns Hopkins University Press, 1977).
34. Ibid.
35. Ibid., p. 243.
36. Leonard Gianessi, Henry Peskin, and Edward Wolf, "The Distributional Effects of Uniform Air Pollution Policy in the United States," *Quarterly Journal of Economics* 93: 281-301 (May 1979).
37. Robert Nozick, *Anarchy, State, and Utopia* (New York: Basic Books, Inc., 1974).
38. Ivan Illich, *Medical Nemesis: The Expropriation of Health* (New York: Random House, Inc., 1976).
39. Ibid., p. 270.
40. Ibid., p. 268.
41. Victor Fuchs, *Who Shall Live? Health, Economics, and Social Choice* (New York: Basic Books, Inc., 1974), p. 151.
42. Milton Friedman, *Capitalism and Freedom* (Chicago: University of Chicago Press, 1962), pp. 137-160; Reuben Kessel, "The A.M.A. and the Supply of Physicians," *Law and Contemporary Problems* 35: 276-283 (Spring 1970); and Reuben Kessel, "Price Discrimination in Medicine," *Journal of Law and Economics* 1: 20-53 (October 1958).
43. Illich, pp. 272-273.
44. John Rawls, *A Theory of Justice* (Cambridge, MA: Harvard University Press, 1971), p. 303.
45. E. Ray Canterbery and Harry G. Johnson, "Justice, Nozick, and Rawls: A Symposium, Introduction," *Eastern Economic Journal* 4: 4 (January 1978).
46. John Bryant, "Principles of Justice as a Basis for Conceptualizing a Health Care System," *International Journal of Health Services* 7: 707-719 (1977).
47. Gerald Rosenthal and Daniel Fox, "A Right to What?: Toward Adequate Minimum Standards for Personal Health Services," *Milbank Memorial Fund Quarterly/Health and Society* 56: 1-6 (Winter 1978).
48. Bryant, p. 709.
49. Rosenthal and Fox, p. 3.
50. Ibid., p. 5.
51. Bryant, p. 715.
52. Leonard Rodberg and Gelven Stevenson, "The Health Care Industry in Advanced Capitalism," *The Review of Radical Political Economics* 9: 114 (Spring 1977).

53.   Richard Edwards, "Who Fares Well in the Welfare State?" in Edwards, Reich, and Weisskopf, *The Capitalist System*, p. 312.

54.   Herman Daly, *Steady-State Economics* (San Francisco: W.H. Freeman and Company, 1977), p. 44.

55.   Ibid., p. 45.

56.   Amory Lovins, *Soft Energy Paths: Toward a Durable Peace.* (New York: Harper & Row, Publishers, Inc., 1977).

57.   Daly, p. 54.

58.   Ibid., p. 56.

5 SOCIAL COSTS OF REGULATION IN THE HEALTH INDUSTRY

Ralph Andreano, Ph. D.
Harold R. Wilde, Ph. D.

INTRODUCTION

The explosion in personal health expenditures in the United States during the past decade and a seeming lack of incentives to control those expenditures have generated an elaborate, albeit often fragmented, regulatory system for the health industry. The market failure represented by the health industry (i.e., the inability of prices to clear markets and allocate resources rationally) has produced an industry in which social costs are entirely out of balance with individual costs. This means that while the burden of rising expenditures on each individual unit (e.g., the consumer, the provider) is nearly zero, the collective burden of these rising costs on society is very large.

The theory of regulation being pursued in the health industry, which has been articulated by few policymakers, is aimed at correcting the substantial imbalance between individual and social costs. The principal components of the regulatory theory, primarily established as a consequence of the passage and recent extension of the National Health Planning and Resources Development Act (PL 93-641), include certificate of need (CON), prospective rate setting for hospitals, appropriateness review, and statewide medical facilities plans. Other traditional regulatory instruments, such as manpower credentialing, rate setting for nonprofit insurance carriers,

121

and quality assurance, must also be included as part of any analysis of the regulatory package applicable to the health industry.

At the outset, a few points should be made about this regulatory framework.

1. Most regulatory attempts have been directed to the supply side — that is, to constrict future resources (e.g., buildings, capital equipment, labor) from going into the industry.

2. Present inefficiencies, due to such things as duplication of services and excess acute and long-term care beds, have not been dealt with systematically. Regulatory efforts could be important in dealing with medical facilities plans and appropriateness review.

3. Almost none of the regulatory framework addresses the demand side of the equation, either through trying to reduce total consumption of health care resources or by encouraging, through the provision of incentives, producers or consumers to substitute less expensive types of care (e.g., preventive versus curative, outpatient versus inpatient care).

Finally, the regulatory framework appears to address the principal elements of the so-called health care crisis—rising costs, unequal access by groups and regions, and quality. The time has come to start asking some hard questions about health regulation, both the newer elements and the more traditional components. Will regulation reduce personal health expenditures? Will it improve the distribution of health care resources? Will it improve access? Will it improve equity? Who will gain? Who will lose?

First, this chapter addresses some of the key elements of regulatory policy under PL 93-641. These, as will be seen, are supply side policy instruments. The second half of the chapter reviews demand side regulatory possibilities. The focal point for this analysis is the health insurance, or third party financing, mode. Although the financial system of the American health care industry is frequently cited as the most effective point for policy intervention, this analysis reveals that even on demand side interventions, it is not always clear that the benefits of society exceed the costs.

REGULATION OF RESOURCE SUPPLY UNDER PL 93-641

Hospital Regulation

There are many possible dimensions of hospital regulations. The discussion focuses on three—CON, prospective rate setting, and utilization review (UR).

CON. Under PL 93-641,[a] states are required to approve all capital expenditures for hospitals, nursing homes, home health care agencies, and in certain cases, physicians' offices in excess of some threshold amount, usually $100,000 to $150,000. Any new or change of service, regardless of the amount of capital expenditure involved, also requires approval. States and health systems agencies (HSAs), which are regional planning bodies created by PL 93-641, have norms or guidelines that govern their activities, but the use of national health-planning guidelines, which outline national norms for beds, services, and the like, usually in quantitative terms (e.g., so many beds per thousand population, utilization rates for certain services) is encouraged.

The underlying theory behind CON regulation is that by constricting the supply of new resources (e.g., beds, services, equipment) going into the hospital sector, (1) the competition among hospitals for new capital will be slowed; (2) the future bed supply will be reduced; and (3) duplication of services, especially highly specialized and costly ones, will be potentially reduced. Theoretically, the result of these combined effects will be to contain the financial requirements hospitals generate from patient revenues and thus reduce the pace at which per diem rates increase. Overall, the net effect should be the production of a constant or declining level of personal health expenditure devoted to the hospital sector.

Unfortunately, there are some conceptual as well as practical problems with this theory. Conceptually, it deals only with the flow of new capital to the hospital sector and not the capital already invested in beds, equipment, and services. Thus, the effective reduction in the available supply of capital goods will take a long time, if it is effec-

---

a. About half of the states had a CON program prior to enactment of PL 93-641.

tive at all. More importantly, the theory depends on the initiative of the institutions to require less capital in the future than in the past. This is a doubtful assumption.

A second conceptual difficulty is that awarding CONs is akin to awarding limited monopolies—that is, it precludes other potential entrants. Health care providers will thus (1) fight fiercely to be first in their area in the provision of a new service or an expansion of existing capacity or service or (2) react protectively or defensively in trying to accelerate long-term plans for new services or planned construction in order not to be precluded in the future from doing so because of planning guidelines or norms. The net result is that hospitals in particular will try to anticipate application of CON standards by planning agencies and will selectively overbuild or overextend specialized services. The collective effect of this interinstitution competition against the CON planning standards is—especially in urban areas—to force short-term hospitals to try to be full service or complete hospitals.

Given the strength of the planning and CON agencies, how could this happen? In any given community, local political dynamics plus the provider domination of HSA boards and project review committees will make it difficult to reject large numbers of CON project applications. Indeed, the Salkever and Bice study shows that the 1122/CON[b] approval rates exceed 90 percent nationally.[1] Thus, the anomalous result produced, or likely to be produced, by this component of health regulatory policy is just the opposite of its intention. Instead of creating a tendency to reduce beds, consolidate, and/or share specialized services, the tendency for each hospital to become a full line department store is reinforced. Thus, regulation, in this sense, is producing an unanticipated social cost; society bears a larger cost because of the regulation than it would without it.

Some will argue that in the absence of regulation, hospitals would normally move in this direction anyway (and indeed have already done so, thus giving rise to CON type regulation in the first place) and that if regulation now is only marginally successful, it will still be socially cost effective. The results thus far do not appear encouraging, but more time is needed to evaluate CON laws and to examine

b. Section 1122 of the Social Security Act (PL 92-603) enacted in 1972 constituted a federal CON type of program required of organizations receiving Medicare funds. In 1974, the CON legislation, requiring the establishment of individual state CON laws, was enacted as part of PL 93-641.

the approximate allocative results produced from the interplay of competitive market forces.

Another unintended social cost of awarding a limited number of franchises (i.e., a CON) is that it may retard new innovations in service delivery. Requirement of CON approval for such new services or delivery mechanisms, such as surgicenters and health maintenance organizations (HMOs), frequently meets resistance among local and state planning bodies. These innovations have cost containment possibilities, and their widespread adoption should be encouraged rather than retarded by planning agencies. The typical hospital response to surgicenters has been to expand outpatient surgery services at charges slightly above those of surgicenters but below those for the same services provided in inpatient settings. Thus, the net effect of the regulatory policy is to reduce prices to consumers, but by less than the reductions produced through competition.

Prospective Rate Setting. This regulatory tool, encouraged by PL 93–641 and now being implemented in many states in one form or another, has a similar objective as CON—hospital cost containment. The theory of prospective rate setting is simple. A hospital should budget for a year, have its budget and its average per diem (or some other measure or price) compared to similar hospitals, justify its rates for the year relative to competition, and be required to operate for the year within those rates. In some rate-setting systems, hospitals are rewarded if they perform under their respective budgets for the year (i.e., accumulating surpluses), and of course, they may be penalized if they exceed their budgets (i.e., absorbing the deficits).

Prospective rate setting encourages hospitals to play accounting games. First, no good hospital administrator wants to understate the budget. Making group comparisons will not provide the discipline of the market; administrators will try to keep their budgets flexible enough to continue their chosen approach or style and not suffer penalties for good operation in a preceding or succeeding year. Occasionally a price cutter emerges in any hospital grouping. Since price cutting in a community hospital confers few competitive advantages, one can presume that like all price cutting, it is a momentary rather than a structural event.

In some states (notably, New York, Massachusetts, and Maryland) where prospective rate setting is already well-developed, recent evaluations suggest that the method may have some effect in containing hospital expenditures. While the effectiveness of rate setting may be doubted, perhaps awaiting the availability of more empirical data would be worthwhile.

Rate setting may alter the mix of the hospital product without decreasing total expenditures. For example, the length of hospitalization and other UR variables may decline, but the intensity of care may increase. Thus, rate setting requires that careful attention be given to both sides of the equation contributing to total expenditures (i.e., price times quantity). In addition, rate setting requires very tight norms and standards for input use, for peer group comparison, and for building incentives for efficient patient management with fewer resources at less total cost. Rate setting, as a regulatory tool, also must be linked integrally to the CON process; that which is lost by a hospital in a CON process must not be easy to win through loose setting of standards and norms.

Possibly the major conceptual problem with prospective rate setting for hospitals is that the burden of performance is placed on the hospital administrator. Rate setting suffers from an additional conceptual flaw in that it does not account for or incorporate physician inputs into a hospital or for variations in those inputs across hospitals. In reality, a hospital is two production units. One produces the manpower, material, and technical inputs; the other, operated by the physician, produces the patients and the care of the patients by combining the resources available.

The primary responsibility of the hospital administrator is to assure the availability of inputs needed by physicians to perform their functions. The income that physicians generate from a hospital, based upon the amounts of their inputs (and the complexity and length of them) and the prices charged for their services, is not under discretionary control of the administrator. Rate setting, therefore, is really dealing with an incomplete set and will produce long-range difficulties in containing total expenditures unless physician inputs and prices are incorporated into the forecast of financial requirements and anticipated revenues. These are the data a rate-setting commission should have and from which control of total expenditures can be achieved.

UR.   Most of the regulation directed toward the physician's contribution to increasing hospital expenditure is in the area of UR, either through Professional Standards Review Organizations (PSRO) or in combination with hospital-based UR committees. UR has two general objectives — (1) quality assurance and (2) cost containment. The evidence is still not conclusive as to whether these two objectives are mutually consistent. It is clear, however, that one of the major cost impacts of UR is the reduction in the length of actual hospitalization (i.e., the average length of stay). However, this tends to work counterproductively toward reducing total hospital expenditures. Operating capacities have declined and have forced hospitals to generate more income from occupied beds than before. Second, the intensity of service increases, with most of the intensity occurring in the first forty-eight hours of hospitalization. While UR as a regulatory tool may be having a salutary effect on maintaining quality, it is primarily rearranging resources used in the hospital setting and not reducing their total amount.

The Regulatory Package

Many people believe that these instruments of regulation — CON, prospective rate setting, and UR programs — must be taken as a package. Each one taken separately has deficiencies as a regulatory tool, and as noted, many may produce results contrary to those intended. Taken as a package, the three instruments could balance the inefficiencies produced by each when operating alone.

Our own review, however, goes further. We believe the regulatory package must include some demand side parameters. In addition, it must more directly acknowledge the key role of the physician as the gatekeeper to the hospital and other components of the health delivery and services system. One alternative may be a market control theory of regulation, in which large buyers of health services (e.g., insurance companies, the states, the federal government) amass all of their buying power and negotiate directly with providers. Amassing the buying strength of Medicare alone would produce substantial market leverage over physicians and the hospitals in which they practice.

In a final analysis, regulation is not a real substitute for the interplay of market forces in which the price system allocates resources. The present system, as discussed, has imperfections and is producing distortions in allocative efficiency and distributive equity. Coupled with a market control theory of regulation—the base outlines of which were suggested above—the present system could produce some real results in containing total expenditures. It should be emphasized, however, that this would be a less desirable alternative than market forces alone. There are real limits to leaving the health industry unregulated; there are also limits to overregulating it and failing to perceive that in certain limited yet important ways incentives and disincentives (i.e., normal market behavior variables) can be used effectively.

HEALTH INSURANCE AND DEMAND SIDE REGULATION

Any review of the demand side of the health care question must begin with the mechanisms—in addition to consumer needs and expectations—that foster that demand. The most significant of these at the primary level are government programs (most notably Medicare and Medicaid) and private health insurance (particularly group health insurance). The most crucial secondary demand source is health care providers (specifically physicians), who serve as guardians of passage into the world of high health care expenditures (e.g., hospitalization, surgery, diagnostic tests, and pharmaceuticals).

The relationship between government and private insurance coverage and consumer demand for health care services is well documented. Recognition of this relationship in the development and refinement of various public health insurance programs has caused various quasi-regulatory cost containment features—for example, deductible and co-payment requirements, reasonable and customary standards for physician payments, and numerous screening measures for procedures and courses of treatment—to be included within the benefits and administrative framework of Medicare and Medicaid. Furthermore, it is worth noting that public health insurance programs have borrowed many of their approaches from the experience of private insurers, most notably from Blue Cross/Blue Shield (BC/BS) plans.

Private health insurance is not federally regulated. It is subject to a patchwork quilt of state insurance regulatory commissions, laws, and approaches that range from government approval or setting of

BC/BS plan rates, to strict scrutiny of policy language, to a series of statutorily mandated coverages and treatments, to an environment of almost total laissez-faire concerning rates and policy features. The sheer variety of these approaches makes any generalization about their effectiveness in controlling costs or their relationship to demand impossible.

In recent years, some state insurance commissioners and legislatures have taken measures to emphasize health care cost containment in the review of BC/BS rates and structures and have gone as far as to mandate specific provider programs (e.g., concurrent inpatient review and second opinion requirements). Given the market power of Blue Cross and Blue Shield (often nicknamed "the Blues") and their special relationship with providers, such initiatives would appear to be a well-targeted use of limited regulatory resources. But like many of the regulatory efforts designed to control health care supply, they may be largely an exercise in futility.

The problem with attempts to affect the cost of health care through regulation of third party payers, who in turn discipline suppliers, is that such efforts should logically flow from the marketplace itself. In theory, consumers (e.g., a large corporate employee group) should seek to maximize the amount of health insurance protection they can obtain for their dollars. Cost containment features within particular insurance plans make such plans more competitive than others. This realization should induce insurers to develop more health care cost containment programs (without the assistance of regulatory mandates).

That the marketplace has frequently not performed this way is a reflection of the fact that consumers have many demands that are simply not cost effective (e.g., convenience, first dollar coverage), but to which they nevertheless give a high priority. In addition, it reflects structural impediments and discontinuities in the health insurance market—the relationship between providers and some insurers, the distorting role played by government insurance (and private health insurance), the discounting factor that results in favorable federal tax treatment for health insurance costs. Most importantly, however, it suggests that despite the large number of licensed health insurers, certain kinds of competition—in particular, that provided by HMOs—have not occurred naturally. A significant reason for the lack of competition may have been regulatory structures that precluded or impeded the formation of alternative plans, while at the same time providing legitimacy for near monopolistic or noncompetitive health insurance arrangements (e.g., BC/BS plans).

The HMO is both a new delivery mode and potentially a new and competitive insuring mechanism. The distinguishing characteristics of HMOs (in theory at least) include their provision of economic incentives for doctors to manage their patients' health economically; their emphasis on prevention rather than cure; and their reduction of unnecessary tests, procedures, and hospital stays. Per capita payments utilized in HMO supplier reimbursement may be contrasted to the fee for service reimbursement systems utilized in most service insurance plans. Per capita payments to the provider neither expand nor contract with the costliness of the services rendered. To the extent that costly programs and approaches are repeatedly used, the provider is at risk. Insurance reimbursements on a fee for service basis remove the critical tension on providers to manage patients as if not only their health problems, but also their dollars, were their own. Neither physicians nor patients are punished for the use of the most extravagant treatment alternatives (except to the extent that they share in the larger social cost produced by escalating demand).

An alternative to attempting to contain costs through the control of supplier-induced demand (i.e., either through regulatory measures or HMO type economic incentives) is to go directly to the source of that demand—namely, the consumer or the patient. Third party payer mechanisms, both governmental and insurer, address the problem of controlling consumer demand through features such as co-payments and deductibles or through an indemnity approach to benefits in which fixed payments are made (e.g., $50 a day). The theoretical justification for such benefit gaps or limitations is to encourage more national consumer behavior in the marketplace, since such a mechanism will not shield consumers from the economic consequences of their actions. The real justification, however, at least in the case of private insurers, may be quite different. They may simply offer a product that looks good competitively, not because it contains underlying health care costs, but rather because it has eliminated costly benefits.

The notion of rationality in the health insurance marketplace may not square with either human nature or the structure of that marketplace. Approximately half the senior citizens in America have chosen to supplement Medicare with some form of private health insurance precisely because they do not want to leave gaps (i.e., initial deductible, co-payments) unfilled. These gaps do not serve, therefore, as an effective disincentive for demand—as studies of the impact of Medicare since its inception on health care costs in this country demonstrate.² The availability of a variety of inadequate individual health insurance alternatives (e.g., cancer policies), poorly understood by the consumer, further clouds the clarity with which a high deductible, co-payment approach might otherwise relate to consumer choice behavior. Consumers with two or three health insurance policies may act as if they have first dollar coverage, even if their policies taken together are riddled with gaps that should moderate their behavior.

Finally, the most expensive elements of the health care system are treatments and procedures over which the consumer has little input or choice. It is not the office visit that is costly, it is the surgery that the physician recommends. Regardless of deductible or co-payment features, it is a rare consumer who will reject a doctor's recommendation for serious treatment and a rare doctor who incorporates discussion of the costs of that treatment into a judgment of its merits.

If first dollar insurance coverage were banned and consumers were forced to assume the responsibility of making medical decisions at least partly based on economic costs, it is likely that over time, demand patterns (both for individuals and for insured groups) could change significantly. A major structural constraint would be the nature of the marketplace that the rational economic health consumer would then confront—a marketplace that is in a number of ways closed, because of a different kind of government regulatory initiative, with a different goal from any discussed thus far.

Historically, all the medical professions have developed various forms of licensure and employment regulation. These licensing restrictions prevent, for example, just anyone from practicing medicine. On the one hand, such restrictions on entry are proposed by various professions as a way of insuring the public from quackery. On the other, however, such restrictions insulate the health professions from rational behavior on the part of consumers. How are consumers, for example, to know which physician is least expensive if physicians are not allowed to advertise their prices?

If consumers do not like what one physician says, how can they find an inexpensive diagnostic center from which to get a second opinion? Are inexpensive health care choices, ranging from routine generic drug substitution to the use of paraprofessionals (e.g., physician assistants, nurse practitioners) and the establishment of ambulatory surgery centers, even permissible under the maze of regulatory boards, commissions, and planning agencies that exist in many states to protect the public from chicanery and unprofessional practices?

Where consumer choices are limited, either by government regulatory efforts (one consequence of which is the absence of useful consumer cost information) or by third party programs that reward one kind of behavior over another (e.g., hospitalization instead of outpatient treatment), demand will be distorted.

SUMMARY AND CONCLUSIONS

It is possible to envision a marketplace where demand would, over time, lead to a more efficient distribution of resources. Physicians would be required to post fee schedules. Entry into professional and paraprofessional areas of activity would be eased. Barriers to pharmacists writing some kinds of prescriptions or substituting generic drugs would be removed. Large groups would use their market power to negotiate fixed rates at efficient hospitals and to establish per capita funding mechanisms with providers. Individual insurance would be standardized in benefits and deductibles, so that consumers could shop and compare policies on the basis of price (insurance efficiency), but could obtain no policy in which they would not have to share in the cost of treatment. Government insurance programs for the elderly and the poor would be structured in a comparable fashion, with voucher payments utilized where necessary to satisfy the deductible (and the recipient who does not utilize those payments rewarded with cash at the end of the year).

Would this approach lead to a more inequitable distribution of health care resources than our current system, to more unequal access by groups and regions, to a reduction in the quality of care? It is doubtful. Both the regulatory and the programmatic efforts of government to address these problems over a generation have proven to be as much a part of the problem as of the solution.

Still, it is unrealistic, and perhaps disingenuous, to argue for a marketplace model that can never exist and that implies its own pattern of government constraints (e.g., a restriction on the kinds of insurance that can be written) and interventions. Social cost cannot be measured just in monetary expense. A community's defense of a dying, inefficient hospital may not be rational from an economic perspective; neither is it irrational, depending upon the weight given to other concerns, such as accessibility and the prestige of housing a community hospital. It only becomes irrational at the point where the money being spent to support the inefficient institution is displacing money needed for other life necessities (e.g., food, shelter) or where the quality of care is demonstrably defeating the purpose for which the institution is being kept alive.

The best role for government in this period of conflicting judgments concerning the social cost of inefficient health care is to pierce through the professional mystique that surrounds the nation's health provider institutions and the veil of reimbursement mechanisms that obscures the true individual consumer cost of extravagances such as inefficient hospitals. With adequate public perception, it is hoped that a willingness to draw the line will come, along with a refusal to further expand that proportion of the gross national product going to health care. Such an awareness has already come to many large group buyers. When it is widely shared by individual consumers, alternative products, competitors, and/or regulatory structures will soon follow. If the social cost of the current health care structure has not yet reached that point, it does not have far to go. Thus, when this happens, we hope that the search for alternatives will include all elements of the existing regulatory mix and not be limited to them or by them.

NOTES TO CHAPTER 5

1. David S. Salkever and Thomas B. Bice, "The Impact of Certificate of Need Controls on Hospital Investment," *Milbank Memorial Fund Quarterly/Health and Society* 54: 185–214 (Spring 1976).
2. U.S. Congress, Congressional Budget Office, *Expenditures for Health Care: Federal Programs and Their Effects.* (Washington, D.C.: U.S. Government Printing Office, August 1977).

6 NATIONAL POLICY IN THE PROMOTION OF HEALTH

Lawrence W. Green, Dr. P.H.

The purpose of this chapter is not so much to address what governments can do, but more importantly, to discuss what they cannot do. Recognizing the necessary limitations and the potential of government policy, five paradoxes, four cycles, three causes, and several proposals are described.

Paradox 1: Every decision involves risk, but then, not to decide is also to face risks. It is the nature of policy and in the nature of decisionmaking—indeed, it is definitional—that a decision involves risk. Whichever way one turns, sideways, up or down, there are certain risks and uncertain risks.

Paradox 2: Every decision requires a choice between competing values. Every time people are asked to make a choice, especially in relation to health policy matters, they are asked to choose between values. Each has a degree of attraction, a certain implied benefit or value to them, and it becomes a choice then between competing risks and competing values. One cannot have all things all ways. One cannot have his or her cake and eat it, too. As clearly stated by Victor Fuchs,[1] policymaking decisions require choices; choices will have to be made between competing values as well as risks.

An earlier version of this chapter appeared in the *International Journal of Health Education* 22: 161–168 (1979).

Paradox 3:   Today's solution may be tomorrow's problem. However, the corollary is that today's problem may become tomorrow's solution, as in the case of people who find that consuming a small quantity of alcohol now may be helpful rather than harmful.

Paradox 4:   The proposed solution for some may become a problem for others. As the problems of some are solved, problems for others are created in the process. Understanding this, will lead to greater care to seek representation, advice and consent in the policy-making process.

Paradox 5:   A public solution is only as viable as the public perception that it is doing some good. No matter how important the program may be in objective terms, if the public does not have feedback from the policies for which they have consented, if the public does not understand why they are regulated, coerced, or persuaded to do required things, to participate in certain activities, to cooperate in certain programs, they are not likely to support such policies for long. This is a paradox for public health, health education, health promotion, and prevention, because most of the prevention and health promotion initiatives do not eradicate easily perceived problems. Most of them have to do with anticipated problems, problems that might develop in the future, and hence, to expect people to perceive the benefits readily is to expect of them a degree of foresightedness that can only be attained through education.

To cope with these several paradoxes in policymaking, two things are needed—facts and a process. A process of information dissemination and decisionmaking that allows relative risks, relative benefits, values, and the time frames to be weighed by an educated public is necessary. A process that will allow the public to participate in as decentralized a way as possible in the formulation of policy is required. From where will these facts come, and how will they be related to policy in health education?

THE INFORMATION CYCLE

First, a historical fact applies to health promotion generally.[2] Health education has followed a poverty cycle that started with inadequate support in the past, which led to programs that were diffuse and of questionable quality; these resulted in modest and scattered impact, which in turn resulted in benefits that were either undetectable or nonexistent. Without demonstrated benefits, health education fails to gain any further support, and the cycle therefore becomes continuous. It is a cycle that is only beginning to be broken with new facts provided by research and evaluation.

How do facts intervene to affect this poverty cycle of health education? At the first level, where programs are poorly developed, facts can provide process evaluation; they can help in the development of clearer, more explicit, more definitive goals, purposes, methods, and procedures of health education. Quality assurance, peer review, and clarification of the objectives and methods of health education are the types of facts needed in order to clearly document what is being done at the very least, how it is being done, and what level of health education is being delivered. Quite independent of its effect, at least what is being done, how it is being done, and how proficiently it is

Figure 6-1.   The Information Cycle in Health Programs.

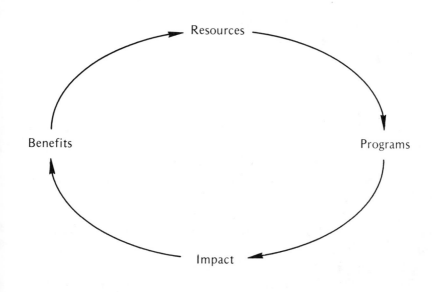

being done as judged by professional standards of quality ought to be documentable.

At a second level, where the immediate effects of programs are unknown, impact evaluation should be used to contribute facts to policy. What effects in terms of changes in knowledge, attitudes, beliefs, and values that motivate health behavior are being realized in the short run? What changes in the organization of health services will enable people to gain greater access to them? What changes in the social climate, support, and reinforcement will enhance behavior change? These are immediate outcomes, including some short-range behavioral changes, that one should be able to document in programs.

The third kind of facts needed to advise policy is information about the outcomes or benefits of health education in the longer run. These include longer lasting behavioral change, the maintenance of changes in lifestyle as well as in the structure of services and the delivery of service in the environment, and also the health outcomes themselves. What improvements can be detected in health, economic, or social problems as a result of health education programs and interventions?

THE DECISION CYCLES

If factual information could be provided at those three levels, policy could be much better advised. But all the facts in the world are not going to advise policy adequately unless there is also a process that allows people to participate in weighing those facts and in assessing the relative benefits, risks, values, and time frames in relation to their perceived problems and the subsequent actions recommended. Thus, there is another cycle—actually, two overlapping cycles—that deal with policy (see Figure 6-2). One is a cycle of professional and organizational behavior, the behavior of providers and deliverers of services. In health education, this cycle includes policy that influences practice, which influences research and evaluation, which influences information and theory. Theory and policy also influence training, which influences practice and evaluation.

On the public side, there is another cycle that overlaps with the professional decision cycle. The public begins with certain social concerns. These concerns lead to demands for improvements in the quality of life. These demands result in certain policy initiatives

Figure 6-2. The Decision Cycles in Health Programs.

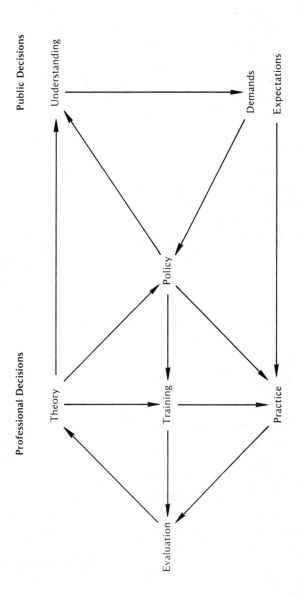

through elected legislators, representatives, and officials. Such policy changes also are influenced by facts—information and theory that comes out of the professional domain—the research, the state of the art, the literature that reports what works, what is possible, and what has been the previous experience with policy in this area.

Policy, in turn, influences practice, the delivery of services, the delivery of health education. Practice is also influenced by the public. Professionals are directly influenced, not just through policy, but by their interaction with the public. The doctor interacting with the patient, the nurse interacting with the patient, the health educator in the community interacting with students or citizens of that community—each influences the way health services are delivered. Practice, in turn, results in the satisfaction of certain needs, which results in a modification of the public's perception of those needs: Expectations will be modified, and policy will be supported or contested. Practice creates a situation in which research and evaluation may be conducted to determine the effects of the implemented methods or techniques. Research and evaluation feed into the knowledge pool, adding facts to theory, which in turn will affect training, policy, and public understanding. If the information can be made known to the public, it can influence the public's understanding of policy issues, which will affect in turn their concerns and demands.

ISSUES IN POLICY FOR HEALTH PROMOTION

As a foundation for an understanding of the paradoxes in policymaking and decisionmaking, the foregoing models identify the actors, issues, and needs involved. If the medical care system is to be turned around in a way that places greater emphasis on prevention and health promotion, then the consumer, the patient, or the citizen must play a larger role in health care both within and outside the system. To what extent can responsibility be placed on individual citizens, not just in relation to changing their lifestyle, but with respect to their participation in policymaking, their participation in self-care, and their participation in affecting the environment? Blaming the victim becomes a risk if the entire responsibility for health is abrogated to the individual.[3]

In attempting to communicate the potential economic benefits of health promotion to the medical community, legislators, administrators, and consumers, it may be interpreted wrongly as a tool of reactionary establishment. Health education may be accused of being primarily a means to save money for the system and the public be damned.

When health education is defined in such a way that a change in behavior is a necessary step between learning and health improvement, its advocates are sometimes accused of having sinister propagandistic intentions. Behavior is the major determinant of health that can be influenced directly by health education. The point that appears to create trouble with this presentation is believing that the only influence on health is behavior and then rather narrowly interpreting behavior to mean lifestyle.

Health education can be defined as any combination of learning experiences designed to facilitate voluntary adaptations of behavior conducive to health. One of the key terms in this definition is "behavior." Voluntary, combination, and designed are the other stumbling blocks in an adequate implementation of health education.

What are the causes of health? The determinants of improved or threatened health fall into three broad categories—environment, behavior, and medical care. Medical care is getting a rather poor reputation as not being a very important determinant of health, even though the public in some countries have been led to believe that it is the primary determinant of health. Increasingly, behavior is being regarded as the major determinant, but attention is also being given to environment—the work environment, the physical environment, the social environment, and the economic environment.

How does behavior relate to the other determinants of health? Where do health promotion and health education fit? Behavior is not only a direct determinant of health, it is also an indirect determinant to the degree that it can influence the environment and the organization and utilization of health care. Behavior should not simply be viewed as lifestyle—those modifications that are expected of people even though they may not be able to afford making them. It also includes behavior directed at the health care system and at the environment—social action, the behavior that people can exercise collectively or individually to influence the health care organization or to guard themselves against environmental risks (see Figure 6-3). Behavior can and should influence health directly as well, through preventive activities, through so-called lifestyle activities, and through self-care in the face of symptoms. Behavior can influence health

Figure 6-3. The Context of Health Promotion.

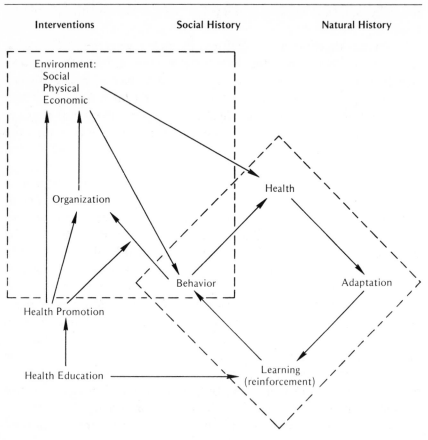

Interventions   Social History   Natural History

through medical care by relating patients more effectively to the medical care system in health examinations, illness behavior, and sick role behavior, as well as in policymaking.[4] An activated, concerned, and knowledgeable public can participate more effectively in the decisions that tend to be made by physicians, nurses, and politicians concerning personal and community health issues as well as national issues such as universal health insurance.

If behavior is able to influence health through all three of the above paths, then a much larger role for behavior than just lifestyle clearly exists. Hence, there is a considerably more significant role for health education than simply affecting lifestyle behavior. Health education will make its major contribution in facilitating voluntary changes in behavior, to be sure, but that behavior should be regarded narrowly as individual lifestyle change. Health education, as part of health promotion, is directed as much at groups, organizations, and communities as at individuals; and it is concerned as much with environmental, economic, and social changes influencing and influenced by behavior as with lifestyle habits and preferences.

GOVERNMENT VERSUS OTHER CHANNELS

What should be the role of government and what should be the role of other agencies in promoting health? When addressing the role of government in health education, it is necessary to inquire about the public's perception of and confidence in government. People do not universally regard the government as the most credible source of communication and advice on health matters. Since the late 1950s, public confidence in the American government as an agency of change or as a servant of the people seems to have eroded. Less than 40 percent of the population may at some point perceive the government as a credible source.

Information can be centralized, but education cannot. Thus, a government can develop knowledge, store it, organize it, retrieve it, and make it available to decisionmakers, but a government by and for the people cannot long make decisions for people or it will soon become a plutocracy or an autocracy. Decisionmaking must be as decentralized as possible.

The Mass Media

If the government cannot do it, perhaps the other broad-based approach to health decisions is through the mass media. Unfortunately, public confidence in the media as a source of information in the United States is only slightly greater than in government. The percentage of people who had hardly any confidence in the people running television increased between 1973 and 1978, and the percentage having a great deal of confidence decreased.

It is the very nature of mass media to produce a message and then to communicate it in such a way that it will appeal to a broad median of the public. The ability to communicate in a tailored, individualized, appropriate way for subgroups in the population is limited with mass media because as soon as the mass media begin to do that, they lose a large segment of their audience. The survival of mass media depends on the ability to communicate broadly to the widest possible audience. Not only do the messages tend to be geared to a magical median that is not appropriate for 40 percent of the population on either end of a normal curve, but the people who regularly attend to the media begin to define their own problems in relation to that average. The result is stereotypes about health and about behavior because they are communicated through the mass media in a way that is applicable to an "average" person. Large masses of the population begin believing they have hypoglycemia or a midlife crisis. Problems get defined in an undifferentiated way, and particular problems of subgroups, of cultural groups, or of geographical regions get glossed over. Worse is the tendency for some mass media to present misinformation, negative role modeling, advertising of junk foods (especially for children), and violence.

Television, or the mass media in general, is not necessarily an inappropriate resource for health education. It is not however, the simplistic, magic bullet answer to all of health education's problems. In fact, the mass media, and television in particular, represent a great untapped resource for health education—not in motivating people as Madison Avenue might suggest (if only it had the money from the health education budget), not in changing people's behavior, but more likely in reinforcing and supporting behavior that is being altered through more decentralized local processes of decisionmaking and change.

The final limitation seen for the mass media is that television in particular, and the other media in general, tend to portray health matters in the context of high drama about high medical technology, heart transplants, bypass valves, and other advanced technological and heroic interventions that only apply to a small proportion of the total population. To this extent, they give the public a false belief that technology will save them no matter how they abuse themselves in the meantime, no matter what else may be going on in the environment. People are thereby lulled into a false sense of security about their responsibility to themselves or to their environment in trying to effect change.

Whose Values and for Whom?

There are other problems with centralized decisionmaking and communication in health. One has to do with values—whose values for whom? If the government, especially a centralized one, makes decisions on health matters (e.g., behavior in relation to health), to what extent can that government reflect the wide range of values of the subgroups in the population? For example, in focusing on risk taking, many values come into play. What is risky behavior, and who is to decide if an individual's behavior is too risky? At one extreme there is suicidal behavior, that which is so dangerous in relation to the benefits that might be derived from it that anyone who engages in it is risking almost certain self-destruction. At the other extreme, however, there is a neglected range of behavior that is pathologically safe. Such behavior is so affected by fear of risk, regardless of potential benefits, that people will not leave their homes, will not take any chances, will take no risks in life. The quality of life for such individuals probably suffers as much as for those who take suicidal risks.

Between the two extremes (i.e., the suicidal and pathologically safe) is a wide range of behavior, some of which is dangerous and some of which is ultrasafe. Even between these two moderate extremes is a "normal" safe range of available behaviors that yields modest benefit relative to the minor risks that people have to take. People must take some risks in order to gain some benefits.

Helping People to Understand
Risk-Benefit Ratios

What benefits do people want in life? Health promotion is an area in which values become extremely prominent and in which it is very dangerous for a national (or other highly centralized) government to attempt to make decisions for its citizens. This is where health education has its most significant and important role to play—helping people to understand risk-benefit ratios, helping young children to think in problematic terms, helping people to sort through the competing risks and competing values that they must assess in making decisions in their daily lives.

To the extent that centralized governments can provide assistance in developing the knowledge base to permit people the opportunity to make such choices, they have a major role in health education. But to the extent that these decisions are made by that government, prefabricated for the individual, the government has overstepped its useful and even safe role in health education.

People will take a different amount of risk relative to the benefit depending on whether the behavior that is at issue is voluntary or involuntary, whether the risk is controllable or not controllable, whether it is new or familiar, whether it is known or unknown, whether it is delayed or immediate. In relation to each of these contrasts that help to determine the degree of risk people are willing to assume, there is a differential that works in many ways to the disadvantage of what one is attempting to accomplish through health education. To the extent that the benefits of health education are more distant than immediate and that the risks are less controllable and less familiar, the task becomes more arduous.

The Carrot or the Stick?

One other issue that government must grapple with in health is the question of incentives versus regulation. Should the government, where it does have to play a role in behavior, do so with the carrot or the stick? The contrast between the policies of Indira Gandhi and her successor, Prime Minister Desai, in the family-planning program of India illustrates the dilemma. Gandhi had put emphasis on the stick because of the urgency of the population problem. Her successor, to relieve political pressure, has placed more emphasis on the carrot and less on the stick, with similar results in birth control.

The emphasis on the latter appears to be the approach assumed by the U.S. Congress on health issues. The stick is only used when the behavior in question influences the health of many rather than that of the individual. To the extent that behavior is only a risk to the individual, the carrot should be maximized rather than the stick. However, when the behavior threatens the health of society, use of the stick must be maximized (i.e., regulation as opposed to incentives).

It becomes less and less a matter of health education once the decision to regulate has been made. The decision to regulate, however, must involve health education because people must participate in deciding whether to regulate, whom to regulate, and by what means to regulate. If there is too little participation of people in such a decision, the regulation will be coercive and without adequate public representation.

CONCLUSIONS

The foregoing analysis implies a set of definitions for health, health education, health promotion, and health behavior. These words are included in the 1976 federal legislation (PL 94-317) that mandates the Office of Health Information, Health Promotion and Physical Fitness and Sports Medicine. Since some of the words are included in the title of the office, it is necessary to acknowledge the distinctions intended by the use of these terms.[5] Health is the ability of a system (e.g., a cell, an organ, an individual, a family, or a community) to adapt its equilibrium in response to change. Health behavior, then, is personal adaptation to anticipated challenges or risks to health. Health education, as defined earlier, is any combination of learning experiences designed to facilitate voluntary adaptations of behavior conducive to health. This, then, leads to the definition of health promotion as any combination of health education and related organizational, economic and environmental supports for behavior conducive to health.

The above definitions are consistent with the activities and efforts that a government can deploy in the name of health education and health promotion. It will be the task of health professionals to assure that their governments are held accountable for these activities while preserving the integrity of individuals to assess their own values, risks, time frames, and options.

NOTES TO CHAPTER 6

1. Victor R. Fuchs, *Who Shall Live: Health, Economics, and Social Choice* (New York: Basic Books, Inc., 1974).
2. Lawrence W. Green, Marshall W. Kreuter, K.B. Partridge, and Sigrid G. Deeds, *Health Education Planning: A Diagnostic Approach* (Palo Alto, CA: Mayfield Publishing Co., 1979).

3. Lawrence W. Green, "Health Promotion Policy and the Placement of Responsibility for Personal Health Care," *Family and Community Health: The Journal of Health Promotion and Maintenance* 2: 51–64 (November 1979).

4. Lawrence W. Green and Connie C. Kansler, *The Professional and Scientific Literature on Patient Education: A Guide to Information Sources* (Detroit: Gale Research Company, 1980).

5. Lawrence W. Green, "Healthy People: The Surgeon General's Report and the Prospects," in Walter J. McNerney, *Working for a Healthier America* (Cambridge, MA: Ballinger Publishing Company, 1980).

▮▮ BEING A PATIENT
Rights in Question

What is it like being a patient in America's health care system? Do beneficence (i.e., doing good) and nonmaleficence (i.e., not doing harm) truly guide the actions of health care professionals? Or does the sick role force patients to forfeit certain individual rights and thereby lose autonomy?

Should the rights of individuals who become patients be put in question? In this regard, do patients want to know about their conditions, their recommended treatment plans, and their prognoses regarding recovery or would they prefer physicians to withhold all or part of this information from them or even to lie? Should minors and the aged be forced to forego certain rights? Since these groups commonly are viewed as nonproductive members of society—that is, they are often dependents and not in the work force—some argue that they are not entitled to the same right to self-determination as those who are actively contributing to society (e.g., through payment of taxes, social security).

With most medical care being paid for by third party payers, have Americans relinquished their right to privacy and confidentiality to insurance companies or the government? Should these rights be voluntarily surrendered for reasons of gaining employment, attending college, obtaining credit, seeking justice and security? What price should individuals have to pay to maintain their self-respect and dignity?

149

In the first part, the chapters share a common orientation to the overall health care system that may be labeled a macro-orientation. In this second part, the common theme transcending the chapters is the individual patient. The reader commonly is asked to weigh the value of individual rights against what is best for society. A common element found in these five chapters is a strong sense of patient rights evolving from ethical principles of autonomy and respect for persons that may come into conflict with a utilitarian perspective focusing on the common good for society. In addition, it is not atypical to see a clash of ethical values between those advocating beneficence and those advocating autonomy. Such conflicts typically arise between physicians and patients in many cases. Using the paradigms discussed in Chapter 1 may assist in the clarification of values and their assigned priorities.

While being a patient in itself precipitates certain questions of rights and responsibilities and hence a set of issues common to all, special populations demand more sensitive considerations due to their special vulnerabilities. In entering a physician–patient relationship, to what degree are (or should) patients be appraised and sensitized to the dynamic state of this encounter, its benefits, and its risks? To what degree do patients maintain their unique identities, values, and rights, and ought they assume certain responsibilities as well? What rights and responsibilities fall upon the attending physician and other members of the health care team?

In Chapter 7, Hiller and Beyda examine the critical issue of privacy as society embarks on a love affair with the computer. Although distinct advantages in medical treatment, research, and management may be attributed to advances in computerization, the authors identify major risks and document cases of violations in personal autonomy. The chapter concludes by examining the legal and ethical issues related to privacy and confidentiality and recommending both institutional and public policies to remedy weaknesses in existing systems.

In Chapter 8, Ronald Green examines the debatable topic of truth telling—a topic closely related to the principle of patient autonomy and the role of the beneficent physician. He asks the poignant question, Should physicians or other responsible members of the medical team tell dying patients the truth about their conditions? He carefully investigates the ethical implications of decisions to fully inform patients of their health status on the basis of their having a right to know. In addition, he explores the reasons prompting untruthfulness.

Meisel (Chapter 9) provides readers with a comprehensive review of the legal and broader ethical justifications for informed consent. He pays close attention to the troublesome area of judging the competency of persons, as is required for informed consent. In his thorough analysis of a topic that clearly represents an area of merger among the disciplines of law, ethics, and medicine, Meisel cuts across many traditional disciplinary barriers. He depicts those conditions and factors that impinge upon and require careful ethical evaluations in the process of obtaining informed consent. For readers concerned about this complicated subject, the author accomplishes the difficult task of clarifying the issues, the conflicting opinions, and the debate on a topic of significant relevance in the 1980s.

The final two chapters in this part explore issues associated with the traditional, albeit wrong in the authors' opinions, limitations of rights of two large segments of our population. Hiller (Chapter 10) discusses selected rights that commonly are sacrificed in the delivery of health care in college health programs around the nation. Among these are rights of privacy and confidentiality—of patients and medical records, the right to informed consent, the right to treatment—even as a minor, and the right to respect. Hiller argues that a failure to reassure these rights to college students and minors in general precipitates poor consumer behavior and attitudes about the health care system later in life. Furthermore, he reports that due to their stage of late adolescence and the unique environment of the college campus, students have particular needs. Hence, he suggests that college health programs should direct additional special attention to the physical, mental, and emotional problems of students.

In Chapter 11, Kleppick finds that long-term care institutions and their administrators often fail to protect their residents. Suggesting that the aged may have special needs and even be somewhat more vulnerable does not provide justification for the failure to respect and protect them. Kleppick argues that health professionals responsible for caring for the nation's elderly need to become more sensitive and humane to those entrusted to them. However, this should not result in either a failure to maintain beneficence or a violation of aged persons' autonomy.

7 COMPUTERS, MEDICAL RECORDS, AND THE RIGHT TO PRIVACY

Marc D. Hiller, Dr. P. H.
Vivian Beyda, M. P. H.

INTRODUCTION

With the growth of our information-oriented society, coupled with increasing demands for financing and quality assurance, the collection, analysis, and storage of data related to medical care have grown more complex. Over the past fifty years, medical record keeping has evolved to keep pace with the changes and growth of the health care system, and many of the significant advances have resulted from the adaptation of modern computer technology to the health industry.

Recent advances in computer technology permit the accumulation, analysis, and storage of an unlimited quantity of medical records and medical record information (or data),[a] thereby seriously compounding existing controversies surrounding patient confidentiality and privacy.[1] With the vast technology at hand, it is not surprising that the benefits of its use are being expanded from more

The authors wish to thank Lee F. Seidel, Ph.D., chairperson, Health Administration and Planning Program, School of Health Studies, University of New Hampshire, for his constructive inputs into an earlier version of this chapter.

a. In this chapter, a "medical record" is defined as a record, file, document, or other written material relating to an individual's medical history, diagnosis, condition, treatment, or evaluation that is created or maintained by a health care provider; "medical record information" or "medical record data" constitute information obtained from a medical record or from an individual patient or from his or her spouse or legal guardian for the purpose of making a nonmedical decision about him or her.

153

simple data systems to more complex management information system models.

COMPUTERS AND MEDICAL RECORDS

Patient care management systems (PCMS) as discussed in this chapter constitute the combination and expansion of computerized medical record systems (such as PROMIS, based on the problem-oriented record developed by Lawrence Weed) and basic management information systems (such as those developed and widely used in business and industry). Their continuing evolution and refinement mark the linkage between the delivery of clinical patient care services and the management and financing of organizations providing such services. This junction is growing because of the need to render detailed bills for patient services, which has stimulated the development of fully integrated PCMS that can capture, store, and report every significant episode of treatment provided to a specific patient and its associated cost. Whereas ethical standards involving the release and use of patient care information traditionally constitute one of the linchpins of the medical records profession, computerization of medical records and the integration of medical and financial data have effectively diluted this traditional safeguard.[b]

Hospitals and health centers across the United States are systematically progressing toward the computerized medical record–most commonly commencing with business office information and then moving toward index classifications and medical abstracts. A survey of 5,912 hospitals conducted by the American Hospital Association (AHA) in 1975 reveals that 1,441 had in-house computers, and the number undoubtedly has increased in the past five years with the advent of minicomputers and the growing experimentation with information systems.[2] Thus, it is apparent that PCMS have become almost inevitable in hospitals.

b. Members of the medical records professions have strong ethical codes, such as those of the American Medical Record Association, adherence to which assures confidentiality and privacy. With the advent of computerized record systems, many nonhealth professionals have been employed to provide technical computer and management skills. Many of these individuals are neither aware, sensitive, nor as concerned about maintaining complete patient privacy. Hence, they represent a potential threat that was nonexistent prior to the adoption of computerized systems.

For health care administrators, therefore, dependence on PCMS will continue to grow in importance, with increased efforts to gain efficiency, control, and cost effectiveness in management and decisionmaking. In the decade of the 1980s, advances in health services management probably will overshadow the clinical applications of such systems; the application of computer technology to health care management will be primary amidst an era of cost containment, fiscal restraint and responsibility, and government intervention through financing and regulation. For many of the same reasons that automation is attractive to other sectors of society, computerization and the development of management information systems has gained, and continues to gain, popularity and use in the health care industry. This expansion in use is due to increasing demands and expectations for medical care services, heavy increases in the volume of paperwork, the need for rapid transmission of data, increases in annual hospital admissions and ambulatory care services, and increased mandatory reporting to government. When used properly, the computer, through its ability to handle large amounts of data quickly and accurately, can disseminate information to the appropriate people at the proper time and thus benefit the patient individually and society collectively.

From an institutional care perspective, few large hospitals or medical centers can successfully operate in the 1980s without complex and intricate computer data systems. Some institutions already have expanded their systems to maintain patient charts with daily entries made directly into the computer by physicians, nurses, laboratory personnel, and other patient care departments. For physicians, increasing reliance on computers in routine diagnoses and clinical decisionmaking is on the horizon.

Additional positive outgrowths of using computers in medical treatment and research include the development of new therapies, more prompt diagnosis and treatment of illness, the matching of appropriate organ transplant donors and recipients, the determination of drug interactions and protocols, the study of genetic diseases, and the discovery of life-saving technologies, to cite only a few. Somewhat removed from the actual use of computerized patient care data in the administration and delivery of medical care is the increased demand for and subsequent use of such data in utilization and standards reviews; epidemiological studies; program evaluations; and biomedical, behavioral, and health services research. Thus, the societal trend toward dependence on computers for the collection, maintenance, storage, management, and analysis of patient care data appears to present significant opportunities and positive advances in the health care industry.

However, the computer also poses major threats to privacy and increases depersonalization and dehumanization in the practice of medicine, the management of health facilities, and the conduct of research. This expanded use of computers—albeit initially solely for medical record purposes and subsequently for institutional management—has introduced new and complex social and ethical dilemmas into hospital-based care.

Universal concern[3] is expressed about what data are being tabulated and used, the extent of their accuracy, the necessity to control their dissemination, and the extent to which patients may have access and opportunity to verify and correct their personal records. Although the issues of privacy and confidentiality did not arise with the invention of computers,[4] increased interest has developed with the proliferation of data handled by them due to their increasing technological capabilities.[5]

According to a recent position paper on "The Confidentiality of Medical Information" issued by the American Medical Record Association (AMRA):

> Economic and social issues, together with technological advances, have resulted in an erosion of the confidential relationship traditionally existing between the patient and health care professional. Substantiation of claims for payment has generated an ever increasing number of requests for information from the patient's health care record. At the same time, the tremendous growth of computerized health data, the development of huge data banks and the advancements in record linkage, pose an enormous threat to the privacy of medical information. The public is generally unaware of this threat or of the serious consequences of a loss of confidentiality in the health care system. Adequate measures to control medical privacy, in light of the electronic information processing, can and must be established.[6]

Furthermore, current trends toward still greater reliance on computers in health data and record systems generate increasing attention to issues of confidentiality and privacy for which sound governing institutional policies have not yet been established.[7]

Hospitals and nursing homes are being subjected to increased demands for patient records more than ever before. Hence, it is difficult to maintain the confidentiality of medical records without strong institutional policies to which health professionals and all other technical personnel must adhere. Furthermore, necessary access to records for management and insurance purposes is increasingly being given to nonhealth professionals such as computer analysts, as well as to many hospital business office personnel. These individuals, unlike physicians, nurses, and medical record librarians, often are neither sensitive to patient concerns over confidentiality and privacy or bound by strong professional codes of ethics regarding the use of such information. To alleviate this problem, a representative of the AHA strongly recommends that hospitals conduct frequent in-service education and indoctrination programs in medical ethics (and specifically, in confidentiality) for employees who are not directly involved in patient care.[8]

Although the Constitution, federal and state statutes, and judicial interpretations all serve as limited vehicles to assure the protection of patient privacy, significant internal efforts must still emerge from within hospitals and other health care institutions to ensure adequate safeguards. In essence, these institutions should view the promulgation of standards to ensure adequate protections as institutional responsibilities rather than simply patient rights that require legal enforcement. Policies must be designed to balance personal privacy and confidentiality while not offsetting the need to make necessary information quickly and easily available to physicians who legitimately require it and to other users who may have legitimate claims to it.

Westin reports that the flow of medical record information between hospitals and third parties is already heavily automated and likely to become more so. He concludes that the creation of large automated information systems, such as PCMS, poses new problems and opportunities from a privacy protection perspective. The problems center around the need to specify the rules under which hospital personnel shall have access to all or part of an automated medical record and the necessary levels of security for records that contain sensitive, personal information (e.g., psychiatric records, abortion records, venereal disease treatment records). The opportunities arise from the fact that an automated record can be adopted to a need to know policy more easily than a traditional, manual record.[9]

Clearly, a one sentence confidentiality oath, such as the Oath of Hippocrates, can no longer be the sole source on which to rely. Physicians, hospitals, and others need more guidance, and patients must be given additional protection.[10] For as the Privacy Protection Study Commission reports:

> The real danger is the gradual erosion of individual liberties through the automation, integration, and interconnection of many small, separate record-keeping systems, each of which alone may seem innocuous, even benevolent, and wholly justifiable. Dramatic developments in computer and communications technology, which both facilitate record-keeping functions previously performed manually and provide the impetus and means to devise new ones, can only exacerbate this problem.[11]

Never before has a society possessed such a wealth of health and medical knowledge, equipment, and technology for conquering disease and preventing human suffering. Never before has the right to privacy of health care confronted such peril. Thus, due to the changing conception of the medical record and its increasing computerization, there is a critical need to establish—and where necessary to enforce—public and institutional policies that ensure privacy protection safeguards for medical records. In turn, such protections contribute to the integrity and efficacy of the physician–patient (or the hospital–patient) relationship.

To a certain degree, the computer introduces change into the traditional relationship between physicians and patients. The increasing participation of subspecialists in the care of an individual requires that more people have access to medical records. Although automation is not responsible for medical specialization and it does not qualitatively affect relationships between patients and health providers, the gathering of scattered medical data into a single file does create potential new problems. The efficiency of an automated system makes violations easier. Furthermore, the comprehensiveness of the files leads to more damaging results when violations do occur.

However, it is not the intent of this chapter to advocate the abandonment of computer-assisted advances in the health care field, for as previously discussed, they provide a critically important set of functions:

• Medical surveillance systems allow for the protection of the public's health—physical and mental.

• The computerization of medical records fosters improvements in assuring quality of care, continuity of care, and accessibility and availability of care.

- The development of PCMS provides for necessary documentation and collection of fees and for the successful planning, operation, and management of health care institutions.

- Computerized data systems allow for conducting significant, highly beneficial research—biomedical, epidemiological, health services, and evaluation.

However, none of the positive values associated with the legitimate infringements of personal privacy to accomplish the above benefits are warranted or acceptable if administered without stringent guarantees and the best of motives and ideals. Failing to assure such protections of privacy destroys those protective barriers that insulate individuals from larger institutions. To this end, Rule and his colleagues call for "[p]rocedural guarantees [that] could ensure such things as confidentiality, access rights, and due process in the use of data . . . scrupulous efforts would have to be made to minimize intrusiveness."[12] Furthermore, they warn that the social and political implications of the incremental growth of computer data banks, such as those maintained by the Social Security Administration, should not go unnoticed or unchallenged. Such arrangements "would destroy the sense of aloneness and autonomy which most people count as essential ingredients to life."[13]

PRIVACY RIGHTS AND HEALTH CARE

The analysis of privacy rights in health care, specifically with respect to medical records, raises three major, interrelated issues, including (1) sources of a right to privacy, (2) the accessibility and disclosure of medical records, and (3) the assurance of adequate safeguards. A major intent of this chapter is to review these issues and to suggest several public and institutional policies that could better protect the privacy and confidentiality of patients in general, with a focus on physicians and hospitals. The ensuing discussion is limited to problems encountered in a clinical, therapeutic environment and does not expound on the additional set of problems encountered in the use of records for strictly research purposes.

Sources of a Right to Privacy

From an ethical perspective, it is relatively clear that based on the principle of respect for persons, individuals have a right to have the confidentiality of their medical records preserved.[14] Furthermore, according to Kant, this respect for persons, which reflects a freedom of will, is significant in assuring one's autonomy.[15] Justice Cordozo cites an analogous principle in his 1914 ruling in *Schloendorff* v. *New York Hospital*: "Every human being of adult years and a sound mind has a right to determine what shall be done with his body."[16] Insofar as information generated regarding one's mind and body may be viewed as an extension of one's body, the concept of autonomy dictates that one has a choice to control the uses of that information.

Other practitioners cite the longstanding Hippocratic Oath, the Principles of Medical Ethics of the American Medical Association (AMA), or their right to privileged communication as being more than sufficient to guard their protection of patient privacy and confidentiality. Physicians commonly maintain that they must protect the information provided them in the intimacy of their offices or their patients' hospital rooms. This premise of confidentiality permits patients to speak freely and to openly discuss their symptoms without fear of disclosures about their problems that might cause personal or public embarrassment or prosecution.

However, violations do occur. What is said to physicians during the course of an examination and follow-up care is noted in the medical record and often makes its way to credit companies, employers, or insurance brokerages without the knowledge of the patient. The improper collection and use of medical information may have lasting consequences on the individual. Evidence from recent privacy debates in the U.S. Congress clearly documents several such breaches of confidentiality.[17]

While physicians on the one hand strongly defend their maintenance of patient confidentiality, they also are obligated to weigh the welfare of the community or their legal or societal obligation to reveal or report certain conditions to the appropriate authority. Such a responsibility is circumscribed in the AMA's Principles of Medical Ethics, Section 9:

A physician may not reveal the confidences entrusted to him in the course of medical attendance, or the deficiencies he may observe in the character of patients unless he is required to do so by law or unless it becomes necessary in order to protect the welfare of the individual or the community.[18]

Erroneously, many believe that the doctor–patient privilege categorically ensures the privacy of medical records. However, privilege is a legal concept; it is a statutory provision enacted by individual states and is not recognized under common law. More than forty states have laws designed to protect, to varying degrees, the confidentiality of communications between physicians (including psychiatrists) and patients—the doctor–patient privilege.[19] But such laws only protect physicians from having to testify in court about medical treatment and the content of all communications related thereto without the consent of the patient. These statutes generally are not applicable to most situations in which doctors are allowed or bound by laws, regulations, or longstanding codes of professional practice to release information from patients' medical records to third parties. Hence, privilege applies only to judicial proceedings; it is a legal rule of evidence.[20] Furthermore, since privilege is binding only in courts of law and in relation to the medical treatment that is the subject of litigation, it should not be perceived as a general prohibition against the release of patient information by a physician.[21] For example, if the mental health status of a patient is not the subject of the proceedings, treatment for prior mental health conditions may be revealed.

Despite the existence of state statutes specifying some degree of privilege,[22] physicians are still forced to testify about patients or to reveal their records in many situations. For example, according to Hayden and Novik:

> In a criminal case, medical testimony may be introduced by the prosecution or the defense. In a civil case—such as a negligence or malpractice suit, a divorce or custody suit, or a commitment proceeding—the medical history and condition of the principles may be the primary questions at issue. In any of these situations, a patient's physician may be required by the court to describe his medical history and even produce his records.[23]

Privilege statutes are limited further since they apply only in cases governed by state law. Furthermore, the Federal Rules of Evidence, which govern practice in federal courts, are considerably less protective of patient privacy, since they assure only psychotherapist (as opposed to all physicians)–patient privilege. Under these Rules, physician–patient communications are revealed at the discretion of the court.[24]

In addition, several other situations limiting privilege continue to exist, including (1) public reporting laws; (2) areas involving patient consent to release medical information, which are often vague; (3) situations involving disclosures in the best interests of the patient; (4) situations in which there are supervening interests of society; (5) situations involving the public's right to know; (6) situations arising during the judicial process in which common law principles apply due to the absence of state statutes.[25] Thus, confidentiality of the physician–patient relationship enjoys no sweeping protection unless by specific state statute;[26] in states where such a law does not exist, privileged communication can be recognized only on a case-by-case basis. As previously noted, no privilege is recognized in federal law.[27]

Beyond the individual state statutory protections of physician–patient privilege, only some states have privacy laws that include private record keepers such as insurance companies and hospitals. Generally, it appears as if states are avoiding blanket protection and are awaiting federal action. The Privacy Protection Study Commission reports:

> Nineteen states have regulations, statutes, or case law recognizing medical records as confidential and limits access to them. In 21 states, a physician's license may be revoked for willful betrayal of professional secrets. These statutes do not generally apply to medical care providers other than physicians, and although the codes of ethics of most allied health professions reaffirm the principle of confidentiality, the codes can impose only a moral, not legal, obligation.[28]

Thus, in summarizing their discussion of physician–patient privilege and state law, Hayden and Novik note that although these words

> are often used rhetorically to describe the principle of confidentiality that is popularly attributed to the relationship between doctor and patient, the privilege is in reality a narrowly drawn rule of evidence, not even recognized in the common law (as is, for example, the attorney–client privilege), but available only where it is specifically provided by statute.[29]

Since the right of privacy is so cherished, some advocate that it is protected in the U.S. Constitution by provisions of the Bill of Rights, most notably by the First, Third, Fourth, Fifth, and Ninth Amendments, as well as by the Fourteenth.[30] A survey of the literature on privacy reveals multiple interpretations and uncertainties.[31] The common element to all is the absence of a firm constitutional statement upon which to pin the privacy concept. The Constitution neither mentions the word privacy nor discusses the privacy concept.

Privacy is considered a reserved right, implicit in a constitutional government that is limited to the exercise of only those powers expressly conferred upon it. The federal Constitution expresses an interest in privacy, but not a constitutional mandate to protect it in all situations. It competes with other sometimes conflicting constitutional interests and social values such as free speech, freedom of the press, and the public's right to know. However, many aspects of personal privacy have been protected against governmental interference in court decisions through judicial interpretations of the special provisions of the Bill of Rights.

Between 1965 and 1973, several landmark and far-reaching decisions of the U.S. Supreme Court confirm that states may not interfere with intimate personal decisions that fall within zones of privacy emanating from several constitutional amendments. These significant opinions give substance to privacy arguments, although they revolve chiefly around debates over contraceptive use and abortion.[32]

Federal statutes are somewhat broader and specifically address the use and misuse of medical information. The Freedom of Information Act (FOIA) of 1967 mandates disclosures of data maintained in governmental files, but specifically exempts medical records from such disclosure.[33] Seven years later, the FOIA was followed by the Privacy Act of 1974.[34]

Enactment of the Privacy Act codified, for the first time in American history, principles to protect privacy in the collection and handling of recorded personal information by federal agencies.[35] It marked the culmination of many years of public and congressional hearings and investigations of threats to personal privacy by the acquisition of vast quantities of computerized personal data by the federal government. Because the Act applies to all federal agencies, it includes medical facilities, health insurance, and payment records (e.g., Medicare) maintained by the federal government. These agencies must grant patients access to their records, since no exception is cited in the regulations for medical records.[36] The Act provides guidelines for the collection, maintenance, and use of personal data, including medical records (computerized and manual). Although designed to guard against abuse in the dissemination of private data, the Act is limited due to its numerous exceptions.

A major shortcoming of the Privacy Act is that it does not apply to state or local governments or to private agencies.[37] Furthermore, it applies only to systems of records from which information is retrieved by the name of the individual or by some other identifier.[38] Access is not granted if information is filed under an organizational name or as aggregate information without the use of a form of personal identifier. Weaknesses aside, the Privacy Act of 1974 is a landmark. It acknowledged the hazards of uncontrolled collection, storage, retrieval, and exchange of personal information as well as the wrongfulness of not granting individuals access to inspect their own records.

However, both the right to know the contents of one's medical record and the right to control who else may gain access to it are within the state's discretion. According to the law in the fifty states, the medical record is the property of the hospital, not the patient. However, this property right has been qualified somewhat over recent years, largely through judicial interpretation and by some state statutes, such as those in Massachusetts and Connecticut.[39] Hospitals and other institutional providers retain the right of ownership to the physical record (the paper, tape, fiche, or film on which the record is recorded), but patients have the right to the information contained therein. Furthermore, while a hospital may assert property rights to patient medical records, in general it has no legal authority to release those records to other parties.[40] There are no general statutory provisions that pertain to medical records maintained in private medical or health facilities other than licensed hospitals or clinics, such as visiting nurse services, drug addiction treatment centers, alcoholism centers, or associations for the blind. In such institutions, professional and ethical codes establish the rules and regulations.[41] In the absence of individual state statutes assuring patient access, the only absolute means by which patients may gain access to their medical records is to file a law suit against the health facility or physician to obtain the record by court order.[42] As noted, regulations and statutes regarding medical access vary from state to state. They also vary within reference to their requirements for contents and maintenance.

Accessibility and Disclosure of Medical Records

In the early 1900s, 85 percent of medical care services were delivered by physicians, most practicing without partners. Today, less than 5 percent of health care providers are physicians.[43] In the hospital, only one-third of the hospital record is contributed by attending physicians.[44] Much is recorded by other members of the health care team who participate in the comprehensive care of the patient. In addition, the Bureau of Health Manpower of the U.S. Department of Health, Education, and Welfare (now the Department of Health and Human Services) estimated that 53,000 individuals were employed in the management and administration of medical records in 1974.[45] Hospital records are routinely available to hospital employees on request; although most of these individuals are health professionals who need such access to fulfill their jobs, not all of them do.[46]

Applicable legal provisions and ethical codes of the AMA, AMRA, and AHA restrict disclosure of medical records. Disclosures have been consistently deemed justifiable only if made either in the best interests of the patient or to foster a supervening societal interest.

Within the nature of the health care relationship, most of the health care professions argue that their discretion in making disclosures is not a significant source of abuse.[47] It is the role of the physician and the hospital to assure that a patient's legitimate expectation of confidentiality is not breached as a consequence of negligence on the part of health care professionals themselves.

Although protection of the confidentiality of medical records is properly the responsibility of the health care provider and patient authorization is usually obtained prior to disclosure, evidence suggests that this safeguard is weak.[48] Indeed, dramatic and troubling breaches of medical record security have become public in the past few years.

The theft and release of Daniel Ellsberg's psychiatric record, the publicizing of Senator Thomas Eagleton's prior medical history, and the recent exposure of the Factual Service Bureau (a firm that specialized and was highly successful in obtaining medical record information through subterfuge)[49] mark three examples of blatant neglect for the confidentiality of medical records.[50] Such findings led the Privacy Protection Study Commission to conclude: "That a firm like Factual Service Bureau (now known as Innerfacts) could be successful, at least until it came under the scrutiny of the Denver grand jury, appears to have been due in no small measure to the laxity of hospital security measures."[51]

Evidence gained from the Factual Service Bureau case demonstrated that similar problems exist elsewhere throughout the country.[52] Since patients cannot control access to or use of their records within the institution, the institution must assume the responsibility. Thus, each hospital must take affirmative action to assure that the medical records that it maintains are available only to authorized recipients. Furthermore, any disclosures to users should be made only on a need to know basis.[53]

According to the Joint Commission on the Accreditation of Hospitals (JCAH):

> Every individual who enters a hospital or other health care facility for care retains certain rights to privacy, which should be protected by the hospital without respect to the patient's economic status or the source of payment for that care. Thus, representatives of agencies not connected with the hospital, who are not directly or indirectly involved in the patient's care, should not be permitted access to the patient for the purpose of interviewing, interrogating, or observing him in any way detrimental to his condition or obstructive to the care being provided . . .[54]
>
> Another important aspect of the patient's right to privacy relates to the preservation, within the law, of the confidentiality of his disclosures. . . .[55]

Although the above excerpts reflect an acknowledgment by the hospital industry of the need to ensure the privacy of patients, including their medical records, it fails to mandate such an institutional policy or to provide a mechanism for its enforcement by translating this objective into a standard measured during JCAH accreditations. However, while not including privacy as a standard, JCAH has established the following standard relating to medical record services: "*STANDARD III*—medical records shall be confidential, secure, current, authenticated, legible, and complete."[56] Hence, the intent of protecting the confidentiality of medical records is stated. However, the degree to which individual institutions go to assure and uphold confidentiality varies. Furthermore, JCAH interpretation of this standard allows for wide latitude in determining who may have access to patient care data or to whom they may be disclosed.

Written consent of the patient or his legally qualified representative is required for release of medical information to persons not otherwise authorized to receive this information. This shall not be construed to require written consent for use of the medical record for automated data processing of designated information; for use in patient care evaluation studies, such as retrospective audit and medical staff monitoring functions; for departmental review of work performance; for official surveys for hospital compliance with accreditation, regulatory, and licensing standards; or for educational purposes and research programs.[57]

To allow use of medical records for any of the cited functions without placing strict controls on the users and the potential uses of the information risks infringements on the rights of patients. As stated earlier, this is particularly true in light of nonhealth professionals currently engaged in administrative roles in hospitals today. In addition, there is a plethora of third parties (e.g., employers, prospective insurers, and educational institutions) who attempt to gain access to confidential records through questionable or illegitimate means. Having weak standards or policies that are difficult or impossible to enforce only contributes to the success of such efforts. Furthermore, no standards or interpretation are offered by JCAH regarding the management or security of computerized record systems.

Despite the violations of confidentiality precipitated by weaknesses in authorization procedures, the majority of patients on whom hospitals and physicians maintain records risk the loss of their confidentiality due to general, nonspecific release forms. These forms, which many patients are routinely requested to sign to authorize disclosure of their records, are worded so broadly that they more or less sign away all of their rights to control the release of information contained therein. Existing evidence suggests that better, more effective safeguards are needed to protect the confidentiality of records maintained by their primary users from disclosure to third parties.

The three most common types of disclosure over which patients have little or no control include (1) disclosure to private and government insurers; (2) disclosures for health evaluation, planning, and research; and (3) disclosure for purposes totally unrelated to medical care or evaluation of research. Although some disagreement exists among privacy advocates, most agree that there are legitimate uses of data generated from PCMS. Table 7–1 summarizes major current users of medical records and the principal purposes for which the

Table 7-1. Users of Medical Records.

Categories of Users	Examples of Users	Examples of Uses of Information from Medical Records
Primary users	Health care providers, including institutional (hospitals) and individuals (physicians)	Purposes related to treatment; training of health professionals; evaluating quality of care; complying with licensure and accreditation standards; conforming to government regulations; research directed at improvement of diagnosis and treatment; promoting effective and efficient use of health resources
Secondary users	Payers for service, including private insurance companies (Blue Cross/Blue Shield, the commercials) and government insurance (Medicare and Medicaid)	Substantiating patient claims for payment; claim audits for service and fees; monitoring quality and equality of care rendered to insurees; assessing and controlling costs
Tertiary users	Health service evaluators; health planners; public health agencies; medical and social research agencies; occupational health and safety agencies	Health planning; allocating scarce health resources; epidemiological surveillance; occupational health and safety efforts
Other users[a]	Employers, educational institutions; law enforcement agencies; credit bureaus; media; judicial system	For determining employment suitability; for determining admission to colleges and universities; for criminal and civil investigations; for determining credit eligibility; for creating sensational headlines; for assessing legal matters

a. In most, if not all, cases of these disclosures (except those resulting from court orders in judicial proceedings), such uses are either unethical, illegal, or both.

data are used. Least disagreement revolves around records used for diagnosis and treatment of trauma and disease and quality assurance by primary users.

However, controlling access to medical data and defining the limits of such authorized access mark the two major means of preventing abuse of computerized medical records. Patients, physicians, and other primary users should be fully aware of those individuals and organizations (i.e., secondary and tertiary users) that will have access to confidential medical records. With respect to computerized records this is even more critical, since large amounts of data can be transferred with relative ease from one computer to another. Policies and procedures should be developed to ensure patient and physician approval prior to the release of any information from a medical record to secondary and tertiary users. Due to the complexity of the health care environment, these latter groups of users are becoming more prevalent. As a result, patients should be notified in advance of any release of information or of any agency or individual having access to it.[58]

Such disclosure is common to secondary users directly engaged in the financing of care and is generally acceptable. Regardless, however, patients need to be duly informed and to voluntarily consent to the release of their medical records to specific financing agencies prior to the initiation of treatment whenever possible. Such a policy represents an acknowledgment by both parties of the trade-off of patient autonomy for third party reimbursement of valid claims.

Where problems may arise is in subsequent use of confidential information by nonprimary users. In other words, what happens to an individual's medical records after their receipt and verification by the financing agency? Once confidential records are disclosed to other parties, effective control over subsequent use of the data is minimal. Hence, such parties should be sensitized to the confidentiality of the information and prudently limit its use. Furthermore, all legitimate recipients of information (e.g., PSROs, peer review bodies, HSAs, and third party insurance carriers) should be advised that authorized release of data to them does not constitute their right to further release the data to other parties.[59]

Disclosure of confidential information for purposes unrelated to patient care and financing, quality assurance, and health-planning activities should be restricted. If desired for valid research purposes, the research design and compliance with institutional review board review and stipulations should be considered carefully before release of data. Since data seekers will have different needs for access, it is important that the level of access and other appropriate limitations be specified and enforced. Furthermore, data, when released, should be in aggregate form without traceable identifiers unless valid claims for identifiable data are agreeable to the institution and to the patients involved. Most uses of information from medical records for nonhealth purposes (i.e., other uses and users shown in Table 7-1) represent clear violations of privacy and confidentiality unless voluntary informed consent (without any form of coercion) of patients (or former patients) is obtained in advance.

Assurance of Safeguards

Custodians of health care records and managers of health care data systems must take measures to ensure the protection of personal information not only against deliberate or accidental destruction of data but also against unauthorized access or modification of data. The sensitivity of health and medical information requires the establishment of policies and procedures that will limit access to those institutional personnel who possess a legitimate need to see the information. Furthermore, it requires a monitoring system to detect unauthorized use and to impose sanctions against intruders. Procedures should be flexible enough not only to safeguard records from unauthorized disclosure but also to permit their release on the written request of the patient.

Threats to data privacy and confidentiality range from accidental release of information to intentional penetration of a health record data bank system. All elements of the system—managers, custodians, users, technicians, and recording personnel—pose threats to the security of the system. Intrusions may also come from outside the system; such intrusions could come from an individual or institution that deliberately attempts to gain unauthorized access to data bank records. Regardless of the level of safeguards, no system, be it manual or computerized, is 100 percent secure.

Health care institutions have been negligent in establishing controls governing who has access and for what purposes. The problem is not limited to controlled access. When access is permitted for a specific purpose, in response to a legitimate request, often the entire record is transmitted because such transmittal is less costly than extracting only the necessary information.[60] In an automated system, this could be corrected with a small investment in software packages—albeit one that probably will not be made until the ethical implications of current practices are exposed.

Threats to security of data can be blocked by a variety of procedures and techniques. However, even the best designed system cannot prevent authorized users from browsing or maliciously using accumulated information. The first safeguard, simple and easy to implement, is controlling input into the system. Data acquisition should be use related. The release of more than the specifically needed data may contribute to an undesired release of very personal, highly sensitive information. Although such data may be entirely accurate, it may be socially undesirable to disclose, such as treatment for a venereal disease or a mental disability.

A second safeguard, the prevention of unauthorized access to a data system, should be the primary objective of access management techniques. Such techniques include authorization, identification, codes, passwords, and authentication. This reduces threats from external sources and from those having no legitimate need of access. Unfortunately, such efforts do not prevent the illegitimate use of data by personnel who have legitimate access to the system.[61]

Hence, safeguarding a health care data system involves two areas of protection—the protection of the system itself and the protection of the confidentiality and privacy of the records contained therein. The risk to personal data increases as data are centralized, as the number of users of the information grows, and as greater volumes of data are shared. Personal privacy should always be a paramount concern.[62] In the spirit of informed consent, it is possible to provide the patient with choices concerning the release of personal information. Society as a whole benefits from the responsible management of data systems that store personal, sensitive information.

POLICY CONSIDERATIONS: PUBLIC AND INSTITUTIONAL

Privacy issues must be addressed through prudent, ethical public policies that reflect a balance between the need for information flow and the right of privacy. These policies should be formulated through consensus of all parties concerned and should govern both manual and computerized systems. Privacy issues cannot be resolved on technical grounds alone. The shaping of public policy is a shared responsibility. The formulation and implementation of public policy regarding this issue requires the input of legislators, governmental agencies, data users, computer manufacturers, and private citizens. Furthermore, when necessary, ethicists should be consulted to help clarify issues and values.

The privacy issue has become a matter of concern because of the ever-increasing demands for services and information. Personal histories are no longer purely personal. Although most data-gathering activities are intended to achieve socially desirable goals, electronic tracks are left for computer personnel to store, retrieve, analyze, exchange, and transmit—almost at will.

Within the broad spectrum of records maintained on individuals, the medical record is special. Its unique characteristics require careful consideration in the formulation of policies that deal with the right of privacy. The medical record is subjected to greater and stronger demands for the release of information. However, many questions arising over the release of information are not covered by the law, court decisions, or regulations. Hospital or medical care institutional policies serve as guidelines for making information disclosure decisions. Fundamental to the establishment of any privacy policy is the question as to whether individuals will be regarded as special entities with unique needs or whether they are mere objects of society to be dealt with as such by data-keeping institutions to satisfy institutional needs. In other words, health institutions confronted with the choice of releasing patient care information or losing fiscal reimbursement must recognize that the choice has more than simply a fiscal dimension. Breaches of privacy can be avoided by restricting the flow of medical information to health care providers. If this is not the case, policy directives may be written with little regard for confidentiality as an inviolate element of health care practice.

Another consideration is the long-term societal need, which appears to be in conflict with the short-term desire among patients for confidentiality. Vital health and medical information, properly managed in a data system, can enhance efforts to improve general patient care and contribute to medical and health services research. As an information-based society, we need a public policy on information processing that will ensure the proper circulation of data. However, there must be a clear delineation of policies and practices governing the acquisition, analysis, storage, exchange, and transmission of this data.

A public policy for health data information should balance individual and societal needs and interests, identify the special priorities, and determine the degree to which computer technology will be utilized within the system. Although industry cannot be faulted for embracing new technologies, these must be more responsive to privacy issues. Since it is a human problem, the potential for privacy invasion is continually present regardless of the advances in computer technology. Computers are products of their makers and subject to human instruction and control. In the absence of public policy, there is little to prevent private organizations or government agencies from collecting more information than they need or from exchanging vast quantities of personal data.

No single approach will provide solutions to the social problems inherent in information data systems. However, those who handle personal data do have an obligation to guard the privacy of patient records and to ensure their accuracy and completeness. For public policy to safeguard personal privacy and to create a standard of fair health information practices, it is essential that certain issues are addressed. Privacy experts agree that certain recurring objectives for such policies should exist and they may be grouped as follows.

1. Patient Needs and Interests

- An enforceable qualified right for patients to review and copy records;

- An opportunity for patients to have erroneous entries in their records corrected and/or amended;

- Limitations on access to records and files;

- Regulations forbidding the collection and recording of unverifiable information;

- A duty of confidentiality in the health professional–patient relationship;

- Notice to patients of record-keeping organization receiving a subpoena;

- Public procedures specified whereby patients can challenge the contents of their records.

2. Agency Needs and Interests

- A defined retention period and provisions for expunging obsolete data;

- Authorization to provide relevant abstracts and/or summaries to organizations having a legitimate claim to information rather than releasing entire medical records;

- Enforcement of rules for data-sharing practices;

- Established standards for identifiers and indexing systems;

- Clarification of record ownership;

- Policies and procedures to ensure data and system security;

- Clear assignment of responsibilities for administration and security to specific individuals;

- Designation of one person directly responsible for the system;

- Provision to all employees of detailed information about the system and the legal consequences of breaches of confidentiality or leakage of information.

3. Societal Needs and Interests

- Notice to data subjects of the identity of the persons or organizations to whom information is transmitted and the conditions under which such a transfer is conducted;

- An enforceable code of conduct for data collectors and keepers;

- A policy of informed consent governing secondary and tertiary use of records, accompanied by a dated, witnessed, signed authorization for the release of a record;

- Implementation of a complete and accurate system of access, entries, uses, corrections, deletions, and other modification of the record;

- Public notice describing the system;

- Established procedures for reporting data in which the identities of patients are not divulged to funding sources.

Good judgment and self-regulation of the information-gathering and using agencies are obligations. The privacy of the persons to whom benefits and services are rendered must be protected. Intrusions on personal privacy occur every time an individual is required to furnish more information than needed, when these data are subsequently reused for unrelated secondary purposes, and when such uses violate promises of confidentiality. While computers provide many advantages, they should not further dehumanize the practice of medicine. Rather, they should be used as tools for improving patient management.[63]

From a public policy perspective, an ethical framework should be constructed that will permit the exploitation of the advances in computer technology and the manipulation of information for individual and societal benefit while assuring that no one is treated unfairly or harmed by a record system.[64] For the question is not whether computer technology will be used in the coming decade of medical practice, but rather, how and how much. Basic privacy rights cannot be allowed to become a casualty of technology. To allow this to occur is to abrogate social responsibility.

Not all of the identified issues are, however, exclusively in the realm of public policy per se. Many are best resolved, at least on an ad hoc basis, by individual health care institutions that have developed mechanisms to evaluate considerations involving patient, agency, and societal needs and interests. The need for such an approach increases as automated medical record systems merge with the financial and business systems (i.e., management information systems) of health care institutions and as third party payers increasingly claim a need for more and greater detail involving financial transactions.

Although many potentially appropriate approaches exist to assist an individual health care institution to adjudicate competing needs and interests involving patient care information, it is essential that the development of any PCMS be governed by a broad-based committee of health professionals, including financial experts. Furthermore, this committee, charged with the responsibility of developing institutional policy concerning information release, should also hold a watchdog responsibility once the system is operational. To do less discounts many issues previously cited in favor of administrative convenience. The inclusion of such a requirement in appropriate accreditation standards by JCAH is worthy of further consideration and action.

SUMMARY AND CONCLUSIONS

In providing privacy safeguards without infringing upon the legitimate interests of data keepers, it is necessary to develop policies that define situations under which medical information is disclosed to other parties; that provide procedures by which patients may gain access to their records; that determine ownership of records; that ensure anonymity in aggregating data for research or statistical purposes; and that carefully balance society's long-term goals and the legitimate need of organizations to have access to medical records with patients' short-term desire for and right to privacy. Balance is what is needed—making available to society the benefits of medical science and research while at the same time making certain that privacy and confidentiality are protected. To achieve this balance, computerization of health data must protect the rights of patients to limit information flow about themselves (privacy) and respect the duty of physicians to restrict the information flow (confidentiality). Even when individuals disclose personal information in order to receive health services, they maintain a continuing interest in this information beyond its original disclosure.

Patients should be able to exercise some control over their records, particularly since these records are so commonly available to third parties. Patient authorization, in the spirit of informed consent, coupled with personal access to their records, offer some protection against misuse and abuse. Such access allows patients to ensure that the information contained in their records is accurate, complete, and relevant to their care. Accuracy is important because records are used for many purposes. A statute of limitations for the retention of medical records is of increasing importance because medical information is reused over long periods of time. There should also be a procedure by which records in their entirety or in part can be expunged.

Privacy is a multidimensional problem. While generally in consonance with other rights, it has introduced stress between society and technology. There is a responsibility to share ideas and facts contained in record-keeping systems in an effort to advance education, research, and knowledge. There is an individual right to be let alone, to be autonomous, and to have a personal right to self-determination. There is a collective right to ensure the accountability of the government's operation.

There are obligations, legal and social, that require the disclosure of medical data. These disclosures are pertinent to solving medical and public health problems, preventing occupational hazards, conducting medical research, and evaluating health programs. As health care systems are reshaped to respond to governmental mandates and societal demands for services, they will make increased use of computer and information technologies.

Privacy issues have arisen because concern for individual dignity has been markedly sensitized by the civil rights and consumer movements. Social movements have demanded research on community and social problems, including those generally viewed as private matters. In addition, increased government funding for social research has increased the scope of programs and has heightened tension between vital public purpose and individual privacy. Increased public awareness of obtrusive uses of computer and information collection technologies has led to a demand for accountability.

The conversion from manual systems to computers has generally led to a tendency to collect more information; to share and exchange information; and for more people to have access to records. All of these have heightened the many difficulties in safeguarding the system, since there are more points of access. There must be more sophisticated surveillance than that which existed before the proliferation of computers and the accompanying technology.

The very nature of health information requires an environment that preferentially encourages the development of desirable systems. Laws pertaining to the issue of privacy are only in their infancy. This situation presents opportunities for health care institutions to contribute to the creation of their own codes of ethics and the formulation of rules and regulations to protect privacy.

Restrictions must be placed on the contents and release of personal information. If future laws restrict the use, amount, and type of data to be extracted from individuals, there will be constraints on the delivery of services. Nonetheless, such restrictions will create an environment that enables individuals to exercise their constitutional rights without worrying about "big brother."

Although the Privacy Act of 1974 appears to be serving as a catalyst for the passage of additional federal and state legislation, both federal and state legislatures should find it incumbent upon themselves to confront the issues of privacy and confidentiality. They must resolve the problems presented by a technology—increasingly refined—that can be used to do ill as well as good. Furthermore, any voluntary accrediting body (e.g., JCAH) should be encouraged to further develop and implement standards necessary to ensure patient privacy amid expanding computerized record systems. In the meantime, dependence on judicial interpretations of constitutional protections, existing ethical codes, and institutional policies appears to be the best, albeit temporary and less than ideal, alternative.

NOTES TO CHAPTER 7

1. Daniel K. Harris and George J. Polli, *Computers and Medicine: Special Report* (Chicago: American Medical Association, 1979), p. 2.
2. Marcia Opp, "The Confidentiality Dilemma," *Modern Health Care*, May 1975, p. 52.
3. *Data Security—Threats and Deficiencies in Computer Operations*, A Report on a Completed Study, translated from IBM Svenska Publication No. G320-5646 (White Plains, NY: IBM, 1975); G.B.F. Niblett, *Digital Information and the Privacy Problem* (Paris: Organization for Economic Cooperation and Development, 1971); K. Younger, *Report of the Committee on Privacy* (London: Her Majesty's Stationery Office, 1972); Commission on Human Rights, *Human Rights and Technological Developments: Uses of Electronics Which May Affect the Rights of the Person and the Limits Which Should Be Placed on Such Uses in a Democratic Society* (Geneva: United Nations, Publication No. E/CN, 4/142 English, January 1974); A. Pentages and G.R. Pipe, "A New Headache for International DP," *Datamation* 23: 115-126 (June 1977); "Confidentiality, Records, and Computers," *British Medical Journal* (March 10, 1979), pp. 698-699; Alan F. Westin: *Computers, Health Records, and Citizen Rights*, National Bureau of Standards Monograph No. 157 (Washington, D.C.: U.S. Government Printing Office, 1976).
4. S.D. Warren and L.D. Brandeis, "The Right to Privacy," *Harvard Law Review* 5: 193-219 (December 1980).
5. R.M. Davis, *Government Looks At: Privacy and Security in Computer Systems* (Washington, D.C.: Computer and Business Equipment Manufacturers Association, 1973); William J. Curran, Barbara Sterns, and Honora Kaplan, "Privacy, Confidentiality, and Other Legal Considerations in the Establishment of a Centralized Health Data System," *New England Journal of Medicine* 281: 243 (July 1969).
6. American Medical Record Association, "Position Paper on the Confidentiality of Medical Information," *Medical Record News*, December 1974.
7. U.S. Congress, House, Committee on Government Operations, *Right to Privacy Proposals of the Privacy Protection Commission, Hearings*, 95th Cong., 2d sess. (Washington, D.C.: U.S. Government Printing Office, 1978); Marc D. Hiller and Maureen J. McHugh, "Patient Rights: An Advo-

cate's Perspective," *Journal of the American College Health Association* 27: 124–129, 138 (December 1978).

8. Opp, p. 51.
9. Westin.
10. Richardson Preyer, "Federal Privacy of Medical Information Act," *Congressional Record*, (November 16, 1979), p. H 10964.
11. Privacy Protection Study Commission, *Personal Privacy in an Information Society: The Report of the Privacy Protection Study Commission* (Washington, D.C.: U.S. Government Printing Office, July 1977), p. 533.
12. James Rule, Douglas McAdam, Linda Stearns, and David Uglow, *The Politics of Privacy* (New York: The New American Library, Inc., April 1980), p. 150.
13. Ibid., p. 151.
14. Karen Lebacqz and Robert J. Levine, "Respect for Persons and Informed Consent to Participate in Research," *Clinical Research* 25: 101–107 (1977).
15. I. Kant, "Fundamental Principles of Metaphysics of Morals," in T.M. Greene, *Selections* (New York: Charles Scribner's Sons, 1929), p. 234.
16. Schloendorff v. Society of New York Hospital, 211 N.Y. Rep. 125, 129–130, 105 N.E. 92, 93 (N.Y. 1914).
17. U.S. Congress, Senate, Committees on Government Operations and the Judiciary, *Privacy: The Collection, Use, and Computerization of Personal Data, Part I, Hearings*, 93rd Cong., 2d sess. (Washington, D.C.: U.S. Government Printing Office, 1974); U.S. Congress, House, Committee on Government Operations, *Privacy of Medical Records, Hearings*, 96th Cong., 1st sess. (Washington, D.C.: U.S. Government Printing Office, 1980), pp. 1129–1140.
18. American Medical Association, *Principles of Medical Ethics* (Chicago, 1957).
19. Privacy Protection Study Commission, p. 284.
20. Ibid., pp. 283–284; Westin, p. 21.
21. Jonathan Brant, Gail Garlinger, and Rene Tankenoff Brant, "So You Want to See Our Files on You," in Gerald P. Koocher, *Children's Rights and the Mental Health Professions* (New York: John Wiley and Sons, 1976), p. 214.
22. Privacy Protection Study Commission, p. 284.
23. Trudy Hayden and Jack D. Novik, *Your Rights to Privacy* (New York: Avon Books, 1980), p. 70.
24. Ibid.
25. Westin, pp. 21–27.
26. William J. Curran, "Protection of Privacy and Confidentiality," *Science* 182: 797 (1973).
27. Ann Laurence O'Sullivan, "Privileged Communication," *American Journal of Nursing* 80: 947–950 (May 1980).

28. Privacy Protection Study Commission, p. 284.

29. Hayden and Novik, p. 71.

30. Richard B. Parker, "A Definition of Privacy," *Rutgers Law Review* 27: 275–296 (Winter 1974).

31. Ruth Gavison, "Privacy and the Limits of Law," *The Yale Law Journal* 89: 421–471 (January 1980).

32. Griswold v. Connecticut, 381 U.S. 479 (1965); Eisenstadt v. Baird, 405 U.S. 438 (1972); Roe v. Wade, 410, U.S. 113 (1973); Doe v. Bolton, 410 U.S. 179 (1973); Kenneth R. Wing, *The Law and the Public's Health* (St. Louis: The C.V. Mosby Company, 1976), pp. 55–69.

33. 5 U.S.C. 552 (1967).

34. PL 93–579, 5 U.S.C. 552a (1974).

35. *Weekly Compilation of Presidential Documents*, vol. II, pt. 1 (Washington, D.C.: U.S. Government Printing Office, 1975), p. 7.

36. Privacy Protection Study Commission, p. 296.

37. U.S. Congress, Senate, Committee on Government Operations, *A Citizen's Guide on How to Use the Freedom of Information Act and the Privacy Act in Requesting Government Documents*, 95th Cong., 1st sess. (Washington, D.C.: U.S. Government Printing Office, 1977), p. 5.

38. James Beverage, "The Privacy Act of 1974: An Overview," *Duke Law Journal* 1976: 303 (May 1976).

39. Jon Meyer, "Patients' Rights of Access to Medical Records—Summary of the Law," typewritten opinion submitted to Marc D. Hiller (Concord, NH: New Hampshire Civil Liberties Union, April 1980); Patrick R. Carroll, "Re: Patient's Bill of Rights," *MHA Bulletin Number 15* (Boston: Massachusetts Hospital Association, June 1979).

40. William H. Getman, "Access to Medical and Psychiatric Records: Proposed Legislation," *Albany Law Review* 40: 580–617 (May 1976).

41. Barbara L. Kaiser, "Patients' Right of Access to Their Own Medical Records: The Need for a New Law," *Buffalo Law Review* 24: 317–330 (Winter 1975).

42. Alan F. Westin, "Medical Records: Should Patients Have Access," *Hastings Center Report* 7: 23–28 (December 1977).

43. Alfred M. Freedman, "Protection of Sensitive Medical Data," in Michael A. Jenkin, *Patient-Centered Health Systems.* (Minneapolis: Society for Computer Medicine, 1975), p. 3.

44. Privacy Protection Study Commission, *Medical Records, Hearings,* June 10, 1976 (Washington, D.C.: U.S. Government Printing Office, 1976), p. 84.

45. U.S. Department of Health, Education, and Welfare, *The Supply of Health Manpower* (Washington, D.C.: U.S. Government Printing Office, 1974), p. 144.

46. Privacy Protection Study Commission, *Personal Privacy in an Information Society*, p. 304.

47.   Ibid., p. 305.

48.   Ibid., p. 285.

49.   Privacy Protection Study Commission, *Medical Records*, p. 474.

50.   The limited length of this discussion precludes a further documentation of violations. However, for a comprehensive sampling of abuses, readers are referred to (1) U.S. Congress, Senate, Committees on Government Operations and the Judiciary, *Privacy: The Collection, Use and Computerization of Personal Data, Joint Hearings*, 93rd Cong., 2nd sess. (Washington, D.C.: U.S. Government Printing Office, 1974; (2) Maurice Grossman, *Confidentiality and Third Parties* (Washington, D.C.: American Psychiatric Association, 1975), pp. 53–59; and (3) the National Commission on Confidentiality of Health Records, 606 National Press Building, Washington, D.C. 20045.

51.   Privacy Protection Study Commission, *Personal Privacy in an Information Society*, p. 285.

52.   Privacy Protection Study Commission, *Medical Records.*

53.   Privacy Protection Study Commission, *Personal Privacy in an Information Society*, p. 304.

54.   Joint Commission on Accreditation of Hospitals, *Accreditation Manual for Hospitals* (Chicago, 1976), p. 23.

55.   Ibid., p. 24.

56.   Ibid., p. 98.

57.   Ibid.

58.   Harris and Polli, p. 5.

59.   Ibid.

60.   Carol Levine, "Sharing Secrets: Health Records and Health Hazards," *Hastings Center Report* 7: 13–15 (December 1977).

61.   Eric Springer, *Automated Medical Records and the Law* (Pittsburgh: The Health Law Center, Aspen Systems Corporation, 1971), p. 75.

62.   Carmault Jackson, "Guardians of Medical Data," *Prisms* 2: 43 (June 1974).

63.   G.A. Ryan and K.E. Monroe, *Computer Assisted Medical Practice: The AMA's Role* (Chicago: American Medical Association Center for Health Services Research and Development, 1971), p. 9.

64.   Willis Ware, *Public Policy Aspects of an Information Age* (Santa Monica, CA: The Rand Corporation, 1977), p. 9.

8 TRUTH TELLING IN MEDICAL CARE

Ronald M. Green, Ph.D.

INTRODUCTION

Iván Illich's chief suffering was from a lie. This lie, for some reason accepted by all, was this, that he was only sick and not dying, and that he needed but to be calm and be cured, and then all would go well. He knew full well, no matter what they might do, nothing would come of it but still more agonizing suffering and death. And he was tormented by this lie and by this, that they would not confess what all; and he, too, knew but insisted on lying about him in this terrible situation, and wanted and compelled him to take part in this lie. The lie, the lie, this lie which was perpetrated on him on the day previous to his death and which was to reduce this terrible solemn act of his death to the level of all their visits, curtains, sturgeon at dinner, was dreadfully painful for Iván Illich. And strange to say, often while they were perpetrating their jests on him, he was within a hair's breadth of shouting out to them, "Stop lying! You know, and I, too, know that I am dying,—so stop at least your lying." But he had never the courage to do it. . . . This lie all around him and in himself more than anything else poisoned the last days of Iván Illich's life.[1]

Should physicians or other responsible members of a medical team tell dying patients the truth about their conditions? As Tolstoy's moving treatment of the death of Iván Illich makes clear, this question is not new. Nevertheless, for many it is the paradigmatic question of truth telling in medical practice. It is also a question raised for each new generation of health care professionals whenever the

183

well-being of a patient appears to be jeopardized by a true knowledge of his or her condition.

Until recently, the view that the seriously ill or dying patient should not be told the truth and, where necessary, should even be actively deceived, has predominated in the medical community. Not all physicians agree with Joseph Collins' opinion that the doctor should cultivate lying "as a fine art"[2] or with Oliver Wendell Holmes' view that the face of a physician, like that of a diplomat, should be inpenetrable.[3] At least until recently, a large majority of physicians appeared to believe that truth is a commodity to be dispensed very sparingly to sick or dying patients, especially those suffering from dread diseases like cancer. In 1953, a study by Fitts and Radvin indicated that nearly 70 percent of Philadelphia physicians chose never (or usually never) to tell patients that they had cancer,[4] and similar percentages are reported in other studies.[5]

REASONS FOR NOT TELLING THE TRUTH

Several major reasons are usually advanced by physicians for their reluctance to tell the truth. Where cancer is involved, for example, there is understandable concern for the severe emotional distress patients may suffer on learning that they have a potentially fatal disease. Knowledge of cancer is "a death sentence," "a Buchenwald," "a torture," in the words of various physicians, while others term communicating such information "the cruelest thing in the world," "like hitting the patient with a baseball bat."[6] An apocryphal story illustrates this medical viewpoint: In the course of grand rounds, a medical school professor allegedly asked the students whether any of them would tell cancer patients the truth. When one replied in the affirmative, the professor grew angry, berated the student for being insensitive, and then abruptly expelled him from medical school and from a medical career. Frightened and in tears, the student was about to leave when the professor called him back and said, "Now you know what it is like to be told you have cancer."[7]

Apart from the painful emotional impact of learning about a serious illness, physicians commonly point to the damaging consequences such information can have for patients as a further reason for withholding the truth. Following disclosure of serious illness, sometimes suicide is alluded to, and if patients do not go this far, they may still experience a loss of hope or severe depression that makes further treatment or care difficult.[8] To many physicians trained in a tradition in which the Hippocratic maxim *Do no harm* is the supreme ethical imperative—and in which truth telling has no correspondingly hallowed place[9]—the mere possibility of such consequences seems an adequate reason for silence or deception.

Nevertheless, while these concerns certainly motivate many well-intentioned physicians to withhold the truth from their patients, they appear to lack a solid empirical foundation. A variety of different studies show that seriously ill or dying patients are apparently able to learn the truth of their condition without suffering major harm. For example, Litin reports that ten years of suicide reports from Rochester, Minnesota,[a] reveal only one such case in which there was a temporal relationship to the patient being told he had cancer.[10] Other studies suggest that although terminal cancer patients usually suffer intense anxiety and depression on learning the true nature of their illness, these symptoms dissipate in a short time in most cases.[11] Hence, as one writer states, the truth may not be entirely "innocuous,"[12] but it is far less damaging than would be suggested by the opinions and past practices of many physicians.

DEEPER MOTIVATIONS FOR UNTRUTHFULNESS

The most important reasons commonly advanced for withholding the truth do not meet the test of experience. Indeed, one study indicates that for many physicians these reasons are not drawn from experience in the first place.[13] This suggests that the reluctance to tell the truth may be based less on direct concern for patients than on the fears and anxieties of physicians associated with this difficult medical situation. Certainly, no one likes to be the bearer of bad news, and there is understandably a constant temptation for physicians (or any member of the health care team) to cloak the bitter truth in a fabric of euphemisms or deception. On a slightly deeper level, terminal illness and dying patients symbolize physicians' helplessness and the limits of their personal skills. As one writer said, "To a doctor committed to life . . . a patient's death—no matter how inevitable—is a

---

a. The diagnosis of cancer has been made thousands of times at the Mayo Clinic, located in Rochester, Minnesota.

form of failure."[14] Among the medical specialists dealing with cancer, those (e.g., dermatologists) able to provide effective treatment report a much higher willingness to reveal the truth. This lends support to the claim that medical truth telling is related to the physician's own sense of competence more than to a patient's immediate reaction.[15]

Some speculate that the typical character structure of physicians may help explain their unwillingness to deal frankly with dying patients. One study reports that physicians display unusually high anxiety when confronted with the subject of death.[16] Becoming a physician, therefore, may be related to an effort to overcome a deep personal problem. Another writer suggests that "part of the psychological motivation of the physician is to cure himself and live forever. . . ."[17] If this is true, it would help explain why repeated studies show that physicians tend to avoid dying patients[18] and why physicians may be less than candid in communicating with such patients.

Finally, the reluctance to tell the truth may be linked to the social role and status traditionally enjoyed by the medical profession in our society. The fact that physicians alone know what is wrong with the patient and are able to dispense information in a limited and paternalistic fashion tends to reinforce the power both of individual physicians and the profession as a whole. As McIntosh observes: "The doctor's authority is in part based upon the esoteric nature of his knowledge. Therefore, because increased knowledge and perceptions of his work may lay it open to evaluation and criticism . . . doctors may, in general, have a predisposition to restrict information available to patients."[19] Some support for this observation is found in a study that shows that physicians working in the cancer wards of a Veterans Administration hospital, where many of the patients are poor and possess no alternative to the care they are receiving, tend to tell the truth to patients far more often than do physicians in other hospital settings. Glaser and Strauss comment: "Since the captive lower class patients cannot effectively threaten the hospital or the doctors, the rule at this hospital is to disclose terminality regardless of the patients' reaction."[20]

Taken together, these considerations suggest that the case against telling dying or seriously ill patients the truth is not as strong as some have claimed. Not only is much of the explicit evidence against truth telling merely speculative and unsupported, but the real motivation for withholding the truth may often derive from an array of psychological and sociological factors that are irrelevant to determing the rightness or wrongness of the act itself. In view of this, the reasons for full disclosure and honesty assume importance and deserve close attention.

REASONS FOR TELLING THE TRUTH

Foremost among the arguments for full disclosure is the claim that, quite apart from the subsequent benefits or harms of learning the truth, patients have a right to know what is wrong with them. Not sharing the truth with patients is to treat them as children, thus depriving them of their freedom to choose whichever course of therapy they wish to take and to reduce their status as moral persons. As Isaiah Berlin observes in the context of a discussion of freedom: "to lie to men, or to deceive them, that is, to use them as means for my, not their own independently conceived ends, even if it is for their benefit, is, in effect, to treat them as subhuman. . . . "[21]

In this connection, it is interesting to note that recent changes in conceptions of the physician-patient relationship and of patients' rights within it may be partly responsible for an increasing willingness of physicians to tell the truth. Whereas an earlier paternalistic conception of this relationship, with physicians having full control over treatments, appears to have supported a policy of untruthfulness, a developing understanding of this relationship as a partnership (in which decisionmaking is shared and patients have responsibility for their own health) appears to be associated with a greater willingness of physicians to tell the truth. One recent study suggests a more positive attitude toward truth telling among younger doctors, those most likely to be influenced by newer attitudes toward the therapeutic relationship.[22]

Closely related to this broad kind of moral assertion of the patient's autonomy and right to know the truth are several pragmatic reasons favoring full disclosure. Patients denied knowledge of their respective conditions can no longer make informed choices concerning their treatment or care and may even withdraw cooperation from beneficial treatment procedures. In addition, terminal patients may have important personal or financial matters that require attention, and ignorance may lead them to neglect these responsibilities.[23]

Obvious considerations such as these help to explain the findings of numerous studies that patients and prospective patients strongly affirm the desire to know the truth about their condition, Kelly and Friesen revealed that eighty-nine of one hundred cancer patients interviewed preferred to know they had cancer, whereas eighty-two of one hundred noncancer patients expressed the same preference for learning the truth.[24] Branch found that 88 percent of a group of noncancer patients said they would want to know the truth if they had cancer,[25] and Samp and Curreri reported that 80 percent of a mixed group of patients and nonpatients favored truth telling.[26] However, as one writer observes, these studies probably should be treated with caution. Cancer patients who were told the truth might have reasons of pride and self-respect for supporting this policy, while the views of those who have not yet suffered a serious illness may be unreliable.[27] At least one study of cancer patients who were not openly informed as to their condition suggests that such patients may not want to know more. However, the meaning of this conclusion is obscured by the fact that many of these patients were already independently aware of their conditions.[28] With these qualifications in mind, however, the fact that patients and prospective patients consistently report a desire to know the truth in itself constitutes at least one additional valid reason for generally supporting a policy of frank disclosure.

Further justification for telling patients the truth is derived from a complex set of psychological problems precipitated by the fact that most seriously ill or dying patients appear to know how sick they really are. Several studies document that terminally ill patients are usually aware of their condition.[29] Family or medical personnel commonly offer various clues about the conditions of such patients, ranging from facial expressions to transparently counterfeit efforts at optimism. Even children, it appears, are able to see through a veil of deceit to know when they are seriously ill. In their discussion of young hospitalized leukemia patients, Vernick and Karon comment that despite efforts to conceal the frequently fatal outcome of this disease, the true nature of death on the ward is promptly known to every child. Hospital wise, the children are able to discern the meaning of the sudden absence of a playmate or the removal of an oxygen tent from a room. As a result, they readily come to mistrust adults' bland assurances about their condition.[30]

Patients intimating the nature of their condition but who are surrounded by medical staff or family members denying their state of serious illness are placed in a curious position. Like Tolstoy's Iván Illich, they find themselves the main players in an elaborate farce designed to protect them, and they come to believe that they in turn must spare others the seemingly unbearable knowledge of their own awareness. One physician has described the unfortunate result of this conspiracy of silence:

> When the stage has been set by distrust and denial of the personal right to know the truth, all participants play their assigned roles through to the end, and the patient usually lives and dies in isolation and loneliness. . . . By withholding the truth the doctor and family think they are being kind. The terrible irony of this situation is that the patient, who has the greatest need for their love and concern, is left in loneliness and isolation through their kindness.[31]

Elisabeth Kübler-Ross[32] and others have led in the recognition that the dying process can be an important part of life, a time when personal self-examination and communication with loved ones can be most intense. In view of this, the forced isolation and abandonment created by practices of deceit and untruthfulness exact a very heavy toll. Almost a century ago Tolstoy's artistic genius helped him identify a major reason for adopting a policy of openness and full communication with the seriously ill or dying patient.

Up to this point, the discussion of reasons for disclosing the truth has dealt primarily with the needs of patients themselves. But clearly, practices of deception or untruthfulness have wider implications than the good or evil done to individual patients. As moral philosophers have long recognized, a single lie or evasion, however well-intentioned, has the effect of reducing everyone's confidence in the veracity of the spoken word. In a medical context, this is a serious problem. When benevolent deception is practiced, all patients—even those with good prognoses—must ask themselves whether they are being told the truth and whether the encouraging words from their physician are not part of a pattern of deception. Therefore, even if a lie benefits the seriously ill patient, this gain must be offset by the wide circle of unnecessary suspicion and anxiety that the practice of deception itself generates. According to Bok, "the entire institution of medicine is threatened by practices lacking in candor, however harmless the results may appear to be in some individual cases."[33]

To physicians trained in the Hippocratic tradition in which the welfare of the individual patient being treated is presumed to come first, this concern with the larger institutional ramifications of untruthfulness may seem of slight importance. However, it should be remembered that the wider consequences of deception touch individuals who are or will be patients themselves, and these consequences may even fall back on the patient whom the lie was meant to benefit. A poignant instance of this is recounted by Vernick. Apparently, children suffering from leukemia in one pediatric ward were frequently spared the knowledge of death by being told that certain of their friends, "had gone to the thirteenth floor." When space limitations made it necessary to transfer one nine year old to the thirteenth floor, the child suddenly became completely unmanageable and had to be restrained by the staff. It took more than an hour before he confessed that the reason he did not want to go to the thirteenth floor was because, "That's where kids go to die."[34]

Therefore, a variety of substantial and well-founded reasons work to support a policy of candor and openness in the medical setting. It would probably be rash to say that patients must always be told the truth. Moral decisions are usually "balancing judgments,"[35] with various goods and evils weighed against one another, and certainly one could speculate on cases where everything conspires to support a policy of evasion or even deception. One such situation might involve mentally disturbed patients who insisted on knowing the truth about their condition but who were clearly unable to bear the truth safely. (Exceptions in cases like these are deemed justifiable by otherwise strong defenders of a policy of truth telling.)[36] However, cases like these are rare, and the considerations thus far suggest that in the very great majority of instances, even including those in which there is concern that the patient may not initially respond well to frankness, a policy of truth is best for all concerned. As Bok illustrates, the substantial value of openness in medical communication generally means that the great burden of proof must always lie on those who advocate dishonesty.[37]

HOW SHOULD THE TRUTH BE TOLD?

The conclusion that honesty is the best policy in medicine raises one final major question of just how the truth is to be told. For example, must physicians actively communicate all the essential facts of the patient's condition, or are they merely required to answer truthfully when questioned? Must they reveal all the bitter details of an illness and all the intracacies of its treatment, or may they withhold some facts? And what are they to do with the patients who do not want to know the truth? Does truth telling require informing patients against their will?

Each of these questions has received some attention from writers on this problem. It is generally conceded that physicians are obligated to do more than passively await questions, that their responsibilities extend to giving patients a full understanding and a true impression of their condition. Although volunteering information is not ordinarily required to fulfill the obligation to tell the truth, a more active role is usually proscribed in situations in which information is known and expected and where a silence is very likely to be interpreted as meaning that nothing is wrong. In such situations, the creation of false inferences by silence can be as deceptive as outright lying.[38] These considerations are compounded in medical conditions that are often so complex that patients cannot be expected to know which questions to ask.

Full and frank disclosure, however, does not necessarily mean a painful detailing of every possible facet of a disease or treatment. Many aspects of a disease process or therapy are irrelevant to the choices that patients must make or to their understanding of what is happening. In discussions of informed consent (see Chapter 9), it is generally held that unless patients specifically inquire, they need to be actively informed only of those facts that a reasonable person might require. This standard, albeit indefinite, suggests that every remote possibility or side effect of therapy and every conceivable suffering of a disease need not be itemized. In addition, full and frank disclosure is not inconsistent with efforts at encouragement and the maintenance of hope. The notion that a physician can bluntly say, "You have six months to live," is not supported by the genuine doubt and uncertainty that attends any illness and its treatment.[39] New discoveries or spontaneous remissions can spare any patient's life. While many of these possibilities are usually too remote to justify withholding the truth of less favorable outcomes, they certainly provide an honest foundation for encouragement and hope.

The patient who plainly does not want the truth poses a special problem. For example, some seriously ill or dying patients, though aware of their condition, do not want to be verbally assaulted with explicit facts. These patients are able to make their wishes clear either by asking in so many words not to be told or by repeatedly forgetting what has already been told them.[40] When such denial exists, it is relatively apparent and probably should not be confused with patients' presumed general reluctance to know the truth. Such patient reluctance has sometimes wrongly been offered as justification for extensive medical deception. In clear cases of denial, however, the duty of truth telling certainly cannot extend to forcing unwanted truth on a patient. In fact, the very principles of self-determination and personal autonomy that underlie a policy of honesty would appear to support respecting a patient's expressed wish for silence.[41]

How the truth should be told raises one final complex issue—perhaps the most important point in this whole area. This is the obvious but easily forgotten wisdom that truth is no substitute for care. One of the most significant findings of studies on dying patients is that very often these patients' principal fear is not death itself as much as the loneliness, isolation, and abandonment that often accompany the dying process.[42] This fear may help explain the common observation by physicians in the past that patients "do not want to know the truth." To ward off abandonment, many patients aware of their condition, but also aware that the living—especially medical personnel—tend to avoid the dying, may have unwillingly entered into conspiracies of deceit.[43]

However, if this is true, then it is not deception patients seek, but rather care. And if what has been discussed to this point is correct, then openness in communication and care are potentially complementary and mutually reinforcing. Ideally, a commitment to telling the truth grows out of care, including genuine respect for the dignity and autonomy of patients. Truth telling in turn assists in the care of patients by eliciting their full cooperation in whatever treatment course is adopted and by removing many of the barriers created by fear and silence. Fresh air and sunlight have long been recognized as remarkable healers. Perhaps today, thanks to changing conceptions of medical practice and a more careful attention to facts rather than opinion, we are learning that the openness of truth also has an important place in medical care.

NOTES TO CHAPTER 8

1. Leo Tolstoy, *The Death of Iván Illich*, Leo Wiener, trans., in *The Complete Works of Count Tolstoy*, vol. XVIII (Boston: Dana & Estes Co., 1904), p. 56.

2. Joseph Collins, "Should Doctors Tell the Truth?" *Harpers Monthly Magazine* 155: 320-326 (August 1927); reprinted in Stanley Joel Reiser, Arthur J. Dyck, and William J. Curran, *Ethics in Medicine: Historical Perspectives and Contemporary Concerns* (Cambridge, MA: The MIT Press, 1977), p. 221.

3. Sissela Bok, *Lying: Moral Choice in Public and Private Life* (New York: Pantheon Books, 1978), p. 220.

4. William T. Fitts and I. S. Radvin, "What Philadelphia Physicians Tell Patients with Cancer," *Journal of the American Medical Association* 153: 901-904 (November 7, 1953).

5. Donald Oken, "What to Tell Cancer Patients," *Journal of the American Medical Association* 175: 1120-1128 (1961); H. Feifel, "The Function of Attitudes toward Death," in Group for the Advancement of Psychiatry, *Death and Dying: Attitudes of Patient and Doctor* (New York: Group for the Advancement of Psychiatry, 1965), pp. 632-641, 654-655.

6. Oken, p. 1126.

7. Robert M. Veatch, *Death, Dying and the Biological Revolution* (New Haven: Yale University Press, 1976), pp. 205-210; William S. Appleton, "The Importance of Psychiatrists' Telling Patients the Truth," *American Journal of Psychiatry* 129: 742 (December 1972).

8. Collins.

9. Bok, p. 223.

10. Edward M. Litin, "Should the Cancer Patient Be Told?" *Post Graduate Medicine* 28: 473 (1960).

11. K. A. Achte and M. L. Vauhkonen, "Cancer and the Psyche," *Omega* 2: 45-46 (1971); Jim McIntosh, "Processes of Communication, Information Seeking and Control Associated with Cancer: A Selective Review of the Literature," *Social Science and Medicine* 8: 174 (1974).

12. Richard C. Cabot, "The Use of Truth and Falsehood in Medicine: An Experimental Study," *American Medicine* 5: 344-349 (1903); reprinted in Reiser, Dyck, and Curran, *Ethics in Medicine*, p. 217.

13. Oken.

14. M. Mannes, *Last Rights* (New York: New American Library, 1973), p. 32.

15. Fitts and Radvin, p. 902.

16. H. Feifel et al., "Physicians Consider Death," *Proceedings, American Psychological Association* (Washington, D.C.: American Psychological Association, 1967), pp. 201-202.

17.   Richard Schultz and David Aderman, "How the Medical Staff Copes with Dying Patients: A Critical Review," *Omega* 7: 12 (1976).
18.   Ibid.
19.   McIntosh, p. 168.
20.   B. Glaser and A. Strauss, *Awareness of Dying* (Chicago: Aldine Publishing Company, 1965), p. 134.
21.   Isaiah Berlin, *Two Concepts of Liberty* (Oxford: The Clarendon Press, 1958), p. 22.
22.   M. Priscilla Rae et al., "Physicians and the Terminal Patient: Some Selected Attitudes and Behavior," *Omega* 6: 295 (1975).
23.   R. Renneker and M. Cutler, "Psychological Problems of Adjustment to Cancer of the Breast," *Journal of the American Medical Association* 148: 833 (1952); William D. Kelly and Stanley Friesen, "Do Cancer Patients Want to be Told," *Surgery* 27: 825 (1950); Sissela Bok, "Truth-Telling: Ethical Aspects," *Encyclopedia of Bioethics* 4: 1683 (1978).
24.   Kelly and Friesen, pp. 824–825.
25.   C.H. Branch, "Psychiatric Aspects of Malignant Disease," *CA: Bulletin of Cancer Progress* 6: 102–104 (1956).
26.   Robert Samp and Anthony Curreri, "A Questionnaire Survey on Public Cancer Education Obtained from Cancer Patients and Their Families," *Cancer* 10: 383 (1957).
27.   Thurstan Brewin, "The Cancer Patient: Communication and Morale," *British Medical Jorunal* 2: 1625 (1977).
28.   Jim McIntosh, "Patients' Awareness and Desire for Information about Diagnosed but Undisclosed Malignant Disease," *The Lancet*, August 7, 1976, pp. 300–303; Robert M. Veatch, "Truth-Telling: Attitudes," *Encyclopedia of Bioethics* 4: 1678 (1978).
29.   Renneker and Cutler, p. 836; J.M. Hinton, "The Physical and Mental Distress of the Dying," *Quarterly Journal of Medicine* 32: 565 (1963).
30.   Joel Vernick and Myron Karon, "Who's Afraid of Death on a Leukemia Ward?" *American Journal of Diseases of Childhood* 109: 394 (1965); Joel Vernick, "Meaningful Communication with the Fatally Ill Child," in E. James Anthony and Cynille Koupernik, *The Child in His Family*, vol. 2. (New York: John Wiley and Sons, 1973), pp. 113–116; Ruth Frank Baer, "The Sick Child Knows," in Samuel Standard and Helmuth Nathan, *Should the Patient Know the Truth?* (New York: Springer Publishing Company, 1955), pp. 100–106.
31.   L. Beaty Pemberton, "Diagnosis: CA—Should We Tell the Truth?" *American College of Surgeons Bulletin* 56: 8–12 (1971).
32.   Elisabeth Kübler-Ross, *On Death and Dying* (New York: The Macmillan Company, 1970).
33.   Sissela Bok, "The Ethics of Giving Placebos," *Scientific American* 231: 17–23 (November 1974), reprinted in Reiser, Dyck, and Curran, *Ethics in Medicine*, p. 252; Bok, *Lying*, pp. 61–68.

34. Vernick and Karon, p. 394.

35. Paul Ramsey, *The Patient as Person* (New Haven: Yale University Press, 1970).

36. Litin, p. 475; Beth Simmons, "Problems in Deceptive Medical Procedures: An Ethical and Legal Analysis of the Administration of Placebos," *Journal of Medical Ethics* 4: 172 (1978).

37. Bok, *Lying*, p. 239.

38. Bok, "Truth-Telling," p. 1684.

39. H. Clay Trumbull, *A Lie Never Justifiable* (Philadelphia: John D. Wattles, 1893); Brewin, p. 1624.

40. Litin, p. 475; Charles C. Lund, "The Doctor, The Patient and the Truth," *Annals of Internal Medicine* 24: 959 (1946); Kübler–Ross, pp. 26–27.

41. Robert M. Veatch, *Case Studies in Medical Ethics*. (Cambridge, MA: Harvard University Press, 1977), p. 154.

42. Kübler–Ross, pp. 26–27.

43. Ibid.

9 INFORMED CONSENT
Who Decides for Whom?

Alan Meisel, J. D.

INTRODUCTION

What is informed consent? Since its birth about two decades ago, the doctrine of informed consent has spawned untold controversy in the courts, among legal scholars, and within the medical profession. Although often condemned by the medical profession as a myth[1] and a fiction[2] and the subject of parodies designed to illustrate its absurdity,[3] generally it is favorably received by legal scholars. The doctrine promotes significant individual rights, and many practicing lawyers regard it well, though possibly for less altruistic reasons.[4]

Informed consent is an ethical command. It has deep and strong roots in the individualistic tradition of the English common law, a tradition reflected in and reinvigorated by the American Constitution. Informed consent is a legal mandate. Nearly half the courts of American jurisdictions have adopted it as law, and only one—

This work was supported by PHS Research Grant No. MH27553, NIHM Center for Studies of Crime and Delinquency and Mental Health Services Development Branch. The author is also indebted to Loren H. Roth, M.D., M.P.H. for his critical comments on earlier drafts of this chapter.

Portions of this chapter are reprinted, with permission, from Alan Meisel, "The Expansion of Liability for Medical Accidents: From Negligence to Strict Liability by Way of Informed Consent," *Nebraska Law Review* 56: 51–152 (1977); and Alan Meisel, "The Exceptions to the Informed Consent Doctrine: Striking a Balance Between Competing Values in Medical Decisionmaking," *Wisconsin Law Review* 1979: 413–488 (1979).

197

Georgia—has rejected it;[5] more recently, twenty-four state legislatures (Alaska, Delaware, Florida, Hawaii, Idaho, Iowa, Kentucky, Louisiana, Maine, Nebraska, Nevada, New Hampshire, New York, North Carolina, North Dakota, Ohio, Oregon, Pennsylvania, Rhode Island, Tennessee, Texas, Utah, Vermont, and Washington) have enacted statutes dealing with it.[6] In addition, informed consent constitutes a response to the mid-twentieth century demands of citizens for protection of their rights as consumers and for recognition of their civil liberties.

Informed consent reflects one of our highest ethical values—individual autonomy; it implicates strong emotional needs both for control over our own lives and for dependence upon others; and it deals with a subject of fundamental importance, our health. It is little wonder that it is a source of so much conflict, confusion, and strongly held positions.

Informed consent is comprised of two legal duties imposed on physicians—to inform patients about treatment and to obtain their consent for it.[a] These duties are imposed in order to assure that a person's right of self-determination—that is, the right of all free citizens to govern their own destiny—may be maintained in one particular sphere of human activity, the acquisition of medical care. In addition to safeguarding the right of self-determination, the informed consent doctrine encourages, but does not require, patients to make informed or intelligent decisions about medical care.

Viewed broadly, the duties of making disclosures and obtaining consent enable the patient to play the role of primary medical decisionmaker—that is, these duties allocate primary decisional authority to the patient in making decisions about whether and how to be treated. The physician's role in decisionmaking is to determine, from a medical perspective, (1) what the patient's problem is (i.e., diagnosis); (2) how, if at all, it may be ameliorated; and (3) what the possible pitfalls of treatment may be. Next, the doctor's role is to

---

a. It is worth stating clearly that there is one thing that informed consent is *not*: It is not the same as traditional medical malpractice. A physician may be liable to a patient for injuries to the patient caused by a procedure that the doctor has administered if the doctor was negligent in one of several ways—(1) the failure to possess a reasonable degree of learning and skill; (2) the failure to exercise reasonable care and diligence in the exercise of skill; (3) the failure to use best judgment in the exercise of skill and application of knowledge; (4) the failure to keep abreast of developments in medicine; and (5) a departure from generally approved or used methods. Pike v. Honsinger, 155 N.Y. 201, 209–210, 49 N.E. 760, 762 (1898).

communicate this information to the patient, who will then utilize it in the context of his or her own personal values and subjective preferences.[7]

The physician's role in medical decisionmaking is primarily cognitive, medical, and technical; the patient's role is primarily affective, personal, and subjective. Informed consent, therefore, views medical decisionmaking as a mix of technical and personal considerations. Decisions about medical care are not to be made exclusively by doctors because they do not, indeed they cannot, have access to other information highly relevant to the making of the decision. Only the patient has access to such information.

Although decisions about medical care involve nontechnical considerations, this fact does not necessarily compel the conclusion that primary decisional authority reposes in the patient. Two other logical alternatives are available. Rather than requiring physician disclosure of information that the patient does not have but that is relevant to decisionmaking, there could be a requirement that the patient disclose the subjective information that the doctor lacks. The doctor then could decide whether and how to treat. Or, both the doctor and the patient could be required to disclose the information available to them to a neutral third party who, on the basis of both kinds of information, would render a decision about treatment.

To a very limited extent, each of these alternative forms of medical decisionmaking does operate and legitimately so, the first under the aegis of "waiver" and the second when the patient is incompetent. Both situations are discussed later in this chapter. However, the general rule is that in the vast majority of cases, disclosure is made by the physician to the patient, and the patient then exercises final decisional authority.

Why is this? Because it is the patient who will, in the most personal way, reap the benefits or experience the failures of treatment. It is the patient's body, mind, and being that must endure the pain, the uncertainty, the anxiety, and the cost of medical treatment. Certainly, physicians experience benefits and failures from rendering care. But the effect upon them is less direct, intense, and personal; it is not critical to every aspect of their lives that a particular treatment on a particular patient succeeds or fails; involves pain and suffering; and entails sacrifice of time, money, and other resources. Thus, it is the patient to whom primary decisional authority is ordinarily entrusted.

The legal rules governing the doctrine of informed consent have undergone and continue to undergo a slow metamorphosis, beginning with what is usually recognized as the first true informed consent case in 1957,[8] to the rash of legislation in the mid-1970s.[9] Although the development of informed consent began as early as the eighteenth century,[10] most of the development did not take place until the 1960s and 1970s. This slow metamorphosis was marked by periodic bursts of activity. First in 1960, with the cases of *Natanson* v. *Kline*[11] and *Mitchell* v. *Robinson*;[12] next in 1972, with the central case of *Canterbury* v. *Spence*,[13] followed by important cases in California[14] and Rhode Island.[15] The third period of activity began in 1975 and subsided in 1977, when half of the state legislatures enacted statutes dealing with informed consent. Most likely there will be another flurry of judicial activity as the courts begin to construe these statutes.

One informed consent case, *Canterbury* v. *Spence*, stands far above all others in discussing, if not establishing, the rules governing the obtaining of informed consent. Although the rules established in *Canterbury* have been adopted in only about half of the jurisdictions and explicitly rejected in an equal number of others that have considered the issue,[16] this case more comprehensively than any before it discusses almost all facets of the doctrine: (1) what must be disclosed, (2) how it must be disclosed, (3) when informed consent need not be obtained, and (4) who makes the decision when a patient cannot.

ELEMENTS OF DISCLOSURE

There is little dispute over the kind of information a physician must tell a patient—the so-called elements of disclosure. The central informational component is the possible negative results that may occur from undergoing a particular procedure. While this concept can be expressed in several ways, it is generally referred to as the risks of the procedure (some courts refer to these risks as hazards, or discomforts, or side effects). Although disclosure of the risks neither guarantees that the patient will utilize the information in making a decision nor assures that the decision reached will be a reasonable one,[17] without disclosure most patients are unable to make an informed decision.

Physicians must also explain the nature of the procedure—for example, is it surgical, pharmacological, or radiological; is it diagnostic or therapeutic; is it experimental or established; and what part of the body is involved. Closely related to the nature of the procedure is the benefit that the patient may reasonably expect to gain from treatment. Although in many cases the benefit of the treatment is self-evident (i.e., the amelioration of the problem for which the patient sought medical care), in many other cases, something less than a total cure can be expected; there is always a possibility that no benefits may accrue. That is, the treatment may bring neither good or bad results, but simply produce no results at all.

Finally, the patient is entitled to be informed of any possible alternative kinds of treatment that might be employed, as well as the consequences of these alternatives (i.e., the benefits and the risks likely to be entailed). Since one alternative to any proposed treatment is no treatment, the patient also should be apprised of the likely consequences of totally foregoing treatment. These requirements—risks, benefits, alternatives, and nature of treatment—are the classical elements of informed consent and constitute the basis from which the corpus of informed consent rules and exceptions have developed.

THE STANDARD OF DISCLOSURE

Describing the elements of informed consent in general terms is quite simple, and perhaps this is why there is so little debate in the law and so little objection from the medical profession as to what kind of information should be disclosed to patients. But when it comes to determining in the context of a particular patient with a particular illness or injury and a particular treatment what particular information should be disclosed, the debate increases, and the controversy mounts. The issue of how much information a physician must disclose about benefits, alternatives, and especially about risks causes considerable concern among all interested parties.

Although the informed consent cases often speak in terms of requiring full disclosure, they also acknowledge that the physician is not obliged to tell the patient everything that is medically known— let alone everything that ought to be known—about the procedure.[18] There are several reasons for this. First, some of what the physician knows is too complex to be communicated meaningfully to the layperson. The courts have made it quite clear that the physician does not have to disclose such complex information. However, if one chooses to do so, simple language must be used that is reasonably calculated for the patient to understand. Second, the process of disclosing all information, if carried to its logical extreme, would involve providing the patient with the equivalent of a medical school education, and time and practicality simply will not permit this. "The patient's interest in information does not extend to a lengthy polysyllabic discourse on all possible complications. A mini-course in medical science is not required . . ."[19] Even then, there is no assurance that the patient has been apprised of all of the information that conceivably could fall under the elements of informed consent. Again, the courts have addressed this objection to full disclosure and have concluded that practical considerations preclude giving the patient all information about a particular procedure. Finally, some of the information that could be disclosed is irrelevant or only marginally relevant to the patient's decisionmaking process and therefore need not be disclosed.

If the problem of defining the standard of disclosure were the only issue, the full disclosure standard would be the one to accept, since it most promotes the patient's decisional authority. However, since necessity clearly dictates that disclosure be something less than full, there is a need to define the extent of disclosure that is required so that physicians will have some idea of how to fulfill their duty and patients will know how to determine if their right to information is being denied.

The courts have agreed that the physician need not make total disclosure, but must make reasonable disclosure of that information that is material to making a decision about treatment. However, the consensus immediately breaks down over the issue of how materiality is to be determined, and two separate factions emerge—those courts that believe that materiality should be measured from the physician's perspective and those that believe that it should be viewed from the patient's perspective.[20]

The early informed consent cases never acknowledged the issue and simply assumed that materiality should be determined from the doctor's perspective. One case indicates that the degree of disclosure made to the patient is "primarily a question of medical judgment,"[21] and consequently that "the duty of the physician to disclose . . . is limited to those disclosures which a reasonable medical practitioner would make under the same or similar circumstances."[22] This rule closely parallels that in medical negligence cases, since the standard to which the physician is held not only in the exercise of skill but also in the disclosure of information to the patient is what is customary and usual in the profession.[23] The courts of several jurisdictions have explicitly adopted this rule and few seriously questioned it before 1972.[24] A corollary of this so-called professional standard of disclosure was the requirement that expert medical testimony was needed to establish the standard of disclosure to which the physician would be held, despite the problems associated with such a requirement.

Beginning with *Canterbury* v. *Spence* and the second wave of informed consent cases, a substantial number of courts began to establish a new standard of disclosure based on a different view of materiality. These cases discarded the professional standard of disclosure and replaced it with a lay- or patient-oriented standard, which effectively withdrew from the medical profession the right to determine what information must be disclosed to the patient. A fair statement of the rule that emerged—and there are several different statements in the *Canterbury* case alone—is that the physician is required to disclose all information about a proposed treatment that a reasonable person (in the patient's situation) would consider material to a decision either to undergo or to forego treatment.[b] The scope of the duty to disclose is to be determined by "the patient's right to self-decision,"[25] rather than by the custom or practice of either the particular physician making the disclosure or the medical profession as a whole.

The dust from the storm that this issue has created has not yet settled, and it is unlikely that one rule will emerge to the exclusion of the other. Rather, these two different standards of disclosure probably will remain, with some jurisdictions subscribing to one and the remainder to the other. Despite the problems inherent in the patient-oriented standard—primarily, how a physician is to know what a reasonable patient would want to know, not to mention how a reasonable patient is to know what he or she would want to know without first knowing all there is to know—it is the preferable standard of disclosure because it is most in keeping with the values

b. The courts have clearly rejected a subjective patient-oriented standard. Hence, the physician is not obliged to disclose what the particular patient would have wanted to know, but what a reasonable patient would want to know.

underlying the informed consent doctrine and the goals that the doctrine seeks to promote (especially that of assuring patient privacy in decisionmaking).

However, the failure of the doctor to make reasonable disclosure to the patient (regardless of whether a professional or lay standard of disclosure is applied) is not sufficient to constitute a violation of the patient's rights under the informed consent doctrine. Rather, two things must be shown apart from breach of duty—(1) that some harm occurred to the patient, and (2) that this harm was caused by the doctor's failure to disclose information. The first is referred to as the materialized risk requirement, and the second is discussed under the aegis of causation.

MATERIALIZED RISK REQUIREMENT

If the physician fails to inform the patient that a particular treatment carries certain risks or has alternatives, the patient's rights have not been violated unless some bodily injury was suffered.[26] For example, if the patient agrees to and undergoes surgery without having been informed that the operation may produce paralysis, there is no violation of rights unless the patient is actually paralyzed. In other words, the risk that the doctor failed to disclose must materialize in order for there to be a violation of the informed consent doctrine giving rise to a right to recovery of damages.

The materialized risk requirement has received severe criticism[27] for failing to "recognize that a citizen can be wronged without being harmed, that his dignity as a human being has been violated and that an assault has taken place the moment the deceiving authority commences therapy . . . , even if beneficial. . . ."[28] This criticism goes to the heart of the question of just what rights are actually promoted and protected by the informed consent doctrine.

If the doctrine's avowed individualistic purposes—the promotion of individual self-determination, human dignity, and rational decisionmaking—are to be honored, then the failure to disclose information disserves these purposes. It makes no difference that the patient incurred no bodily harm; the failure to disclose is a harm, and the failure of the cases to recognize this is a betrayal of the lofty ideals of the informed consent doctrine.

CAUSATION

Not only must the risk that the physician failed to disclose material-ize in order for the patient to recover damages for a lack of informed consent, but the cases uniformly hold that this failure must be the cause of the harm that befalls the patient. There is agreement that causation exists only when disclosure of risks to the patient would have resulted in a decision to forego the treatment in question. How-ever, controversy exists as to whether causation is found by refer-ence to an objective standard—that is, would a reasonable person have decided not to undergo treatment had he or she been properly informed?—or to a subjective standard—namely, would this patient have decided not to undergo treatment had he or she been properly informed? The earlier cases seemed unaware of the difference be-tween the two tests,[29] and some commentators assumed that the subjective test should be applied.[30] Surprisingly, since it is otherwise so protective of patient's rights, *Canterbury* and most other cases that have specifically confronted this issue reject the subjective test.[31] However, some courts appear to have adopted a subjective standard of disclosure.[32]

This trend undermines a fundamental purpose of the informed consent doctrine—the protection and promotion of human dignity. Since the doctrine is premised on the right of the individual to make decisions concerning the kind of medical care (if any) that one wishes to undergo or forego, regardless of the soundness of one's reasons, the subjective test of causation is far more consonant with the underlying rationale for informed consent than the objective test.[33] By conditioning the availability of compensation on the con-gruence between the patient's own decision and that of a reasonable person under the same or similar circumstances, the objective test undercuts the patient's right of self-determination.

It is not difficult to understand why this development has oc-curred. As *Canterbury* indicates and other cases have agreed, it is highly unlikely that medical accident victims would thwart oppor-tunities for obtaining compensation by testifying that had they been properly informed, they still would have consented to treat-ment. There is, however, a serious flaw in this reasoning. Under an objective test of causation, the plaintiffs could testify as to what they actually would have done had they been properly informed. Although such testimony would no longer be determinative of the causation issue, the jury would be able to consider the plaintiffs' subjective views. *Canterbury*, in rejecting a subjective test of causation, was skeptical of the ability of plaintiffs to admit that they would have elected treatment even with adequate disclosure. It is reasonable to assume that jurors would share the skepticism of the *Canterbury* court. Since it is the jury's function to evaluate all the evidence and to weigh the credibility of witnesses, it would have ample opportunity to apply this natural skepticism. Thus, the fear of a subjective standard is overstated, if not entirely misplaced.

THE EXCEPTIONS TO INFORMED CONSENT

Physicians labor under duties and patients possess rights other than those imposed by the informed consent doctrine. Some duties are imposed by law, such as the duty to practice technically proficient medicine (i.e., not to commit malpractice); some find their source in the ethics of the profession (e.g., the duty to do no harm); and some are derived from professional ethics that are accorded legal recognition as well, such as the duty of confidentiality.

Some of these duties may come into conflict with the doctor's duty to disclose and to obtain consent. In so doing, they impose limitations on the informed consent doctrine and help to shape its boundaries. Other limitations on the doctrine also exist. Practical considerations often require a more abbreviated (or even nonexistent) disclosure than contemplated by law, and consent is sometimes not obtained when it should be. Of more immediate concern are those limitations imposed on the doctrine by the other legal and ethical duties of the physician rather than by practical constraints.

Limitations are imposed on the informed consent doctrine by certain exceptions that have developed and acquired judicial or legislative recognition. Although the contours of each of the exceptions are relatively unclear, as are the appropriate consequences of the invocation and application of each of them, their existence is beyond dispute. There are four recognized exceptions that limit the doctor's duty either to disclose or to obtain consent or both—(1) an emergency, (2) incompetency, (3) a waiver, and (4) the therapeutic privilege. Each of these exceptions recognizes that the individualistic values that the informed consent doctrine seeks to promote—self-determination, autonomy, privacy—are not the only significant concerns in medical decisionmaking despite their being primary ones. Of concern also are health values—the interest in the individual's health for his or her own sake, the interest that others have in the maintenance and promotion of the health of family and friends, and the concern with assuring that health professionals are not unduly hampered in exercising their skills. The four exceptions are the means by which the law permits these concerns to be interjected into the process of medical decisionmaking.

The Emergency Exception

In an emergency, the doctor may render treatment without the patient's informed consent. The rationale for this rule is that since a reasonable person would consent to treatment in an emergency if able to do so, it is presumed that any patient would give consent under such circumstances.[34]

Since there appears to be an intuitive notion of what an emergency is, many courts have refrained from attempting to define an emergency while still finding one to exist. Those that have considered the question of how an emergency should be defined range from a very stringent definition, such as the medical care needed to preserve life or limb,[35] to a very broad one, such as the medical care needed simply to alleviate suffering or pain.[36] The definition of an emergency used in determining when the requirements of informed consent should be suspended must consider the extent to which their abandonment or relaxation undermines the values that the doctrine promotes.

If informed consent is suspended in an emergency, it should be done because the patient is incapable of either giving consent or receiving information or both. Otherwise, it should be suspended only if the time required to make disclosure and/or to obtain the patient's decision might be very disadvantageous to the patient's personal health. To permit treatment without obtaining informed consent in situations in which the patient is incapable of giving it allows health to be restored or possibly a life to be saved. Such a practice promotes the social value in health at no expense to the interest in individualism. However, if the consequence of withholding treatment due to the patient's inability to give informed consent is merely that the patient suffers pain with no risk of permanent physical detriment, then permitting treatment without informed consent seriously undercuts individualism without any substantial countervailing gain in promoting the societal interest in health. If the patient in such a situation is having severe enough pain that there is no interest in listening to the physician's disclosure, then the right may be waived.

The Incompetency Exception

Closely related to the emergency situation is the exception granted for incompetent patients. Certain individuals recognized as incompetent to consent to treatment may consequently be treated without their consent. Similar to the emergency exception, the only thing certain about the incompetency exception is its existence. There is no single, or even well-accepted, definition of incompetency. However, there are several general ways in which the determination of incompetency can be approached, each of which has been utilized, or its appropriateness suggested, in court decisions, statutes, administrative regulations, or scholarly commentary.

Incompetency may be of two different types—general or specific. The individual who is intoxicated, actively psychotic, severely mentally retarded, or senile may fall into the general incompetency category. Since such individuals bear so little resemblance to the average person, they are considered incompetent to make important decisions about their own lives, including decisions about medical care. In contrast, incompetency may be specific in that one may be incompetent to make certain kinds of important decisions and yet competent to make others. What is relevant to a determination of specific incompetency is not the individual's general qualities of intellect, affect, and reasoning, but one's actual ability to make a decision (in this case, a decision about medical care). Specific incompetency may be determined by reference to (1) the person's mere ability to manifest a decision, (2) the manner in which the person makes a decision, (3) the nature of the decision itself, or (4) the person's understanding of the information disclosed by the doctor.[37]

In addition, it is necessary to distinguish between de jure (or legal) and de facto (or actual) incompetency. One is de jure incompetent by either being a minor or being determined to be incompetent by a court. Minors are legally generally incompetent; an adult may be adjudged either generally or specifically incompetent. Some persons who are legally competent may in fact be incompetent; therefore, their assent to treatment is not a valid authorization for it, nor is their dissent a valid refusal. In contrast, individuals adjudicated as generally incompetent may in fact be specifically competent to make a medical decision, or persons adjudicated incompetent in the past may in fact have regained their competency. In summary, although the incompetency exception exists, what it involves is quite unclear.

The Waiver Exception

Several cases and recent statutes,[38] have acknowledged that a patient may relinquish, or waive, the right to give an informed consent to treatment. However, the cases and statutes do little more than recognize the existence of waiver and do not address several important problems relating to its definition and application.

Although the notion of waiving one's right to give an informed consent is relatively new, the waiver of other rights has long been recognized and thus provides substantial guidance in determining what a waiver of informed consent should look like. To be valid, a waiver must be an intentional and voluntary relinquishment of a known right.[39] Therefore, in order to validly relinquish the right to be informed or the right to decide or both, the patient must know that one possesses these rights, one must intend to give them up, and there must be no undue pressure on one to do so.

It is unlikely that the average patient will possess this knowledge. Therefore it is incumbent upon the physician to tell the patient of the right to waive informed consent when one expresses a desire not to participate in the decisionmaking process (either by indicating a disinterest in information or in deciding or both). Statements such as "Please don't tell me about that, it will only upset me" (the functional equivalent of a relinquishment of the right to be informed) and/or "Doctor, you decide what is best for me" (the functional equivalent of a relinquishment of the right to decide) should activate the physician's duty to tell the patient that an individual has both a right to the information and a right to decide. However, the patient should also be informed of a right not to hear and a right not to decide—namely, a right to waive.

A properly obtained waiver is in keeping with the individualistic values promoted by the doctrine of informed consent. The patient remains the ultimate decisionmaker, but the content of the decision is shifted from the decisional level to the metadecisional level—from the equivalent of "I want this treatment or that treatment or no treatment" to "I don't want any information about the treatment" or "I don't want to decide; you make the decision as to what should be done." Waiver permits taking care of a patient's health without the patient's actual participation in the process of medical decisionmaking or at least without his or her full participation.

The Therapeutic Privilege

It is well established in case law and commentary that the physician, in appropriate circumstances, may be excused from compliance with the requirements of informed consent by the therapeutic privilege. Of all of the exceptions to the informed consent doctrine, the therapeutic privilege is the most well known and discussed, despite the fact that few cases turn on its application.

Although the contours of the privilege are unclear, the general purpose of the privilege is to "free physicians from a legal requirement which would force them to violate their 'primary duty' to do what is beneficial for the patient."[40] In practice, however, the privilege may legitimate the physician's natural reticence to disclose unpleasant information to the patient. Therefore, if the privilege is not severely circumscribed in its scope, it threatens to swallow the general obligation of disclosure. If the harm to the patient from disclosure is viewed broadly as including the risk that the patient may choose to reject medical care, the privilege would, in effect, permit the physician to substitute his or her own judgment for that of the patient's in every instance of medical decisionmaking.

The most stringent formulation of the privilege permits information to be withheld from the patient only when its disclosure would be so upsetting that it would render the patient unable to rationally engage in decisionmaking. However, the physician is accorded more extensive latitude by a definition of the privilege that allows the withholding "of information regarding any untoward consequences of a treatment where full disclosure will be detrimental to the patient's total care and best interest."[41]

Although disclosure of treatment information and patient decisionmaking are important (if not compelling) values, they should not be so singlemindedly pursued that they become self-defeating. When disclosure reasonably threatens to impede rather than to promote patient decisionmaking, consideration must be given to dispensing with it. Indeed, some authorities suggest that disclosure must be suspended when it poses a reasonable threat of harm to the patient.[42] However, a loose formulation of the privilege is inconsistent with the values underlying and the functions of the doctrine of informed consent.

Other Exceptions

In addition to the above four exceptions, it is arguable that there are a few others. Some courts have spoken about an exception to the consent requirement for the unconscious patient.[43] However, the unconscious patient is viewed most adequately as a subcategory of either the emergency or the incompetency exceptions.

Courts have also suggested that there is an exception to the disclosure requirement for common risks—risks of which the reasonable person ought to be aware—and for known risks—namely, risks of which the patient is actually aware.[44] However, these two situations should not be viewed as exceptions to the disclosure requirement, but as constituting an integral part of the definition of the degree of disclosure that is required of the physician.

PROXY DECISIONMAKING

When one of the four exceptions to informed consent is properly invoked and applied, the consequence is that the decision about medical treatment will be made by someone other than the patient. The problem of who should make the decision when the patient is disqualified from doing so—a problem referred to as either proxy consent, substituted consent, or third party consent[c]—has received

c. The National Commission for the Protection of Human Subjects of Biomedical and Behavioral Research has eschewed the use of the term "consent" when a research subject is unable to participate in decisionmaking. Instead, it speaks of "permission," when given by a third party. For a further discussion of consent when research subjects are involved, readers are referred to The National Commission for the Protection of Human Subjects of Biomedical and Behavioral Research, *Protection of Human Subjects—Research Involving Children* (Washington, D.C.: U.S. Government Printing Office, 1978) and to Chapter 20.

only scant analysis by the courts and legislatures. One of the few generalizations that can be made is found in legal treaties suggesting that when the patient cannot give consent, the proper practice to follow is to obtain the consent of a close family member, if available,[45] and most physicians and hospitals routinely follow this practice.

There are several general options available for making a medical decision in situations in which the patient appropriately is disqualified from participation. First, the physician could be legally empowered to make the medical decision in all cases in which an exception is invoked, as is now the case in an emergency. However, to so empower the physician may be to foreclose the interjection of personal values into the decisionmaking process, resulting in a decision made exclusively on the basis of technical considerations supplied by the physician.

A second method of proxy decisionmaking involves the use of a family member or a friend of the patient. In theory, this method permits the interjection of nonmedical values into the decisionmaking process by a party whose primary allegiance is not to the medical profession. However, there is no guarantee that a family member or friend will have only the patient's best interest at heart; that person may be motivated by self-interest.

A third general way of making a medical decision without the patient's participation is for the case to be brought to the attention of governmental authorities, either administrative or judicial. Either by making the treatment decision itself or by reviewing the decision of the proxy, the governmental authority could provide a forum in which individualism as well as society's interest in the patient's health may be explicitly brought to bear in the decisionmaking process.

In present practice, when the patient is disqualified from participation in medical decisionmaking, sometimes the physician makes the decision, sometimes a family member is called upon to do so, and sometimes judicial proceedings are instituted by the physician, hospital administrators, or family members. The only relatively clear situation is an emergency in which the physician out of necessity makes the treatment decision. Although the heavily debated *Quinlan*[46] and *Saikewicz*[47] cases suggest that the courts provide the proper forum for decisionmaking when the question involves the administration or cessation of treatment to the terminally ill, no similar guidance exists for the large number of cases involving medical decisions in more ordinary contexts. Furthermore, the *Quinlan* case suggests that in situations other than those involving the treatment of the terminally ill, one does not need to resort to the courts; however, it offers no guidance as to how and by whom such decisions should be made.

SANCTIONS FOR FAILURE TO OBTAIN CONSENT

Until this point, the discussion has revolved around the obligations imposed by the informed consent doctrine on the physician and the correlative rights accorded to the patient. Unless some remedy is available to the patient who has been denied one or the other of them, these rights represent mere words.

The doctrine of informed consent is a branch of the law of torts, which deals with the victims of accidental injuries. The remedy ordinarily available to the aggrieved tort victim is an award of monetary damages, and the doctrine of informed consent is no exception. Historically, the purposes of awarding damages to the victim against the person who committed the tort are several: (1) to deter the same conduct in the future both by the tortfeasor and by others, (2) to punish, (3) to serve as a substitute for revenge, and (4) to compensate victims for the losses that they have suffered. The last—compensation—is the primary goal of contemporary tort law. In part, this is because it is not clear that any of the other goals are actually served by the awarding of damages. Additionally, today's wide availability of insurance both undercuts some of the other purposes and promotes compensation. Thus, patients able to show the violation of their rights under the informed consent doctrine may collect damages from physicians (or their insurance companies)[d] for their actual, out of pocket expenses occasioned by the materialized risk; for the pain and suffering consequent to this risk; and for other economic damages such as lost wages or the cost of hiring a housekeeper.

As in the remainder of the Anglo–American civil legal system, the initiative is on patients to pursue a remedy. If they fail to assume this initiative, it is highly unlikely that anyone else will. The problem is

---

d. The physician usually will be indemnified by an insurance company. In some jurisdictions, an insurance company may be sued directly by the patient for damages.

that if patients were inadequately informed or if consent was not obtained, they may simply be unaware of being wronged. Only if the treatment fails to produce the desired results may some feel aggrieved, seek satisfaction, and then possibly learn (most likely from a lawyer who has been consulted) of the rights of patients under the informed consent doctrine. Thus, even in those instances in which the materialized risk requirement is not a prerequisite to recover (e.g., where the patient has not even given consent or possibly in a jurisdiction that has not chosen to adhere to such a requirement) patients may be wronged—in the sense of having been denied their rights under the informed consent doctrine—without knowing it because there are no bad results to tip them off.

The failure to obtain the patient's informed consent could conceivably lead to other sanctions against the offending doctor. To the extent that hospital bylaws require the doctor to comply with the law in general—or more specifically, with the doctrine of informed consent—a physician might lose staff privileges or be subject to less onerous sanctions for failing to obtain informed consent. Similarly, the physician might be subject to sanctions by the state licensing authorities if the licensing statute and/or regulations make it an offense to fail to obtain informed consent. In a rare case, the failure to obtain the patient's consent might provide the basis for criminal proceedings. However, this would only be in the most extreme cases—not merely where the doctor failed to obtain consent, but where under nonemergency conditions, medical treatment was rendered over the patient's express prohibition.

CONCLUSION

Although more than twenty years old, informed consent is still in its infancy. The fundamental duties imposed by the doctrine—making disclosure and obtaining consent—have become clearly delineated, as have the more particular rules dealing with the standard of disclosure, materialized risk, causation, and exceptions. Additionally, the purposes of informed consent—to promote individual self-determination and rational decisionmaking—have been so often reiterated that they are almost commonplace, yet problems of application of the rules constantly pose dilemmas for doctors called upon to make disclosure and obtain consent and for judges who must determine in retrospect whether the doctor's efforts were adequate. Only if physicians and, especially, judges are able to keep in mind that the individual's "right to determine what shall be done with his own body"[48] is as important as the preservation of health will the lofty ideals of the informed consent doctrine be reflected in practice.

NOTES TO CHAPTER 9

1. Henry K. Beecher, "Consent in Clinical Experimentation—Myth and Reality," *Journal of the American Medical Association* 195: 34–35 (January 3, 1966).
2. Eugene G. Laforet, "The Fiction of Informed Consent," *Journal of the American Medical Association* 235: 1579–1585 (April 12, 1976).
3. Preston J. Burnham, "Medical Experimentation on Humans," *Science* 152: 448–450 (1966); William P. Irvin, "Now, Mrs. Blare, About the Complications . . . ," *Medical Economics* 40: 102–108 (1963); Edmund B. Middleton, "Informed Consent," *Journal of the American Medical Association* 233: 1049 (September 8, 1975); Mark M. Ravitch, "Informed Consent—Descent to Absurdity," *Medical Times* 101: 164–171 (1973).
4. Alan Meisel, "The 'Exceptions' to the Informed Consent Doctrine: Striking a Balance between Competing Values in Medical Decisionmaking," *Wisconsin Law Review* 1979: 413–488 (1979). Specific reference is made to p. 413, n. 3.
5. Young v. Yarn, 222 S.E.2d 113 (Ga. App. 1975); Georgia Code Ann. §88-2901 *et seq.* (Supp. 1977).
6. Alan Meisel and Lisa D. Kabnick, "Informed Consent to Medical Treatment: An Analysis of Recent Legislation," *University of Pittsburgh Law Review* 41: 407–564 (Spring 1980).
7. "Informed Consent and the Dying Patient," *Yale Law Journal* 83: 1632–1664 (1974).
8. Salgo v. Leland Stanford Jr. University Board of Trustees, 317 P.2d 170 (Cal. App. 1957).
9. Meisel and Kabnick.
10. Slater v. Baker and Stapleton, 2 Wils. 359, 95 Eng. Rep. 860 (K.B. 1767).
11. Natanson v. Kline, 350 P.2d 1093, *opinion on denial of motion for rehearing*, 354 P.2d 670 (Kan. 1960).
12. Mitchell v. Robinson, 334 S.W.2d 11, *opinion on denial of motion for rehearing*, 360 S.W.2d 673 (Mo. 1962).
13. Canterbury v. Spence, 464 F.2d 772 (D.C. Cir.) *cert. denied* 409 U.S. 1064 (1972).
14. Cobbs v. Grant, 502 P.2d 1 (Cal. 1972).

15. Wilkinson v. Vesey, 295 A.2d 676 (R.I. 1972).

16. "Modern Status of Views as to General Measure of Physician's Duty to Inform Patients of Risks of Proposed Treatment," *Annotated Law Reports, 3rd ser.* 88:1008–1044 (1978).

17. Meisel, p. 421.

18. The physician is required to know about those risks which a reasonable medical practitioner would know. For a further discussion of the term "reasonable," see: Natanson v. Kline, 350 P.2d 1093, 1106 (Kan. 1960).

19. Cobbs v. Grant, 502 P.2d 1, 11 (Cal. 1972).

20. "Modern Status of Views as to General Measure of Physician's Duty to Inform Patients of Risks of Proposed Treatment."

21. Natanson v. Kline, 360 P.2d 1093, 1106 (Kan. 1960).

22. Id.

23. William L. Prosser, *Handbook of the Law of Torts, 4th ed.* (St. Paul: West Publishing Company, 1971), p. 165; David W. Louisell and Harold Williams, *Medical Malpractice* (Albany: M. Bender, 1969), p. 200.

24. For further references to these jurisdictions and cases and for discussion of this issue, the reader is referred to Alan Meisel, "The Expansion of Liability for Medical Accidents: From Negligence to Strict Liability Way of Informed Consent," *Nebraska Law Review* 56: 51–152 (1977).

25. Canterbury v. Spence, 464 F.2d 772, 768 (D.C. Cir. 1972).

26. Id. at 790.

27. Joseph Goldstein, "For Harold Lasswell: Some Reflections on Human Dignity, Entrapment, Informed Consent, and the Plea Bargain," *Yale Law Journal* 84: 683–703 (March 1975).

28. Ibid., p. 691.

29. Shetter v. Rochelle, 409 P.2d 74, 83 (Ariz. App. 1965).

30. Marcus L. Plant, "An Analysis of 'Informed Consent'," *Fordham Law Review* 36: 639–672 (May 1968); Comment, "Informed Consent in Medical Malpractice," *California Law Review* 55: 1396–1418 (1967).

31. Cobbs v. Grant, 502 P.2d 1 (Cal. 1972); Funke v. Fieldman, 512 P.2d 539 (Kan. 1973); Fogal v. Genesee Hospital, 344 N.Y.S.2d 552 (App. Div. 1973); Scaria v. St. Paul Fire and Marine Insurance Company, 227 N.W.2d 647 (Wis. 1975).

32. Poulin v. Zartman, 542 P.2d 251 (Alaska 1975); Wilkinson v. Vesey, 295 A.2d 676 (R.I. 1972); Shetter v. Rochelle, 409 P.2d 74 (Ariz. App. 1965).

33. Scaria v. St. Paul Fire and Marine Insurance Company, 227 N.W.2d 647, 655 (Wis. 1975).

34. Prosser, p. 103.

35. Dunham v. Wright, 423 F.2d 940 (3d Cir. 1970); Mohr v. Williams, 104 N.W.12 (Minn. 1905); Moss v. Rishworth, 222 S.W. 225 (Tex. App. 1920).

36. Sullivan v. Montgomery, 279 N.Y.S. 575, 577 (Bronx Cty. City Ct. 1935).
37. Loren H. Roth, Alan Meisel, and Charles W. Lidz, "Tests of Competency to Consent to Treatment," *American Journal of Psychiatry* 134: 279–284 (1977).
38. Meisel and Kabnick.
39. Miranda v. Arizona, 384 U.S. 436, 475, 476 (1966).
40. Comment, "Informed Consent: The Illusion of Patient Choice," *Emory Law Journal* 23: 504 (1974).
41. Nishi v. Hartwell, 473 P.2d 116, 119 (Haw. 1970).
42. Ferrara v. Galluchio, 152 N.E.2d 249 (N.Y. 1958); Kraus v. Spielberg, 236 N.Y.S.2d 143 (Sup. Ct. Kings Cty. 1962); Williams v. Menehan, 379 P.2d 292, 294 (Kan. 1963).
43. See, for example, Franklyn v. Peabody, 228 N.W. 681 (Mich. 1930).
44. See, for example, Wilkinson v. Vesey, 295 A.2d 676, 689 (R.I. 1972).
45. Health Law Center, *Hospital Law Manual* (Germantown: Aspen Systems Corporation, 1974), p. 58; Joseph H. King, *The Law of Medical Malpractice in a Nutshell* (St. Paul: West Publishing Company, 1977), p. 140.
46. In re Quinlan, 355 A.2d 647 (N.J. 1976), *cert. denied*, 429 U.S. 922 (1976).
47. Superintendent of Belchertown State School v. Saikewicz, 370 N.E.2d 417 (Mass. 1977).
48. Schloendorff v. Society of New York Hospital, 105 N.E. 92 (N.Y. 1914).

10 PATIENT RIGHTS AND COLLEGE HEALTH

Marc D. Hiller, Dr. P. H.

INTRODUCTION

The majority of students attending American colleges and universities are relatively healthy and seldomly viewed as patients. While this segment of the population traditionally constitutes a young, healthy cohort, experience demonstrates that college and university (hereafter referred to only as college) health services play an important role in facilitating student health maintenance, completion of school, consumer health education, and the development of sound health practices and behaviors.

Although college health services cater to a select population with a reasonably well-circumscribed set of needs, they constitute an important component of the overall health care system in the United States. As a collective group, these facilities provide primary and preventive physical and mental health care services to more than eleven million students attending American colleges and universities. Having a commitment to high quality services and continually being constrained by institutional budgeting and financing limitations,[1] internal and external politics, and available health resources, college health programs lead the way in the design of many innovative prototypes for the delivery and financing[2] of health care services — group practice arrangements, shared services, prepayment and third party insurance plans, health maintenance organizations,[3] and self-insurance programs, among others. In addition, recognition of the unique contributions and cost-effectiveness of preventive health education and health promotion programs first implemented in college health programs has been instrumental in the development of similar endeavors on a much larger scale. While this chapter focuses for the most part on many ethical dilemmas involved in delivering student health services, it is important to appreciate that in many ways these settings constitute microcosms of and models for the system as a whole. Additionally, issues are examined that pertain to student rights (and responsibilities) as patients and the professional responsibilities of practitioners in college health programs around the United States.

In the normal activities of college health services, many health providers repeatedly violate the individual rights of students. Often these violations are inadvertent, but in some cases they are deliberate. They may be well- or ill-intentioned. Sometimes they are carefully conceived or executed to serve student welfare; sometimes they occur only as an expedient to cut through red tape; too often they reflect persistent stereotypes ingrained in professional education and training programs or outdated practices.

Problems of patient rights are further magnified in that student mental health services may be delivered by practitioners from diverse backgrounds with multiple levels of both formal and informal education, training, and experience. Such practitioners may have a background in psychiatry, clinical or educational psychology, counselor education, counseling, social work, public health, or peer advising. They may have reached the doctoral, master's, or baccalaureate level; they may still be at the undergraduate level.

Regardless of background, providers of all college health services (physical and/or mental) must be aware that their actions, attitudes, and personalities may be crucial influences on student development. Particular attention is needed in maintaining confidentiality and obtaining informed consent. The different stages of adolescence cause both societal and individual confusion and conflict with respect to the rights and responsibilities of young people regarding health services, their families, and themselves.

Intricate and highly sensitive issues of patient rights exist throughout the sphere of student health care. Despite the increasing complexities and scope of knowledge in areas of college health, problems related to patient rights in the delivery of such services too often precipitate an environment of fear and anxiety, distrust and avoidance, or insensitivity and uneasiness within college health programs.

This chapter addresses selected legal and ethical issues related to confidentiality and consent that have come into conflict in college health programs during recent years. The discussion focuses on the responsibilities of health care providers bound by either law or their own respective professional ethical codes. Furthermore, the problems discussed are not unique to student health services, but in a more generic sense relate to violations of patient rights in general—and particularly in cases involving minors. The examination of the ethical and legal principles of confidentiality defines areas in which breaches are most likely to occur and suggests ways of preventing their occurrence.

PRIVACY, CONFIDENTIALITY, AND PRIVILEGE: AN OVERVIEW

Initially, for purposes of clarity and the prevention of misunderstanding, it is important to define the concept of a right. In addition to the legal rights guaranteed by the Constitution and by common or statutory law, patients are entitled to ethical and common sense considerations. In other words, the reference to rights extends beyond the limited and elusive nature of the legal right to include the moral obligation of the provider to assure the privacy of the patient and the confidentiality of medical records. Thus, with the acknowledgment of the welfare and rights of patients as their primary concern, practitioners hold a professional obligation to protect the privacy of their patients and to maintain the confidentiality of all communications whether verbal or written.

Before proceeding, one should distinguish among confidentiality, privacy, and privilege. The doctrine of confidentiality has its roots in earliest medicine. It was promulgated to reassure the patient that any information volunteered to the health professional would go no further. The Oath of Hippocrates[4] initially established the duty of maintaining patient confidentiality. For the profession of medicine, its more modern interpretation can be found in the Principles of Medical Ethics of the American Medical Association (AMA), Section 9: "A physician may not reveal the confidences entrusted to him in the course of medical attendance, or the deficiencies he may observe in the character of patients unless he is required to do so by law or unless it becomes necessary in order to protect the welfare of the individual or the community."[5]

The ethic of confidentiality, however, extends beyond medicine to many health disciplines. Most codes of professional ethics governing conduct maintain principles of privacy and confidentiality. However, a wide degree of variation exists among individual practitioners regarding adherence to such ethical postures. In addition to self-imposed professional codes, there are several areas of law[a] that support the right of patient privacy. These include the right to privacy, privileged communications, and regulation of medical records.

In a legal context, a breach of confidentiality by physicians might make them liable for damages in a tort action since information obtained in the treatment process and communicated to others may be construed as defamatory.[6] Most states acknowledge the legal right of individuals to be let alone—that is, to be protected from wrongful interference in their private lives. If the disclosure of confidential medical information occurs without the consent of the patient, damages may be sought on the grounds of invasion of privacy. Generally, rights of privacy pertain to the physical or mental status of the individual or to written or published records or materials. Hence, an action for the invasion of privacy relates to the mental peace and comfort of the individual. Usually, an action for a breach of confidentiality solely concerns the reputation of the individual at stake due to the release of information given in confidence to others. In addition, the right to privacy relates to the right to be protected from defamation, and usually both are discussed when a problem of confidentiality arises.[7]

Privilege is a legal concept: It is a statutory provision based on the patient's right to privacy and confidentiality of consultation that protects physicians from testifying about medical treatment and the content of all communications related thereto. A communication is viewed as privileged if the person to whom the information is given is forbidden by law from disclosing it in court without the consent of the patient. Hence, privilege applies only to judicial proceedings: It

---

a. While many areas of law hold strong implications for all mental health disciplines, most statutory or common law references are specific for psychiatrists or covered in medical practice acts. Current trends, however, suggest that these interpretations and governing rules are broadening to include other mental health practitioners.

is a legal rule of evidence. It is a legal right that belongs only to the patient, not to the physician or other health care providers.[8]

Since the physician–patient privilege is binding only in a court of law and relates only to the medical treatment that is the subject of the lawsuit, privilege should not be perceived as a general prohibition against the dissemination of patient information by physicians.[9] Thus, for example, if the mental health status of the patient is not the subject of the proceedings, delivery of prior mental health treatment may be revealed. Major prohibitions against general dissemination are not derived necessarily from statutes; more often, protection emanates from ethical principles recorded in professional codes such as the Hippocratic Oath, the Pediatric Bill of Rights,[10] the Principles of Medical Ethics of the AMA,[11] Recommended Standards and Practices for a College Health Program,[12] or tort law created through precedent-setting decisions by appellate courts.[13]

Since the physician–patient relationship is not recognized as privileged under common law, as is the attorney–client privilege, it exists only in states that have such a statute.[14] Moreover, there are several circumstances limiting physician–patient privilege, including (1) public reporting laws; (2) areas involving patient consent to release medical information, which are often vague; (3) situations involving disclosures in the "best interests of the patient"; (4) situations in which there are "supervening interests of society"; (5) situations involving the public's right to know; and (6) situations arising during the judicial process in which common law principles apply due to the absence of state statutes.[15] Confidentiality of physician–patient relationships and medical records—the latter being the property of the physician or the hospital and considered part of confidential communications (and privileged communications where privilege is established by law)—enjoys no sweeping protection unless by state statute.[16]

PRIVACY AND STUDENT MENTAL HEALTH CARE

Although the fundamental ethical principle underlying confidentiality is the right to privacy, many related legal issues are extremely difficult to resolve clearly and therefore depend upon professional judgment. Strong policy statements in support of the rights of students (including those under the age of legal majority) have emerged from well-established professional, community service, religious, and governmental organizations and have influenced the trend toward a greater assurance of student autonomy.[17]

While most areas of health care require professional sensitivity and confidentiality, such assurances in psychotherapy are essential.[18] In reiterating this need in the delivery of mental health services, the American Psychiatric Association reports that "It is the very essence of the profession to deal with the most private corners of the patient's personal life, and scrutiny from abuses of privacy form a condition without which it would be difficult to practice psychiatry and psychotherapy at all."[19]

In a college health setting, guaranteeing the right of privacy to students may be more difficult due to their different maturational stages of development, their generally perceived low status in the college community, and frequent institutional administrative pressures. Some strong critics of student mental health programs argue that the assurance of confidentiality is impossible in a college environment. For example, Szasz views college psychiatrists as double agents with loyalty divided and confused between students and the administration.[20]

In an effort to avoid such a double agent status, the American College Health Association (ACHA)[b] is quite explicit in its recommended standards pertaining to confidentiality of health records in general and mental health records even more specifically:

> It is of critical importance that health records be processed and stored in a manner which will insure maintaining strict confidentiality regarding all information at all times. Students, no less than others, are acutely aware of how important this is in maintaining high quality care and they are quick to sense carelessness in the manner in which information is handled. It should be recognized that, in the eyes of students, an apparent breach of confidentiality will be equally as serious as an actual documented indiscretion. Every effort should be made to maintain the appearance as well as the reality of continuing dedication to confidentiality.[21]

Noted legal authorities[22] and leading college health officials[23] agree that the establishment of a sound, confidential relationship

---

b. The American College Health Association is the professional health association in which a majority of the nation's student health services and related professionals hold membership. It has established recommended standards and practices for all college health programs and until 1980 was engaged in providing formal accreditation to institutions meeting these standards and seeking such acknowledgment.

between student and therapist is fundamental in any college mental health program. According to Farnsworth, "No information about the student gained in confidence should be divulged without explicit permission. Psychiatric records should be kept separate from the other medical records and extreme care taken to protect them."[24]

ACHA officially supports this position and advocates separating actual mental health records from general health records to further protect confidentiality:

Any psychiatric, or other sensitive data should be kept separate in confidential files during treatment, and should be filed in its entirety in confidential files on completion of treatment. The general policy of not releasing information from treatment records, and the exceptions to that policy, are applicable to confidential files. However, when information is released from health records, information from separate, confidential files should not be included unless the material is specified in the request or subpoena. Any release of information should be made only after consultation with the patient. There is nothing illegal or administratively improper in the maintenance of separate confidential files for certain types of information. . . .

Notation of contact with or the date of each visit to the mental health service in the general health record is a matter of some controversy. The value of coordinated total health care must be weighed against the special importance of confidentiality of mental health contacts, including the fact of their having been a contact at all. In practice, it is often doubtful that treatment of the patient by other health service staff members is enhanced by their knowing that the patient has had one or more visits to the mental health service. No feature of the mental health service is of greater importance to students than their perception of the level of confidentiality which is practiced. No effort should be spared to establish scrupulous observance of carefully established practices and to communicate this concern to all members of the college community.[25]

Since universities and colleges create a self-contained community with an increased opportunity of acquaintance, the risk of even inadvertent breaches of confidentiality becomes more likely. College health and counseling centers often have a policy disallowing discussion of case materials among professional staff members in any location other than in the privacy of the individual practitioner's office. In fact, however, such policies rarely are adhered to in a strict manner. Colleagues often discuss mutual concerns of patients and seek advice or alternatives in an informal way in the larger clinic setting, in dining areas, around the campus, or on the street. These practices may compromise a student's privacy, are often not even done for beneficent purposes, and should be strongly discouraged. In contrast to this view, some suggest that collegial consultation should be promoted rather than stifled. Should any such limited discussion occur, it should occur only after obtaining the voluntary informed consent of the student.

In a survey of 488 ACHA-affiliated institutions, from which 173 responses were received, findings reveal a high degree of respect and endorsement of the principle of a professional, confidential relationship between student and therapist. Most health service directors identify the need to maintain confidentiality as paramount to the successful operation of any college health program.[26]

COMMUNICATION WITH OUTSIDE ORGANIZATIONS

On closer examination, Curran identifies different practices among schools in several areas, the most problematic being communication with outside organizations wanting information about selected students or access to their college health records. Problems are identified with respect to three main groups:

1. Informing parents—Only eight of 153 schools refuse to inform parents of treatment provided students under any circumstances and these are all graduate schools (in which most are either twenty-one or over and/or married). Most inform parents only in situations requiring hospitalization, of serious illness, or attempted suicide. However, twenty schools inform parents of any treatment.[27]

2. Informing the administration—Although replies vary, the majority of schools favor maintaining confidentiality. However, when students are referred to the health service by the administration, most report that students are informed at the outset that a report would be made to the dean.[28]

3. Informing outside organizations—Only eight schools report release of information to outside organizations without student consent. Nineteen release only a specific request with student permission. Refusal to release psychiatric information, even with the consent of the student, to an outside body is cited by thirteen universities.[29]

Communication and thus a breakdown in confidentiality between the health service and the administration is an extremely difficult area in which to achieve a satisfactory policy.[30] However, such communication must be avoided, since it gradually erodes the entire ethical structure and generates distrust of college health programs in the student community.[31] In this area, ACHA recommends that:

> The only information which may be given to appropriate members of the administration and faculty without the specific permission of the individual is the fact that the individual was seen at the health service, and the date and time of the visit. Inasmuch as information can be verified by others in the building at the time, this is not confidential. It should be the responsibility of the student to inform faculty, administrative officers, residential counselors and advisors, and others as needed.[32]

However, ACHA policy should be strengthened. Although the time and date of visits might be obtainable elsewhere in the college, this does not remove the ethical responsibility to maintain the confidentiality of student visits. Hence, there should be no acknowledgment to third parties by the health service of any past or forthcoming visits. More importantly, such a policy should be adopted in certain more sensitive cases, such as visits to psychiatrists or gynecologists. Any disclosure—even of limited information—should never be made without first obtaining written consent from the student.

In certain situations, particularly those in which student dismissal is pending due to academic failure or alleged misconduct or misbehavior, the college administration may send students to the health service or counseling center for evaluation and/or therapy. Their involvement, however, must occur only after their role is defined clearly to all parties. Although students may be referred, the students alone must elect to accept treatment or to undergo therapy. Coercion can never be a prelude to successful therapy.

It is of paramount importance that a clear and distinct separation exists between the administration (which has the responsibility for disciplinary action) and the health professionals involved. Rarely can disciplinary and therapeutic services emanate from the same office without seriously compromising effectiveness of the latter due to the inevitable threat, real or potential, of a breach of confidentiality.[33]

It is important for the administration to understand that college health professionals have neither a right nor an obligation to order or force therapeutic measures on students. Furthermore, the right of students to refuse treatment, especially if not under emergency conditions, is well established in law.[34]

Although the health service may be expected to verify the delivery of health care to a given student, such practices should never become routine. Furthermore, verification of treatment to the administration should be noted in advance and never forwarded prior to the proper written student authorization.[35] Failure to adhere to these policies leads to undesirable results for both students and the institution.

> For the health service to be cast in the role of disciplinarian or even to appear to assume this role, is in opposition to its purpose and is contrary to the principles of medical ethics. Matters of felony should be reported in accordance with state laws. In other disciplinary matters, as part of the management of a problem, the health professional may counsel the patient to report the matter or to take action, but the therapist's primary responsibility remains to the patient and not to any institution.[36]

Furthermore, reporting confidential information within the administrative structure of a school requires adherence to complex legal principles including privilege, responsibility to insurers, unprofessional conduct, and laws of privacy and defamation that vary among states.[37]

With respect to communication of patient information to outside organizations or to individuals other than parents or legal guardians, most colleges widely respect student rights, at least when dealing with requests from private bodies. Strict adherence to maintaining total confidentiality is often tested—and in some cases questionably compromised—in matters involving official agencies and insurance companies. According to Brown, the Peace Corps tested the limits of confidentiality through overzealous concern for their trainees during the 1960s. Student activists feared their confidentiality was not always being fully maintained by their schools.[38]

In situations involving confrontation with legal authorities, flexible policies pertaining to those given access to confidential records often arise; a mild threat of subpoena, too frequently causes information to be released prior to court order or official subpoena. Colleges seldom stand as firm student advocates by calling on their own legal counsel or outside legal resources (e.g., the American Civil Liberties Union, Neighborhood Legal Services, or other public interest law groups) to protect student privacy and confidentiality.

From theoretical and official standpoints, confidentiality in mental health care, at least, remained essential and absolute until the 1976 decision of the California Supreme Court in the case of *Tarasoff* v. *the Regents of the University of California*, which limited this principle by ruling that "the protective privilege ends when the public peril begins."[39] As a result of this ruling, at least psychiatrists, including those in college health programs, must now weigh their responsibility to protect the public from the potentially violent patient against their more familiar responsibility to treat students and to maintain their confidentiality. Due to the potential impact of this decision, Roth and Meisel warn that "rather than attempting to walk a tightrope between conflicting imperatives, the psychiatric profession might prefer to abandon its obligation of confidentiality to the patient or its role in protecting the community."[40]

COMPUTERIZATION OF STUDENT RECORDS

With the advent of computerization and collection of aggregate data,[c] related issues of disclosure of confidential information to third parties arise. Governing bodies and funding sources frequently request computerized tabulations of student data to maintain accountability and justify budgetary expenditures. State governments often mandate collection of data pertaining to the utilization of health services in educational institutions receiving public support.

Recent trends toward machine processing and computerization introduce new problems of confidentiality in health record systems. Moving away from manual tabulations, large schools have prompted the growth of centralized data banks containing personal, sociological, and academic data on students.[41] In turn, the accessibility of such sources of aggregate data fosters increasing interests in research and evaluation of college health programs around the country.

Although less apparent in other situations, the release of aggregate data in research raises a classical ethical dilemma, the conflict between individual rights and social obligations. The use of medical records for research in highly sensitive areas of counseling and mental health treatment, which have become popular areas of investigation, creates particular problems in protecting confidentiality and privacy. Assuming that there is no risk of disclosing individual student identity, sound research that will potentially benefit large seg-

---

c. For a more indepth discussion of this issue, readers are referred to Chapter 7.

ments of society—for example, the student population of a large university—poses a relatively easy decision. However, in research that may result in a loss of student confidentiality without prior consent, such intrusions may not be warranted. Such cases must be measured in the context of the potential social benefits and the individual costs and risks associated with the loss of confidentiality. More simply, do the possible social gains to be achieved by the proposed research warrant the abrogation of a student's right to autonomy?

Aggregate data for research purposes may be released under limited, well-defined, and closely supervised conditions. Again, the release of data, however, should only be authorized when there is no risk of student identification. No blanket release policies should exist, and access to aggregate data should be granted only for scientifically-sound planning and evaluation research studies focusing on issues such as financing, prevention, and health promotion. In addition, release of confidential data which could reveal student identities should never occur without obtaining prior written consent of students. Students refusing to consent, for whatever reason, ought to be assured in advance that their decision will in no way jeopardize future receipt of service.

In addition, ACHA suggests several basic principles for maintaining confidentiality of computerized records. They address issues such as preventing incorporation of medical data into central data systems, limiting identification of computer tapes or cards to numerical codes with their retention by the health service, focusing attention on possible leaks of original source material into centralized data banks, and assuring that records intended for data processing are void of sensitive information.[42]

In addition to researchers, funding sources, and governing bodies, further concerns relate to the storage and accessibility of confidential medical records within college health services. Who should have or has access to the information that they include? Should students be able to gain access to their own files both due to personal interest and to assure that no mistaken or erroneous data are included in them? What happens to the medical records when students graduate? These and many other sensitive and complex questions relate to the protection of student confidentiality and privacy and demand greater consideration and careful thought. More effective methods of securing and maintaining privacy rights should be designed, and more strictly enforced policies should be delineated to address these troublesome issues.

As health care institutions designed to meet student needs, college health and counseling programs should be aware of all options in establishing their respective standards. Requests for data can be denied without exceptions; requests can be directed to individual students in question, making any response their responsibility; requests can be reviewed jointly by provider and patient and the discussion of which can even constitute part of the treatment process; records simply can be duplicated or summarized for distribution to a third party. In summary, the policy selected by the health service will be influenced by its ethical stance as an institution and by the individual ethical codes of its director and staff.

MINORS AND THE RIGHT TO TREATMENT

Due to the importance and continual debate surrounding the provision of health care to minors without obtaining prior parental consent, particularly in sensitive areas such as sexual and mental health services, this topic deserves special attention. Most often viewed as an extension of the right to privacy, fundamental ethical and legal issues exist with respect to the treatment of minors without parental consent. As the unique needs of young people, and particularly those of minor students attending college away from home, have become more widely articulated, one of the major barriers between students under the legal age of majority and their access to and benefit from medical treatment remains individual state laws.[43]

Although most of the problems impinging on privacy rights discussed thus far relate to varying degrees to all segments of the population, the requirement of parental consent in the treatment of minors clearly invades their right to privacy. The law governing the rights, privileges, obligations, and protections of minors presents a complex, continually evolving picture and remains in a state of flux.[44] However, there appears to be an almost unanimous consensus in existing laws that minors do possess the necessary right to privacy to assure access without parental consent. When this right is challenged, there is ample precedence for litigation between a student and the institution refusing services without parental consent.

Despite the changing status of the law, numerous exceptions to the general rule arising from both common law and statutory law emerge. Unfortunately, these changes produce considerable confusion, misinterpretation, and fear of professional liability.[45] Thus, accessibility to care for students who are minors in many college health services without parental consent is somewhat limited, albeit improving. Within the past ten years, nearly every state has enacted legislation enabling defined groups of minors to consent to some or all of their own health care needs, and the trend to expand the scope of these statutes appears to be accelerating, particularly in light of recent decisions of the U.S. Supreme Court.[46]

However, practices have not fully followed modernization of the law. Many institutions continue to refuse to provide physical or mental health services to minors without parental consent, even in situations in which students fall into an emancipated minor status or in which colleges still view themselves as acting in loco parentis. A vast majority of states still recognize few if any instances when minors can be treated for medical or psychiatric conditions without parental consent according to at least one recent report.[47]

In his study of confidentiality in college mental health services, Curran found that only a small minority (8.3 percent of the 173 schools surveyed) considers that parents have a right to know about referrals and treatment in college health services.[48] It appears, however, that many students, particularly freshmen and sophomores entering college directly from high school, are unaware that they may receive health care without parental consent, which is commonly unavailable in the nonacademic community. College policies governing the right to treatment in college health facilities must be publicized widely through all available channels, or many students will remain unaware of services available on their campus. Thus, despite accessibility, the existence of perceived barriers will inhibit utilization.[49]

THE RIGHT TO INFORMED CONSENT

Arguments supporting the validity of and the need to assure informed consent[d] continue to be waged as a matter of legal discourse

---

d. For a more indepth analysis of the issue of informed consent, readers are referred to Chapter 9.

based on statutory and judicial sources of law and simply on the basis of moral or ethical command to protect individual autonomy. Further discussion relates to the division of responsibility for assuring it between the provider and the health care consumer. Based on analysis of the generally agreed upon five elements included in the informed consent process (i.e., voluntariness, provision of information, competency, understanding, and consent or refusal), clearly the most significant role must be exercised by health professionals.[50]

Students, like other patients, have both a legal and an ethical right to be fully informed and to voluntarily consent prior to initiation of any particular therapy or procedure. Unfortunately, in consenting, students often remain ill informed about the variety of dimensions or risks associated with possible treatments offered by college health services.[51] Efforts to assure total compliance with the five elements in the consent process must be advocated; appropriate protocols—and if necessary proper enforcement—should exist or be established. The importance and understanding of these five critical elements warrant an examination of their implications for college health.

Voluntariness

Students considering treatment must be able to act voluntarily. They must be free from coercion and from unfair persuasions and inducements from college administrators, faculty, parents, health service professionals, and all other parties. Furthermore, they must be aware that they alone are responsible for any decision to accept or to reject treatment or other services. Additionally, they must be instructed that acceptance or rejection of any particular treatment will have no effect on their subsequent use of health service facilities and that their interaction with the health service or its staff will be maintained in strictest confidence. In sum, students must be free actors.

Provision of Information

Students must receive all necessary information in a manner that they will understand and comprehend. This information should explain (1) the risks, discomforts, and side effects of proposed treatments; (2) the expected benefits of such treatments; and (3) any available alternative treatments and their corresponding risks, disforts, and side effects. This element of the informed consent process, in essence, constitutes the informed aspect of any future decision. Responses to any student inquiries should include a full disclosure of pertinent facts, results of clinical trials, and existing conflicting medical opinions.

Competency

Most students attending college possess the capacity to comprehend the information provided to them assuming it is presented in an uncomplicated, not overly technical manner—that is, it should not consist of professional or scientific jargon that an average person would not understand. Furthermore, when conditions such as intoxication, blindness, severe emotional upset, or others that inhibit competency to some degree are apparent, additional efforts and approaches to ensure competency must be undertaken. For example, in a college health setting, the level of a student's maturity sometimes poses a difficult question in assuming competency, particularly with respect to young freshmen and sophomores. This should not be interpreted as grounds for requiring parental consent, since the right of privacy is paramount; however, in questionable situations, it does suggest the need to expend additional efforts in the giving of information and assistance in understanding. If competency is not ascertained, any consent is tantamount to none at all. Thus, the assurance of student competency is a critical element of the process to be borne by the health service provider.

Understanding

Most judicial decisions implicitly assume that a free actor, provided with adequate information, who is competent, will understand the information and be able to make a reasonable decision with respect to the proposed medical treatment. However, in acknowledging the combined elements of competency and understanding in a college health setting, there may be some reason for concern. Where questions arise as to the assurance of competency or whether the provided information is understood, the importance of a student's understanding becomes heightened. Another distinguishing characteristic of this element is student responsibility. If students do not clearly understand all aspects of any proposed treatment, they are obliged to seek additional information, clarification, explanation of alternatives, and so forth. While the provider holds a legal and ethical obligation to provide the necessary information at a level of reasonable comprehension, students have a concomitant responsibility to be sure that they understand it prior to giving consent or rejection of any proposed treatment. Decisions by students who fail to understand the information provided mark acceptance of the paternalistic practices common in the health professions.

Consent or Refusal

Finally, the fifth element of the process calls for each student actually to make a decision—either to accept or to reject the proposed treatment. Regardless of this decision, it should not be overridden by the health service, the physician, parent(s), or any other party. In addition, students should be permitted, like other patients, to change their original decision voluntarily. Of particular importance in a college environment, however, is the guarding against undue social (e.g., peer) pressures, while acknowledging that to some degree they are avoidable. Furthermore, in this light, it is important that health service providers support whichever decision is made by students.

Hence, informed consent, predicated on an individual's right to self-determination, may be summarized as a dynamic process assuring the autonomy of patients. In sum, it constitutes a process in which information is given to a competent individual, resulting in his or her understanding. The precondition for this process is that the individual is a free actor; its culmination is understanding that will result in a decision (consent or refusal).[52]

Consent for Mental Health

One area of college health care that warrants special mention, since it commonly precipitates a misunderstanding of the joint responsibilities of providers and patients in the informed consent process, is the mental health component. Mental health professionals have particular expertise in addressing special problem areas, such as alcohol and drug abuse, family crisis, troubled relationships, birth control and pregnancy, and human sexuality, among others. However, difficulties may arise due to the preferred orientation among individual therapists, such as ego psychology, Gestalt therapy, Rogerian counseling, or an eclectic approach. In addition, different therapists commonly possess different levels of experience and seniority within the service delivery system, from junior trainees and interns to senior and supervisory positions. Further variation is generated due to the multiple treatment processes, which can range on a continuum from short-term and issue-specific to open ended and self-exploratory.

In reality, students usually enter a therapeutic relationship with the therapist available at the time they seek help. The availability of therapists holding certain orientations usually is limited by the administrative policy of the college health service based on its physical plant, its staff size, and their schedule and constraints. Offering students initial access to treatment with the practitioner of choice, while preferable, admittedly would become problematic in many cases and simply impossible in others. The dissemination of information about treatment options, therapist expertise and experience, the facilitation of the selection process, and the delivery of effective service without undue delays frequently preclude individual choice by students. Nonetheless, both students and college health professionals must share responsibility for insuring adequate opportunity for choice of treatment to maintain the students' right to self-determination and personal responsibility. As stated by Tancredi and Slaby:

> In sum, the first point along the trajectory of mental health care delivery for heightened ethical awareness is that at which a consumer must make the choice of whom to ask for help. . . . It is incumbent upon caregivers to alert consumers to the variety of treatment options for a given problem, and to who may provide these services in a way consistent with personal preferences and economic circumstances.[53]

CONCLUSION

It is unfortunate that too frequently, policies governing college health fail to support the rights of student patients. Commonly lacking is an effective mechanism to assure the protection of students and the opportunity to positively influence policymakers in a college health setting.

Even when affirmation of student rights is embodied in administrative policy, the application of college health practices frequently is inconsistent and often arbitrary. Thus, further standardization needs to be established without further delay. Then, efforts must focus on the promotion of these standards among colleges across the country. To a large extent, ethical institutional guidelines are circumscribed for college health services in the ACHA's Recommended Standards and Practices for a College Health Program. However, these standards are only recommended, and their adoption is voluntary. The next task is to achieve their more widespread adoption and some authority through which they may be programmatically enforceable.

Meanwhile, greater focus must rest with the identification of ethical responsibilities by individual college health service practitioners. Undoubtedly, personal ethical positions and value judgments will vary to some degree with policies established by health service directors and among practitioners themselves in terms of both basic stance and specific issues. However, these differences must be minimized in the students' best interests. Some mechanism to resolve inevitable conflicts that arise needs to be identified and examined amidst the plethora of existing service delivery systems. Based on such an evaluation, a formal document proposing guidelines for ethical practices and clinical integrity in the delivery of student health services should be promulgated. Such a policy statement would stipulate, clarify, and initiate the implementation of a more unified system of both the rights and the responsibilities of students and practitioners. Furthermore, the process of developing such a document facilitates (and almost necessitates) the defining of priorities by both groups. Undoubtedly, it assists in establishing a clearer understanding of the primary importance of the physician–patient (student) relationship.

An example of an effort to ensure the rights of patients at the University of New Hampshire (UNH) Student Health Service recently was developed by the University's Health Services Advisory Committee.[e] The Patient's Bill of Rights, as it has become known, is shown in Table 10-1. Endorsed by the UNH Health Services and the stu-

e. A joint committee, consisting of eight students, three faculty, and three administrative staff, including the directors of the health services and of the counseling and testing center, that advises the UNH vice-president for student affairs on campus student health and related issues.

Table 10-1. University of New Hampshire Student Health Services Patients' Bill of Rights.

1. The patient has the right to considerate and respectful *care.*

2. The patient has the right to complete and current *information* from the health care provider concerning diagnosis, treatment, and prognosis in language that the patient can readily understand.

3. The patient has the right to receive sufficient information (e.g., type of procedures to be used, risks involved, probable duration of incapacity) and to expect a stress-free situation (e.g., privacy, time to think) in order that he/she may grant *informed consent* prior to the start of any treatment. Further, the patient has the right to continued sharing of pertinent information throughout the course of treatment so that informed consent may be maintained.

4. The patient has the right to know the *names* and pertinent *qualifications* of the health care provider handling the patient's case.

5. The patient has a right to direct access to his/her *medical records.* The patient has the right to have these records explained by a health care provider and the right to have copies of these records made at his/her own expense.[a]

6. The patient has the right to *refuse* treatment, change health care providers, or seek a second opinion. This includes the right on the part of the patient to be informed by the health care provider of the possible consequences of any of these choices.

7. The patient has the right to *privacy* that includes discreet and respectful conduct of examinations and treatment, and confidentiality in the discussion of the patient's case. Further, the patient has the right to grant or deny permission for anyone not directly involved in the patient's care to be present at discussions, consultations, examinations, or during treatment.

8. The patient has the right to have all communications and records regarding the patient's care kept *confidential,* within the limits of the law.

9. The patient has the right to expect a reasonable response to a request for *services,* subject to the capacity of the health care facility and to the urgency of the case. Should transfer to another health care facility be prescribed, the patient has the right to complete information as to the reasons for such a transfer along with the information about alternative plans.

10. The patient has the right to know if the health care facility engages in or intends to engage in *experimental methods* (e.g., use of experimental drugs) in handling cases like the patient's own. Where there are experimental options available, the patient has the right to choose whether or not to participate.

Table 10-1. continued

11. The patient has the right to expect reasonable *continuity* of care; this includes knowledge of the times that health care providers are available for appointments, and the right to know the specific nature of health care requirements between visits and/or following discharge.

12. The patient has the right to examine the medical *bill* and to have it explained in simple language, regardless of who is responsible for payment.

13. The patient has the right to know the health care facility *rules* and *regulations* which govern conduct as a patient.

14. The patient has the right to available and reasonable *recourse* to a person of responsibility through normal grievance procedures within the health care facility and, if necessary, within the University so that the patient may speak of specific problems or perceived violations of these patients' rights.

a. Author's note: The status of this provision is in a state of flux and negotiation due to technical difficulties and currently is being reviewed by the University's legal counsel and Board of Trustees. Meanwhile, due to its unanimous support of this provision, the UNH Health Services Advisory Committee has sought an opinion from the New Hampshire Civil Liberties Union on this provision. A similar right has become law in neighboring states, including Massachusetts and Connecticut.

Source: University of New Hampshire Health Service (Durham: University of New Hampshire, September 1979), p. 18.

dent government, it was forwarded by the vice-president for student affairs to the University's president and board of trustees. Although unofficially in effect since 1979, it became official institutional policy with its publication in the 1980 edition of the UNH *Rights and Rules.*[54] Such model policies mark major steps toward helping to guarantee that students will receive quality health care services delivered in an ethical and professional manner through college health services.[f]

In cases involving third parties, whether from within or outside of the college or university, the college health service should assume the role of patient advocate when administrative policy and/or conflicting positions appear to threaten or infringe upon the patient's rights to privacy, confidentiality, or treatment. Although in most cases legal support is explicated clearly for only physicians, all other health practitioners face similar issues and, at least from an ethical point of view, share the same responsibilities. Furthermore, recent

f. For further details on the development of a Patients' Bill of Rights, readers may contact the author.

legal decisions have aided in the enunciation and clarification of the rights of students and of minors in particular.

Finally, many of the major legal, ethical, and clinical issues associated with the delivery of college health care have been identified. Yet much more work needs to be done. The clear delineation of consumer rights and responsibilities in health care is a popular topic, particularly among today's youth, both on and off the campus. Unfortunately, even with this added attention and advances in law and ethics, many issues remain unresolved. In some, the law supports ethical stands; in others, taking an ethical stance creates conflict with existing laws and regulations. Hence, college health policies must revolve around the promotion of the physical and mental well-being of the student population in an environment that maximizes the highest ethical codes while protecting the legal rights of patients.

NOTES TO CHAPTER 10

1. For a more extensive discussion of the budgeting and financing restrictions common to college and university health services operated under the confines of an academic-oriented environment, readers are referred to American College Health Association, "Recommended Standards and Practices for a College Health Program, Third Revision," *Journal of the American College Health Association* 25: 27–29 (March 1977); Marc D. Hiller, "The Responsible Involvement of Students in University Health Services," *Journal of the American College Health Association* 26: 132–135 (December 1977); Maurice M. Osborne, Jr., "That's Not Where the Problem Is, But That's Where It Hurts," *Journal of the American College Health Association* 21: 287–295 (April 1973).

2. Marc D. Hiller, Peter H. Patterson and Richard J. Kaufman, "A Comparative Study of Financing Rural New England University Health Services." (Presented at the 58th Annual Meeting of the American College Health Association, San Diego, California, April 10, 1980).

3. Barry W. Averill, "Planning and Development of an HMO in a University Community," *Journal of the American College Health Association* 28: 247–253 (April 1980).

4. Alan F. Westin, *Computers, Health Records, and Citizen Rights* (Washington, D.C.: U.S. Government Printing Office, 1976), p. 19.

5. American Medical Association, *Principles of Medical Ethics* (Chicago, 1957).

6. J.P. Cattell, "Position Statement on Guidelines for Psychiatrists: Problems in Confidentiality," *American Journal of Psychiatry* 126: 1543–1549 (1970).

7. Ibid.
8. Westin, p. 21.
9. Jonathan Brant, Gail Garinger, and Rene Tankenoff Brant, "So You Want to See Our Files on You," in Gerald P. Koocher, *Children's Rights and the Mental Health Professions* (New York: John Wiley and Sons, 1976), p. 124.
10. Planned Parenthood Federation of America, *The Positive Policy Handbook* (New York: Planned Parenthood Federation of America, 1975).
11. American Medical Association.
12. American College Health Association, "Recommended Standards and Practices for a College Health Program, Third Revision," *Journal of the American College Health Association* 25: 1–35 (March 1977).
13. Alan F. Westin, "Medical Records: Should Patients Have Access," *Hastings Center Report* 7: 23–28 (December 1977).
14. Westin, *Computers, Health Records, and Citizen Rights*, p. 21.
15. Ibid., pp. 21–27.
16. An example of such a specific statute was drafted for New York State to protect computerized, psychiatric patient records. See: William J. Curran, "Protection of Privacy and Confidentiality," *Science* 182: 797 (1973).
17. Planned Parenthood Federation.
18. J. Dubey, "Confidentiality as a Requirement of the Therapist: Technical Necessities for Absolute Privilege in Psychotherapy," *American Journal of Psychiatry* 131: 1093–1096 (1974); Group for the Advancement of Psychiatry, *Confidentiality and Privileged Communication in the Practice of Psychiatry, Report 45* (New York, 1960), pp. 89–112; E.A. Plaut, "A Perspective on Confidentiality," *American Journal of Psychiatry* 131: 1021–1024 (1974).
19. American Psychiatric Association, *Confidentiality and Third Parties, Task Force Report 9* (Washington, D.C., 1975).
20. Thomas S. Szasz, "The Psychiatrist as Double Agent," *Trans-Action* 4: 16–24 (1967).
21. American College Health Association, p. 18.
22. L.J. Cass and William J. Curran, "Rights of Privacy in Medical Practice," *Lancet* 2: 783–785 (1965).
23. Dana L. Farnsworth, "Confidentiality," *Harvard Medical Alumni Bulletin* 43: 29 (1968).
24. Ibid.
25. American College Health Association, p. 19.
26. William J. Curran, "Policies and Practices Concerning Confidentiality in College Mental Health Services in the United States and Canada," *American Journal of Psychiatry* 125: 1520–1530 (1969).
27. Ibid., pp. 1522–1523.
28. Ibid., pp. 1523–1524.
29. Ibid., pp. 1524–1526.

30. Ibid., p. 1524; see also Szasz.
31. American College Health Association, p. 32.
32. Ibid.
33. Ibid., p. 9.
34. Laurence R. Tancredi and Andrew E. Slaby, *Ethical Policy in Mental Health Care: The Goals of Psychiatric Intervention* (New York: Prodist, 1977), pp. 102–103.
35. American College Health Association, p. 32.
36. Ibid., p. 34.
37. Ibid., p. 32.
38. James R. Brown, "Patient Rights: The Berkeley Experience (Abstract)," *Journal of the American College Health Association* 27:42 (August 1978).
39. Ibid.; Tarasoff v. Regents of the University of California, et al. 131 Cal. Rptr. 14, 551 P.2d 234 (Cal. 1976).
40. Loren H. Roth and Alan Meisel, "Dangerousness, Confidentiality, and the Duty to Warn," *American Journal of Psychiatry* 134: 508–511 (1977).
41. American College Health Association, p. 20.
42. Ibid.
43. Lee J. Dunn, Jr., "The Availability of Abortion, Sterilization, and Other Medical Treatment for Minor Patients," *University of Missouri–Kansas City Law Review* 44:1–22 (Fall 1975).
44. Adele D. Hofmann, "A Rational Policy Toward Consent and Confidentiality in Adolescent Health Care," *Journal of Adolescent Health Care* 1:9–17 (September 1980); Marc D. Hiller, *U.S. Family Planning Policy: Its Effect on the Support, Organization, and Delivery of Services to Teenagers in Pittsburgh, PA.* (Ann Arbor: Xerox University Microfilms, 1978); Adele D. Hofmann and Harriet F. Pilpel, "The Legal Rights of Minors," *Pediatric Clinics of North America* 20: 989–1004 (November 1973); W. Wadlington, "Minors and Health Care: The Age of Consent," *Osgoode Hall Law Journal* 11: 115–124 (1973); L.P. Wilkins, "Children's Rights: Removing the Parental Consent Barrier to Medical Treatment for Minors," *Arizona State Law Journal* 1975: 31–92 (1975); Angela Roddey Holder, *Legal Issues in Pediatrics and Adolescent Medicine* (New York: John Wiley and Sons, 1977), pp. 135–157.
45. Holder, pp. 135–157.
46. Ibid.; Eve W. Paul and Harriet F. Pilpel, "Teenagers and Pregnancy: The Law in 1979," *Family Planning Perspectives* 11:297–302 (September/October 1979).
47. Brant, Garinger, and Brant.
48. Curran, "Policies and Practices Concerning Confidentiality."
49. Marc D. Hiller, *The University of Pittsburgh Student Health Survey: The Evolution of a Student Health Care Facility* (Pittsburgh: University of Pittsburgh Graduate School of Public Health, 1976).

50. Loren H. Roth, Charles W. Lidz, and Alan Meisel, "Summary of Study of Informed Consent" (Pittsburgh: University of Pittsburgh School of Medicine Department of Psychiatry, 1975), pp. 3-5.

51. Marc D. Hiller, "Informed Consent—Ethical Issues in Determining Responsibility" (Presented at the 57th Annual Meeting of the American College Health Association, Washington, D.C., May 24, 1979).

52. Roth, Lidz, and Meisel, p. 4.

53. Tancredi and Slaby, pp. 51-52.

54. University of New Hampshire, *Caboodle/Rights and Rules* (Durham, 1980), pp. 35-36.

11 ETHICS AND ADMINISTRATIVE PRACTICES IN LONG-TERM CARE

Annabelle L. Kleppick, Ph.D.

Long-term care administrators, in common with other organizational managers, are faced with a variety of ethical problems in managing their institutions. Some cause little or no controversy. To illustrate, since an organization's lawful continuance depends on its goals being in consonance with societal aims, an assumption may be made that those that have public acceptance are meeting this standard and that occasional disagreements usually involve degree and not kind. With others, there is constant disagreement, which may involve employees, owners, and consumers. In addition to these problems of a business nature, long-term care administrators have a circumstance specific to their type of institution that brings them increasingly under consumer and governmental scrutiny and censure. Their distinctive problem lies in the nature of the population they serve. Long-term care patients are characterized by chronic ill-health, dependency, agedness, limited resources, and institutionalization over a period of years, if not for the balance of their lives.

This chapter discusses selected ethical issues relevant to administrative practices in the care of the institutionalized aged. The examination of ethics for administration is not based on any specific philosophical theory of ethics. Rather, it focuses on the attitudes and values of those persons and institutions providing care for the aged from the perspectives of both society and the individual and on how, either singly or in combination, they affect ethical practices in the administration of long-term care institutions.

RIGHTS AND VALUES

Ethics relates simply to the rightness or the wrongness of certain actions and of the motives and the ends of such actions. Values, which are more germane to this discussion, refer to the desirable — either the means to an end or the end in itself. They connote an evaluation of moral or social good.[1] As codes attached to things or events and fashioned through historic circumstances, values reflect changing priorities of society over time. Although the worth of a thing or object may not change (i.e., its essential goodness or badness), its priority varies as the level of development of a society advances or regresses.

Values are at the root of choices and behavior. The behavior of individuals in general reflects the values of the society in which they live. However, there may be differences in the congruence between the behavior of some individuals and the priority of society's values attached to that which individual behaviors are directed.

Good health, for example, is a value that has always been widely recognized but applied differentially across social classes. The history of its antonym, illness, indicates that society through the centuries has regarded illness variously as a sign of unworthiness (as in the Greek tradition), as a punishment for sins (as in the Hebraic interpretation), or as a means of grace with a concomitant obligation for caring (as in the Christian view). Today, good health is considered by many to be so important that it has become regarded as a human right of every person regardless of social or economic worth.

Concepts of who has a right to good health and the appropriate agencies through which health services are delivered have had a reciprocal influence on society and its health institutions. Hospitals exemplify a favorable shift in attitudes and values. During the present century, attitudes have changed from low to high esteem as the curative functions of these institutions became a reality, which in turn contributed to their assuming a position of predominant value for society. Today, hospitals are viewed as valuable resources for diagnosis, treatment, and recovery of patients. They contribute to the common good by returning people to their productive functions in society.

Long-term care institutions, by contrast, occupy a different place on the value continuum. A portrait of patients packed into every available space in a ramshackle building and being constantly physically and mentally mistreated, while Medicaid is charged for services poorly or never performed, is commonly projected by critics of nursing homes. Accompanying this picture is a stereotyped image of the long-term care administrator as a venal self-server making money from defenseless, friendless, resourceless, and apathetic old people. Once regarded as a necessary social invention, the basis for the existence of long-term care institutions is coming under increasing attack.

The latter part of the twentieth century sees the American philosophy of a "fundamental belief in the uniqueness of the individual, in his basic dignity, and as a human being"[2] as far from a reality. There are numerous accounts documenting the rejection of the aged and the low value attached to the quality of oldness by society in general. Recently, Donahue poignantly described the status of the aged in America: "In the American value system old men and old women have long since depreciated in worth; in consequence, when they become dependent on others to care for them and to determine in large part the quality of their lives, they are doomed to suffer many indignities from those who consider them to be without value."[3] Reflecting the ambivalence of society toward aging and the aged, long-term institutional care, in spite of the efforts of both its supporters and its critics to effect necessary changes, has numerous unresolved ethical issues of a humanistic, business, and social nature.

Since problems generally have historical roots, a brief review of the past may help in an understanding of the reasons why ethical issues continue to plague these institutions. Long-term care as a societal concern originated in the provision of shelter for the powerless — namely, the poor, the homeless wayfarer, the mentally disabled, the physically handicapped, and the orphan, among others. The major concern of religious orders historically has involved the giving of charity.

As society passed from a religious to a secular orientation, the provision of shelter was shared by the public and private sectors through the development of poor farms, county workhouses, orphanages, insane asylums, and other institutions for individuals unable to be self-sufficient. Such institutions were usually located away from the cities and towns intentionally; their inhabitants, viewed as intrinsically worthless, were isolated and rejected by the rest of society. Only the barest of services, supervised by unqualified persons, were provided, and abuses proliferated and went unchecked. Society's concerns were elsewhere—in a productive work force; in an entrepreneurial free enterprise system that has no place for misfits; and in expanding and building in the social, economic, and political realms. The provision of subsistence for the nonproductive was not, for the most part, motivated by charity or philanthropy. It was viewed simply as a societal responsibility. Quality was not an issue, since the people to whom it was directed were seen as having little if any redeeming social value.

The Depression, enactment of social welfare legislation intended to give people financial resources in their old age, establishment of a mandatory retirement limit, and the general aging of the population overall led to a shift in social philosophy. Medical advances following the Second World War had a dramatic effect on the average life expectancy and the growth in the numbers of the aged. More persons were living longer. Unfortunately, many of them had no families nor a place to live because the family structure had undergone significant changes, and they suffered from chronic diseases for which medical care was needed. Through a variety of routes, these people became nursing home residents or patients.

Preceding the enactment of Medicare and Medicaid in 1965, concern grew for the treatment of the aged in old age institutions. Medicare to some extent, and Medicaid to a much larger degree, have provided funds and established minimal standards for nursing home operations, and all states have adopted licensure laws.

Abuses and problems, however, continue to be uncovered, particularly in areas of patient care. The media have provided extensive coverage of these acts. This chapter focuses on those acts that are administrative in nature—specifically, the intrusion of institutions through their administrative practices on the rights of the patients as human beings, their failure to respect the dignity of patients, and their failure to protect patients from being used as subjects of research.

THE ADMINISTRATOR AND THE INSTITUTION

An institution, as a form of organization, is a social invention that bears the obligation to contribute to the public good, to conserve its resources through just allocation and responsible use, and to be responsive to the welfare of its human resources. An institution in operation is not an inanimate legal creation—it is a group of people working in concert to achieve a specific mission. Although the institution is more than the administrator (i.e., it comprises a board of directors, employees, and patients), this person, as its chief operating officer, is its primary decisionmaker and leader. As such, administrators exert the most pervasive influence on the ethical actions practiced in institutions. Thus, neither an institution nor its administrator can be viewed apart from each other.

Long-term care institutions have been castigated for failing to provide an ethos that recognizes the unique characteristics of their residents and their multifaceted needs. Gerontologists and other human service professionals have conducted lengthy research on numerous aspects of institutional environments, including staff, patients, and structure. Their findings have revealed poor quality of care and staff inadequacies.[4] Ethical practices of institutions have also been researched in terms of accountability. Conclusions suggest problems ranging from reimbursement deficiencies, to staff insensitivity, to community intervention, to weaknesses inherent in an institutional model.[5] Representative of the variables whose investigation has indicated the multidimensional nature of ethical problems confronting long-term care administrators are those concerned with practices of patient care staff and management personnel.

Employees in health institutions have a variety of emotions and ambitions that they bring to a formal work setting.[6] This explains why some staff use their jobs solely as a means of career advancement while others view them simply as a means to generate an income. In both of these situations, patients receive the lowest priority.

Lack of qualified, well-trained staff at the aide level, that which is most crucial for the daily interaction with patients, was documented by the Subcommittee on Long Term Care of the U.S. Senate Special Committee on Aging.[7] Staff often believe that they perform a more professional job when patients are submissive and simply follow orders. Such an environment can contribute little to the goal of humane treatment, which requires concentration on the distinctively human aspects of the individual, involving concepts of integration, goal setting, and self-actualization.[8]

Researchers also identify institutional faults. For example, institutions are more responsive to societal awareness of a rundown building or lack of supplies than to the apathy or hopelessness manifested by the residents.[9] The usual organizational goals of maximum efficiency and productivity are seen as the antithesis of humane care. Rigid adherence to administrative rules is another dehumanizing factor, because it prevents older persons from exercising any sense of control over their environment. The administrative process is viewed as unsupportive of the patients' best interests. Accordingly, when the power balance between providers and patients is disturbed and providers dominate the control of decisions affecting patients, abuses occur.[10] Similarly, if the affairs of institutions receive priority over the needs of the patients, then the values may be on efficiency and effectiveness rather than on individuation of care.

A crucial issue in long-term care administration is the determination of the appropriate area and level of administrative intervention in patient care. Certainly, administrators are not to be involved in the process of care—that is, that set of activities involving what is to be done to or for a patient with respect to a specific disease, complaint, or episode of illness, together with an evaluation of the efficiency of the care.

Bergman fashioned a role for administrators when he declared that "[t]he nursing home administrator neither can nor should be exempted from involvement in the on-going search for a moral and ethical framework to use in the definition of responsibilities of human care."[11] He perceived this kind of responsibility as one of the components of long-term care administration, notwithstanding the fact that it is still not widely recognized as such.

Tessaro, Kleppick, and Sumner, in formulating a mechanism to ensure better patient care, proposed an advocacy role for administrators through institutional policies.[12] Without question, administrators bear a moral and ethical responsibility to be advocates for patients in cases of staff abuse. Furthermore, administrators should intervene as advocates for patients in gaining more control over their lives and in participating in decisions about their care.

The managerial function of controlling, including evaluation, can be a mechanism for improving quality of care through reappraising the institution's structure and organization and examining the use, qualifications, and attitudes of patient care staff. When dealing with the welfare of patients, sensitive management and clearly written policies and rules ought to be used. Sensitizing staff to the needs of the aged can curb undesirable staff conduct.

The profit motive in a health care institution applies to the predominant form of nursing home ownership—the proprietary nursing home. In their book, *The Value Issue of Business*, Elbing and Elbing discuss the problems of applying the various theories of sound ethical practices to business and their implications for those engaged in business. They observe that "those who wish to promote values in addition to profit may sometimes have to do so at the potential risk or actual loss of some profit. Some situations force us to make a choice among values, and we take risks for what we value most."[13]

Unquestionably, through the process of administration, administrators have a major impact on the quality of care. Their values influence their institutions' programs, policies, and personnel and their allocations of limited resources. Their leadership efforts influence the quality and the nature of the activities of their personnel in attaining institutional goals.

THE PATIENT AS A PERSON

An ethical principle relevant to the care of the elderly is respect for persons. Albeit implicit in the preceding discussion, such respect is a moral obligation of administrators and institutions. The fact that many patients live multiple years in long-term care facilities (as opposed to in acute care institutions) is a distinctive characteristic of long-term care institutions. Hence, there is an added responsibility to provide an environment based upon a sound moral and ethical framework—involving all personnel—to assure that the behavior and practices of all parties support an institutional policy of respect for persons. All too often, long-term care institutions dismiss this need of patients as being too costly to provide or being simply unnecessary in the provision of long-term care services.

The fundamental ethical basis for such care is respect for the dignity of patients. Dignity means merit or worth. It includes recognition of one's worth both by others and by one's self. Respect means recognizing the worth and/or the rights of others. Bandman and Bandman link the concept of rights with dignity and describe rights as "an indispensably valuable moral possession."[14] Having rights, they say, is "to have dignity and respect and is the basis of self-respect as well."[15] Jonsen defines respect for persons as "the principle that each individual be seen . . . as equal to every other."[16]

Another ethical principle that is central to the idea of respect is autonomy. Autonomy, or the right to self-determination, must be assured if dignity and a sense of self-worth are to accompany long-term care of the elderly. Alternatively, the opposite of autonomy—dependency—is fostered in the care of the elderly. Jonsen views the creation of dependency as an "essential immorality of treatment of the elderly."[17] To ensure respect of the elderly as individuals and as a class, their unique needs and desires should be determined, and their traditional categorization, amounting to a stereotyped image, must cease.

Institutional living generally increases the likelihood of suffering indignities. The environment of most nursing homes is impersonal, and the atmosphere is sometimes sterile and demeaning. Patients have to relinquish much of their freedom and autonomy and most of the control of their affairs. Termination of usual routines, former lifestyles, and linkages with family and friends affects decrementally the dignity of the aged. The lack of respect for institutionalized patients has negative effects both on them and on their ability to adjust to an institutional environment.[18] Negative attitudes beget negative attitudes. Staff with poor attitudes toward the aged and aging foster maladaptive behavior among the elderly.[19] A probable reflection of staff attitudes toward the aged is the cause of the increase in their negative self-image after institutionalization.[20]

The lack of staff respect for each other may further extend to patients; problems in the personal lives of staff may also affect their treatment of patients.[21] A recent "Special Report on State Long Term Care Activities" revealed that in a six month period in 1978, there were eighty-nine cases of physical abuse reported and sustained in residential health care facilities. More than 150 additional cases were reported but not sustained.[22]

Lack of respect for patients is also demonstrated through administrative conduct. In March 1979, after a careful review, the comptroller general of the United States reported that the personal funds of patients were being mishandled. Deficiencies cited included shortages, unauthorized charges, and withholding of funds.[23]

Reservations have been expressed about achieving respect and dignity for the aged. Viewing the problem as one of the values of the total society rather than one specific to institutions, Donahue concludes:

It is questionable whether prescription and proclamation alone can dissipate the deep seated personal rejection of aging and agedness and substitute an ethic of dignity which will so permeate the American value system that conscience will automatically inhibit indignities and mistreatment of elderly patients.[24]

PROTECTION OF PATIENTS IN RESEARCH

Biomedical research and, to a greater degree, social science research view nursing homes as a valuable source of fruitful populations for investigations in general and those involving the aged in particular. The expressions of concern for the protection of human subjects in these kinds of research are of relatively recent origin. In the course of clarifying legal and ethical responsibilities in the conduct of research using human subjects, special populations have been identified for whom an additional protection of rights must be guaranteed. The aged were not among these populations identified by federal agencies.

Wales and Treybig[25] and Reich[26] have documented that the aged are not protected against abuses by special administrative or regulatory provisions. In reviewing legislative enactments from 1962 to 1977, Wales found none that established the aged as an especially vulnerable group.[27] In 1978, Reich further noted that absent from the extensive studies conducted by the National Commission for the Protection of Human Subjects of Biomedical and Behavioral Research were any dealing with ethical and policy dimensions of using the aged in research.[28] These investigators questioned whether the aged had distinctive characteristics or circumstances that increased their vulnerability as research subjects. Wales and Treybig suggested that the question of special risk be investigated from the viewpoint of how the aged might be at risk. For example, is age itself a hazard? Age could indeed be a risk factor from the physiological standpoint, as well as from a social one.[29]

Reich identified a number of ethical issues having relevance for research with the aged. Inasmuch as the conduct of research within long-term care facilities requires the consent and cooperation of the respective nursing home administrators, key issues arise in which they should be involved on behalf of their institutionalized patients— namely, the goals and purposes of the research, the selection process of subjects, and the problem of competence of and the ability to obtain voluntary informed consent of the aged patient. In addition, the usefulness, necessity, and applicability of the research, from both the institutions' and patients' standpoints should be assessed. Moreover, the motivation of the researchers and their ability to protect the research subjects from unnecessary physical and mental risk need to be established.

The selection process itself raises a number of important ethical issues. Being a patient in an institution, as evidenced by the National Commission's interest in research in prisons and in mental institutions, increases the possibility of selection as a research subject. One proposed criterion for selection of subjects ought to be the principle of equity in the selection process—that is, involving all segments of society and avoiding discrimination against captive populations such as the institutionalized. Patients are especially vulnerable to selection as research subjects on variables of age, disease entities, locus of residence, mental impairments, and types of inducements that may make participation attractive because of the interaction of some of the above factors. Furthermore, they constitute ideal subjects, since with the exception of death, they are seldom lost to follow-up.[30]

Competence and informed consent are vitally important problems for researchers, subjects, and administrators of institutions. Serious negative factors can greatly impair competence and negate free consent. The aged have a high incidence of physical and psychiatric impairments and chronic illnesses. These conditions, which from the viewpoint of researchers appear attractive, can produce a reduction in the aged population's competence to judge the personal advantages of their participation (if any) and even whether they have the freedom to consent or refuse. Increased feelings of dependency and helplessness may obscure the abilities of patients to make independent judgments about the personal or societal value of the research, especially that of a biomedical nature.

In addition to functional losses, the aged also suffer from those of a social and economic nature. These, too, may influence the decision to be a research subject. Institutionalized elderly are especially vulnerable because as captive populations, they can be manipulated by subtle, covert pressures without recourse to any protecting mechanism, agency, or intervention.[a] Coercion to consent can take many

a. For a more in-depth discussion of the possible uses (and abuses) of covert research, readers are referred to Chapter 19.

forms, including conformity to institutional expectations. Research documents that institutionalization leads to psychological dependence on staff and that resistance to institutional staff contributes to fears of (or actual) loss of privileges.[31] Under such conditions, free or informed consent is nonexistent. Wales and Treybig further question whether the older generation possesses sufficient knowledge to make judgments, since they come from an era in which the uses and abuses of research were not as widely publicized as they are now.[32]

In summation, protection from exploitation is an important component of humane care of the aged. Failure to protect elderly patients from inappropriate research forces one to question the quality of life in long-term care institutions and the ethical stance of their administrators. In not exercising an advocacy role and by not standardly employing institutional research committees[b] to review all research proposals, administrators fail to define their role with patients and to use standard management practices in their decisionmaking.

CONCLUSION

Ethical practices in long-term care facilities serving the aged are complicated by societal ambivalence on the value of a nonproductive segment of society. Further complicating the situation is a lack of clarification of the role of administrators in patient care.

There are many kinds of people and organizations involved in long-term care, each of which commonly represents a different value hierarchy. Conflicts between and among the care givers and their constituents—or consumers of the services—are resolved through compromise, most likely reached in the political arena. Since this manner of development proscribes arriving at a consensus on ethical values, multiple codes of ethics have proliferated: Thus, there is no single code governing long-term care. In addition, federal and state regulations have proliferated and govern many actions in the delivery of long-term care. Ethical problems have in many cases evolved into legal matters, and thereby questions of right (or ethical) conduct have become questions of lawful conduct.

b. Such committees, charged with the responsibility of reviewing research protocols for projects seeking the use of human subjects, are commonly referred to as institutional review boards (IRBs). IRBs have been the subject of extensive study, particularly by the National Commission for the Protection of Human Subjects of Biomedical and Behavioral Research. A further description of them is provided in Chapter 20.

Although research on long-term care institutions has examined both structural and administrative details and components of patient care, the centrality of the administrator's role in planning, organizing, staffing, and controlling patient care services has not been clearly identified. With respect to the residents of long-term care facilities, this role needs clarification. The multiple societal and personal values that comprise integral parts of work settings must also be included in such a definition. Both administrators and their staffs are acted upon by internal and external social and ethical systems; in turn, they act upon these systems. A role that does not recognize these interrelationships will be inadequately conceived.

There are many explanations of why individuals often find themselves being censured for previously accepted practices. One significant reason may be their failure to keep abreast of new concepts or values that affect their particular work environment. Although the problem is too complex to discuss in the context of this study, it is a fact that regardless of reason, a gap has developed between ethical practices in long-term care institutions and society's evaluation of their morality.

In appraising their institutions, administrators must understand that having qualified professional staff and modern, high quality equipment does not ensure the delivery of humane treatment. Furthermore, administrators must question an institutional ambience that fosters dependency, deterioration, and other behavioral manifestations associated with a loss of self-image. They must realize that legislation or prescriptive measures cannot fully change or prevent such situations. The mission of each institution must be examined and related to its overall management philosophy, including the role of the administrator in patient care. They are all part of what must be viewed as a total pattern.

Thus, long-term care administrators must assume dual roles in conducting their professional responsibilities. Their initial set of functions consists of exercising the usual managerial tasks necessary for the provision of patient care services. The second set, as defined in this chapter, includes those that call upon administrators to serve as patient advocates. This will not be an easy task, since at times it may bring them into conflict with those who render direct patient care or even with some who may serve on their board of directors. However, the tendency to organize the institution around the delivery of medical services (i.e., following the traditional medical model found in most acute care institutions) must be overcome. Long-term care administrators must critically examine the administrative practices that reinforce this medically-oriented concept in many nursing homes.

In seeking long-term care, the whole person comes for care—in contrast to the patient seeking solely physical treatment, who comes to the acute care institution. The long-term care patient must be treated from physical, social, and psychological perspectives. An overemphasis on medical care can and has acted as a deterrent to the creation of supportive psychosocial aspects of patient care that are important components of humane care.

It may never be possible—or even necessary—to establish a single code of ethics for long-term care. However, it is desirable and possible for administrators to bring a sense of the just and the right to bear on the relationship between long-term care institutions and patients. In so doing, the care provided will be most appropriate to the individual needs of the patients and will be delivered in an environment of support and respect.

In conclusion, it should be reemphasized that not all of the values discussed in this chapter can or should be legislated. Laws and regulations are aimed at preventing the behavioral manifestations of questionable ethics, such as physical abuse. They do not correct the basic cause of the immoral or inhumane action, nor can they require a choice among alternatives when the options are not basically immoral.

Thoughtful criticisms have been made about legislating ethics. Lawton suggests that true ethical standards develop more through evolution than from enforced legal decisions.[33] Herbert illustrates that ethics formalized into law may still not be adhered to. He argues that morality is conformity to the rules of right conduct, regardless of whether they have or have not been cemented into law.[34] Hence, as many who are concerned about ethics and the aged agree:

Few of the issues raised by aging and the existence of the aged and those with chronic diseases requiring special care will be solved by dollars alone or by politics as usual. Solutions will be found when the people of the nation start relating their Judeo-Christian ethic to all social issues in a sincere and meaningful way.[35]

NOTES TO CHAPTER 11

1. J. Elbing and C. Elbing, *The Value Issue of Business* (New York: McGraw-Hill Book Company, 1967), p. 7.
2. W. Donahue, "Maintaining Dignity of Patients," in W. Winston and A. Wilson, III, *Ethical Considerations in Long Term Care* (St. Petersburg, FL: Eckard Gerontology Center, 1977), p. 167.
3. Ibid., pp. 159–160.
4. J. I. Kosburg and S. S. Tobin, "Variability among Nursing Homes," *The Gerontologist* 12: 214–219 (1972); S. Levey, H. S. Ruchlin et al., "An Appraisal of Nursing Home Care," *Journal of Gerontology* 28: 222–228 (1973); N. Anderson, "Approaches to Improving the Quality of Long-Term Care for Older Persons," *Journal of Gerontology* 14: 519–524 (1974); J. G. Zimmer, "Characteristics of Patients and Care Provided in Health-Related and Skilled Nursing Facilities," *Medical Care* 13: 992–1010 (1975); M. W. Linn, "Predicting Quality of Patient Care in Nursing Homes," *The Gerontologist* 14: 225–227 (1974).
5. J. L. Barney, "Community Presence as a Key to Quality of Life in Nursing Homes," *American Journal of Public Health* 64: 265–268 (1965); R. Penchansky and L. J. Taubenhaus, "Institutional Factors Affecting the Quality of Care in Nursing Homes," *Geriatrics* 20: 591–598 (1965); L. E. Gottesman, "Nursing Home Performance as Related to Resident Traits, Ownership, Size and Source of Payment," *American Journal of Public Health* 64: 269–276 (1974).
6. D. Schwartz, "The Patient's Bill of Rights and the Hospital Administrator," in E. Bandman and B. Bandman, *Bioethics and Human Rights* (Boston: Little, Brown, and Company, 1978), pp. 277–280.
7. U.S. Congress, Senate, Special Committee on Aging, Subcommittee on Long Term Care, *Nursing Home Care in the United States: Failure in Public Policy, Supporting Paper No. 4, Nurses in Nursing Homes: The Heavy Burden—The Reliance on Untrained and Unlicensed Personnel* (Washington, D.C.: U.S. Government Printing Office, April 1975).
8. E. Kahana, "The Humane Treatment of Old People in Institutions," *The Gerontologist, Part I* 13: 282–289 (Autumn 1973).
9. Ibid., pp. 284–285.
10. Laurence R. Tancredi and Andrew E. Slaby, *Ethical Policy in Mental Health Care* (New York: Prodist, 1977), p. 96.
11. S. Bergman, "Conversation with a Gerontologist," *The Journal of Long Term Care Administration* 3: 10 (Summer 1975).
12. E. Tessaro, A. Kleppick, and W. Sumner, "Protecting Patients' and Facilities' Rights: The Advocating Administrator" (Pittsburgh: University of Pittsburgh Graduate School of Public Health, n.d.).

13. Elbing and Elbing, p. 36.
14. B. Bandman and E. Bandman, "General Introduction," in Bandman and Bandman, *Bioethics and Human Rights*, p. 8.
15. Ibid.
16. Albert R. Jonsen, "Principles for an Ethics of Health Services," in Bernice L. Neugarten and Robert J. Havighurst, *Social Policy, Social Ethics, and the Aging Society* (Washington, D.C.: U.S. Government Printing Office, 1976), p. 98.
17. Ibid.
18. M.I. Spetter, "Growing Older in America: Can We Restore the Dignity of Age," in Bandman and Bandman, *Bioethics and Human Rights*, p. 203.
19. R. Bennett and J. Eckman, "Attitudes toward Aging: A Critical Examination of Recent Literature and Implications for Future Research," in C. Eisdorfer and M. Lawton, *The Psychology of Adult Development and Aging* (Washington, D.C.: American Psychological Association, 1973), pp. 575-597.
20. R. Bennett and C. Eisdorfer, "The Institutional Environment and Behavior Change," in S. Sherwood, *Long Term Care* (Holliswood, NY: Spectrum Publications, 1975), pp. 406-407.
21. Schwartz, p. 279.
22. "State Roundup: A Special Report on State Long Term Care Activities," *Long Term Care* 8: 3 (July 6, 1979).
23. Office of the Comptroller General, *Report to the Senate Subcommittee on Long Term Care Special Committee on Aging* (Washington, D.C.: U.S. Government Printing Office, March 18, 1976).
24. Donahue, p. 168.
25. J. Wales and D. Treybig, "Recent Legislative Trends Towards Protection of Human Subjects," *The Gerontologist* 18: 244-249 (1978).
26. W. Reich, "Ethical Issues Related to Research Involving Elderly Subjects," *The Gerontologist* 18: 326-337 (1978).
27. Wales and Treybig, p. 244.
28. Reich, p. 326.
29. Wales and Treybig, pp. 247-248.
30. Marc D. Hiller, "The Administrator and Research Involving Human Subjects." Durham, NH. 1980 (unpublished).
31. J. Makarushka and R. McDonald, "Informed Consent, Research and Geriatric Patients: The Responsibility of Institutional Review Committees," *The Gerontologist* 19: 61-65 (1979); S. Berkowitz, "Informed Consent, Research and the Elderly," *The Gerontologist* 18: 237-243 (1978).
32. Wales and Treybig, p. 248.
33. A. Lawton, "Issues for Medical Care Personnel," in Winston and Wilson, *Ethical Considerations in Long Term Care*, pp. 147-156.

34. Victor Herbert, "Acquiring New Information While Retaining Old Ethics," in Philip H. Abelson, *Health Care: Regulations, Economics, Ethics, Practice* (Washington, D.C.: American Association for the Advancement of Science, 1978), p. 231.
35. Lawton, p. 155.

▌▌▌ CONFLICTING VALUES IN MENTAL HEALTH

Probably few areas of health care are more misunderstood or carry such a strong negative social value as mental disability. Historically, society has chosen an "out of sight, out of mind" philosophy characterized by the lack of both public and private commitments to the mentally disabled and the system to provide the necessary services for them. Dramatic accounts of the plight of those so labeled appear in such classic works as Irving Goffman's *Asylums*[1] and Frederick Wiseman's "Titicut Follies."[2] Still today, individuals confronting mental health problems commonly must choose whether to go without adequate treatment, to seek therapy amid a veil of secrecy, or to openly risk public scorn. Those who may not have had a choice to voluntarily elect treatment, in some cases, have confronted institutionalization without appropriate treatment, without any treatment, or with inhumane incarceration, largely due to instances of society's and the health professions' neglect.

Social pressure often continues to push mental health into a closet as if it were the plague despite evidence that up to 15 percent of the U.S. population may be in need of some form of professional mental health services at any one time.[3] Furthermore, the stigma and fear attached to mental illness can harm, or destroy, one's professional career and irreparably damage one's personal life. Noted public figures, such as U.S. Senator Thomas Eagleton, and countless others,

261

have paid high dues for undergoing mental health treatment and risking public disclosure.

Individuals seeking short-term or intermittent therapy for minor conditions related to emotional upsets, depression, or other common neuroses risk encountering less than sensitive and understanding public reaction; those institutionalized—either voluntarily or involuntarily—for more severe, chronic conditions such as character disorders, psychoses, or mental retardation often face public scorn and unprofessional (and inhumane) practices. Of particular concern in the delivery of mental health services is the violation of patient rights—to respect, dignity, and compassion, to confidentiality and privacy, to informed consent, to receive or to refuse treatment. Furthermore, issues involving the use of the mentally disabled or the institutionalized infirm in human experimentation commands public attention.[4]

Fortunately, major changes have and are continuing to occur during the second half of the twentieth century. During the last thirty-five years many modern, effective therapies have undergone development; society has begun to become more aware of the broad based needs for a wide range of mental health care. While the mental health movement will long remember the sensitivity and commitment of its early crusaders such as Dorothea Dix who led the early battles of the mid-1800s, more recent public policy reminds us of John F. Kennedy's drive to establish a national community mental health and mental retardation program. Most recently, history has recorded the efforts and sensitivity of Rosalynn A. Carter in advocating the establishment of and then serving as the honorary chairperson for the President's Commission on Mental Health in the late 1970s.

Despite the advances and the work of private citizen-action and public interest organizations in assuring more human and legal rights, much remains to be done. Deinstitutionalization efforts and the establishment of group homes continue to meet strong, harsh community resistance. Many institutionalized mentally infirm are still at the risk of unethical and inhumane practices, particularly some who become nonconsenting subjects of biomedical and behavioral research. More recently, human experimentation involving psychosurgery has generated considerable debate in professional, scientific, and public arenas. The practice of involuntary institutionalization is undergoing significant discussion, particularly when issues of privacy rights and questions of competency are raised. Dramatic accounts of failures in mental health treatment have been portrayed in several documentaries and have been the subject of several investigations during the 1970s. Possibly the popular film, "One Flew Over the Cuckoo's Nest," under the technical direction of Dean K. Brooks, M.D., Superintendent of the Oregon State Hospital (the site where the film was made) and the news media coverage of several successful court battles waged by such groups as the Mental Health Law Project in Washington, D.C., have heightened public awareness. Furthermore, the documentation of individual cases, such as Kenneth Donaldson's personal recollection of his long-term involuntary commitment in a Florida state mental institution in his book, *Insanity Inside Out*,[5] has contributed to an increased public appreciation and understanding of the problems and conflicting values in mental health.

From the perspective of the mental health professional, additional problems associated with ethical and legal dilemmas exist. In some medical circles, psychiatrists are shunned by their professional colleagues in comparison to the recognition heaped upon many in more traditional specialities—such as surgery, internal medicine, or pediatrics. At the same time, the image of psychiatry is tarnished by headlines describing the unprofessional behaviors of some psychiatrists (e.g., the popular tale of the male psychiatrist taking sexual advantage of his female patients under the guise of therapy). Further, the modern psychiatrist is often cast in a dual role—on one hand, as a physician, he or she is bound by a professional code of ethics to maintain patient privacy and confidentiality; on the other, the psychiatrist is instructed by the court to violate at times the previously assumed confidential physician–patient relationship in cases in which the patient may be considered "dangerous" to himself (or herself) or to others. This latter obligation does little to allow the psychiatrist to garner the necessary trust among patients demanded by such a sensitive profession. Hence, no other set of health care issues have precipitated as much legal intervention, litigation, and judicial and legislative review as have ones related to mental health and disability. Clearly, no other area demands the application of sound ethical principles and humanistic values. Despite the problems—many that still remain unsatisfactorily resolved—a societal obligation to provide the necessary network of health and human services associated with mental health care remains before us. As summarized by the President's Commission on Mental Health, "despite shortcomings and inequities, the foundation exists for reaching a goal of making high quality public and private mental health services available at reasonable cost to all who need them . . . we must assure that mental health services and programs operate within basic principles protecting human rights and guaranteeing freedom of choice."[6]

However, amid the needs and rights of individuals, other complex ethical issues arise. In Chapter 12, Roth tackles one of the most difficult, controversial dilemmas confronting mental health patients, physicians, and society in general—involuntary commitment. Early in his study, he examines the roots and justifications of competing claims— the rights of the individual (not to be involuntarily institutionalized) versus the rights of society (to be protected by the state from harm). The psychiatrist's role creates a somewhat unresolvable conflict as to whether one ought to adhere to patient rights related to autonomy or whether a higher level of allegiance is owed to the protection of the society at large. Furthermore, does involuntary institutionalization exhibit more beneficence, or at least nonmaleficence, to the patient or to society? Following a thorough analysis, Roth develops a model of compromise that he refers to as safeguarded paternalism. He views this as an alternative to the trend toward the proof of dangerousness approach that he considers more of a political remedy than a medical one.

In Chapter 13, Tancredi and Slaby choose to examine a much wider range of ethical issues in contemporary psychiatry, which they group into three categories—patient–therapist relationship conflicts, issues associated with the allocation of limited resources and distributive justice in mental health, and psychiatry's responsibility to society as a whole. They conclude that psychiatry as a profession and the field of mental health in general must confront a particularly challenging period in the short-term future.

NOTES TO PART III

1. Erving Goffman, *Asylums: Essays on the Social Situation of Mental Patients and Other Inmates* (Chicago: Aldine Publishing Company, 1961).
2. Edgar Z. Friedenberg, "Ship of Fools," *The New York Review of Books*, Vol. 17, October 21, 1971.
3. President's Commission on Mental Health, *Report to the President from the President's Commission on Mental Health* (4 vols.) *Vol. 1: Report and Rec-*

ommendations to the President (Washington, D.C.: U.S. Government Printing Office, 1978), p. 15.

4. National Commission for the Protection of Human Subjects of Biomedical and Behavioral Research, *Report and Recommendations: Research Involving Those Institutionalized as Mentally Infirm.* DHEW Publication OS 78-0006 (Washington, D.C.: U.S. Government Printing Office, 1978).

5. Kenneth Donaldson, *Insanity Inside Out* (New York: Crown Publishers, Inc., 1976).

6. President's Commission on Mental Health, *Vol. 1*, p. viii.

12 A COMMITMENT LAW FOR PATIENTS, DOCTORS, AND LAWYERS

Loren H. Roth, M.D., M.P.H.

Man cares because it is his nature to care.
Man survives because he cares and is cared for.[1]

INTRODUCTION

Recent clashes among the parties to mental health commitment have been inevitable and heuristic. Not unlike Greta Garbo, many mental patients want to be alone.[2] Their point of view should be respected. In the absence of their incompetency to consent to or refuse treatment, or absent an emergency, mental patients should not be treated involuntarily.[3]

Next come the mental health lawyers, who are keen to advocate for clients (and to protect civil rights for all persons) and who are reluctant to recognize the legitimate role that paternalism must play in a caring society. But no caring society can ignore the health needs of persons demonstrably unable to care for themselves. As Marcus noted, "You can degrade people by taking care of them and you can degrade people by not taking care of them and I see no simple answer to such questions."[4]

Reprinted with the permission of the *American Journal of Psychiatry* 136:1121–1127 (September 1979), in which the original manuscript appeared.

Finally come the physicians, who understandably want to treat severely mentally ill individuals who can benefit from treatment and are frustrated by the new laws emphasizing patient dangerousness as a prerequisite for involuntary treatment.[5] However, physicians at times also fail to acknowledge the bankruptcy of past commitment approaches that sanctioned hospitalization of the mentally ill solely on the basis of their need for care and treatment.

As a consequence of the failed dialogue among these parties, the stakes have escalated. Recent trends in mental health law, for example, point in a paradoxical direction. Judicially committed mental patients may soon be permitted to refuse customary psychiatric treatments that are likely to reverse or stabilize their respective conditions.[6] The risk is that the mental hospital will again become custodial, which would ensure the patient's civil rights while failing to restore health. Such a scenario seems all the more paradoxical when one considers that the severely mentally ill are more treatable now than ever before.[7]

It is the thesis of this chapter that a new synthesis for the law of commitment is possible.[a] The following approach to the law of commitment is one that respects persons and gives credence to both medical and legal values. In addition, it may be acceptable to all parties concerned, except the most vocal groups of disaffected ex-mental patients and the abolitionists, who would do away with commitment altogether.

PARENS PATRIAE COMMITMENT: SAFEGUARDED PATERNALISM

The *parens patriae* approach to mental health commitment described herein modifies and tightens considerably an approach previously suggested by Stone.[8] Brief periods of mental health commitment are permitted based upon the principle of parens patriae, the interest of the state in caring for persons unable to care for themselves. As envisioned here, commitment under the parens patriae power explicitly sanctions the formerly implicit; commitment is based on the specific legal incompetency of the patient to consent to or refuse treatment. It is an acknowledged period of temporary guardianship in the best

---

a. Considering that both doctors and lawyers are increasingly viewed by the public as instrumentalities of disgraced professions, the time may be opportune to establish some common ground between the warring parties.

interest of the patient. Procedural protections are afforded the parens patriae patient. The aim is to reconcile mental health commitment with other state laws, which have always permitted substitute permission for treatment of medical patients who are demonstrated incompetent to consent to or refuse medical treatment. This is the medical model for mental health commitment. It ensures that mental patients would be treated similarly to other medical patients—that is, in the absence of their incompetency to consent or refuse, or absent an emergency, patients may not be treated against their will.[9]

Proposed Procedures for Parens Patriae Commitment

If the person suffers from a severe and reliably diagnosed mental illness (e.g., a psychosis), and (1) absent treatment the immediate prognosis is for major distress of the person, (2) treatment is available, (3) the diagnosed illness substantially impairs the person's ability to understand or to communicate about the possibility of treatment, and (4) the risk–benefit ratio of treatment is such that "a reasonable man would consent to it," then a brief trial of treatment in the patient's best interest is both ethically proper and legally sanctioned.[10]

Most state commitment hearings do not at present adjudicate specific legal incompetency to consent or refuse. They are therefore defective, although some might dispute this assertion. In the past the hidden competency addressed by most commitment statutes has concerned the ability of patients to judge their own need for treatment. Rather than a more elemental approach to competency (compatible with informed consent doctrine and evaluating whether or not patients understand the consequences of treatment), a *judgment about treatment* standard was applied. If the person's judgment was so defective that he or she did not voluntarily seek or willingly accept psychiatric treatment, then the patient was committed and involuntarily treated. In operation this standard (and its legal meaning) is vague and imprecise. This approach is heavily susceptible to value judgments, so that unlike other medical patients, mentally ill patients may be treated simply because they need such treatment, whether they want it or not or are capable of deciding for themselves.

The ethical, legal, and practical problems in implementing this approach have accounted for its rejection by civil libertarians and for a return to *dangerousness* to self or others as the only acceptable standard for civil commitment. Inspection of the wording of the 1966 Pennsylvania Mental Health statute (now repealed) illustrates this problem. Persons were committed and involuntarily treated upon a finding that mental disability "lessen[ed] the capacity of the person to use his customary self-control, judgment, and discretion in the conduct of his affairs and social relations" so as to render the person in "need of care or treatment by reason of such mental disability."[11] The approach to competency to consent proposed here attempts instead to clarify the standard for determination of competency, bringing the determination for psychiatry more into line with that of general medicine and making this determination more viable.

The approach proposed here acknowledges that absent a specific adjudication of incompetency, even those patients properly judicially committed have the right to refuse subsequent treatment. The proposed parens patriae system would therefore alter future commitment hearings to address, at the time of commitment, the patient's specific competency to consent to or refuse treatment. Absent patient incompetency to consent or to refuse, no patient may be committed under the parens patriae power, because a requisite step in the logic of involuntary medical treatment is missing.[12]

Recent developments in the law commend such an approach. The report of the National Commission for the Protection of Human Subjects of Biomedical and Behavioral Research advocates that greater reliance be placed on the concept of limited incompetency in adjudicating the rights of the mentally ill.[13] The National Commission cites with favor the statute of Washington State, which includes the following wording: "[T]he court shall impose . . . only specific limitation and disabilities on a disabled person to be placed under a limited guardianship as the court finds necessary for such person's protection and assistance."[14]

It is proposed that such limited incompetency be adjudicated at commitment. Thus, such patients remain generally competent. They therefore lose no other civil rights as a consequence of commitment but the right to refuse customary treatment, which is the only civil right that should be abridged by commitment.

There are today no universally accepted criteria for adjudicating a patient's competency to consent to or refuse treatment.[15] However, the following criteria have been proposed for trial application. The three-pronged standard for competency to consent or refuse is as follows:

1. Does the patient understand the generally agreed upon consequences (the potential benefits and the potential risks) both of being treated and of not being treated?

2. Does the patient understand why a particular form of treatment (e.g., psychotropic medication) is being considered or recommended?

3. Does the patient express a choice for or against treatment?

Patients who fail on one, two, or three of the three competency criteria may, at the discretion of a legal decisionmaker, be adjudicated incompetent to consent to or refuse treatment. A major purpose of the commitment hearing is to adjudicate the patient's competency or incompetency to consent to or refuse treatment, but the legal decisionmaker, in sanctioning commitment for the patient, attends to other requisite elements in the logic of commitment. This approach is practical. Based on outpatient or inpatient evaluation (e.g., following three to five days of emergency psychiatric treatment), professional opinion is usually clear as to whether or not a patient requires treatment with, for example, psychotropic medications. Such plans are part of the patient's general treatment plan. While the professional may later recommend either increases or decreases in medication (or even a change of medication), the general purpose of receiving psychotropic medication is explored with the patient prior to the commitment hearing. The patient's capacity or incapacity to utilize this information is then presented to the judge or other legal decisionmaker in order to adjudicate the patient's competency.

The court does not order that treatment be given. Whether or not the patient is subsequently treated is a matter for further in-hospital deliberation between the patient's physicians, the appointed substitute decisionmakers (i.e., the temporary guardians), and the patient. The court appoints others to act as limited guardians for the patient for the duration of the commitment order. The patient's relatives, the patient's friends, two or more physicians, a treatment evaluator,[16] an interdisciplinary institutional treatment committee, or a human rights committee might each, under differing circumstances or jurisdictions, be appropriate as substitute decisionmakers (i.e., temporary limited guardians) for the patient.[17]

The physician solicits an informed permission to treat the patient from the substitute decisionmaker. The substitute decisionmaker is empowered to elect or to reject treatment for the patient that is objectively in the patient's best interest or, under a more subjective approach,[18] to make the decision that the patient would have made were he or she competent to consent. While ethical considerations and the demands of good clinical practice dictate that the physician continue attempts to secure an informed consent for treatment from the patient (and to explore variations in the patient's treatment plan that may be more acceptable to the patient), ultimately it is the physician's prerogative, assuming substitute informed permission is obtained, to treat the patient nonconsensually. In-hospital advocacy service is provided for the patient, but the deliberations of the substitute decisionmaker are fact finding and information gathering rather than adversary in nature.

Commitment under the parens patriae power is for brief periods of time—for example, six weeks. The court order is renewable for an additional six weeks only if it is shown to the court or an equivalent legal decisionmaker (e.g., a court-appointed Master) that the patient is benefiting or is likely to benefit from continuing treatment.

At the conclusion of a twelve week period of treatment under the parens patriae power, the court order for commitment and for specific incompetency to consent to or refuse treatment is automatically terminated. If the patient has not by this time agreed to voluntary treatment, it is unlikely he or she will do so. Subsequent periods of hospitalization are permitted only if it shows that the patient constitutes a clear and continuing danger to others or to self.

The purpose of parens patriae treatment is to restore the patient to functioning (i.e., competency) over a relatively brief period of time, using common and accepted methods of therapy. Once this is accomplished, the person is in a position to evaluate whether or not he or she has been helped by the interventions that were made over his or her initial objection. This type of help should not be forced again and again in the name of a person's best interest or because of incompetency to consent. The patient should in fact, and not only in theory, say "thank you."[19] If the patient recovers, he or she should be allowed to declare, when no longer a patient, that no such treatment is desired in the future. There should be a living will for involuntary treatment delivered under the parens patriae power.[b]

The initial parens patriae court hearing is a full legal hearing with the usual due process protections afforded the patient. The patient is afforded counsel, the right to an independent mental health examination, the right to question his or her physicians as to their rationale for treatment, and so forth.[20] Parens patriae hearings may occur at two times—after a period of outpatient examination or, alternatively, three to five days following a period of emergency control for the patient under the police power of the state.

Comment

As here proposed, a parens patriae commitment makes explicit and legally sanctioned what is now implicit and only questionably legally sanctioned under the law of commitment. The purpose of involuntary commitment is to provide those patients with demonstrated functional incapacity the treatment they need. A parens patriae commitment would be a proper medical approach to the involuntary treatment of some patients who are acutely psychotic or schizophrenic, severely and/or delusionally depressed, or manic or who have confusional or other organic syndromes that compromise orientation and understanding. Failing a trial of treatment that benefits the patient and absent the patient's consent to continue treatment, involuntary commitment is subsequently permitted only under the dangerousness to others or self rationales.

EMERGENCY COMMITMENT

Under emergency circumstances, and before a formal court adjudication of specific competency, involuntary treatment with medication is permitted only to the extent necessary to control the emergency. The purpose of emergency treatment, similar to all medical

b. There are complex philosophical problems here concerning the definition and duration of personhood along the life arc. In logic (assuming that repetitive treatment is required for efficacy and that newly restored persons are not yet in a good position to understand what should or would be their future choice were they to become ill again), parens patriae might justify involuntary treatment on more than one occasion. However, this has the potential for a shell game and should not be permitted to go on indefinitely.

treatment under the emergency exception to informed consent law (in which the patient's consent is implied),[21] is to preserve the patient's health and/or to protect others until the court is able to rule on the suitability of a parens patriae or a dangerousness type commitment.

POLICE POWER COMMITMENTS

Is commitment justified for mentally ill patients who are a danger to others? While some psychiatrists have understandably discounted the appropriateness of this approach for the mental health system,[22] few legislatures are willing to ground involuntary commitment solely on the basis of parens patriae. There remains the question of how to handle mentally ill persons who do not profit from brief treatment and who at the time of expiration of a parens patriae commitment may still constitute a danger to others. While some argue that a single system of social control for deviant behavior should be sufficient for society[23] (e.g., the criminal justice system with mental health treatment offered opportunistically), this point of view has not been accepted. A second rationale for commitment, with a differing procedural approach, is therefore proposed.

A major problem with commitment under the dangerousness to others approach is that such patients, many of whom manifest character type problems, are not incompetent to consent to or refuse treatment. It is therefore both legally and ethically unclear whether such mentally ill but competent persons may be treated against their will with, for example, psychotropic medications.

> Police power commitments . . . are based on potential dangerousness but do not necessarily require a level of mental disability amounting to incompetency. Police power patients, therefore, may be in a position to refuse intrusive treatment, although . . . their continuing confinement while dangerous may, for public protection purposes, be constitutionally affirmed.[24]

The physician's identity as a helping person is both distorted and degraded when treating competent objecting patients at the behest of society. Furthermore, the patient's rights are violated. It is thus no surprise that recent and ongoing lawsuits have questioned this point, asserting that in the absence of a clear-cut emergency (i.e., imminent danger), involuntary treatment with medication, even for patients committed under the dangerousness to others rationale, is not consti-tutionally permitted.[25] The problem here is one of imminent danger versus dangerousness over the long-term or the proclivity for danger-ous behavior. Under the police power, there is no doubt as to soci-ety's right to restrain dangerous persons and to prevent the continu-ation of violent behavior. However, it is not clear that preventive treatment may continue once the emergency is controlled. This leaves in limbo the treatment of mentally ill persons who have been assaultive, who are judicially committed, but who are not assaultive in the hospital. Unfortunately, this type of person, rather than the person who can profit from treatment, is the paradigm of commit-ment under the dangerousness to others approach, honestly applied. While treatment is presumably part of the purpose for commitment, it is argued that such patients cannot be treated against their will without additionally being adjudicated incompetent to consent or refuse.[26]

Roth[27] and Meisel have previously described a *segregation model* for the commitment of dangerous, competent, and mentally ill per-sons. Under this model the purposes of commitment are served by segregating such persons so as to decrease the risks for others. Treat-ment is offered but cannot be compelled. The mentally ill, compe-tent, dangerous person may choose to refuse treatment at the risk of continuing confinement. The patient, not the doctor, balances the risk for the patient of continuing confinement as opposed to un-wanted treatment. Under the proposed commitment law described below, this approach (that is believed to be both legally and ethi-cally compelled for dangerous competent persons) is given formal recognition.

Proposed Approach to Commitment of Dangerous, Competent Patients

Dangerousness is adjudicated by a court only when it is shown that the patient has perpetrated a recent act of violence, either a threat or (preferably for purposes of reliable ascertainment) an attempted or an accomplished act. Future dangerousness is difficult to predict. Courts will no doubt continue to rely on past dangerousness in estab-lishing the likelihood of future dangerousness (for purposes of equity if for no other).

The due process protections of the criminal justice system are afforded the patient at the court hearing. Dangerousness must be proved beyond a reasonable doubt. Commitment is for a ninety-day period. The commitment is renewed only after another court hearing establishes the reoccurrence of dangerous behavior during the previous ninety days.[c]

If competency is not adjudicated at the time of commitment (as is the present approach in most state laws), the dangerous, competent, committed patient has the right to refuse all treatment except for that treatment necessary to control an ongoing emergency (i.e., imminent danger to others or self) in the hospital. Forced treatment for purposes of making treatment more definitive requires an additional finding of incompetency. To treat nonconsensually the dangerous committed patient, physicians would need to return to court (or to present their recommendations to some other not yet identified legal decisionmaker) for a second due process competency hearing. This scenario is no pipe dream. It is an approach analogous to that recently proposed by most of the members of the Task Force on Legal and Ethical Issues of the President's Commission on Mental Health[28] and may be constitutionally required depending on the outcome of ongoing legal actions.[29]

The dangerousness to others approach might be modified to include adjudication of competency at the time of the commitment hearing, but clinical experience suggests that the proposed standard for competency (honestly applied) would adjudicate most patients who are dangerous to others as competent to consent or to refuse. Under a combined approach (i.e., dangerousness plus incompetency), many patients who are dangerous to others would not be committed. Alternatively, if found competent but nevertheless committed, the dangerous patient has the right to refuse treatment. The willingness of physicians to provide treatment and to work in mental institutions under these circumstances is problematic,[30] and there is the additional problem of ensuring that dangerous patients do not harm other patients. The dangerousness to others approach may force the creation of a new type of quasi-penal setting for the long-term detention of the dangerous mentally ill patient who refuses treatment.

c. Elaboration of this rule is necessary for the treatment of mentally abnormal offenders (e.g., persons found not guilty by reason of insanity). Discussion of this point is beyond the scope of this study.

COMBINED COMMITMENTS:
DANGEROUSNESS TO SELF

Commitment under the dangerousness to self rationale combines elements of both parens patriae and police power. Most patients dangerous to self (e.g., the suicidal and delusionally depressed patient or the patient with an acute confusional psychosis) would be treated under the parens patriae approach as above. Persons who are gravely disabled due to mental illness and therefore pose a danger to themselves over the long run may instead be committed under the dangerousness to self system. Such cases, which clinically include some cases of chronic schizophrenia and functional impairment or with organic brain syndromes (e.g., alcoholic dementia, senile dementia with psychosis) resemble more nearly care than treatment type cases. In such cases, a ninety-day renewable court commitment is permitted contingent upon a finding in court that the patient is or continues to be a danger to self.

Commitment under the dangerousness to self rationale is permitted only when the following criteria are satisfied.

1. The person's preference for no care or treatment whatsoever is respected unless it is likely that serious harm to the person's physical health will ensue without care and treatment.

2. Although the person may not be fully treatable, treatment will be attempted.

3. The diagnosed illness impairs the person's ability to understand or to communicate about the possibilities of care and treatment (i.e., the patient is incompetent to consent or to refuse care and treatment).

4. The quality of care and treatment available (and subsequently delivered) is clearly superior to that care and treatment the person would otherwise receive were he or she not committed.

5. The locus of care is that environment least restrictive of the person's freedom, is that which is medically and socially advisable, and is consistent with the person's needs. A person's preference of choice of environments where care is to be received is given great weight.

The patient who is dangerous to self, since he or she must also be found incompetent to consent or to refuse care and treatment, is not permitted to refuse subsequent care or treatment necessary to maintain health and to stabilize his or her condition. A system for substitute decisionmaking similar to that previously discussed under parens patriae commitments is put into place for patients who are dangerous to themselves. The dangerousness to self approach to commitment is a system of protective services for chronically disabled patients. Much of the care and treatment delivered under this system might be community rather than institutionally based.

DISCUSSION

This study cannot review in depth here the philosophical arguments that justify an approach of *safeguarded paternalism* in the treatment of mental patients.[31] It is clear that some alternative to the dangerousness approach is required, however, if the helping potential of the mental health system is to be realized and if treatment is to be afforded severely mentally ill persons who can profit from treatment and who may be unable, because of their illness, to understand their need for treatment. Unless specific incompetency to consent or to refuse is adjudicated at the time of commitment, the custodial and social control functions of the mental hospital are elevated at the expense of its treatment functions. Allowing commitment without permission to treat is essentially the abolitionist position in disguise.

Complementing the parens patriae approach is a back-up system for patients dangerous to self or to others over the long run. A finding of dangerousness (and not solely treatability and incapacity) is required if persons are deprived of freedom for long periods of time. Patients must have committed or be likely to commit a criminal act; alternatively, their physical health as well as mental health must be at obvious jeopardy. Dangerousness, which is a political and not a medical concept, is the sole justification for long-term commitment.

Standards and procedures concerning mental health commitment must be assessed in terms of their pragmatic impact as well as through a consideration of attendant societal values. Over the last few years, some studies have pointed to the value of brief involuntary treatment for the psychiatric patient. They have suggested that most patients are helped, not victimized, by involuntary treatment.[32] A substantial proportion of patients continue to participate in treatment voluntarily following a period of involuntary treatment.[33] Furthermore, the course of involuntary treatment is usually fairly brief. In one recent study, 67 percent of the involuntary patients were discharged within thirty-eight days.[34] Follow-up interviews with the patients suggested "that although the committed patients were generally hospitalized against their will, with the advantage of hindsight they tended to have a positive attitude toward their hospitalization."[35] Another study found that 63 percent of the involuntary patients were discharged in less than three months.[36] While more and better controlled research is needed, not all studies are as encouraging (for example, readers are referred to note 37). However, this is the type of findings that should help to justify brief trials of involuntary treatment for mentally ill patients who are genuinely incompetent to consent to or to refuse it, where such treatment is available. The paradigm case for evaluating the law of commitment is not the harmless eccentric who receives indefinite segregation and overtranquilization in a medieval institution, but the previously functioning person, with an acute or subacute mental decompensation, where the possibility of improvement with treatment can be assessed readily.

The proposed parens patriae system treats the psychiatric patient similarly to any other medical patient. In the absence of a formal court adjudication of incompetency to consent or refuse (or absent an emergency), the adult, competent mental patient has the right to refuse treatment. For the incompetent patient, procedural protections are provided, and durational limits are defined.[38]

Patients who are dangerous to others and competent to consent to or refuse treatment are committed for detention so that they may be offered an opportunity for treatment and in order to decrease societal risk. The types of acts required to establish dangerousness to others under the dangerousness system are also violations of the criminal law. Such patients in fairness may, and arguably, should be handled in the criminal justice system and not in the mental health system.

A final virtue of the proposed system is that it would facilitate research and evaluation of the commitment process. From the outset, all commitment cases are clearly defined and labeled as either of the parens patriae type or of the dangerousness type (either to self or to others). Absent this type approach, precisely directed evaluation studies of the commitment process have been difficult to perform. The type of law proposed above would be modified on the basis of empirical data.

If the mental health bar were to accept the proposed approach, it would be necessary to concede that the reliability of psychiatric diagnosis is improving,[39] that customary treatment should be made available for patients who are incompetent to consent to or to refuse it, and that the principle of beneficence[40] (not misplaced authority) underlies the desires of mental health professionals to provide trials of treatment for persons who are severely mentally ill and functionally impaired. We do no less for kith and kin.

The traditional mental commitment approach, wherein two physicians declare that the patient is ill and that he or she will be treated at the doctor's discretion (i.e., doctor knows best), must also give way. Substitute decisionmakers, and not solely physicians, must give informed permission for the patient to be treated. Physicians must be willing to participate in formal court hearings that adjudicate patient competency and to subject themselves to cross-examination about their opinions. Perhaps most importantly, physicians must recognize that while it is one thing to want to help the impaired patient, if there is evidence that help is not forthcoming, it is time to quit.

NOTES TO CHAPTER 12

1. W. Gaylin, *Caring* (New York: Alfred A. Knopf, 1976), p. 13.
2. Judi Chamberlin, *On Our Own: Patient-Controlled Alternatives to the Mental Health System* (New York: Hawthorn Books, 1978).
3. Loren H. Roth, "Involuntary Civil Commitment: The Right to Treatment and the Right to Refuse Treatment," in R.J. Bonnie, *Psychiatrists and the Legal Process: Diagnosis and Debate* (New York: Insight Communications, 1977), pp. 332–345.
4. I. Shenker, "Milk of Kindness Sours, Experts Find," *The New York Times*, March 8, 1976, p. 22.
5. Roth; Alan A. Stone, *Mental Health and Law: A System in Transition*, DHEW Publication ADM 75–176 (Washington, D.C.: U.S. Government Printing Office, 1975).
6. R. Plotkin, "Limiting the Therapeutic Orgy: Mental Patients' Rights to Refuse Treatment," *Northwestern University Law Review* 72: 461–525 (1977).
7. D.F. Klein and R. Gittelman–Klein, *Progress in Psychiatric Drug Treatment* (New York: Brunner/Mazel, 1975).

8. Stone.
9. Roth.
10. Stone.
11. Alan Meisel, "Pennsylvania Civil Commitment Procedures—A Practical Guide," *Pennsylvania Medicine* 77: 47–50 (1974).
12. "Developments in the Law—Civil Commitment of the Mentally Ill," *Harvard Law Review* 87: 1190–1406 (1974).
13. National Commission for the Protection of Human Subjects of Biomedical and Behavioral Research, *Report and Recommendations: Research Involving Those Institutionalized as Mentally Infirm*, DHEW Publication OS 78–0006 (Washington, D.C.: U.S. Government Printing Office, 1978), pp. 53–90.
14. Ibid., p. 80.
15. Loren H. Roth, Alan Meisel, and Charles W. Lidz, "Tests of Competency to Consent to Treatment," *American Journal of Psychiatry* 134: 279–284 (1977).
16. P.B. Hoffman and R.C. Dunn. "Guaranteeing the Right to Treatment," in Bonnie, *Psychiatrists and the Legal Process: Diagnosis and Debate*, pp. 298–322.
17. "Position Statement on the Right to Adequate Care and Treatment for the Mentally Ill and Mentally Retarded," *American Journal of Psychiatry* 134: 354–355 (1977).
18. Superintendent of Belchertown State School v. Saikewicz, 370 N.E.2d 417 (Mass. 1977).
19. Stone.
20. "Report of the Task Panel on Legal and Ethical Issues," in *Task Panel Reports Submitted to the President's Commission on Mental Health, Volume 4, Appendix* (Washington, D.C.: U.S. Government Printing Office, 1978), pp. 1359–1516.
21. William L. Prosser, *Handbook of the Law of Torts, 4th ed.* (St. Paul: West Publishing Company, 1971), p. 103.
22. Stone.
23. John T. Monahan, "The Psychiatrization of Criminal Behavior: A Reply," *Hospital and Community Psychiatry* 24: 105–108 (1973).
24. David B. Wexler, *Criminal Commitments and Dangerous Mental Patients: Legal Issues of Confinement, Treatment, and Release*, DHEW Publication ADM 76–331 (Washington, D.C.: U.S. Government Printing Office, 1976), p. 15.
25. The Mental Health Association, The Civil Liberties Union of Massachusetts, and The Mental Patients Liberation Front, "Brief for Amici Curiae in Okin v. Rogers," *Mental Disability Law Reporter* 2: 43–50 (1978).
26. Ibid.; Plotkin.
27. Roth.

28. "Report of the Task Panel on Legal and Ethical Issues."
29. The Mental Health Association et al.
30. Roth.
31. "Report of the Task Panel on Legal and Ethical Issues"; J.G. Murphy, "Incompetence and Paternalism," *Archiv Für Rechts-Und Sozialphiloso-phie* 60: 465–485 (1974).
32. W.R. Gove and T. Fain, "A Comparison of Voluntary and Committed Psychiatric Patients," *Archives of General Psychiatry* 34: 669–676 (1977); L.S. Sata and E.E. Goldenberg, "A Study of Involuntary Patients in Seattle," *Hospital and Community Psychiatry* 28: 834–837 (1977); H.M. Ginzburg, J.R. Rappeport, and D. Paskewitz, "A Follow-Up Study of Involuntary Commitments" (Paper presented at the 130th Annual Meeting of the American Psychiatric Association, Toronto, Canada, May 11-15, 1977).
33. J. Spensley, J.T. Barter, P.H. Werme et al., "Involuntary Hospitalization: What For and How Long?" *American Journal of Psychiatry* 131: 219–222 (1974); R. Peele, P. Chodoff, and N. Taub, "Involuntary Hospitalization and Treatability: Observations from the District of Columbia Experience," *Catholic University of America Law Review* 23: 744–753 (1974).
34. Gove and Fain.
35. Ibid., p. 675.
36. C.J. Tomelleri, N. Lakshminarayanan, and M. Herjanic, "Who Are the 'Committed'?" *Journal of Nervous and Mental Diseases* 165: 288–293 (1977).
37. I. Zwerling, T. Karasu, R. Plutchik et al., "A Comparison of Voluntary and Involuntary Patients in a State Hospital," *American Journal of Orthopsychiatry* 45: 81–87 (1975).
38. "Report of the Task Panel on Legal and Ethical Issues."
39. Stone; J.E. Helzer, P.H. Clayton, R. Pambakian et al., "Reliability of Psychiatric Diagnosis. II.: The Test/Retest Reliability of Diagnostic Classification," *Archives of General Psychiatry* 34: 136–141 (1977).
40. National Commission.

13 ETHICAL ISSUES IN MENTAL HEALTH CARE

Laurence R. Tancredi, M.D., J.D.
Andrew E. Slaby, M.D., Ph.D.

INTRODUCTION

The developments in medical ethics that have occurred over the past ten years have had a profound impact on virtually every facet of medical research and care. Some aspects of biomedicine have come under careful ethical scrutiny earlier than others. The problems of experimentation with human beings were the most conspicuous during the early 1960s, with the widespread application of random clinical trials and the increasing outlays of national funds for medical research. The National Institutes of Health (NIH) took a leading role during those years in reflecting on its guidelines for human experimentation and using consultants to radically restructure ways of maximally protecting patients in these studies. Abuses like the Tuskegee affair and the injections of cancer cells into elderly patients in a Brooklyn hospital rapidly gained national attention and intensified both the focus and the debate on the ethics of experimentation. Similarly, certain technologies that were in the early stage of application and that held a promise of major steps toward eradications serious diseases became the subject of ethical analysis; hence, the use of artificial organs, advances in reproductive medicine, and the extraordinary discoveries in genetics resulted in the creation of various policy groups. Such groups looked at the social, ethical, and

283

economic consequences and examined methods for approaching new technologies as they emerge in the medical field.[1]

The mental health field has been relatively free of this focus on ethics—with the exception, perhaps, of psychosurgery, which drew attention to itself in the *Kaimowitz*[2] case in 1973[a] and the experience in Russia where psychiatry has been used conspicuously for the purpose of societal control.[3] The issues surrounding psychosurgery are similar in kind to those in the human experimentation area and are in fact a logical extension of that inquiry: The Russians' abuse of psychiatry for political control is so egregious and of such a major threat to a free society that it induced negative reactions throughout the world. Beyond these striking abuses, the mental health field has not, until recently, come under the examination of social ethics. Since the 1960s, legal reform of mental health has been led by such liberal patient-oriented groups as the American Civil Liberties Union and the Mental Health Law Project located in Washington, D.C. The issues raised in the case involving involuntary commitment, and especially the right to treatment, are sound arguments consistent with those that would be considered by scholars who centered their attention on the ethical aspects of psychiatric care. The law concerns itself not only with the tightness of legal reasoning and the wisdom of precedents, but also the pervasive values of society.[b]

In addition to the issues surrounding psychosurgery, the abuse of psychiatry, and patients' rights as reflected in involuntary commitment and right to treatment, there are a wide range of very important social ethical issues in the mental health field that characterize the responsibility of the therapist to the patient as well as to society

a. The case involved the study of the effects of amygdalectomies on violent behavior in criminals. The court claimed there could not have been an informed consent due to the nature of the experimental treatment and the vulnerability of the particular research group—prisoners.

b. A crucial distinction is often made among terms such as taste, ethics, and politics. Taste refers, for the most part, to an individual's preferences. One person may prefer football, another baseball; or one person may prefer vanilla sherbet and another chocolate ice cream. Ethics, in contrast, involves how an individual's values may affect others in the social system. If values are easily commenserable (i.e., no real distinction exists), then one could argue that there is no moral issue. The difficulty occurs when options are available, though not all will be available to everyone, and underlying values will be determinative. In contrast, the political process influences over and beyond ethics and taste. The political process may produce positions that are constant with ethical consideration. On the other hand, the government may provide large amounts of money for specific treatment programs due to the exertion of political pressures, with no consideration of the underlying values and the extent to which various groups may be precluded from expressing their options.

at large. Many of these issues have been addressed in other than a context of ethical analysis; few, if any, have been analyzed in any depth from the standpoint of values and social morality.

ETHICAL ISSUES IN CONTEMPORARY PSYCHIATRY

The ethical issues in contemporary psychiatry fall along three clusters of concern—(1) those conflicts that emerge in the patient–therapist relationship; (2) the issues of allocation of limited resources, both money and talent, in the mental health field; and (3) the responsibility that psychiatry as a profession has to society as a whole.

The Therapist–Patient Relationship

A great deal of attention has been given during the past several years to the nature of the physician–patient relationship in medical care. In large part, the emphasis has been on the extent to which the prerogatives of the patient are equalized with those of the physician around specific decisions in the treatment of medical disabilities. In the general field of medical care, informed consent has gained prominence as one of the most significant and powerful instruments for the patient in the physician–patient relationship.[4] Not only must patients now be informed about the nature and possible effects of possible treatments, but they must also be informed of the risks, benefits, alternatives to treatment, and contrasts among various treatment modalities. When a patient goes to a physician for a gynecological condition, for example, the obstetrician–gynecologist must now clearly inform the patient of the alternatives to hysterectomy or a radium implant to treatment through hormones, so that the patient can wisely enter into the decisionmaking process around the treatment of choice. This expansion of the doctrine of informed consent in clinical practice finds its roots in the application of that doctrine in the field of human experimentation. Before the 1960s, patients virtually always accepted without question not only the physician's decisions regarding specific treatments but the fact that they would be unable to understand the complicated language and concepts of medicine. Medicine is no longer the province of the physician alone, and the lay public is becoming aware of its capacity to understand biomedical concepts as they relate to diagnosis and treatment. With this growing familiarity with medical terminology, the public has rightfully demanded a greater role in medical decisions.

In the mental health field, the application of the concept of informed consent in both the experimental and the treatment arenas is much more difficult and problematic. To begin with, many of the patients by virtue of their mental condition are unable to give an informed consent on either an experimental or a treatment issue. Studies[5] dealing specifically with voluntarily admitted patients demonstrate that even in those cases where the competence of the patient is not in question, there is often misunderstanding and misperception of the nature of informed consent. Palmer and Wohl demonstrate that the number of patients able to recall and understand the provision of the forms for voluntary admission, for release of information about hospitalization, and for having been informed of legal rights is very small.[6] In this study, forty patients entering into a mental hospital in Ohio for a first admission were interviewed to determine the extent to which they understood the provisions of the forms. Half were interviewed between one and three days after admission and the other half between seven and ten days. Their findings suggest that a higher percentage of those hospitalized for the longer period of time prior to being confronted with the forms could read all three forms acceptably. Overall, it appears that the study group's comprehension of the significance of the forms was minimal.

Olin and Olin investigated the understanding that one hundred mental patients had of a voluntary admissions form signed by them on entering a hospital.[7] They determined that only eight of the patients could be considered completely informed of the terms of the application that they signed on admission. Thirty-three of the patients at one of the hospitals were interviewed ten days after admission, and of these, fifteen showed increased understanding of the terms of the form. However, the overall results of this study corroborate those of Palmer and Wohl in demonstrating that few patients voluntarily admitted to a hospital fully understand that which they sign to give an informed consent.[8]

For the most part, voluntary patients are not as emotionally and mentally disorganized and disturbed as involuntarily committed patients. However, there are exceptions. Often, efforts will be made to have patients voluntarily admit themselves to an institution to avoid the process of involuntary commitment and to enhance the likelihood of their more positively entering into a treatment program. In addition, with the shift in the laws around involuntary commitment, which are based increasingly on the objective standard of dangerousness to oneself and/or to others, it is conceivable that a patient may be disorganized mentally and in even more distress than an involuntarily committed patient and yet not fall within the established criteria and, therefore, be accepted voluntarily into an institution.[9] Nonetheless, involuntarily committed patients are generally in more serious mental and emotional distress than voluntarily admitted ones. If voluntarily admitted patients have not demonstrated a significant degree of comprehension of forms in an informed consent context, then it is unlikely that involuntarily committed patients will be able to do any better; more than likely, they will do significantly worse.

Informed consent as a protective instrument, therefore, in the physician–patient relationship is considerably attenuated in its effect in the mental health field. Seriously decompensated schizophrenics, who are convinced that everyone they come across is a member of the CIA or the FBI, would not be able to comprehend the nature and consequences of an informed consent application. The components of informed consent—voluntariness, competency, and a level of knowledgeability about the treatment procedure that is being recommended—require a high degree of mental and emotional integration.[10]

In the *Kaimowitz* case, a Michigan judge suggested that prisoners deciding to enter into an experiment on psychosurgery for violent behavior could not give informed consent, because among other things, the alternative of entering into the experiment was continued confinement in the institution. The court saw this as highly coercive and emphasized the vulnerable position of these prisoners. In the mental health field, especially when dealing with involuntarily committed patients, this argument may also apply.

Involuntarily committed patients are in a particularly vulnerable position, since the nature of their mental illness may preclude their understanding of the experimental or treatment procedures for which their agreement is sought. Involuntarily committed patients are also vulnerable because decisions pertaining to their gaining release from the institution rest in part on the nature of their conduct as it is interpreted by the psychiatric staff. If patients become particularly argumentative or belligerent in their reluctance to accept treatment, they may alienate the authority figures (i.e., the psychiatrists). Such a response may be perceived by patients as negatively affecting their ease in gaining release from the custody of the mental health care institution. The coercive nature of being involuntarily committed, comparable to that which applies to the prisoners in the *Kaimowitz* case, might reasonably be viewed as negating the possibilities of a truly informed consent.

The issues of information disclosure and consent become more problematic in cases involving the care of patients who are not necessarily voluntarily or involuntarily committed to an institution, but who rely on the support, care, and even financial backing of family members. The family, in frustration, may take a patient to a psychiatrist for treatment and subtly coerce the patient into accepting whatever treatment the psychiatrist proposes.[11] The nature of the psychiatrist's bias (e.g., as among psychotherapy, behavioral modification, biological treatment, or even psychosurgery) may not be known to the patient or the family, but it will inevitably significantly effect the way in which that patient is treated in the psychiatric system.

For example, assume a patient with severe obsessive compulsive disease sees a psychiatrist who believes in psychosurgery as the appropriate treatment of that condition. The family, frustrated and confused by the patient's condition and burdened by his or her unceasing activities symptomatic of obsessive compulsive disease, would have a strong incentive to engage the patient in whatever treatment the psychiatrist recommends. The patient, therefore, would be dealing not only with the psychiatrist's particular bias but also with the coercive effects of family pressures to accept whatever treatment is provided. Families, not operating out of malevolent designs but rather simply desiring relief from the burdensome aspects of patients' conditions, may actually thrust patients into consent for a treatment about which not only have they not been fully informed but also in which they must rely solely on the judgment of the psychiatrist as to its scientific merits.

There are an infinite variety of circumstances similar to the one described in which patients may formally enter into informed consent agreements without being fully and completely informed of the nature of the treatment, the alternatives available, and the consequences or risks and without being able to voluntarily and freely give consent to accept that therapy.

Extending informed consent even further, some jurisdictions have incorporated it into the procedures for involuntary commitment. The recent *Lessard*[12] and subsequent *Suzuki*[13] decisions on application of the procedural rights available to criminals for those in mental health treatment systems acknowledge the importance of information disclosure. As mentioned previously, the tendency has been strongly in the direction of using an objective standard of dangerousness to oneself and others as the criteria for involuntary commitment. There seems to be very little evidence that psychiatrists are good at determining not only the current or present dangerousness of the patient but also the predictable dangerousness of the patient. Dershowitz,[14] Ennis and Litwach,[15] and Monahan[16] in respective articles discuss various epidemiological studies that indicate that psychiatrists, psychologists, police officers, and social workers are not very successful at predicting dangerousness to self and others.[17] Notwithstanding the fact that dangerousness, as a criteria for involuntary commitment, is an important attempt at significantly constricting the scope of patients who would be subjected to this abridgement of personal freedom, the new cases in the mental health field involving involuntary commitment also focus on Fifth Amendment rights against self-incrimination. The *Lessard* case—and even more fully, the *Suzuki* case—insist that patients be informed by the psychiatrist evaluating them for the purposes of commitment that anything they say can be used against them.[18] This requirement is an overt acknowledgment of the importance of informed consent in the care of mental patients. Patients must be informed of the purposes and potential ends of the interview with the psychiatrist and give their consent for full cooperation with the diagnostic evaluation in order for there to be any basis for arriving at the required criteria for involuntary commitment.

The issues of information disclosure, of course, take on a curious twist in the areas of confidentiality of information and create a host of questions that have not been resolved or fully addressed by the psychiatric and legal communities.[19] The *Tarasoff* case,[20] which involves the placing of an affirmative obligation on the psychotherapist or psychiatrist to inform those who are potential victims of actions by their patients, retreats somewhat from the position that the patient should be informed at all points in the course of treatment and be given the opportunity for consent.[21] The *Tarasoff* case does not consider whether the therapist has an obligation to inform the patient that whatever is said during the course of treatment, such as the fact that a third party may be victimized by the patient, must be reported by the therapist to potential victims. With regard to the issues discussed in *Tarasoff*, the power prerogatives in the therapist–patient relationship are balanced strongly in favor of the therapist. It could be argued, from an ethical perspective, that where the *Tarasoff* principle is applicable, psychiatrists have an affirmative obligation to so inform their patients (perhaps at the initiation of treatment).

Because of the sanctity of the patient–physician (therapist) relationship, which completely frees patients to disclose personal information, informed consent remains as the most sensitive and powerful tool for patients in the assertion of their rights in the treatment system. Every effort should be made not only to maintain the validity of that theory regarding any treatment or diagnostic decision made by the therapist, but also to assure that, wherever possible in the system, patients have the final decision as to the information that will be disclosed to third parties by the therapist. The importance of this is only underscored by the fact that many third parties (e.g., insurance companies, hospital records committees, employers) are constantly clamoring to obtain specific data about patients and that the widespread use of computers for storage and rapid retrieval of personal information makes this easily available for and susceptible to indiscriminate dissemination.

In addition to informed consent, two other issues are important ethical concerns in the patient–therapist relationship. The first of these is the issue of consumer education, particularly of the options in mental health care, as well as responsiveness by the providers of care to consumer patterns of using psychiatric services. The second involves the phenomenon of labeling, which refers to a process by which patients are placed in a certain diagnostic category, which in turn affects the ways others will perceive them and ultimately how they will perceive themselves.

Consumers of mental health services are for the most part unaware of the many possible causes of their troubled behavior and of the options that are available within the mental health field for treatment. Disorders of mood, thought, and behavior can have a wide variety of causes and be of varying degrees of severity. A patient suffering from an ended love affair or the termination of a marital relationship may receive treatment and support from a psychiatrist or from a number of professionals who have some training in psychotherapy. Highly trained individuals who provide care in a formalized setting, such as a mental health clinic, include psychologists, psychiatric social workers, and psychiatric nurses, in addition to psychiatrists. In an informal setting, family members, clergy, or a sensitive and understanding friend may provide the necessary support for an individual in the midst of a family or relationship crisis. Of course, the skill and sophistication of understanding mental health issues varies with the educational background and the sensitivity of the practitioner.[22]

Many disturbances that affect individuals can be handled through crisis-oriented therapy by nonmedically trained clinicians. On the other hand, some conditions, like schizophrenia and manic-depressive illness, are aided more directly by biological intervention, such as the antipsychotic and antidepressive agents. These medications are essential in the acute phases to ameliorate the disturbing systems, and psychotherapy may at best help such patients to adjust to their social setting. The neuropsychiatric evaluation and the biologic components of treatment in particular remain the purview of the medical profession. It is important, therefore, that the limits of the use of psychotherapy clearly be defined and presented to consumers, so they may have the necessary information to determine the professional wanted for therapy and the available treatment options.

To a large extent, psychiatry, as a profession, has colluded in the existing vagueness of the types of treatment that are available and their respective degrees of effectiveness. It is true that much psychotherapy surrounding crisis issues, loss of job, and problems of living may be accomplished effectively by the use of nonmedically trained psychiatric professionals. On the other hand, the limits of that therapy and the importance of neuropsychiatric evaluations and biological treatment in the cases of the severely mentally ill require the delineation of some boundaries of when psychotherapy is and is not appropriate.[23]

In keeping with the importance of informing the consumer of available mental health service options, it is also the institutional and professional responsibility to adapt the mental health care delivery system to consumer patterns of use.[24] If a mental health facility is only open during the day, blue collar workers may not be able to avail themselves of the facility. Jobs may preclude their getting away during the day to see a psychiatrist. Furthermore, such workers may be more reluctant to enter into psychiatric treatment due to the stigma that various groups often attach to such therapy.

Lower socioeconomic and elderly patients also need to have the health care system shaped to their individual needs. Those in lower socioeconomic groups tend not to make appointments for help; rather, they commonly use the facilities sporadically at the time of the crisis during periods of emotional upset.[25] Elderly patients, who frequently are limited in mobility and often are under the care of others, cannot meet the rigidly defined patterns of health care facilities. A primary health care delivery system that attends to patients' neuropsychiatric and social problems as well as medical needs and that is available at the odd times during the day when many need to use its facilities, would be a major step in the direction of dealing ethically with the consumer needs of the population.[26]

The second major ethical issue in addition to informed consent is that of labeling. As discussed earlier, this is a process by which an individual is categorized into a certain diagnostic group. This process inevitably influences the way others will respond to labeled patients and the way they will perceive themselves. Thus, labeling has many dangers.[27] First, there will be a tendency by mental health professionals to attribute all changes and modifications in the mental and emotional state of such patients to the label that has been applied. For example, patients labeled as psychiatrically ill who may be seen in an emergency room will often be treated as though they were complaining of a mental condition even though they may have a legitimate medical ailment. Second, once labeled, patients may be treated with less respect and attention even with respect to legitimate problems. Patients may be kept in the wrong course of treatment for a long period of time because of a label. For example, patients suffering from migraine headaches may be viewed as schizophrenic since their behavior may become bizarre and they may manifest some of the symptoms of schizophrenia during periods of an attack. To prevent this distortion, labels in psychiatry must be periodically reevaluated—despite the certainty of the original diagnosis—by a professional highly skilled in diagnosis and aware of the available therapeutic options.

A third conceptual difficulty that results from labeling is that mislabeling can lead to specious conclusions about the efficacy of treatment interventions. For example, if patients are mislabeled as schizophrenic, one might erroneously assume that the chosen treatment is highly effective when in fact such treatment may not really be that effective on confirmed schizophrenics. Cost efficiency and effectiveness studies in psychiatry cannot be undertaken with any degree of validity if strict criteria are not used for assigning patients to particular diagnostic and research groups.[28] Furthermore, a medical discipline fails to have any validity if it cannot clearly define diagnostic categories and the effectiveness of various treatment modalities.[29] Mislabeling of patients may inflate the benefits of a particular treatment or devalue the efficacy of a therapy. In either case, mislabeling undercuts the scientific basis of the discipline.

Distributive Justice Issues in Psychiatric Care

The ethical issues involving the patient–therapist relationship are complex and have been the object of considerable scrutiny during the past decade. Issues involving distributive justice in psychiatric care are relatively new, but they are becoming particularly important with the increasing interest in the development of a national health insurance system. Issues of distributive justice in psychiatry deal with major policy and ethical questions such as who gets what and how much of it is available. With respect to the provision of care, a New Haven study done in the 1950s by Hollingshead and Redlich disclosed the inequitable distribution of psychiatric care as it involved social classes.[30] Srole[31] and Leighton[32] later demonstrated that there is a great prevalence of psychiatric symptoms with compromised functioning in the general population.

In a reevaluation of the New Haven population originally studied by Hollingshead and Redlich, Myers and Bean identified a series of factors that contribute to the inequitable distribution of services by social class.[33] They demonstrated that certain factors are attributable to the nature of lower socioeconomic patients. Having a limited amount of sophistication in psychiatric matters, these patients often do not identify the early signs of mental illness. Their family structures are so compromised that even if such patients are treated, there is no support system available to assure them continued follow-up and medication maintenance.

If patients from the lower socioeconomic group are evaluated in a mental health facility and found to require hospitalization, they are often sent to state hospitals. Such institutions are usually very poorly staffed and are often located significantly far from the community. Lacking the social matrices of family, school, and church and given the far distance of most institutions from the community, poor patients often rapidly decompensate on return to the community and consequently enter a revolving door phenomenon with the mental health facility. When such patients from lower socioeconomic groups are treated, both through a state hospital or a clinic, they often receive the services of significantly less experienced clinicians or those in the early stages of psychiatric training.[34]

The inequities of distribution and availability of psychiatric services are by no means only related to social class issues. The inequities are also associated with differences in age and severity of illness. The difficulty of caring for the elderly in our society has already been cited. The barriers to accessibility to mental health facilities for the severely psychiatrically ill are, on some levels, even more significant than those for lower socioeconomic groups. Few private clinicians or public clinics are available when these patients require immediate intervention. Even where facilities are available for patients in need of immediate intervention, many clinicians will not invest the time and care in treating acutely ill psychotic or suicidal patients. Chronically ill psychiatric patients, such as chronic schizophrenics, are often handled even more curiously in the psychiatric treatment system. In effect, there is a differential of accessibility of patients to mental health treatment facilities. The lower socioeconomic classes, the severely psychiatrically ill, and the elderly are particularly discriminated against in psychiatric treatment. They are often subjected to fragmented patterns of care and limited community support.

In addition to the problems discussed regarding provision of care, distributive justice issues also involve an analysis of the mental health care budget. The way in which medical resources are allocated largely determines society's commitment to the higher values of social justice. In 1974, the cost of direct care of the mentally ill in the United States was estimated at $14.5 billion. This represented approximately 15 percent of all direct health care expenditures and 1 percent of the gross national product.[35] This constitutes a strikingly inadequate sum of money when viewed from the perspective of the amount allocated for research purposes in mental illness. The inadequate expenditures in the mental health field are easy to demonstrate. According to Daniel X. Freedman, based on the four million Americans considered seriously psychiatrically ill who are receiving care, as a nation we spend an outer limit of $28 per patient for research.[36] This is in contrast to an estimated ratio in the research allocations for cancer and heart disease that run as high as $200 per patient under treatment. The 1976 budget of NIH allocated $572 million for cancer research and only $127 million for research into mental illness.[37] This analysis suggests that the nation's priorities are directed at the more easily identified—and hence researchable—problems of physical illness rather than mental illness. In large part, this may also reflect the fact that seriously mentally ill patients cannot as readily engage in the political process for the purposes of politicking and influencing legislators vis-à-vis the allocation of resources. In contrast, cardiac or cancer patients (or even more graphically in recent years, patients suffering from end stage renal disease) are mentally alert enough to be able to actively lobby for a higher percentage of the national health care budget. It is ironic that the main stresses that may precipitate not only a host of psychiatric illnesses but medical conditions as well are of a psycho-social nature. Considerable research findings demonstrate the close association between stress and psycho-social factors and the development of cardiovascular illnesses.[38] Some research also shows a relationship between depression and stress and the development of certain forms of malignancies.[39]

In addition to the social and ethical issues in the distribution of national health care resources, it is important to examine the way in which resources are distributed within the mental health care system.[40] This includes investigating the way moneys are spent for training psychiatrists and paraprofessionals in light of the contributions made by these groups to those in the population who are in need of mental health services. In addition, there should be an examination of how money is being spent for different treatment programs. Some programs, such as suicide prevention centers, have yielded highly equivocal results. It is important that the effects of these treatment programs and the number and kinds of people who are being affected by them are examined. The priorities for the distribution of moneys within the mental health care system, whether through direct services, training, administration, or research, must be evaluated continuously and examined from the standpoint of their responsiveness to community needs and their cost efficiency with respect to quality and outcome of patient care.

The most egregiously ignored group, it would appear, in the mental health field are the mentally ill who are aged.[41] It is estimated that there are twenty million Americans over sixty-five years of age; this is a rapidly growing segment of the population. Robert Butler, director of the National Institute on Aging, reports that the incidence of psychopathology, poverty, and suicide increases significantly with age.[42] He shows projections that over the next four year period, over 75 percent of the elderly who could benefit from psychiatric care will not receive it. It is critically important from the standpoint of social ethics in the distribution of limited services in the mental health field to examine what groups in the population are receiving what kinds of care.

Psychiatry and Society

The last major series of ethical issues in psychiatry deals with the responsibility and accountability of psychiatry as a medical speciality to society. There are two ways in which psychiatry is potentially highly abusive as a mechanism of behavioral control. Historically, psychiatry has been involved in the control of nonpathological deviant behavior. In the Soviet Union in particular, psychiatry has been used by the state for the purpose of quelling dissident political beliefs by confining protestors and advocates of nonmajoritorian views to a mental hospital.[43] In such situations, treatment consists of using therapy and drugs for militating against individuals who engage in political activist positions. The goal of this treatment is to make these individuals less angry, thereby making them satisfied with the system as it exists. In addition to the direct control of political behavior, psychiatry can be involved in controlling behavior that is not intrinsically deviant but that contradicts, on some level, the prevailing values of the society. Some of the most conspicuous current examples of control of this type of deviant behavior include such diverse conduct as suicide, abortion, euthanasia, and various forms of sexual engagement with consenting adults. In *Collusion for Conformity*, the socioeconomic determinants that are in large part responsible for psychiatry's characterization of such behaviors as deviant are reviewed.[44] The fact that the socioeconomic prerogatives of a society can figure so prominently in the way psychiatry as a discipline develops its taxonomy of diseases points rather conspicuously to the abusive manipulation of a system for purposes other than the treatment of mental illness.[45]

The second way in which psychiatry in broad terms can be abusive in a social system is that it lends itself to normalization of features of an individual's personality, which might result in anxiety for the individual but at the same time may be important adherent components to the creative potential of that person.[46] The reduction of anxiety in the individual at the cost of individual creativity or social ethical sensitivity is an important potential abuse of psychiatric treatment. New ideas and creative endeavors rarely have the support of society. In Quinton Bell's description of Virginia Woolf, he alludes to the trauma that she suffered by being individualistic to the extent of deviating too far from the established norm of writers of her day.[47] Psychiatry can often be used as a means of regressing creative, deviant, individualistic behaviors to that of the majority of society. When serving this goal, it enters a function that is diametrically opposed to the care and treatment of the truly mentally ill.

With regard to the integrity of psychiatric theory, this is an area that deserves considerable attention. The way in which psychiatry conceptualizes the etiology and development of mental illnesses has a major impact on the structuring of acceptable social behavior. At one stage in the determination of the etiology of schizophrenia, mothers were often referred to as the primary causative factor. Although inherently contradictory, the so-called schizophrenogenic mother's creation of double-binding situations for the child or the schizmatic family has been alluded to as the major causative factor for the development of this very serious mental illness. Recent genetic studies to determine the origins of schizophrenia demonstrate a high concordance rate among monozygotic twins and less so with high dizygotic twins. Only since these findings has blaming the family and the mothers as primary etiological factors of schizophrenia been considered inappropriate.[48] Because of the far-reaching and painful effects of psychiatric theories on how parents evaluate psychological growth and see their roles in the development of a mentally ill child, psychiatry has an ethical obligation to be exceedingly careful and circumspect in its description of the etiology of mental illness and to maximize its justification of perceptions on the basis of statistically sound scientific observation.

Thus, in keeping with the need for psychiatric theory to be sensitive to the impact of its conceptualization on individuals in society and to be highly aware of the need for a scientific basis for its conceptualization, psychiatry on a practical level has an obligation to periodically assess the efficiency, the effectiveness, and the cost of its treatment modalities.[49] This is among the most paramount of psychiatry's ethical responsibilities to society. It is important when several treatments are being proposed to determine which are most effective, which are most efficient in providing care to afflicted patients in a way that maximizes care to all in need, and which are the least costly yet still achieve high effectiveness for the consumer.[50] To achieve this kind of critical assessment, psychiatry must also be careful in the diagnoses of various symptoms. For example, to overextend the boundaries of manic-depressive illness is to do a disservice to the accuracy and effectiveness of the treatment modality. Giving lithium carbonate to inaccurately diagnosed patients of manic-depressive illness distorts the picture of the effectiveness and efficiency of this treatment for that condition. Hence, studies that deal with cost efficiency effectiveness must not only apply rigid scientific criteria for the diagnostic categories being evaluated but also subject all the modalities of psychiatric treatment, including psychotherapy, psychoanalysis, and behavioral modification, to the same strict epidemiological and statistical analysis.[51]

These studies are critical for improving and maintaining the quality of psychiatric care and for providing consumers with the necessary information so they can enter more fully into the decision-making process around their treatment of choice.[52] Therefore, the obligation of society in general is predicated on the maximum disclosure of information possible regarding what psychiatry can and cannot do, the extent to which it is distorted for societal and other control ends, and the extent to which it can create an information base to provide consumers with a guideline whereby meaningful treatment decisions can be made in a mutual partnership between the therapist and the patient.[c]

c. Included in these studies must be an evaluation of other treatment methods that are not within the domain of psychiatry — for example, other therapies such as self-help methods that frequently are presented to the consumer as options to conventional mental health care. The responsibility of the professions to study, such other treatment methods objectively remains.

CONCLUSIONS

The immediate future of the field of psychiatry is going to be a particularly challenging period. With the increasing sophistication in the use of drugs and the development of refined methods of psychosurgery and behavioral control, psychiatry will be increasingly capable of modifying and channeling human behavior. As in the previously cited *Kaimowitz* case, involving the experimental use of psychosurgery for the control of violent behavior, part of the court's position against the use of such techniques was predicated on the experimental nature of such procedures.[53] As techniques for psychosurgery become more effective and specific for the control of certain antisocial behaviors, there will be strong movements toward employing such treatment in the criminal system — perhaps even at the expense of certain deleterious effects to features of the personality. In the area of the use of medication, the same potentiality for invasion and intrusion by psychiatry into the thinking and feeling process of patients exists. The phenothiazines heralded a new era in psychiatry. For the first time, drugs were produced that actually could affect the very thinking processes of the seriously disturbed, mentally ill patient. Refinements in medication technology in the decade ahead will result in a generation of drugs that should be more effective not only in dealing with variations of mood state, but also with the conceptual process of patients themselves.

A dilemma already has occurred with respect to the increasing invasion of psychiatry on disorders of mood, thought, and behavior. With the right to refuse treatment cases, which found their origins in the Christian Scientist's right to refuse psychotropic medication and now with the more recent cases[54] that will possibly apply this right to any involuntarily committed patient, there has been an affirmation by the court of the individual's right to autonomy, privacy, and individualism. This right has and is being affirmed even in cases in which the individual's perception to reality is distorted. The right to refuse treatment cases may conflict strongly in time with the growing sophistication of psychiatry in the area of behavioral modification and control. The battlegrounds for future major conflicts already are in formation. It appears that the rights of patients and prisoners with regard to these invasive techniques are receiving major priority. However, as more advanced psychiatric techniques are developed, amid an increasing clamor from society for some method of behavior alteration of criminals as well as mentally ill patients, these modification techniques may readily become viewed as the panacea of society's ills. There is no question that the next fifteen to twenty years will be marked by increasing tensions between the rights of autonomy and privacy of the individual patient and the requirements of society for order, conformity, and regression, despite resorting to these highly invasive modern technologies.

The ethical issues discussed in this chapter are of current concern in the field of psychiatry and mental health care. Those issues of behavior modification and control are in part already the object of considerable focus, but the future will see a major expansion of attention to the social conflicts of the rights of the individual in society. The importance of maintaining a society of diverse personalities with a variety of creative interests cannot be underestimated, particularly in the light of progress and productivity. At the same time, the forces for order and conformity in society are all-pervasive.

NOTES TO CHAPTER 13

1. Laurence R. Tancredi and Andrew E. Slaby, *Ethical Policy in Mental Health Care: The Goals of Psychiatric Intervention* (New York: Prodist, 1977).
2. Kaimowitz v. Department of Mental Health, Civ. No. 73-19434-AW (Cir. Ct. of Wayne County, Mich., July 10, 1973), abstracted in 13 Crim. L. Rptr. 2452 (1973).
3. Walter Reich, "Soviet Psychiatry on Trial," *Commentary*, January 1978, pp. 40-48.
4. Tancredi and Slaby, pp. 42-45.
5. A.B. Palmer and J. Wohl, "Voluntary Admission Forms: Does the Patient Know What He Is Signing?" *Hospital and Community Psychiatry* 23: 38-40 (August 1972); G.B. Olin and H.S. Olin, "Informed Consent and Voluntary Mental Hospital Admissions," *American Journal of Psychiatry* 132: 938-941 (September 1975).
6. Palmer and Wohl, pp. 38-40.
7. Olin and Olin, pp. 938-941.
8. Ibid.
9. Laurence R. Tancredi, Julian Lieb, and Andrew E. Slaby, *Legal Issues in Psychiatric Care* (New York: Harper & Row, 1975).
10. Tancredi and Slaby, pp. 42-45, 56-60.
11. Ibid., pp. 20-42.

12. Lessard v. Schmidt, 349 F. Supp. 1078 (E.D. Wisc. 1972), *vacated and remanded*, 414 U.S. 473 (1974).
13. Suzuki v. Quisenberry, 411 F. Supp. 1113 (D. Hawaii, 1976).
14. A.M. Dershowitz, "Dangerousness as a Criterion for Confinement," *Bulletin of the American Academy of Psychiatry and the Law* 2:172-197 (September 1974).
15. B.J. Ennis and T.R. Litwack, "Psychiatry and the Presumption of Expertise: Flipping Coins in the Courtroom," *California Law Review* 62:694-752 (May 1974).
16. John T. Monahan, "Prediction Research and the Emergency Commitment of Dangerous Mentally Ill Persons: A Reconsideration," *American Journal of Psychiatry* 135:198-201 (February 1978).
17. Tancredi and Slaby, pp. 110-114.
18. Lessard v. Schmidt, 349 F. Supp. 1078-1104 (E.D. Wisc. 1972); Suzuki v. Quisenberry, 411 F. Supp. 1113-1135 (D. Hawaii, 1976).
19. American Bar Association, Commission on the Mentally Disabled, *Mental Disability Law Reporter* 2:337-354 (September-December 1977).
20. Tarasoff v. Regents of the University of California, et al., 108 Cal. Rptr. 878 (1974).
21. A recent California Supreme Court ruling, *Bellah* v. *Greenson*, 141 Cal. Rptr. 92 (1977), did not extend *Tarasoff* in ruling that a psychiatrist is not liable to parents under a wrongful death action where a patient—their daughter—committed suicide, which he was aware could occur because of her disposition.
22. Tancredi and Slaby, pp. 71-72.
23. Ibid., pp. 73-74.
24. David Mechanic, *Public Expectations and Health Care* (New York: Wiley Interscience, 1972).
25. Tancredi and Slaby, pp. 63-65.
26. Ibid., pp. 65-69.
27. Ibid., pp. 74-77.
28. Ibid., pp. 73-74, 90-93.
29. E. Robins, S.B. Guze, R.A. Woodruff et al., "Diagnostic Criteria for Use in Psychiatric Research," *Archives of General Psychiatry* 26:57-62 (1972).
30. A.B. Hollingshead and F.C. Redlich, *Social Class and Mental Illness* (New York: John Wiley and Sons, 1958).
31. T.S. Sanger, S.T. Michael et al., *Mental Health in the Metropolis, vol. 1—The Midtown Manhattan Study* (New York: McGraw-Hill, 1962).
32. A. Leighton, *My Name Is Legion—The Sterling County Study of Psychiatric Disorders, A Socio-Cultural Environment, vol. 1* (New York: Basic Books, Inc., 1959).

33. J.M. Myers and L.L. Bean, *A Decade Later—A Follow-Up of Social Class and Mental Illness* (New York: John Wiley and Sons, 1968).

34. L.S. Linn, "Social Characteristics and Social Interaction in the Utilization of the Psychiatric Outpatient Clinic," *Journal of Health and Social Behavior* 8: 3–7 (1967).

35. National Institute of Mental Health, *The Cost of Mental Illness 1974–1975* (Washington, D.C.: U.S. Government Printing Office, 1976); U.S. Congressional Budget Office, *Special Analysis Budget of the United States Government—1977* (Washington, D.C.: U.S. Government Printing Office, 1976).

36. D.X. Freedman, "The Alma Mater Is Smoking—This Is Dangerous to Your Health," *Archives of General Psychiatry* 33: 407–410 (1976).

37. U.S. Congressional Budget Office, pp. 6–22.

38. D.C. Jenkins, "Recent Evidence Supporting Psychological and Social Risk Factors for Coronary Disease," *New England Journal of Medicine* 294: 1033–1038 (1976).

39. S. Greer and T. Morris, "Psychological Attributes of Women Who Develop Breast Cancer: A Controlled Study," *Journal of Psychosomatic Research* 19:147–153 (1975).

40. Tancredi and Slaby, pp. 77–86.

41. Ibid., pp. 125–131.

42. R.N. Butler, "Psychiatry and the Elderly: An Overview," *American Journal of Psychiatry* 132: 893–900 (September 1975).

43. Reich, pp. 40–48.

44. Andrew E. Slaby and Laurence R. Tancredi, *Collusion for Conformity* (New York: Jason Aronson, 1975).

45. Ibid., pp. 1–33; Nicholas Kittrie, *The Right to be Different* (Baltimore: Johns Hopkins University Press, 1973).

46. Slaby and Tancredi, pp. 143–148.

47. Tancredi and Slaby, pp. 86–90.

48. Ibid., pp. 90–93.

49. Ibid., pp. 73–74; A.L. Cochrane, *Effectiveness and Efficiency: Random Reflections on Health Services.* (London: Burgess & Sons, Ltd., 1971).

50. Tancredi and Slaby, pp. 73–74, 131–138.

51. Cochrane, pp. 35–52.

52. Tancredi and Slaby, pp. 117–124.

53. Ibid., pp. 98–110.

54. In re: The Mental Health of K.K.B. 609 P.2d 747 (Okla. 1980); Rogers v. Okin, 478 F. Supp. 1342 (1979); Rennie v. Klein, 462 F. Supp. 1131 (1978).

IV REPRODUCTION, RIGHTS, AND POPULATION PLANNING

Every year the U.S. government imposes laws and establishes programs that affect the balance among births, deaths, and human migration. These actions, consciously or unconsciously, constitute the promulgation of a population policy when viewed collectively. In the absence of an explicit, coherent public policy regarding population, an implicit, unclear policy emerges which fosters a plethora of unfair, inconsistent, and often contradictory results. These disjointed efforts precipitate major ethical and social issues at both societal and individual levels.

In summarizing several major findings and recommendations from reports ranging from *Population and the American Future*[1] (1972) to the *Global 2000 Report*[2] (1980), U.S. Representative Richard L. Ottinger (D-New York) reiterated his call to his congressional colleagues to enact a comprehensive population policy for the United States to address the nation's goals relating to overall size, growth, and distribution of its population changes.[3] There is an increasing awareness of many direct and indirect consequences of not having an explicit population policy in terms of the health care system and existing levels of health. In addition, the lack of such a population policy impinges on a multitude of programs related to education, employment, housing, agriculture, commerce, transportation, communication, and services to senior citizens. Having no such policy disallows many advantages to and social needs for the federal government engaging in population planning at a national level. Although it is not the first such attempt, Ottinger's proposed legislation in the Ninety-seventh Congress seeks demographic change to achieve an optimum balance between population, resources, and the environment.[4] However, regardless of the legitimate need for such legislation, adoption of this or any other national population policy carries certain ethical and social values.

With the ensuing debate at the national level, ethical concerns arise, not only related to the question of whether the government should or should not establish such a policy or whether the goal should be population stabilization,[a] but more importantly with respect to the means through which it is to be achieved. Thus, despite impending discussions at the national level of government, many Americans are concerned with the existing, conflicting reproductive health policies that have emerged over recent decades and that directly affect the lives of individuals and families. These reproductive health policies reflect decisions on fertility related practices such as family planning, abortion, sterilization, and genetic screening, and they collectively constitute a major component of an overall population policy. For a variety of reasons many of these issue-specific laws are inconsistent and in conflict with each other, and many enjoin more general national policy trends.

With respect to reproductive health policies, a wide range of ethical theories (e.g., justice, autonomy, beneficence and nonmaleficence) and personal values (e.g., what is right versus what is wrong) warrant considerable consideration. Conflicting positions reflect the public debate and ensuing policies. On one end of the spectrum arguments support individual liberties, rights, and freedoms; on the other, more deontological justifications suggest that decisions related to procreation should remain solely with God. On another front, the interests of society as a whole relating to broad social and economic impact of given policy decisions are often heard. In most cases the debates never reach amenable resolution due to the nature of the clash between those advocating the right to self-determination and quality of life versus those supporting the sanctity of life.

In this part, five chapters present a wide range of issues related to an overall population policy and several specific reproductive health

---

a. In a national context, the population is stabilized when the number of births and immigration equal the number of deaths and emigration.

issues. The first two essays by Kraft and Oakley, respectively, address critical issues related to and the implications of establishing a comprehensive population policy in the United States. Chapter 14 by Kraft explores a wide range of policy implications of demographic changes in the population. In acknowledging the existing shift towards an aging population and the transition to a slow growth or a no-growth future, Kraft considers some of the major political, economic, and ethical issues precipitated by population stabilization.

In Chapter 15, Oakley depicts the interrelationship and the interdependency of a population policy and reproductive health programs. She critically examines how coercive and noncoercive governmental policies influence reproductive health behavior and childbearing among American women drawing upon comparisons with the Chinese culture. She further explores many of the social and ethical values and implications associated with the promulgation and implementation of a population policy. Oakley argues that assuring equality for women and increasing reproductive choices constitute important, integral components in the establishment of a meaningful and ethically sound national population policy.

The remaining chapters in this part address three highly controversial reproductive health issues. Although each issue—genetic screening, voluntary sterilization, and abortion among the poor—reflects individual (i.e., personal) and societal dimensions in which hard choices must often be made, existing policies generate value conflicts, public debate, and unjustified suffering. In each, ethical and legal questions arise regarding individual rights, social justice, and whether the respective practices are right or wrong, good or evil, or just or unjust. Furthermore, an overriding concern is whether government should even intervene in matters involving such personal value judgments and decisionmaking.

Steele (Chapter 16) invites inquiry about the social and economic costs and benefits of mass genetic screening programs. In addition, he legitimates concerns associated with such programs, particularly those directed at large populations or entire communities. As a physician deeply committed to genetic well-being, Steele cites many advantages made available through appropriate genetic screening and counseling, but also sounds a warning about potential disadvantages and abuses. To this end, he advocates the need for the protection of individuals and populations as a whole from unreasonable exploitations produced by some coercive screening efforts which may be geared more for population research purposes than for individual therapeutic relief.

In Chapter 17, Gonzales and Sansoucie analyze recently promulgated U.S. sterilization policy and related critical issues. Although the authors recognize historical abuses and violations of human rights associated with involuntary sterilization, they argue that the enforcement of overly protective restrictive regulations are equally bad as they serve to impose one group's values on another. In other words, in an effort to protect abusive and coercive practices, they contend that stringent regulations place undue restraints and barriers on individuals who are both competent and desirous of terminating their fertility through voluntary sterilization. Hence, neither economic issues cited by some to support sterilization of the poor and dependent nor religious or social pressures used by others to ban an individual's voluntary decision to seek sterilization are universally valid.

The authors suggest that the federal government has overreacted by imposing overly restrictive federal regulations that strip an individual's right to autonomy and a physician's obligation to practice beneficent medicine. Furthermore, since public policy in this regard is binding only to those dependent on medical assistance for the procedure, they further conclude that such regulations are discriminatory and unjust.

Kaufman tackles possibly the most controversial, ethical dilemma of the twentieth century in Chapter 18 when he analyzes current public policy and abortion. While leaning towards a women's right to self-determination—that is, the right to choose to terminate or to continue a pregnancy to term, he argues that existing public policy on abortion is unjustly discriminatory against a particular segment of the nation's population, namely the poor (who are dependent on public support or welfare). He documents the implications of and negative consequences produced by enforcement of the statutory ban on federal support (i.e., Medicaid) for abortion services for the poor except in certain limited circumstances.

Kaufman provides evidence of the strong impact of a powerful, well-organized minority in affecting the life and well-being of millions of American women. He further notes the failure of society to address adequately the health and welfare problems of children born into poverty. Beyond illustrating the lack of ethical and social values inherent in limiting a woman's right to choose that which violates highly cherished principles of privacy, social justice, equal protection and due process, he illustrates the even greater social injustice of infringing on the lives of the weakest segment of our society—the poor—and forcing them into a state of compulsory pregnancy and parenthood.

NOTES TO PART IV

1. Commission on Population Growth and the American Future, *Population and the American Future* (Washington, D.C.: U.S. Government Printing Office, 1972).
2. Council on Environmental Quality and U.S. Department of State, *Global 2000 Report to the President: Entering the Twenty-first Century* (Washington, D.C.: U.S. Government Printing Office, 1980).
3. Richard H. Ottinger, "United States Needs to Look at Population Changes." *Congressional Record* 127: E382–E383 (February 5, 1981).
4. U.S. Congress, House of Representatives, *A Bill to Establish a National Population Policy and to Establish an Office of Population Policy, H.R. 907,* 97th Cong., 1st sess. (Washington, D.C.: U.S. Government Printing Office January 19, 1981).

14 POLICY IMPLICATIONS OF U.S. POPULATION STABILIZATION

Michael E. Kraft, Ph.D.

Population growth is a relatively new issue on the American political agenda. As recently as 1959, President Dwight D. Eisenhower said that he could not "imagine anything more emphatically a subject that is not a proper political or governmental activity."[1] In July 1969, President Richard M. Nixon sent a message to Congress in which he characterized population growth as: "one of the most serious challenges to human destiny of the last third of this century"[2] and called for the creation of a Commission on Population Growth and the American Future (the Commission) to study the problem and its impact on the nation.

The evolution of governmental attention to population concerns between 1959 and 1969 is remarkable. Since the height of public concern about population growth in 1970, an even more striking development has been a sharp decline in fertility rates in the United States and other developed nations.[3] A few years after the Commission issued its final report in 1972—accompanied by six volumes of scholarly research on the social, economic, environmental, and governmental consequences of population growth—the American public, government policymakers, and professional demographers ceased to consider domestic population growth as a major problem. Indeed,

Editor's Note: Chapter 15 discusses many policy issues related to those addressed here.

concern has been expressed that continued low fertility might lead to undesirable social and economic consequences.[4] Furthermore, some have speculated that in the future the government may choose to adopt pronatalist policies to prevent population decline.[5]

Given these developments during the past twenty years and the fairly widespread consensus among demographers that the near-term future of the United States will be characterized by sustained low fertility, an investigation of the public policy implications of population change seems in order. In particular, if stabilization of the U.S. population is to be a national goal worth pursuing—or is a condition that will come about naturally through personal fertility decisions— public policymaking in the United States should be based on an analysis of the impact of such population change. Major policy choices will have to be made to ease the transition to a slow growth or no growth future. This chapter considers some of the political, economic, and ethical issues raised by population stabilization and by possible governmental actions related to that demographic development.

POPULATION TRENDS

In mid-1979, the U.S. population approximated 220 million. The fertility rate in 1978 was slightly less than 1.8 births per woman, significantly below the replacement level of 2.1 births per woman, and marked the sixth year in which the total fertility rate remained near 1.8. Even at this low rate, however, the country's population is subject to considerable growth. In 1978, the population increased by approximately 1.8 million, due to a natural increase of 1.4 million and the legal migration of 379,000 individuals. Adding illegal immigration, estimated at between 166,000 and one million each year, would raise the growth rate appreciably.

What does the future look like? Several population projections are offered by the U.S. Bureau of the Census, based upon different assumptions regarding fertility and immigration. If childbearing continues at the 1.8 rate, the medium projection of the Bureau, the population in the year 2000 would be 260 million. If the rate declines to 1.7 births per woman and if net immigration is held at 400,000 per year, the current low projection of the Bureau, the population would reach 246 million in the year 2000 and would stabilize at 253 million by the year 2020.[6]

Such estimates of future growth rates and population size depend heavily on the accuracy of forecasting future fertility rates.[7] Although demographers do not know enough about the social, economic, and psychological determinants of fertility to predict future rates with great certainty, there is widespread belief that the current low rates will continue and possibly decrease further. The reasons for this confidence relates to the expected continuation of conditions leading to the present low fertility—increasing education, equality of women, participation of women in the labor force, costs of having and raising children, and the development and extent of use of new contraceptive technologies including sterilization. As Westoff states, "nothing on the horizon suggests that fertility will not remain low. All the recent evidence on trends in marriage and reproductive behavior encourages a presumption that it will remain low."[8]

To the extent that these expectations are valid, current population trends may be summarized as a short-term continuation of a relatively high rate of growth even while the low fertility rate is maintained, followed by a long transition period of continued low fertility and a slowing of the rate of growth, followed by an eventual stabilization of the population (i.e., an achievement of a stable, stationary, or nongrowing population). The time frame for these stages cannot be specified with accuracy, but for present purposes this is not crucial. Population growth may also fluctuate around a zero rate or even decline appreciably for a period of time. This chapter does not address these possibilities, since they would occur in an even more distant and uncertain future.

POLICY CHOICES

What should be the nation's response to these projected population changes? Should stabilization of the American population be welcomed as desirable in an age of resource scarcity or should it be opposed as detrimental to the social, political, and economic welfare of the country? What national policies might be required to adapt to the expected population changes or to attempt to alter them? There could be a wide spectrum of views on the twin questions of the desirability of population stabilization and the need for new public policies:

1. Assuming a strongly positive response suggests that the benefits of stabilization clearly outweigh the costs of continued growth. A national policy declaring stabilization as a goal and providing for rapid achievement of that goal is favored.

2. Assuming a positive to neutral position suggests that the benefits are believed to outweigh the costs, but that a national policy is not needed to proclaim stabilization as a goal or to attempt to alter personal fertility or immigration patterns. Accommodation to the social and economic consequences of continued low fertility may require population planning.

3. Assuming a neutral to negative stance suggests that the negative consequences of stabilization may outweigh the benefits, but that present knowledge of the implications of stabilization is too incomplete to confirm this. Adoption of pronatalist policies or those increasing immigration levels may need to be considered in order to slow the declining growth rate.

4. Assuming a negative position suggests that the costs of stabilization clearly outweigh its benefits. A national policy to maintain a high rate of growth is favored.

The first position is endorsed by Zero Population Growth, Inc. (ZPG);[9] by many environmentalists and limits to growth advocates;[10] by some population studies scholars;[11] and to a limited extent, by the Commission.[12] The second position is favored by many demographers,[13] seems to be shared in part by the American public, and may be supported by many government policymakers. The third position appears to be taken by a few demographers[14] and may characterize the views of a significant minority of policymakers. The fourth position is not currently endorsed by many within the United States, but may increase in importance as stabilization approaches.[15]

Obviously, there are conflicting views on the desirability of population stabilization and on the need for further policy development. The brief history of formulation and adoption of population policies in the United States serves as a useful reminder of the type of political conflict and obstacles to policymaking that will be encountered in the future as the nation decides how to welcome the present trend toward stabilization.

Most simply, public policy is what governments choose to do or not to do about public problems. Population policy has been defined in many ways, but may be considered to be government actions that affect or attempt to affect some component of population change (i.e., births, deaths, migration). However, when population policy is mentioned in the context of national reaction to stabilization, a more explicit conception of public policy is implied, such as a projected program of goals, values, and practices.[16] Hence, population policy is taken to mean a comprehensive, coherent statement of a nation's population goals and the specific means to be used in achieving them.

Using this definition, the United States has no population policy. Instead, it has a collection of policies—direct and indirect, explicit and implicit, population influencing and population responsive—with very little coordination and no detectable commitment to a particular population goal. Population policymaking has been ad hoc, narrowly focused, piecemeal, and incremental. For example, although the Family Planning and Population Research Act (PL 91–572) was enacted in 1970, shortly after President Nixon's message to Congress requesting a population commission, the Act is not a comprehensive statement of policy. It was enacted as a public health measure to help reduce unwanted fertility through the provision of grants to states for the delivery of contraceptive services and for the promotion of research on contraceptive technology and reproductive behavior.[17]

POPULATION POLICYMAKING

A number of efforts to formulate policy proposals and to build political support for action on a comprehensive policy on population goals have been undertaken since 1971.[18] In 1971, the U.S. Senate held hearings on a population stabilization resolution, but the committee did not report out the bill.[19] In 1972, the Commission recommended that the nation "welcome and plan for" an end to population growth and said that population stabilization would contribute significantly to the nation's ability to solve its problems.[20] However,

President Nixon rejected some controversial recommendations of the Commission (e.g., on abortion and on contraceptive services for teenagers) and paid little attention to the rest of the report. Thus, the Commission's recommendations cannot be viewed as a statement of U.S. public policy or as a position clearly endorsed by significant policymakers.[21]

The Select Committee on Population of the U.S. House of Representatives held a total of thirty-seven days of hearings on population problems and consequences in 1977 and 1978. A considerable portion of these hearings was directly relevant to evaluating the desirability of population stabilization and to making policy decisions for population planning. However, the Select Committee was not extended by the House in 1979, apparently because of internal jurisdictional politics and a lack of sufficient political support. The impact of the extensive hearings on policy development in the future remains to be seen.

ZPG sponsored legislation in 1978 and again in 1979, calling for a national policy of coordinated planning for population change and eventual population stabilization. The bill called for the creation of an office of population planning in the White House, mandated an annual report on national population change and planning, and called for all agencies of the federal government to review their present statutory authority, administrative regulations, and current policies and procedures to ensure compliance with the provisions of the bill. No hearings were held. Thus far, the main effect of such legislation has been to help establish the political agenda and to keep the issues incubating on Capitol Hill until sufficient public interest and political support develop in the future.[a] This type of legislation also serves to remind the population community of the omission of such institutional components in the collection of present policies. Formulation of such comprehensive policy proposals and their introduction in Congress mark only the first steps in a lengthy and difficult legislative process, the conclusion of which may be years or decades away.

Why has there been no more success than this brief review indicates? Policymaking is successful when proposals are supported by a

a. Editor's Note: Due to mounting recognition of the need for a U.S. population policy, new legislation to establish a national population policy was introduced into the House of Representatives (H.R. 907) in the 97th Cong., 1st sess. on January 19, 1981. National hearings on H.R. 907 are also scheduled.

large, well-organized, well-financed, or very effective national constituencies. No such constituency calling for population stabilization as an explicit policy goal exists. The American public is not convinced that there is a problem and in any event does not rate population concerns among the most salient of public problems. Furthermore, there is also only a very small constituency concerned about population trends and their consequences and a very small group of representatives and senators interested in this policy area. For most members of Congress, other more pressing and politically rewarding issues receive their limited attention, time, and resources. Partly as a result of this selective inattention, most members of Congress are generally poorly informed about population trends, do not fully understand complex policy issues, or tend to discount the uncertain, long-term consequences of population change as well as the need to plan for resulting policy impacts.[22] Many policymakers also identify population issues as inherently controversial and politically dangerous. To the extent that the politics of abortion and related moralistic concerns influence reactions to population stabilization, attention to the problem and efforts to devise appropriate public policy will be hindered.

In addition to these formidable obstacles, Congress is so fragmented organizationally that any systematic policymaking efforts are exceptionally difficult. Michael Teitlebaum, staff director of the short-lived House Select Committee on Population, calculated that at least thirty committees of Congress (and possibly as many as one hundred) deal with population issues, making coordinated analysis of problems and cooperative or comprehensive policymaking unlikely. His views of the policymaking capacity of Congress were pessimistic following the demise of the Select Committee in 1979: "Chaos is a characteristic of Congress. Much that happens is accidental or not understood by those who make it happen."[23]

Institutional fragmentation, inattention, poor understanding of the facts, and a lack of political incentives to consider and act on proposals may sometimes be overcome through effective presidential and congressional leadership. However, in the population policy area, such leadership has been notably lacking. Policymaking on issues such as population stabilization becomes even more difficult due to the recent decline in public confidence in governmental capacity, loss of public trust in political leadership, loss of a sense of shared concern over the nation's collective interest and its future, and a variety of related political constraints on policymaking that restrain the building of sufficient consensus and support for action.

The overall record of population policymaking in the United States, especially with regard to population planning, does not inspire much confidence in the rationality of the policy process. Ideally, it should be formulated using the best available—albeit incomplete— data on the social, economic, health, and policy consequences of population change. In addition, policymaking needs to include a thorough examination of the political and ethical issues raised by the trend toward stabilization and by alternative policies that governments may consider. Examination of such issues allows clarification of the criteria by which policy alternatives should be assessed. Taken together, these analytical inquiries constitute a basis for rational decisionmaking on population stabilization.

ASSESSING POLICY CHOICES: THE CONSEQUENCES OF POPULATION CHANGE

A review of the limited and still developing literature on the social, economic, and political consequences of sustained low fertility and population stabilization leaves one with the impression that less is known than optimally desirable for the formulation of long-term population policy. However, there does seem to be a consensus that the benefits of stabilization outweigh the costs.[24] There are fewer negative consequences than generally assumed, and these can be significantly ameliorated with proper planning for a gradual transition to a stationary population. The major controversies appear to revolve around how the relative advantages of a stable population with the presumed short-term costs of slowing growth are assessed. At a minimum, the nation needs a forum in which these kinds of issues may be raised and discussed. The expired Select Committee might have provided a particularly important debate forum.

The academic literature on this subject provides at least some tentative answers to the questions posed. Most analyses of the future impact of stabilization begin by acknowledging the expected aging of the population as growth slows. In 1970, the average age of the U.S. population was twenty-eight; in a stationary population it would be thirty-seven. In addition, an older population obviously carries a number of implications for economic conditions and for the type and level of demand for goods and services (public or private), including health care services. Given current fertility rates, the elderly population (ages sixty-five or older) is projected to grow to thirty-four million by 2010 and to fifty-two million by 2030. The proportion of the elderly in the total population was 10.7 percent in 1976, will start to rise rapidly in 2010, and will peak in 2030 at between 14 and 22 percent, depending on future fertility rates.[25]

In addition to the aggregate increase in the aged population, the relative growth in the seventy-five years of age and older cohort is of special interest. Of the 6.9 million increase in the elderly population expected in the 1980s and the 1990s, almost three-quarters will be in this group. In short, as the population moves toward a stable size, the percentage of those eighteen and under will decline appreciably, and the percentage of those aged sixty-five and over will increase appreciably. The old age dependency ratio will increase from 0.18 in 1980 to 0.32 by the year 2030 under the U.S. Census Bureau's Series II projection (medium fertility) and will rise to 0.38 should its Series III (low fertility) projection prove to be more accurate.[26]

What do such populations imply for public policy? This question is more difficult to answer. The Select Committee claimed that more data, analysis, and research are necessary for making informed policy with respect to the elderly. However, the lack of data is not the only problem in predicting the type of impact an aging population will have on the nation's resources. The consequences of an aging population will to some extent be a matter of conjecture because demographic conditions are not necessarily going to be the major determinant of the future quality of life in the United States. For example, economic growth, environmental policies, technological development, and energy supply and demand will significantly affect future resources and thus will shape the nature of the burden of an aging population. The influence of demographic changes is mediated through a complex set of social, economic, and cultural conditions, suggesting that demographic determinism is not an appropriate means to predict the future.[27] Consider the implications of such a perspective with respect to the demand for health care services.

The per capita demand for medical resources is greater for elderly people than for the general population. Thus, with an increasing number of elderly citizens, with an increasing proportion of elderly in the population, and with the aging of the elderly, a significant increase in the demand for health services is expected. Furthermore, depending on the response of Congress, the proportion of the health budget to be used for the provision of health services for the elderly would increase dramatically.[28] As one indicator of the projected cost increases, the Select Committee received estimated expenditures for hospital care of the elderly under two conditions—no inflation and a 10 percent increase per year to allow for inflation as well as for changes in the services offered by hospitals, for new equipment, and so on. Under the first assumption, the cost for the elderly population aged sixty-five and over rises from $12.3 billion in 1975 to $17.3 billion by the year 2000. Under the second assumption (i.e., with inflation), the cost rises to $187.8 billion in the year 2000. In both projections, the rate of increase is much greater for groups aged seventy-five and over and eighty-five and over.

If these projections prove accurate, (1) the costs of stabilization (with an aging population) will be excessive and the transition to a stationary population should be slowed, or (2) the nation must engage in extensive population planning and policy planning in general to allow a smooth transition to an era with considerably different economic and health care costs. An aging of the population does not translate automatically into the presumed increased level of demands for medical services, nursing homes, and so forth. Future demands for such services are dependent on more than the aggregate number implied in the statistics on aging. They depend upon the habits, expectations, and demands of older persons. Aging is a social and psychological process as well as a biological one. To the extent that older persons are encouraged to remain active and useful and have the opportunities to do so, their need for and demand for health care services may be less than the assumed projections.[29] Furthermore, interest groups representing older persons are keenly interested in bringing about changes in attitudes toward aging precisely in this direction. The 1981 White House Conference on Aging will provide a major forum for the discussion of such possibilities.

These remarks are not meant to dismiss the probable increase in demands for health care services that will accompany transition to population stabilization. Rather, they simply acknowledge the great many uncertainties in projecting economic and health care consequences of an aging population. Additionally, they acknowledge that there are important social and political choices that can alter the very projections of future costs that are frequently presented by those who view stabilization as possibly detrimental to the public welfare.

Beyond the case of health care services, what conclusions should be drawn from current research on the economic and social consequences of population stabilization? In 1972, the Commission concluded, in part, that

> in the long run, no substantial benefits will result from further growth of the Nation's population, rather that the gradual stabilization of our population through voluntary means would contribute significantly to the Nation's ability to solve its problems. We have looked for, and have not found any convincing economic argument for continued population growth. The health of our country does not depend on it, nor does the vitality of business nor the welfare of the average person.[30]

Based on a more recent, major review of economic research on this subject, including studies conducted between 1972 and 1978, Espenshade concludes that although many research questions remain unanswered, the overall consensus among economists "would appear to be that the net impact of a decline in population growth would be positive, in terms of a per capita measure of economic well being."[31] The health of a nation depends far more on the adoption of wise economic policies than on its demographic trends. Population change is important, but it is not determinative.

Espenshade's conclusions follow a thorough examination of the impact of sustained low population growth on social security, pensions, education, the spatial distribution of economic activity, the labor force, and levels of consumption (including consumption of health care services). As he notes, the proper questions with respect to population stabilization are not merely whether it is desirable or not, but over what time period and with what type of public policies or other instruments should the goal of stabilization be pursued to minimize social and economic disruptions. Transition to zero population growth will create some problems that necessitate personal adjustments and governmental action. However, there is no reason why such adaptation cannot be accomplished if there is adequate planning for population change and a political process that is receptive to making appropriate policy decisions.

ETHICAL ISSUES IN POLICY CHOICE

To the extent that important policy choices will have to be made in support of, or in response to, population stabilization, serious ethical issues will be raised. For example, should present programs of family planning services be maintained or increased in size? Should existing restrictive policies on abortion be maintained? Should contraceptive services for teenagers be expanded? What are appropriate policies on sensitive issues such as sex education, population education, participation of women in the labor force, and full equal rights for women? Currently acceptable and relatively noncontroversial policies may come under critical review in the future depending on public and governmental reactions to slowing population growth. In Eastern Europe, a number of nations have reacted to such population change by adopting strongly pronatalist policies.[32] Will the reaction in Europe be duplicated in the United States in the future?

Given these types of policy issues, what guidelines or procedures are available for determining the best or most appropriate policy choice in any given case? There are many criteria used in public policy analysis and in public policymaking. These may be explicitly stated or only implicit in the value judgments made. The criteria most often used include expected effectiveness of a policy or program; scientific, medical, and technological feasibility; administrative feasibility; economic costs and benefits; and political feasibility, including social acceptability. Ethical or moral acceptability should be added to this list, even though not all policy debate includes such considerations.

A moral or ethical proposition is a statement reflecting a rank order of preferences among alternatives that is intended to apply to more than one person.[33] Ethical criteria are among those that can contribute to determining which policies—and which social and political processes—are most desirable in terms of the general welfare or most consistent with specific standards of morality. They are not, however, easily applied to the type of questions confronted under conditions of slowing population growth.

What kinds of ethical criteria are especially relevant to population policies in general? Much of the literature on ethical issues in population policy was developed as a contribution to public debate over global population growth. Some of the same considerations, however, should influence domestic policy decisions. The ethical issues include the conflict among and ranking of four major values—freedom, justice and equity, security and survival, and the general welfare.[34] Freedom may be defined as the absence of government coercion; the flourishing of human dignity; or the ability to choose, shape, and implement one's own thinking and action. Justice and equity imply equality of treatment and opportunity or due process and equitable access to resources and opportunities in life. Security and survival refer to physical and psychological safety and a continuation of the ability to exist and to pursue other values. They may also refer to the security of subgroups within a nation, minority groups in particular.[35] The general welfare seems to be a catchall category for the fulfillment of remaining human needs—physical, cultural, psychological, and social.

It is easy to argue that ethical considerations should be an integral part of public discussion and policymaking processes. However, it is more difficult to determine exactly how such ethical norms can be applied to the kinds of policy choices outlined in this chapter. Treatises on the importance of ethics in population policy may not be of much help in clarifying the choices to be made, and ethical discourse may play a very limited role in government policymaking.[36] As noted above, the explicitness and rank ordering of values in policymaking is probably ill defined, and the values concerned are often unclear and subject to varying definitions. Hence, a solution may possibly lie in a procedural approach to decisionmaking.

In his essay on "Population Policies and Ethical Acceptability," Arthur Dyck distinguishes two meanings to ethical acceptability.[37] One looks to normative criteria like freedom, justice, and security. The other relies on decisionmaking procedures rather than a case-by-case determination of morality. In other words, procedures that allow or encourage consideration of appropriate norms may be considered ethically acceptable. It may be that this approach offers a partial answer to the question of how to apply ethical norms to policy choices related to population stabilization.

CONCLUSIONS

The United States should develop a policy on population stabilization. The purpose of such a policy would not be to declare a particular population size as optimal nor simply to favor eventual stabilization of the population—to do so would be like favoring sunrises and sunsets. Rather, the purpose of adopting such a policy would be to indicate a preferred timetable for transition to stabilization and to establish a set of institutional mechanisms and procedures for considering appropriate data and policy measures. The value of establishing this policy lies in meeting a need for planning for and coordination of present policies affecting population change. Additional research is needed on the consequences of slower growth and on alternative paths for adapting to stabilization. An institutional setting for data collection and analysis would improve our capability for weighing the costs and benefits of alternative ways of slowing population growth. For example, the creation of an Office of Population Planning in the White House or in the Executive Office of the President would increase the likelihood that such research, data collection, and analysis would be considered more seriously by national policymakers.

The Select Committee heard testimony from a number of witnesses on the desirability of creating such planning offices and procedures.[38] The appeal of this proposal in an era increasingly characterized by antibureaucratic sentiments and limited government resources is highly uncertain. However, one positive note can be found in a recent budget submitted by the president to Congress. The Office of Management and Budget included in that document a six page discussion of "Population Change and Long Range Effects on the Budget," apparently the first such analysis to appear in a federal budget.[39]

The public debate that would accompany consideration of such a national policy (and equivalent policies at the state and local level) would help insure that a valuative discourse takes place. More significantly, policymaking procedures might be created that call for explicit consideration of social, economic, political, and ethical issues and that ensure widespread public access to decisionmakers during their considerations of major policies. The nation's transition to a future characterized by population stabilization is important enough to suggest that nothing less would serve the public interest.

NOTES TO CHAPTER 14

1. Phyllis T. Piotrow, *World Population Crisis: The United States Response* (New York: Praeger Publishers, Inc., 1973), p. 73.
2. Richard M. Nixon, "The Population Problem—Message from the President," *Congressional Record*, July 18, 1969, pp. S8229-8232.
3. Charles F. Westoff, "Marriage and Fertility in the Developed Countries," *Scientific American* 239: 51-57 (December 1978).

4. William Petersen, "Population Policy and Age Structure," in Michael E. Kraft and Mark Schneider, *Population Policy Analysis: Issues in American Politics* (Lexington, MA: Lexington Books, 1978), pp. 15-26; James A. Weber, *Grow or Die* (New Rochelle, N.Y.: Arlington House, 1977).

5. Westoff.

6. U.S. Department of Commerce, Bureau of the Census, *Current Population Reports*, Series P-24, no. 704 (Washington, D.C.: U.S. Government Printing Office, 1978).

7. Leon F. Bouvier, "U.S. Population in 2000—Zero Growth or Not?" *Population Bulletin* 30:1-32 (1975).

8. Westoff, p. 54.

9. Zero Population Growth, Inc., *A U.S. Population Policy: Z.P.G.'s Recommendations* (Washington, D.C., January 1977); Zero Population Growth Inc., *A Basic Case for Zero Population Growth in the United States* (Washington, D.C., 1979).

10. William Ophuls, *Ecology and the Politics of Ecology* (San Francisco: W.H. Freeman and Company, 1977); Herman E. Daly, *Steady State Economics* (San Francisco: W.H. Freeman and Company, 1977).

11. Leslie Corsa, "Population Policy for the United States," *Sierra*, May/June 1979); Kingsley Davis, "Zero Population Growth: The Goal and the Means," in Mancur Olson and Hans L. Landsberg, *The No-Growth Society* (New York: W.W. Norton and Company, Inc., 1973)

12. Commission on Population Growth and the American Future, *Population and the American Future* (Washington, D.C.: U.S. Government Printing Office, 1972).

13. Lincoln H. Day, "The Social Consequences of a Zero Population Growth Rate in the United States," in Charles F. Westoff and Robert Parke, Jr., *Demographic and Social Aspects of Population Growth* (Washington, D.C.: U.S. Government Printing Office, 1972), pp. 659-673; Lincoln H. Day, "What Will a ZPG Society Be Like?" *Population Bulletin* 33:1-43 (June 1978); Norman B. Ryder, "Two Cheers for ZPG," in Olson and Landsberg, *The No-Growth Society*, pp. 45-62; Thomas J. Espenshade, "Zero Population Growth and the Economies of Developed Nations," *Population and Development Review* 4: 645-680 (December 1978).

14. Petersen.

15. Weber.

16. Howard D. Lasswell and Abraham Kaplan, *Power and Society* (New Haven: Yale University Press, 1950).

17. Carl Pope, "Population," in James Rathlesberger, *Nixon and the Environment* (New York: Village Voice Books, 1972); Dorothy M. Stetson, "Family Policy and Fertility in the United States," in Kraft and Schneider, *Population Policy Analysis: Issues in American Politics*, pp. 103-114.

18. Pope; Peter Bachrach and Elihu Bergman, *Power and Choice: The Formulation of American Population Policy* (Lexington, MA: Lexington Books,

1973); Thomas B. Littlewood, *The Politics of Population Control* (Notre Dame, IN: University of Notre Dame Press, 1977).

19. U.S. Congress, Senate, Committee on Labor and Public Welfare, Special Subcommittee on Human Resources, *Declaration of U.S. Policy on Population Stabilization by Voluntary Means, Hearings*, 92d Cong., 1st sess. (Washington, D.C.: U.S. Government Printing Office, 1971); Natalie Davis Spingarn, "Population Report/Fertility Drop Confuses Debate over National Population Growth Policy," *National Journal*, November 20, 1971, pp. 2288-2301.

20. Commission on Population Growth and the American Future.

21. A.E. Keir Nash, "Procedural and Substantive Unorthodoxies on the Population Commission's Agenda," in Kraft and Schneider, *Population Policy Analysis: Issues in American Politics*, pp. 55-65.

22. Michael E. Kraft, "Congressional Attitudes Toward the Environment: Attention and Issue Orientation in Ecological Politics" (Ph.D. dissertation, Yale University, 1973), pp. 193-200.

23. Population Reference Bureau, *Intercom* (Washington, D.C., May 1979), p. 14.

24. Thomas J. Espenshade and William G. Serow, *The Economic Consequences of Slowing Population Growth* (New York: Academic Press, Inc., 1978); Joseph J. Spengler, *Facing Zero Population Growth: Reactions and Interpretations, Past and Present* (Durham, NC: Duke University Press, 1978); Council of Europe, *Population Decline in Europe: Implications of a Declining or Stationary Population* (New York: St. Martin's Press, Inc., 1978).

25. U.S. Congress, House of Representatives, Select Committee on Population, *Final Report of the Select Committee on Population*, 95th Cong., 2d sess. (Washington, D.C.: U.S. Government Printing Office, 1978).

26. U.S. Congress, House of Representatives, Select Committee on Population and Select Committee on Aging, *Consequences of Changing U.S. Population: Demographics of Aging, Joint Hearings*, 95th Cong., 2d sess. (Washington, D.C.: U.S. Government Printing Office, 1978), p. 51.

27. Day, "The Social Consequences of a Zero Population Growth Rate in the United States."

28. U.S. Congress, House, *Consequences of Changing U.S. Population*, pp. 7-8.

29. Day, "The Social Consequences of a Zero Population Growth Rate in the United States"; Day, "What Will a ZPG Society Be Like?"

30. Commission on Population Growth and the American Future, p. 4.

31. Thomas J. Espenshade, "The Economic Consequences of Sustained Low Population Growth in the United States," in U.S. Congress, House of Representatives, Select Committee on Population, *Consequences of Changing U.S. Population: Baby Boom and Bust, Hearings*, 95 Cong., 2d sess. (Washington, D.C.: U.S. Government Printing Office, 1978), p. 394.

32. Council of Europe.
33. Daniel Callahan, "Ethics and Population Limitation," *Science* 175: 487–494 (February 1972).
34. Ibid.; Robert M. Veatch, *Population Policy and Ethics: The American Experience* (New York: Irvington Publishers, Inc., 1977).
35. Milton Himmelfarb and Victor Baras, *Zero Population Growth—For Whom?: Differential Fertility and Minority Group Survival* (Westport, CT: Greenwood Press, 1978).
36. Thomas G. Sanders, "Ethical Issues in Relating Normative Concerns to the Politics of Population," in Richard L. Clinton, *Population and Politics* (Lexington, MA: Lexington Books, 1973).
37. Arthur J. Dyck, "Population Policies and Ethical Acceptability," in Daniel Callahan, *The American Population Debate* (Garden City, NY: Doubleday and Company, Inc., 1971), pp. 351–377.
38. U.S. Congress, House of Representatives Select Committee on Population, *Consequences of Changing U.S. Population: Population Movement and Planning, Hearings,* 95th Cong., 2d sess. (Washington, D.C.: U.S. Government Printing Office, 1978).
39. U.S. Office of Management and Budget, *The Budget of the United States Government, Fiscal Year 1980* (Washington, D.C.: U.S. Government Printing Office, 1979), pp. 52–57.

15 REPRODUCTIVE FREEDOM AND THE DEVELOPMENT OF POPULATION POLICY

Deborah Oakley, Ph.D.

INTRODUCTION

It is sometimes felt that having children is natural and that government actions or policies taking no stand on the issue of planning births are also natural, thus placing all other governmental stances into a coercive category. In particular, it is often assumed that having a population policy means necessarily having fewer children; in the United States the initial reaction to the words "population policy" for our own country often seems to be the belief that such a policy would disallow couples from having more than two children. The discussion then is channeled into skeptical queries of enforcement, political acceptability, and technological capability.[1] In effect, not being antinatalist is considered natural and thereby noncoercive, while governmental policy that is antinatalist is assumed to be unnatural and coercive.

Equating no government action with freedom and any government action with coercion stems from a biological determinism of the worst kind—viewing women as uteri that seek inexorably to be filled. Rather, the more adequate framework for considering ethical questions in population policy is the model presented in Figure 15-1, which seeks to separate the pronatalist and antinatalist quality from the scale of coercion. This forced compliance, a function of

327

Figure 15-1.   External Forces on Reproductive Choice.

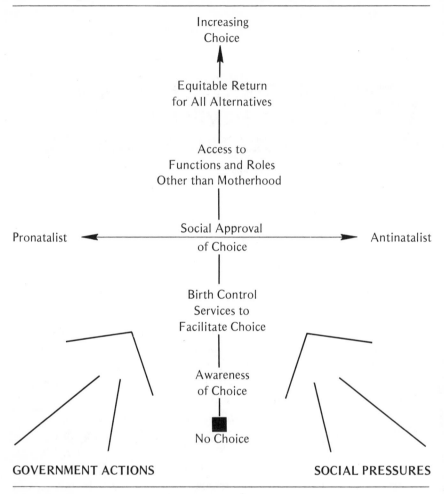

GOVERNMENT ACTIONS   SOCIAL PRESSURES

Source: Adapted from Leslie Corsa and Deborah Oakley, *Population Planning* (Ann Arbor: University of Michigan Press, 1979), p. 382.

anatomy, can require women not to have or to have children. Coercion can be pronatalist as well as antinatalist. That is, the goal itself does not determine whether a population policy is coercive or not. The agent of force can be government or society. Moving up the scale, women can become aware that they can prevent births or cure sterility; they become able to do so through access to services; they perceive increasing social support for using these services; and eventually they even become aware of the inner choice to have or not have children at all. Further up the scale toward full choice is access to roles and functions other than motherhood, and even further along the way toward true choice is equitable reward for these functions. According to this paradigm, women with many or with no children can be equally free as long as they have choice.

Differentiating the number of children from the element of coercion and the policy goal from the coercive or noncoercive means adopted to reach that goal is morally and practically important. While it is true that most population policies discussed today envision reduced population growth or its cessation and that this goal requires lower fertility (because one would not want higher mortality), there are many ways to achieve fertility reduction. According to one observer:

> The most desirable, and for many of us, the only defensible, way is through efforts to guarantee everyone's reproductive freedom and choice.... We select means to achieve policy goals which are consistent with the purpose of the goal—in this case consistent with the enhancement of individuals' well-being and expanded opportunities because that is the ultimate reason for supporting a population policy in the first place.[2]

It is true in every part of the world that women who have increasing choice do indeed choose, on the average, to have fewer children. This means that large families, and the closely spaced births they require, with their accompanying physical drain on the mothers' nutritional balance, should never be taken as prima facie evidence of freedom, particularly from the woman's point of view. Having several children can be a sign of true choice, but in most of the world today, it is not. Most people today live under conditions in which they are subject to predominantly pronatalist forces with little true reproductive freedom (see the bottom half of the lower left quadrant of Figure 15-1).[3] Therefore, the basis for advocating population policy is advocacy of real reproductive choice.

Ethical issues in population policy can be examined productively by contrasting the situations in the United States and the People's Republic of China. In the United States, the cohorts currently in their reproductive years have the highest proportion married and the highest proportion ever recorded with some children. Motherhood is nearly universal among women aged thirty-five to forty-five.[4] Although birth control is widely used during the reproductive years, one can legitimately ask whether childbearing was totally free in the United States for these women or for their successors currently entering their reproductive years. Neither access to alternative functions and roles nor equitable return for these alternatives are assured for all young women today.[5] A subtle form of social coercion through a deprivation of secure alternatives continues to afflict the United States. As society successfully reduces the number of unwanted or unplanned births, it continues to mold definitions of womanhood that depend upon motherhood for social acceptance.[6]

BIRTH PLANNING IN THE PEOPLE'S REPUBLIC OF CHINA[7]

The three slogans that energize and guide the Chinese program are late marriage, prolonged spacing, and few children. In the cities this means that men do not marry before age twenty-six and that women do not enter wedlock before age twenty-four; in the countryside, the respective ages should be twenty-five and twenty-three. In addition, there should be three to five years between births and not more than one or two children.

A representative of the highest governmental office for family planning policy stated that the government currently encourages families throughout China to have no more than two children; previously the goal had been three child families in the countryside and two in the cities.[8] Moreover, in Shanghai and Canton (which are among the most cosmopolitan and advanced cities in China and are the traditional origins of innovations in the republic), municipal governments are said to be warmly welcoming one child families, and decisions to remain childless are publicly acknowledged and accepted. There also appears to be a major program developing to encourage one child families in at least a few local areas.

An important characteristic of the program is the planning of births at the societal level. It appears that at the central level, local reductions have been projected and are communicated to grassroots units. Community groups then meet to gather individuals' desires and to see whether these total or exceed the numbers suggested above. Through a series of discussions between upper and lower echelons, a final number is agreed upon, and that becomes the number of births planned for the year. In past years, however, apparently there was considerable flexibility in achieving the desired target; in 1976, in one commune of about 20,000 people, actual births apparently exceeded the target considerably, but by 1978, they reportedly did not.

This process of planning births in social groups is the central thrust of voluntarism versus coercion. In at least some areas, there seem to be criteria: women must be one year beyond the socially sanctioned minimum age of marriage and second births must follow the first by a minimum of four years. Third births clearly do not meet the criteria and apparently even second births are being discouraged.

What if a couple who does not meet these criteria still wants to have children? According to available information, Chinese propagandists[a] would talk with the couple (or individual member of a couple) and inform them, if they were too young, that there could be greater health hazards to early birth. If more than two children were wanted, the reasons would be examined. For those wanting to have additional children (in order to have their first son), older people and others would attempt to help them understand that while boys may have been necessary in old China, now daughters and sons can be equally productive and helpful because whatever men can do, women can too. For instance, in the past it was considered bad luck for women to irrigate the rice and to fish; now they fully participate in these activities. Additionally, the improved health conditions would be explained, helping to eliminate the fear of child mortality; and support would be expressed for small families, since restraining population growth would help serve the people — the ubiquitous slogan that seems to cover everything in China.[9]

As of 1981, China seems to be involved in a national discussion of more obvious incentives, including allocation of rations, housing, or other perquisites.[b] For example, in at least one local area, a family promising to have only one child is allotted three and a half garden plots, rather than the three plots that would have been received under the old system of per capita allotments. It is hoped that this acquisition of additional assignments of land, grain, and other material goods will discourage large families. Although negative materialistic sanctions can always remain a force because of their potential use, current evidence suggests that the birth planning program today still depends largely on mobilization of social incentives and is evolving toward an emphasis on positive rewards for doing more than is

a. In China, the word propagandist carries a positive connotation.

b. Special gratitude is extended to Pi–chao Chen for providing the latest available information on events in China's program.

required (e.g., having only one child) rather than on negative punishment for doing less.

Are the Chinese prisoners of thought control about childbearing? The real questions are, Are they prisoners to a degree greater than any of the rest of us? What childbearing decisions would U.S. citizens make if such decisions were totally free? These questions are unanswerable, but they are important ones to ask. Through an understanding of the social molding of decisions about births in China, one should gain insight into the presence of a similar process in every culture, including the United States. Although direct sanctions of deviants may not occur in the United States, as they may in China, the leveling of social sanctions in the United States is similar, albeit less overt.

Although the act of procreation is almost always a very private one between two individuals, the determinant of that act and its procreational outcomes are essentially socially conditioned.[c] Hence, whatever the biological component, childbearing decisions are also socially influenced. The agents of conditioning may be the immediate family (e.g., family or in-laws), peers and friends, or society or some political or economic institution of society. The pernicious effect of governmental direction of this conditioning under the totalitarian regimes of World War II must not lead one to deny the general fact that societies do shape childbearing decisions.

The feminist movement has promoted the awareness of a second aspect of this concept: Neither men nor women necessarily want or do not want children. Current thinking that women either have an irresistible maternal instinct or are driven by their lack of a y gene to have babies depicts a relic of outmoded ideology. Today, society accepts women as more than uteri. In fact, the extent to which a woman's image of herself even includes mothering may depend on forces external to herself. At the least, if inborn biological needs do play a part, it is only reasonable to conclude that the trait favoring motherhood would be distributed among the female population in

---

c. That is, the incidence of premarital intercourse differs according to the culture and the particular era within any given society. The use of abortion and of contraception depend on availability as well as on personal and general attitudes toward their use. The frequency of intercourse does not vary significantly during the prime reproductive years in various cultures, at least for married couples. For a more detailed discussion, see Chapter 3 of Leslie Corsa and Deborah Oakley, *Population Planning* (Ann Arbor: The University of Michigan Press, 1979).

a normal distribution; furthermore, since no other trait is universal, there is no reason to assume that desire for motherhood should be. To biologists who argue in support of natural selection and the biological drive to reproduce, the point should be made that selection was made previously according to women's tolerance for children and their ability to accept anatomy as destiny, not according to whether they wanted, much less actively sought, children.

Given this background, the ethical issues in population policy do not emerge as being morally justified. The social need to preserve resources by limiting increases in the numbers of people is not equivalent to or comparable to individual needs to have children. Rather, the more appropriate question is whether it is morally justifiable to continue denying women the full range of options in life and providing full reimbursement and other rewards for each of these options. The answer seems undeniable. It should be the life expectation of women that their options in life be as varied and rewarded as those of men. However, due to the world's cultures of poverty, neither have many life options. Thus, it should further be the expectation that everyone's life options will be expanded and varied to the maximum extent that the world can afford—for men and women equally.

Therefore, an ethically sound population policy requires (1) expansion of social approval of choice in roles and functions for women, (2) access to alternatives as well as to complete control over reproduction, and finally, (3) equitable return for both childbearing and for alternatives. In fact, a population policy of this sort may be a moral imperative, since oppressions or deprivation of more than one-half of the world's population should be a painful chancre, and is not simply justified—it appears to be mandated.

Political reality is something else. The United States has an implicit population policy, and there is marked resistance to converting this disjointed, sometimes conflicting, set of subpolicies into an explicit, coordinated single policy. This resistance is found not only among birth control foes, but also among family and population planners. It appears that the basis for much of the opposition from both sides is a misperception that an explicit population policy necessarily means coercion—that is, forcing people to do what they do not wish to do. Given the motivations from both perspectives, it may be that they would be no more attracted to a population policy predicated on Margaret Sanger's insight that no woman can call herself free . . . until she can choose whether or not to be a mother, but the moral and ethical questions would at least be properly defined, as shown in Figure 15-2.

The United States should adopt a policy that goes beyond established numerical limits to enhance real choice, a policy that is consistent with these freely made choices of women and men. The subject of a population policy for the United States should be taken out of the closet, removed from the list of taboo subjects, and openly examined. In such a discussion, one should avoid the old thinking that people are impelled to have children primarily because of biological needs.

Among women given equitable social and/or monetary return for their varying functions and roles, some will have preference for children and some will not, just as some women prefer to be weavers, some doctors, some athletes, and many choose to combine multiple roles. If society succeeds in recognizing the social influence on the desire to mother, a population policy could emerge on the premise that some women seek several children while others desire only one or none. The balancing of childbearing patterns will become the issue, not a homogeneous requirement to stop at two or any other coercive mandate.

In other words, real choice leads to multiple life options, and all of the evidence from other industrialized countries suggests an outcome of sustained low fertility for couples, on the average. Hence, there is no need to fear goals expressed in numerical terms calling for continued replacement reproduction or lower as long as such

Figure 15-2. Definitions in Population Policy.

Improper Definition

To have a population policy ⟶ Requires coercion

Not to have a population policy ⟶ Does not necessitate coercion

Proper Definition

To have a successful population policy ⟶ Requires increasing freedom of alternative life functions and identities

Not to have a population policy ⟶ Encourages continued socially restricted definitions for women's activities and identities goals are consistent with diversity. Since replacement reproduction leads eventually to a zero rate of natural increase (see Figure 15-3) and since the United States is already in a pattern of replacement reproduction, the achievement of a zero rate of natural increase within the first quarter of the twenty-first century appears to be inevitable. Furthermore, this achievement is consistent with many different distributions of family size. For example, there are many different family size patterns that would produce a replacement of 200 children for 200 parents (i.e., one hundred couples). Ignoring any mortality, some examples may be observed in Table 15-1.

Thus, why not state a zero rate of natural increase by something like the year 2010 or 2020 as a reasonable goal for the United States and design a monitoring system to detect and project into public debate any discrepancies that could arise between this goal and the continued increasing implementation of freedom of reproductive choice? If the freedom of choice begins to reverse the sustained low fertility in the United States (which would eventually balance the nation's low mortality), then a major public debate is necessary. As a nation, the country must decide whether diversity and reproductive

Figure 15-3. Simplified Population Structure.

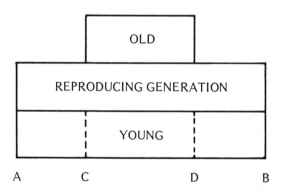

If the population is shown as three age groups, replacement reproduction simply means that the reproducing generation is replacing itself—that is having A-B births. However, this is not *zero population growth*, because deaths are represented by only C-D, a smaller number. Eventually, as the reproducers become old and if replacement reproduction continues, then births will equal deaths.

Source: Adapted from Leslie Corsa and Deborah Oakley, *Population Planning* (Ann Arbor: University of Michigan Press, 1979), p. 24.

Table 15-1. Three Hypothetical Family Size Patterns (distributions) Producing a Replacement of 200 Children.

	Number of Couples		
Children per Couple[a]	Distribution A	Distribution B	Distribution C
0	10	3	3
1	10	4	6
2	50	65	37
3	30	22	40
Total children per 200 Parents	200	200	200

a. Of course, families including more than three children are also consistent in many different patterns of overall replacement population.

freedom should take priority over environmental impact or other considerations. Evidence suggests that continuing trends all lead in the same direction—that is, toward a zero rate of natural increase. (The problems posed by immigration are addressed in a subsequent part.)

Thus, the practical question is whether an explicit population policy statement is possible, and whether it would be useful. If these questions are answered in the affirmative, then the United States must reassess its traditional descriptions of population policy to assess whether these deliberations could contribute any new components or directions. In order to adequately address the above questions, it may be necessary to understand the past proposals for a U.S. population policy.

POSSIBLE POPULATION POLICIES
FOR THE UNITED STATES

At various times, suggestions have been made that the United States should have a population policy:

1. To reach a stabilized population at a projected 100 million, a population size thought to be better than the current 131 mil-

lion (1939) or the projected leveling off figure of 140 to 150 million;[10]

2. To maintain a stabilized population, implying a need to encourage a higher birth rate because of then current low levels.[11]

3. To accept a lower population size than was then projected as the maximum, 115 million;[12]

4. To reach a stabilized population, via replacement reproduction,[13] implying a population size of about 280 million;

5. To reach a stabilized population, but without establishing a timetable,[14] implying a population size of 280 million; and

6. To reach an end to population growth within the first decade of the twenty-first century, at a population size projected as 243 million.[15]

In a search of the literature, no proposals were found to suggest that the United States should adopt a population policy that would promote growth, and there now appears to be a consensus favoring the conclusion of the Commission on Population Growth and the American Future:

> We have examined the effects that future growth alternatives are likely to have on our economy, society, government, resources, and environment, and we have found no convincing argument for continued national population growth. On the contrary, the pluses seem to be on the side of slowing growth and eventually stopping it altogether. Indeed, there might be no reason to fear a decline in population once we are past the period of growth that is in store.[16]

The population policy toward which the United States seems to be moving is one that seeks to end population growth at about 250 million or even less. The major remaining debate is the timing for these goals and whether they can be reached without changing our immigration policies. If the desired goals are viewed as appropriate ends eventually, why not sooner and why not explicitly? While the public debate on this issue has barely begun, it is essential to clarify exactly what a population policy would mean.

Few support an immediate cessation of growth and fewer recommend the reduction of population size within the next few decades. Thus, any differences in policy proposals may amount to little more than an argument over whether to take fifty versus seventy years to reach the goals, or an argument about whether a low U.S. fertility rate can or should compensate for continued legal and illegal immigration.[17] Since every government has a myriad of policies influencing population growth, the only real question about developing population policy is whether it is better to have an implicit or an explicit one. There are both advantages and disadvantages of changing from a current implicit policy to an explicit one. The advantages accrue if the explicit policy produces more coordinated, consistent, and humanitarian outcomes; the disadvantages are associated largely with the supposed trials and errors of arriving at an explicit policy statement.

ADVANTAGES OF AN EXPLICIT
POPULATION POLICY

Currently, multiple governmental agencies make allocation decisions about future needs that are created in part by population growth without even considering population; often one agency uses one set of population projections while another agency uses a different one.[18] One agency plans for a large population; another for only a modest increase. With an explicit population policy, both the utilization and the consistency of population data should improve. As a result, this should lead to better planning and less waste of under-utilized or inappropriate resources, such as schools located in the wrong places or designed for the wrong age groups.

Immigration, a significant part of our population growth,[d] is an important component of the implicit population policy practiced by the United States. Today there are explicit laws limiting numbers and types of entrants, combined with implicit decisions (sometimes non-decisions) to monitor, arrest, or deport entrants who enter or remain in the country without appropriate documentation. These decisions vary by the time of year, enforcement agency, and area of the country.[19] The United States has elected to limit the number of new residents from other countries, but strict consistent adherence to this policy applies only to those attempting to enter legally. An explicit population policy would require examination of the political, eco-

d. A recent estimate shows a net legal immigration of 343,000 in 1978, accounting for 20 percent of U.S. officially recognized population growth, with an estimated 166,000 to one million or more per year further net increase due to entries of undocumented illegal aliens.

nomic, and moral issues involved, and decisions would have to be made to allow these inconsistencies to remain or to take action to resolve them.

Perhaps most important, the current implicit policy of the United States allows inadequate progress toward fulfilling needs for comprehensive reproductive care for everyone.[20] Currently, the federal government attempts to assure American citizens the opportunity to choose the number and the timing of their conceptions. However, the federally funded programs do not reach all of the ten million people over twenty years of age or the two million more under twenty who are in need of organized public services. There is some question whether the stated objectives will be achieved in the near future.

Furthermore, sex and birth control education are often lacking; and social security, education, tax, employment, census enumeration, and other laws and federally sanctioned practices treat women as dependents and second class citizens, thus furthering their lack of choice about departing psychologically from the tradition of multiple motherhood. Amid current debates over new national health policies, the inclusion of a benefit covering contraceptive services remains questionable, and there is little hope that the ultimate protection of choice—abortion—will be covered.

With an explicit and complete population statement, comprehensive and complete family planning programs should be enhanced. In fact, the greatest advantage of an explicit policy would be the implementation of a program that promoted women's rights. Such a policy would guarantee American women a choice of when and how many children to have and even a choice as to whether to have any children at all.

Posing these issues in the context of population policy must not be misunderstood. Reproductive choice is a goal in itself, justifiable and socially valued as an end in itself. Practical considerations of its likely acceptance as an element of population policy as defined in this chapter require their mention in this context.

DISADVANTAGES OF AN EXPLICIT
POPULATION POLICY

With general consensus favoring population stabilization, the major reservation appears to be that the process of discussing and arriving at some explicit policy would provide a focus for opposition to existing family planning and population education programs (and it is primarily Catholic opposition that forms this perceived threat). In other countries with heavily Catholic populations, such as Mexico, Peru, the Philippines, and the Caribbean nations, the adoption of explicit population policies has enhanced, rather than threatened, family planning programs. Furthermore, one factor in any equation does not necessarily determine the outcome. Public discussion also facilitates recognition of limited resources, of the increased costliness of government services due to decreasing economies or diseconomies of scale, of the undesirable demands placed on women and family life, and of other factors that also enter into the equation.

Religious opinions alone are not the only factor; while they must be respected, they should not alone determine the outcome, nor should religious opinions alone determine whether the issue is to undergo public discussion. Public debates over important social questions are never onesided, and proponents of a population policy should not be deterred by the existence of an opposition, since opposition exists on every social issue. It would be naive to expect that opposition will evaporate with delay. Furthermore, it is irresponsible to permit the opposition to determine whether an issue as important as population policy should be an item on the agenda for discussion by public policymakers. To the contrary, the very discussion, because of the clear focus provided by the opposition, should reach more people, stimulate more thinking, and be one of the most productive ways to promote consistency in both public and private actions that form components of population policy and its desired effects. Public opinion polls show that a majority of Americans think population growth is a significant problem.[21]

IMPLEMENTATION PROGRAM FOR A POPULATION POLICY

Given the above discussion, the issue in the formulation of a population policy for the United States becomes the development of an implementation program that illustrates that the proponents are discussing increased freedom rather than coercion. The policy needs to be framed in detail to include:

1. Complete and universal reproductive health care;

2. Comprehensive public information showing the consequences of population growth nationally, locally, and personally;

3. Assurance of legal and de facto equality of opportunity for women and for men;

4. Comprehensive public information on the costs and benefits of sex-specific roles in life and the awareness of the inequities of role limitations for women as compared with men;

5. Public debate on the value of continued population growth and the alternatives available to limit it (e.g., restrict fertility and/or limit immigration); and

6. An advanced monitoring system that provides public information to safeguard against abuse of reproductive choice.

Programs to provide reproductive health services have been analyzed and reported from both the public and the private sectors.[22] Fostering population education programs is an initial step toward better public education about the consequences of population growth, but they must be augmented to assure adequate national coverage within elementary and secondary schools and in the general media to reach adults as well.

The Equal Rights Amendment, affirmative action requirements, and other legal changes are promoting an equality for women and men, but the federal government has yet to initiate a serious effort to transform law into reality. Practical political and ethical issues associated with immigration are currently being examined by a Commission on Immigration.

This chapter proposes the creation of a national initiative to destroy the stereotypes that limit both women's and men's views of themselves and the establishment of a monitoring system to detect and correct any conflicts between increased freedom of choice in childbearing and a goal of sustained low fertility. Most components of an antistereotyping program are well-known and include:

1. Review and change of textbooks and curricula in schools;

2. Review and change of media content;

3. Review and change of decisionmaking hierarchies in which men are allowed to predominate;

4. Assurance of affirmative action in education, training, and hiring; and

5. Provision of child care and other private and public programs to encourage truly equal participation and remuneration for women and men.

What is new is a call for a national commitment that acknowledges, as in China, that women must have the opportunities, take the responsibility, and receive the rewards commensurate with their paid and unpaid work. As part of an explicit population policy, the United States needs to proclaim that women are valued as highly as men and that women are as important and as in control of their own lives to the same extent as men are.

An explicit population policy could actually promote increasing reproductive choice and certainly is consistent with this basic element in women's attainment of equality. A new approach to population policy should remove its association with coercion as a relic of outmoded thinking and turn to a recognition that enhancement of freedom is the basic and pervasive element.

NOTES TO CHAPTER 15

1. Bernard Berelson, "Beyond Family Planning," *Science* 163: 533–542 (1969).
2. Peters Willson, Zero Population Growth, Inc., June 13, 1979, personal communication.
3. Leslie Corsa and Deborah Oakley, *Population Planning* (Ann Arbor: University of Michigan Press, 1979).
4. U.S. Department of Commerce, Bureau of the Census, "Fertility of American Women: June 1975," *Current Population Reports*, Series P–20, no. 301 (Washington, D.C.: U.S. Government Printing Office, 1976).
5. Phyllis A. Wallace and Annette M. LaMond, *Women, Minorities and Employment Discrimination* (Lexington, MA: Lexington Books, 1977); David L. Featherman and Robert M. Hauser, "Sexual Inequalities and Socioeconomic Achievement in the United States, 1962–1973" (Presented at the 1978 Annual Meeting of the Population Association of America, Seattle, Washington, 1978); Juanita Kreps and Robert Clark, *Sex, Age, and Work* (Baltimore: Johns Hopkins University Press, 1975); Orley Ashenfelter and Albert Rees, *Discrimination in Labor Markets* (Princeton, NJ: Princeton University Press, 1973).
6. Jessie Bernard, *The Future of Motherhood* (New York: Penguin Books, Inc., 1974); Constantina Safilios Rothschild, *Toward a Sociology of Women* (Lexington, MA: Xerox Publishing Company, 1972).

7. Frederick Jaffe and Deborah Oakley, "Observations on Birth Planning in China," *Family Planning Perspectives* 10:101-108 (1978).

8. Deborah Oakley, *Journal of a Trip to China* (Ann Arbor: University of Michigan School of Public Health, 1977), pp. 43-46.

9. Victor Sidel and Ruth Sidel, *Serve the People: Observations on Medicine in the People's Republic of China* (Boston: Beacon Press, 1973).

10. P.K. Whelpton, "Population Policy for the United States," *Journal of Heredity*; rprt. Birth Control Federation of America (New York, 1939).

11. Natural Resources Committee, *The Problems of a Changing Population* (Washington, D.C.: U.S. Government Printing Office, 1938).

12. Ibid.

13. American Public Health Association, "Replacement Reproduction and Zero Population Growth," (Resolution adopted by Governing Council, 1971).

14. Commission on Population Growth and the American Future, *Population and the American Future* (Washington, D.C.: U.S. Government Printing Office, 1972).

15. Zero Population Growth, Inc., *A U.S. Population Policy: Z.P.G.'s Recommendations* (Washington, D.C., January 1977).

16. Commission on Population Growth and the American Future, p. 75.

17. Charles Keely, *U.S. Immigration: A Policy Analysis* (New York: The Population Council, 1979).

18. Judith Kunofsky, "The Use of Population Projections by the Federal Government for Programs at the Local Level," in U.S. Congress, House of Representatives, Select Committee on Population, *Consequences of Changing U.S. Population: Population Movement and Planning, Hearing*, 95th Cong., 2d sess. (Washington, D.C.: U.S. Government Printing Office, 1978), pp. 132-136, 508-533.

19. David North and Marion Houston, *The Characteristics and Role of Illegal Aliens in the U.S. Labor Market* (Washington, D.C.: Linton and Company, 1976).

20. Ad Hoc Committee for a Position Paper on the Status of Family Planning in the United States Today, *Planned Births, the Future of the Family and the Quality of American Life* (New York: The Alan Guttmacher Institute, 1977).

21. Charles Westoff and James McCarthy, "Population Attitude and Fertility," *Family Planning Perspectives* 11:93-96 (1979).

22. Ad Hoc Committee, p. 17.

16 GENETIC SCREENING AND THE PUBLIC WELL-BEING

Mark W. Steele, M.D.

GENERAL PRINCIPLES

Genetic screening is that aspect of the field of public health concerned with the impact of heritable disorders on the population. The concept of applying genetic principles and techniques to public health programs for the population is as old as genetics itself and, not surprisingly, has consistently generated profound ethical and legal problems. Some of these concerns are reflected in conflicts between the individual good versus the good of society as a whole; voluntary approaches with informed consent versus coercion—both overt and covert; the individual's right to reproduce; the issue of sterilization (voluntarily or involuntarily); and therapeutic abortion. These ethical and legal problems surround human genetic programs today as much as they did when the eugenecists of the early 1900s first proposed their now discredited views. Detailed treatments of these issues may be found in the 1975 report of the National Academy of Sciences;[1] in books edited by Hilton et al.,[2] Kaback,[3] Milunsky,[4] Milunsky and Annas,[5] and Lubs and de la Cruz;[6] and in an article by Lappé, Gustafsone, and Robbins.[7]

The goals of genetic screening, like Caesar's Gaul, can be divided into three parts. Genetic screening can attempt to identify newborns or older individuals who may be affected with genetic disease. The

345

object is not only therapeutic, but also to provide genetically at risk[a] individuals with counseling to enable them to make informed decisions about future reproductive efforts. Screening for phenylketonuria and hypothyroidism[b] are examples in the newborn period, while screening for sickle cell disease is an example in older individuals.

Genetic screening attempts to identify fetuses effected with genetic diseases prior to birth. This can be done by sonography or fetoscopy,[c] but is usually done by appropriate testing of fetal cells or fluids obtained early in pregnancy through amniocentesis or through blood serum in pregnant women. Testing of amniotic fluid cells allows detection of fetal chromosomal abnormalities such as Down's Syndrome (i.e., mongolism) in addition to about eighty other genetic disorders. Testing of amniotic fluid or maternal serum allows detection of fetal neural tube defects such as myelomeningocele.[d] In these instances, the object of screening is to give couples the option of terminating a pregnancy when the fetus is known to be affected with genetic disease rather than merely at high risk.

Finally, genetic screening can attempt to identify individuals who are prospectively at greater risk than the general population of having offspring with specific genetic defects. The object is to provide those at risk with genetic information so that they can make informed decisions about future reproductive efforts before the birth of a defective child.[e] This chapter focuses only on this third type of genetic counseling.

Mass screening of populations to detect individuals at greater risk than the general population of having genetically defective offspring

a. An at risk individual (or couple) is one who is at greater risk than the general population of having genetically defective offspring. Such individuals (or couples) may or may not be affected with the disease themselves.

b. Phenylketonuria and hypothyroidism are heritable biochemical defects of the newborn that can result in mental retardation unless detected and treated immediately.

c. Sonography is a method of using sound waves to form a pictorial outline of the fetus in utero. Fetoscopy is a technique by which the fetus can be visualized directly by insertion of a lighted optical tube into the uterus through the abdominal wall.

d. A defect in the embryonic development of the spine in which the spinal cord may be exposed to open air. Even with appropriate surgical treatment, death, paralysis, and mental retardation often result as a consequence of this condition.

e. Although most genetic counseling is nondirective, it is assumed that informed at risk individuals will make rational reproductive decisions – that is, they will avoid high risks (> 10 percent) but not be unnecessarily deterred by low risks (< 5 percent). One might expect, thereby, a reduction in the incidence of genetic diseases.

must function within certain limits dictated by scientific, technical, ethical, and legal considerations. The first two limits are not difficult to define; the latter two are more complex. Scientific and technical considerations demand that at least:

1. The defect has a precise medical description;
2. The defect is known to have a specific genetic etiology;
3. Detection of at risk individuals can be determined easily by a safe, reliable, inexpensive test;
4. The population to be screened can be readily identified; and
5. Society at large has the necessary technical and financial resources to conduct the screening program.

SPECIFIC SCREENING PROGRAMS

Sickle cell disease and Tay–Sach's disease (TSD) in the United States and similar nations satisfy these five conditions. Each is well-defined medically; each is known to be an autosomal recessive genetic trait. Thus, affected individuals are homozygous for the sickle cell or Tay–Sach's gene, while parents of affected individuals are respectively unaffected heterozygous carriers of one or the other abnormal genes. Therefore, until the birth of an affected child, such carriers are usually unaware of their offspring being at genetic risk—that is, they are unaware that they carry the defective gene.

However, safe, reliable, and inexpensive blood tests exist to detect carriers of both the sickle cell and the Tay–Sach's genes. Each of the respective populations to be screened is readily identifiable. In the United States, sickle cell disease is found almost exclusively in blacks; TSD is found almost exclusively in Ashkenazic Jews (who are mainly of Polish, Russian or Lithuanian ancestry). Finally, society (be it the United States or other Western industrialized nations) can muster the financial, logistical, manpower, and technical resources to screen its black population for sickle cell disease and its Ashkenazic Jewish population for TSD.

Sickle cell disease is an autosomal recessive genetic trait. Affected homozygotes develop a severe anemia early in life and confront recurring crises of pain and hemolytic collapse. Although modern medical treatment has improved the prognosis for longevity considerably, death usually occurs after ten or twenty years of life. In the United

States, about 1 in 600 offspring of black couples have sickle cell disease; about 1 in 12 blacks are normal carriers (heterozygotes) for the sickle cell gene; and about 1 in 150 black couples are each carriers and therefore at risk of having an affected child.

It is important to understand that only a mating between two carriers can produce an affected child. With each conception, the offspring of a carrier–carrier mating has a 25 percent chance of being affected with sickle cell disease. Each offspring parented by a carrier and a noncarrier has a 50 percent chance of being a carrier, a 50 percent chance of being a normal noncarrier, and no chance of having sickle cell disease. A mating between two noncarriers can produce only noncarriers of the sickle cell gene. For a detailed description of these basic genetic principles, the reader is urged to consult the brief introductory text by McKusick.[8]

Among matings of black Americans, 14 percent are between a carrier and a noncarrier and about 83 percent are between two noncarriers. The frequency of matings between carriers and noncarriers is twenty-one-fold greater than between two carriers. Therefore, it is the reproductive behavior of the former, not the latter, that maintains the frequency of the sickle cell gene in the population. As long as carrier–carrier couples do not reproduce, children with sickle cell disease will not be born, but the potential risk of sickle cell disease among black children in future generations remains the same. This potential risk can only decrease if the frequency of the gene in the black population decreases. Such decreases can occur through outbreeding of blacks with nonblacks; but within the black population, it can occur only if couples consisting of one carrier and one noncarrier refrain from reproducing or if carrier fetuses can be detected in utero and are aborted.

Up to now, safe, reliable antenatal diagnosis of sickle cell disease in the fetus has not been feasible.[f] Furthermore, it is an unlikely probability that either nonreproduction or abortion of normal carrier fetuses would be acceptable to most American black couples, even if it were proposed. Therefore, the only aim of prospective screening of the black population for the sickle cell gene is to identify and then counsel carriers of their genetic risks for having a child affected with sickle cell disease.

f. Rapid technical progress is being made in this area, and reliable prenatal diagnosis of sickle cell disease in the fetus should be available during the 1980s.

Like sickle cell disease, TSD is also an autosomal recessive genetic trait. Affected newborns are normal for the first four months of life, at which time progressive neurological degeneration begins. There is no effective treatment, and death is inevitable by the age of three or four. The frequency of the disease is one hundred times greater among the offspring of Ashkenazic Jewish couples (AJS) than among the offspring of other ethnic or racial groups. About 1 in 3,600 offspring of AJS have TSD; about 1 in 30 AJS are normal carriers of the TSD gene (heterozygotes); and about 1 in 900 matings between AJS include two carriers of the TSD gene.

The frequency of matings between carriers and noncarriers (1 in 16) is fifty-seven-fold greater than between carriers. Therefore, the potential effects of genetic screening on the population for TSD are the same as for sickle cell disease. However, couples at risk of producing a child with TSD now have the added option of antenatal diagnosis and abortion of affected fetuses.

To illustrate how an ideal prospective genetic-screening program might work using TSD as an example, suppose an American community has 60,000 Ashkenazic Jews of reproductive age (50 percent male, 50 percent female). Suppose all matings are within the community. Then 1 in 30 (or 2,000) of these individuals would be normal carriers of the TSD gene and 1 in 900 (or 33) possible matings could be of the at risk carrier–carrier type. To find the 33 at risk couples, one would first test (i.e., screen) the 30,000 females to find the 1,000 carriers. Next, one would test the 1,000 mates of the 1,000 carrier females to find the 33 carrier males (thus identifying the 33 at risk couples).

Now, suppose each at risk couple, after genetic counseling, decided to have two normal children using antenatal diagnosis and abortion to eliminate the risk of offspring affected with TSD. Production of sixty-six normal children would require eighty-eight pregnancies and antenatal diagnoses, with therapeutic abortion of the twenty-two TSD fetuses. Through such a prospective screening program, this particular Jewish community would have no cases of TSD, albeit the frequency of the TSD gene in this population would not be reduced by this genetic screening effort. Thus, if the screening program were discontinued, the frequency of TSD in the community would return to at least the same level as prior to its initiation.

EFFECTS OF SCREENING PROGRAMS

Genetic counseling accelerated in the late 1950s and has become an established medical specialty in the United States, Canada, Great Britain, France, Scandinavia, and other similar countries. Prospective screening for sickle cell gene carriers among American blacks began in the late 1960s and for TSD gene carriers among American and Canadian Ashkenazic Jews in 1969.

The effects of genetic counseling for individuals have been evaluated by numerous retrospective studies in the United States, Canada, and Great Britain. The findings are similar.[9] After genetic counseling, about 33 percent of the couples at relatively high risk (i.e., > 10 percent) for having a genetically defective child elect to continue to reproduce; about 25 percent of the couples at relatively low risk (i.e., < 5 percent) elect not to reproduce. The remaining couples avoid high risks and ignore low risks, but the relationship of genetic counseling to such reproductive behavior is unknown.

It is estimated that genetic counseling influences the reproductive decisionmaking of about 40 percent of couples, while it appears to have little impact on the remaining 60 percent. Interestingly, there is a direct correlation between intelligence, education, and socioeconomic status with understanding genetic information, but no correlation between any of these and actual reproductive behavior. The impact of genetic counseling on reproductive decisionmaking appears to be highly dependent on psychological factors that are still only poorly understood. Twenty-five years experience with genetic counseling of individuals suggests a limited impact on preventing the birth of genetically defective individuals. A more significant improvement will require better behavioral research rather than further advancements in genetics.

In addition, the effects of prospective screening of populations for sickle cell or TSD gene carriers have been evaluated. For example, on the Greek island of Orchomenos, 23 percent of the population carry the sickle cell gene, and 1 percent of the newborns are affected with the disease. Most of the 2,300 islanders are semiliterate, Caucasian farmers whose marriages are arranged. In 1966 a group of American geneticists screened the entire population for the sickle cell gene, followed by genetic counseling for individuals and public health education for the community. The hypothesis was that genetic considerations would influence marriage arrangements—that is, deter carrier–carrier marriages. In 1969, the island was revisited by the study team. Findings revealed that most of the population comprehended the genetics of sickle cell disease and discussed it during marriage arrangements. However, the study also showed that (1) there was social stigmatization of many sickle cell carriers as being inferior and less marriageable;[g] (2) one-third of the population still erroneously believed that a carrier was diseased (mainly because of misinformation from local physicians); and (3) there was no reduction in carrier–carrier marriages, since the partners ignored their genetic status or lied about it.[10]

The experience with prospective sickle cell carrier screening among blacks in the United States has been similar to that found on Orchomenos. There has been little effect of the program on black mating patterns, reproductive behavior, or the incidence of sickle cell disease. However, a significant amount of unwarranted anxiety and negative psychological stress has been found among black children identified as carriers and their parents. Adults identified as carriers have suffered economic hardships due to unwarranted restrictions in job opportunities and have had difficulty in obtaining health and life insurance.[11]

The TSD screening efforts directed at American Jews have not demonstrated any greater positive outcome than the sickle cell program despite the higher socioeconomic and educational status found in the Jewish population. This is even more discouraging, since antenatal diagnosis for TSD is readily available. During the last eight years, about 150,000 Jews of reproductive age volunteered to be screened for the TSD gene. Most resided in the United States and Canada, but some were in Great Britain, South Africa, and Israel. However, these 150,000 screenees represented less than 10 percent of the potential screenees, despite massive community educational and promotional efforts by the medical and rabbinical professionals and enthusiastic Jewish laity. Consequently, TSD screening has had only a minor impact on the worldwide incidence of the disease among Jews (about 2.5 cases per year have been prevented worldwide by therapeutic abortion of affected fetuses). No evidence of socioeconomic stigmatization of TSD gene carriers has been identi-

g. Even though carriers are not diseased and even though a marriage between a carrier and a noncarrier has no risk of bearing a child with sickle cell disease, the negative stigmatization was apparent.

fied, but whether there has been any significant negative psychological effects remains unclear.

Researchers have monitored TSD screening programs extensively, seeking to show some psychological effects. Responses gained from attitudinal questionnaires and interviews of most adult screenees have not suggested significant long-term anxieties or stigmatization. However, some worrisome discrepancies between what screenees say and what they do have appeared.

Between 1972 and 1975, a TSD screening program was conducted among the adult Jewish population in Toronto, Canada. Among the 100,000 Jews in that community, 10,567 adults volunteered to be tested, and twenty-one carrier–carrier couples were identified. After three years, only two of these twenty-one couples had attempted subsequent pregnancies. Another two couples stated that they had achieved their desired family size in any event; the remaining seventeen couples apparently elected to remain childless. As one of the screeners said, "I find it somewhat disconcerting that they [the seventeen couples] seem to have decided not to have any children. Perhaps the anxieties created by carrier screening are greater than we realize." [12]

Between 1974 and 1975, tenth and eleventh grade high school students were screened for the TSD gene in Montreal, Canada. [13] The testing was preceded by an intensive educational program, followed by genetic counseling and attitudinal surveys. In contrast to adults, 75 percent of the students volunteered to be screened. Most students identified as noncarriers said they either were elated or relieved; about 25 percent were simply indifferent. Student attitudes remained largely unchanged when resurveyed eight months later.

One must wonder why 15 percent of these students did not tell their friends of their noncarrier status, why 17 percent of them erroneously felt it was harmful to be a carrier, and even why 10 percent of the noncarriers said their self-image was improved. Since all humans carry three to four recessive genes that are harmful when homozygous, there is no reason for self-image to improve simply due to education in human genetics.

Among students identified as carriers, 52 percent at first said they were worried or depressed, but this fell to 4 percent within eight months. Again, one must wonder, however, why one-third of the students chose not to tell their friends of their carrier status and why 9 percent indicated that their self-image was lowered.

Finally, it is more disturbing that 10 percent of the students who were noncarriers said they would not marry a carrier (despite no risk of producing a TSD offspring) and 12 percent of the carrier students were hesitant to marry another carrier despite the knowledge that affected fetuses are detectable antenatally and could be aborted if desired. Of course, the latter position may be more reflective of a negative stance on abortion than anything else.

LEGAL AND ETHICAL ISSUES

As indicated at the beginning of this chapter, genetic counseling and screening raise many legal and ethical questions, most of which are yet to be resolved. Is the right of the individual to reproduce absolute, or may it be limited by other priorities of society? Is the right of the individual to confidentiality absolute, or is it limited to the right of collateral relatives to know of their genetic risks? Is the right of the individual to choose to bear or not to bear a possibly defective fetus absolute, or is it limited by the consensus of society on abortion? If the rights of the individual are subordinated to those of society, who should bear the burden?

There are, however, more pressing issues that must be addressed. Should genetic screening be voluntary or should it be mandated for the good of the society? If voluntary, does simple lack of coercion suffice, or should consent be informed? The remaining discussion highlights major public policy benchmarks related to genetic screening and raises several ethical issues associated with such programs (e.g., confidentiality and informed consent).

Sickle cell screening among blacks in the United States began in the 1960s. "It evolved in a rapid, haphazard, often poorly planned fashion, generated in large measure by public clamor and political pressure. . . . Some of the programs were well planned with clearly thought out and stated objectives; others were initiated simply because it was fashionable to do so."[14] The objectives of the sickle cell programs varied from one locality to another. Some of the programs were launched primarily for research purposes. Investigators sought to learn about the effectiveness of genetic education and counseling techniques. Others were designed principally to detect and treat individuals affected with sickle cell disease; some concentrated on the detection of both affected persons and carriers. The latter two would then receive genetic counseling for use in their future reproductive decisions.

At first, the programs were organized and financed privately by voluntary nonprofit agencies such as the Sickle Cell Foundation or black awareness groups such as the Black Panthers. In 1972, Congress enacted the National Sickle Cell Anemia Control Act (PL 92–294). Sickle cell disease centers to promote research, screening, counseling, and management were established and supported by the federal government. Federal regulations mandated that state sickle cell screening programs be run on a voluntary basis. Programs found in noncompliance risked the loss of federal support.

Nevertheless, in 1971 the Commonwealth of Massachusetts legislated sickle cell testing as a prerequisite for school attendance. By 1973, sixteen other states (Arizona, California, Georgia, Illinois, Indiana, Kansas, Kentucky, Louisiana, Maryland, Mississippi, New Jersey, New Mexico, New York, North Carolina, Ohio, and Virginia) and the District of Columbia had enacted coercive sickle cell screening legislation.[15] Some statutes were directed at school children; others at marriage license applicants; and a few involved pregnant women or newborns. Most of the statutes did not specify race directly, but contained qualifiers that achieved the same effect. In eight instances there were no penalties for statutory violators. In four states, however, violators could be fined or imprisoned; in four other states, they could be denied marriage licenses or school admission.

Initially, none of the state laws mandated confidentiality of data. Consequently, the sickle cell status of individuals could be made available, without their consent, to insurance companies and prospective employers. As a result, many sickle cell carriers were denied admission to the armed forces and charged higher insurance premiums even though the carrier state is clinically benign. Schools were able to obtain the results of sickle cell screening and used the information irrationally to restrict the physical activities of carrier children. In 1973, public criticism and pressure from the U.S. Department of Health, Education, and Welfare (DHEW) forced four states to amend their laws to ensure confidentiality. Since 1974, similar pressures have forced amendments of other state laws, which to a large extent have restored their voluntary nature. Despite these advances, there remains no legislation to ensure the informed consent of screenees. More recent federal legislation amended the sickle cell screening program and included it in the broader National Genetic

Diseases and Screening Act (PL 94-278) in 1976, with a relative reduction in funding priority.

The experience with screening carriers of the TSD gene has been similar, at least qualitatively. TSD screening began under private auspices in 1969 among Jewish residents of the Baltimore-Washington, D.C., area. The objectives were the same as those for sickle cell carrier screening.

TSD screening programs have been promoted largely through the private sector. Geneticists, Jewish clergy, and lay organizations have combined activities to establish TSD screening programs in many major American and Canadian cities, in Great Britain, and in Europe, South Africa, and Israel. Within the public sector, there has been no state legislation regarding TSD screening. However, limited federal support became available following the enactment of the National Genetic Diseases and Screening Act.

Despite massive community educational efforts and support from local religious and lay Jewish leaders, there has been and continues to be a low voluntary compliance rate among potential screenees. Among the adult Jewish population of the United States, Canada, and Great Britain in their reproductive years, less than 10 percent have consistently elected TSD screening. In South Africa and Israel, virtually no Jews have elected to be screened. As a result, attempts to recruit screenees have become more intensified. One brightly colored publicity display reads as follows:

A SIMPLE BLOOD TEST CAN PREVENT
TAY-SACH'S DISEASE
DETECTION AND COUNSELING ENABLE
CARRIER COUPLES
TO HAVE CHILDREN FREE FROM THIS DISEASE

In a recent *New England Journal of Medicine* editorial, the editor charged that this display could mislead couples to believe there was "some therapeutic maneuver [that] would somehow make the genetically defective child normal"; when in fact, antenatal detection and therapeutic abortion of affected fetuses are the only options offered. Such a disclosure could produce "agonizing personal disappointment," particularly to potential screenees among Orthodox Jewry for whom religious beliefs condemn even therapeutic abortions.[16]

Disturbing evidence of psychological coercion has been found in the TSD screening program in Montreal, Canada.[17] As with some American programs, adult Jews of reproductive age only minimally volunteered to be tested (less than 10 percent) despite intensive community educational efforts sponsored by religious and scientific organizations. Therefore, geneticists in Montreal capitalized on a Quebec law that allows persons fourteen years of age or over to authorize various medical procedures for themselves within the school health jurisdiction.

Accordingly, students in the tenth and eleventh grades, most of whom were aged fifteen to seventeen, were educated about TSD screening. The subject was introduced into the curriculum during biology classes. In addition, all Jewish students received an official letter recommending Tay–Sach's testing from the chief medical officer of the school system, and a special school assembly was held to discuss its benefits. The admitted purpose of all this was to circumvent the manifest continued reluctance of adult Canadian Jews of childbearing age to be tested. The purpose was achieved; 75 percent of the Jewish high school students agreed to be tested. However, when these students enthusiastically informed their parents that they had been tested, there remained no increase in the rate of testing among the parents. The Canadian high school program raises several ethical issues regarding informed consent.[18]

Although it was not illegal to screen high school students without parental consent, was it ethical to use a legal loophole to thwart parental opposition? This law was not to promote genetic screening; rather, it was intended to spare students the embarrassment of seeking parental consent for treatment of venereal disease. Similar statutes continue to gain popularity in the United States and elsewhere due to the assumption that students (i.e., minors) will seek treatment more quickly if such embarrassment is avoided. It is not assumed that parental consent would be denied if requested. The geneticists knew, however, from past experience that parental consent would have been denied in more than 90 percent of the cases.

One must also question whether consent obtained from the high school students was truly voluntary or informed.[19] The combined effects of an official letter to all Jewish students, a special school assembly, and adolescent peer pressure clearly create a somewhat coercive psychological atmosphere. Although the students were educated about the genetics of TSD, did they know that genetic screening programs were still highly experimental? Were they informed that they were experimental subjects whose participation was in part for the purpose of evaluating the effects of genetic screening programs?

One must wonder whether the students were encouraged to appreciate the rarity of TSD—not only in absolute terms but also in perspective to other far more common genetic and nongenetic preventable birth defects and health problems—or told that only 10 percent of their seniors had agreed to be screened or that the effect of a prior screening of 21,000 Canadian Jews had only prevented one case of TSD—at a cost of $100,000—or that this $100,000 expense siphoned scarce, limited funds from other preventive medical programs concerned with more common and pressing health problems.

Finally, one must ask questions not only about informed consent of individuals to be screened, but also about the informed consent of a community to actively support a screening program of itself. The purpose of a TSD screening program is to reduce the incidence of that disease among a community of Jews, just as the purpose of a sickle cell program is to reduce the frequency of that disease among a community of blacks. Before Jews or blacks decide to expend their limited financial and educational resources on promoting genetic screening programs, they should have received sufficient information about the likely effects of such programs on the community as a whole and on them as individuals.

With a continuing decline of the Jewish population in North America, there is concern over the potential impact of TSD screening programs. About 80 percent of the decline has been the result of a relatively low birth rate; about 20 percent, to an intermarriage rate of about 50 percent. If present trends continue, there will be fewer than 10,000 Jews in the United States and Canada in one hundred years. Therefore, a very high priority in many Jewish communities is to encourage reproduction and not to support programs that may in effect precipitate a further reduction in the birth rate.

One effect of screening 21,000 Jews in Canada for the TSD gene was virtual cessation of reproductive efforts by carrier–carrier couples. Indeed, the prevention of one case of TSD in effect deprived the Canadian Jewish community of at least forty potentially normal Jewish children. There is little evidence that Jewish communities being solicited to vigorously support TSD screening are made aware of its genocidal potential.

CONCLUSIONS

A ten year effort at population screening for carriers of abnormal recessive genes may not have had a major impact on the incidence of sickle cell or Tay-Sach's diseases. However, it has demonstrated some of the legal and ethical pitfalls of such programs. At their onset, both the sickle cell and TSD screening programs were voluntary and private, but they soon become more coercive and state-related. Interestingly, attempts at legal coercion such as in the sickle cell program proved to be the least dangerous. The infringement on individual rights in this program was so blatant that public protest, from both the lay and the medical communities, was able to force legal relief through democratic, political processes. Psychological coercion such as in the Tay-Sach's program conducted in Montreal, however, has proven much more dangerous. Such programs may be insidious, difficult to identify, usually not deliberate, and less amenable to effective control.

Although attempts at legislative coercion in genetic screening appear to be fading, a more ominous threat to the voluntary nature of human genetic programs in the future may come from the judiciary. At the 1979 Annual March of Dimes Birth Defects Conference, one speaker indicated that increasingly litigation was arising over the issue of wrongful life. In this situation, genetically defective individuals sue their parents for damages for having conceived them despite their prior knowledge of genetic risks. As of 1979, such cases had not been accepted by the courts. However, disturbing signs among legal circles suggest that this judicial attitude may not always prevail. Should the courts ever entertain the concept of parental liability for wrongful life, then human genetic programs would effectively cease to be voluntary. Under such conditions, individuals would probably actively avoid genetic screening programs. Such an avoidance could lead to tragic consequences for many that could have been prevented. Consequently, efforts should be undertaken through appropriate educational programs to dissuade the pursuit of such a course.

Since the mid-1970s, both the federal government and the scientific community have developed a regulatory system for ensuring the informed consent of individuals participating in human research and for protecting volunteers from unreasonable risk. Since most research using human subjects is done in or by teaching institutions that are heavily dependent on federal support, the government can enforce its regulations by threatening loss of funds for noncompliance. Accordingly, all research involving human research subjects must be reviewed and approved by local institutional review boards (IRBs) composed of concerned scientific experts and laity, to ensure that the potential benefits of the research outweigh the risks, that there is effective provision for written informed consent, and that confidentiality and privacy are insured.

Experiences gained from genetic screening programs demonstrate that similar mechanisms should be developed for population research. Such mechanisms must be designed not only to protect individuals in the population from possible exploitation (even if well meant), but also to protect the population as a whole. IRBs do not appear adequate for this task, since population research is rarely limited to a local area for long periods of time. More likely, a central research review board at the federal level (e.g., within the National Institutes of Health) would be the most efficient and competent body to protect the public from risk and to ensure informed consent to populations in experimental situations.

NOTES TO CHAPTER 16

1. Committee for the Study of Inborn Errors of Metabolism, National Research Council, *Genetic Screening: Programs, Principles, and Research* (Washington, D.C.: National Academy of Sciences, 1975), pp. 1-388.
2. Bruce Hilton, Daniel Callahan, Maureen Harris, Peter Condliffe, and Burton Berkley, *Ethical Issues in Human Genetics* (New York: Plenum Press, 1973), pp. 1-455.
3. M.M. Kaback, *Tay Sach's Disease: Screening and Prevention* (New York: Alan R. Liss, Inc., 1977), pp. 1-433.
4. A. Milunsky, *The Prevention of Genetic Diseases and Mental Retardation* (Philadelphia: W.B. Saunders Co., 1975), pp. 1-506.
5. A. Milunsky and G. Annas, *Genetics and the Law* (New York: Plenum Press, 1975), pp. 1-532.
6. H.A. Lubs and F. de la Cruz, *Genetic Counseling* (New York: Raven Press, 1977), pp. 1-598.
7. M. Lappé, J.M. Gustafsone, and R. Robbin, "Ethical and Social Issues in Screening for Genetic Diseases," *New England Journal of Medicine* 286: 1129-1132 (1972).
8. V.A. McKusick, *Human Genetics* (Englewood Cliffs, NJ: Prentice-Hall, Inc., 1969), pp. 1-221.

360   REPRODUCTION, RIGHTS, AND POPULATION PLANNING

9. C.O. Carter, J.A. Frazer Roberts, K.A. Evans, and A.R. Buck, "Genetic Clinic: A Follow-Up," *Lancet* 1: 281–285 (1971); C.O. Leonard, G.A. Chase, and B. Childs, "Genetic Counseling: A Consumer's View," *New England Journal of Medicine* 278: 433–439 (1972).

10. G. Stamatoyannopoulos, "Problems of Screening and Counseling in the Hemoglobinopathies," in A. Motulsky and W. Lenz, *Birth Defects* (Amsterdam: Excerpta Medica, 1974), pp. 268–276.

11. R. Murray, "Screening: A Practitioner's View," in Hilton et al., *Ethical Issues in Human Genetics*, pp. 121–130.

12. Ibid., p. 126.

13. C.L. Clow and C.R. Scrivner, "Knowledge About Our Attitudes Toward Genetic Screening Among High School Students: The Tay–Sach's Experience," *Pediatrics* 59: 86–91 (1977); N.A. Holtzman, "Genetic Screening: For Better or Worse," *Pediatrics* 59: 131–133 (1977).

14. Committee for the Study of Inborn Errors of Metabolism, p. 117.

15. Ibid., pp. 119–125.

16. F.J. Inglefinger, "Cozening with People with Ambiguous Claims," *New England Journal of Medicine* 297: 334 (1977).

17. Clow and Scrivner.

18. Holtzman.

19. Ibid.

17 STERILIZATION
Issues in Conflict

Betty Gonzales, R. N.
Robert W. Sansoucie, M. Div.

With respect to human rights and public policy, perhaps there is no more volatile an area of concern than contraceptive sterilization. The incendiary emotions of religious and moral conviction that are ignited by almost any discussion of the subject cannot be gainsaid merely on dismissal by opponents of the religious prohibition of sterilization.

Religious prohibitionists as well as proponents are really seeking the same end—namely, the fulfillment of human destiny. If prohibitionists have as their point of thrust the single goal of generational fulfillment under the will of God, then the proponents have the dual goal of relief from the burden of unwanted childbearing and childraising and the conservation of the world's natural resources. In short, one view would fulfill human destiny by letting the population grow naturally; the other would commence planning for the upcoming resources crunch by actively reducing the population that eventually would be affected.

Possibly the most appropriate focus for discussing the opposing views on sterilization is the regulations promulgated by the U.S. Department of Health, Education, and Welfare (DHEW), now the Department of Health and Human Services (DHHS), in November 1978. These regulations codify federal policy pertaining to sterilization in cases in which government funds are expended. Moreover,

361

these rules may produce even more far-reaching effects. At the time of their release, former HEW Secretary Joseph Califano asserted that the new procedures hopefully would become normative for the entire medical field. Such an observation suggests a growing encroachment of government control in the lives of American citizens. Should the intent of DHHS policy be realized, citizens unable to afford the cost of private surgical care could be forced to adhere to conditions that might be repugnant to them.

Prior to any further discussion of the federal regulations pertaining to sterilization, the reason behind their creation should be explained. As highlighted during the nationwide public hearings held during the formulation of the regulations, sterilization abuse is a common reality. Cases were identified in which individuals were sterilized against their will; individuals of limited mentality (i.e., those who could not understand the finality of their decision) were sterilized; some incarcerated in institutions such as prisons were sterilized; some welfare recipients were pressured to undergo sterilization in order to receive obstetrical care. One of the most serious outcomes of these practices was that the public financing of these procedures was contributing to the abridgement of the rights of many disadvantaged citizens.

As a result of many of the above and similar cases, DHHS regulations exemplify both an attempt to protect the rights of those dependent upon government funds for health care and an effort to standardize sterilization procedures. However, the major consideration should be the protection of individual rights. Thus, there needs to be the assurance that the human and legal rights of those seeking voluntary sterilization are as protected as those at risk of involuntary sterilization.

In a field that is so rife with emotion and opposing views, the dual aspects of this subject necessitate fair exposure. Hence, the following discussion offers an analysis of both the positive and negative aspects of the federal regulations and specific recommendations by the authors.

THIRTY DAY WAITING PERIOD

Programs or projects to which this subpart applies shall perform or arrange for the performance of sterilization of a mentally competent individual only if the following requirements have been met: . . . .

At least 30 days but no more than 180 days have passed between the date of informed consent and the date of sterilization.[1]

The above regulation attempts to provide adequate time for consultation with family, friends, and others about sterilization procedures and their irreversible consequences prior to surgery. In addition, it allows sufficient time for the individual to get away from the environment in which consent was given. For instance, if a consent was given in a hospital setting, the individual could benefit from the thirty-day cooling-off period by escaping an atmosphere of possible coercion to review the decision.

However, since there is no waiting period for most privately funded sterilizations, this regulation could be discriminatory against some groups. It could create a hardship for and limit access to residents of rural areas, to migratory workers, and to many low income individuals who must often travel considerable distances to obtain the counseling as well as the surgery.

The purpose of the thirty-day waiting period is to protect women hospitalized for childbirth and women who might be making arrangements for an abortion. Women under such conditions may be subjected to pressures from authoritative individuals in medical settings. In these cases, the waiting period provides a beneficial opportunity for decisionmaking; however, for others it clearly makes voluntary sterilization impossible for those faced with the unexpected need for a Caesarean delivery and who had not previously signed consent forms for the procedure.

The late André E. Hellegers, M.D., serving as director of the Kennedy Institute for the Study of Human Reproduction and Bioethics at Georgetown University and one of the nation's leading bioethicists, said that the thirty-day period:

> means that occasions will arise in which, in order to consent to one sterilization operation, one will have to consent to two operations, which changes the nature of the consent to sterilization. . . . It takes little imagination to conclude that some physicians and patients will put a signed consent "on file" just in case it is needed.[2]

Hellegers also indicated that some abortions would be delayed by the thirty-day waiting policy.

No cases of men being forced into surgery in a vasectomy clinic or of nonpregnant women seeking contraception being forced into a hospital for sterilization have been reported. Insofar as these groups

364 REPRODUCTION, RIGHTS, AND POPULATION PLANNING

have not been subjected to sterilization abuse, one must conclude that the regulations are too broad and prohibitive. Furthermore, the specific period of thirty days was selected arbitrarily, and such a policy does not guarantee prevention of abuse. One might envision a pregnant woman visiting a prenatal clinic monthly, being brainwashed regularly during her pregnancy, and eventually signing the necessary papers. Although this consent could be obtained under a more subtle coercion, it is involuntary nevertheless.

The voice of the medical profession loudly proclaims against this mandatory waiting period on the grounds that it constitutes an excessive control of medical practice. For the government to adopt a thirty-day waiting period solely for sterilization destroys the doctor-patient relationship. While the thirty-day waiting period should be opposed on the basis that the specific number of days between the signing of the consent form and the performance of the sterilization act is mandated, this should not be the matter of prime concern. Rather, proper counseling to assure that patients fully understand and desire this permanent surgical method of birth control should be the major issue of concern.

MINIMUM AGE OF TWENTY-ONE

Programs or projects to which this subpart applies shall perform or arrange for the performance of sterilization of an individual only if the following requirements have been met:

The individual is at least 21 years old at the time consent is obtained.[3]

Due to the irreversible nature of the procedure, establishing a minimum age of consent prior to surgery protects persons under twenty-one who are both more susceptible to coercion and more likely to lack the maturity to make an informed decision. Some studies have suggested a higher rate of regret among younger women.[4]

In reviewing requests for information about sterilization reversal, findings from the Association for Voluntary Sterilization (AVS) show that a significant number of individuals who honestly desired to end their fertility at the time they sought sterilization subsequently found themselves in a different life situation and genuinely regretted their earlier decision. However, nearly all of these patients were over twenty-one years of age at the time they were sterilized.

Thus, a minimal age restriction will not prevent unhappiness. More important than a minimum age limit is the need for thorough, lengthy, and repeated counseling. While such counseling is good practice in general, it especially should be provided to young persons to help them to project themselves not only into a future life situation that might seemingly be better without more children (or any children), but also into one that might include a new mate and more children (or at least the ability to have children).

When most states permit individuals over the age of eighteen to enter into contracts and make legally binding decisions for themselves, the federally imposed requirement that these same individuals must be over twenty-one in order to elect to terminate their fertility appears arbitrary and capricious. There are some for whom this regulation results in hardship—for example, those who have completed their families before the age of twenty-one and those for whom other methods of contraception have been ineffective or are medically contraindicated.

The age of majority for sterilization should conform to the individual state standards used in other situations requiring mature judgment. An across the board prohibition of sterilization for those under twenty-one is discriminatory.

MENTALLY INCOMPETENT INDIVIDUALS

"A mentally incompetent individual" means a person who has been declared mentally incompetent by a Federal, State, or local court of competent jurisdiction for any purpose unless he or she has been declared competent for purposes which include the ability to consent to sterilization.[5]

With respect to sterilization and the mentally incompetent, DHHS regulations state that:

Programs or projects to which this subpart applies shall not perform or arrange for the performance of a sterilization of any mentally incompetent individual. . . .[6]

The words mentally incompetent do not connote a diagnosis. Rather, they constitute a judicial term used to identify individuals unable to handle their own affairs. DHHS should be commended for having foresight to recognize that while some declared incompetent individuals may be unable to handle some of their affairs (e.g., their financial responsibilities), they may be capable of making decisions regarding their own health or contraceptive needs.

The above regulations may be viewed as being protective of mentally incompetent persons, since there is a high likelihood that families or guardians might seek selective sterilization of their wards or children to minimize the burden on themselves. A significant number of sterilization abuse cases currently in litigation deal with such questionable intents.

It is also important to acknowledge that not all mentally incompetent persons are retarded. Some may be suffering from a temporary mental illness and may subsequently improve. The prohibition of federal funds for sterilization of such incompetent individuals is appropriate, since it might hold such surgical procedures in abeyance until individuals return to a state of competency.

Certainly a method assuring proper safeguards should be developed to permit sterilization for some incompetent individuals. However, DHHS has concluded that compliance with complicated safeguards in an area that is as sensitive and susceptible to abuse as sterilization of the mentally incompetent might be unenforceable. Thus, the Department has adopted its current, simpler blanket prohibition policy. Accordingly, the denial of federal funding in such cases deprives some persons of their right not to have children because of their limited intellectual or emotional abilities.

Although limited, many retarded individuals understand that they are emotionally unable to cope with the responsibilities of rearing children, but still seek marriage. Pallister and Perry have studied marriage among the retarded and present a case for voluntary sterilization. According to them:

> There are economic as well as genetic realities to be considered. Most of the retarded who support themselves in the community have minimal incomes at best. If they marry, it is seldom to anyone above their level of intelligence and earning power. The birth of a child poses increased financial burdens that can only cause further deprivation. If the child is retarded, with concomitant medical problems, the impact is often unmanageable. Various social agencies must intervene, and the concept of independent living for the retarded is destroyed.[7]

Thus, the continuing risk of unwanted pregnancies poses a real physical, emotional, and financial burden on both retarded persons and their families. Temporary methods of birth control may be unsuitable for some of these individuals; depriving them of sterilization may cause their parents or guardians to seek their institutionalization to insure the avoidance of unwanted pregnancy.

A total prohibition of federal funds is discriminatory to the 90 percent of mentally retarded citizens who are capable of learning social and work skills, of understanding the idea of having no more babies, and of possibly desiring permanent birth control. Appropriate guidelines should protect this group of mentally retarded persons from involuntary sterilization, but should also provide for a full range of contraceptive options, including sterilization.

Guidelines should be established for sterilizations of mentally incompetent persons who can demonstrate the mental capacity to give informed consent. A review committee could have the responsibility to determine their capacity to make informed decisions. This committee should consist of

1. Qualified professionals, not including the operating surgeon, that accept the general concept of voluntary sterilization as a birth control method;

2. One member from a socioeconomic group similar to that of the patient; and

3. One member designated as patient advocate.

The power of this committee should be limited. Having determined that a person is capable of making informed decisions, the committee should not influence the person toward or against the option of sterilization. The individual alone should be permitted to make this decision. In addition, this committee should hold no power to determine what is in the best interests of the person. Individuals found to be incapable of decisionmaking should be referred to a special committee established to review such cases.

Individuals who are not able to establish their capability of giving informed consent should not be categorically denied the possibility of sterilization. Continued fertility among the severely retarded serves neither their best interests nor those of society. Appropriate guidelines should help protect the sexually active members of this group from pregnancy by permitting a representative to consent to medical procedures on their behalf. These citizens must be permitted to enjoy full expression of their sexuality without fear of unwanted pregnancies, and thus there should be an alternative to the prohibition of sterilization.

Guardians of individuals declared incapable of making informed decisions should have access to a special review committee whose purpose would be to determine whether permanent termination of fertility is in the best interests of the individual. The composition of the committee should be the same as of the original review committee although it may be comprised of different members. The involvement of the court at this point would be advisable, since determination of competence traditionally has been a judicial responsibility.

Counseling should be available for every applicant seeking evaluation. Within this service, all of the elements of informed consent should be explained at a level and pace that individuals could comfortably accept. Repeated sessions may be essential. Patients should have access to this counseling service even prior to their appearance before the review committee.

INSTITUTIONALIZED INDIVIDUALS

"Institutionalized individual" means a person who is (1) involuntarily confined or detained under a civil or criminal statute, in a correctional, or rehabilitative facility including a mental hospital or other facility for the care and treatment of mental illness, or (2) confined, under a voluntary commitment in a mental hospital or other facility for the care and treatment of mental illness.[8]

Programs or projects to which this subpart applies shall not perform or arrange for the performance of a sterilization of any . . . institutionalized individual.[9]

There is little refutation that institutions exert control over those in residence. This control often leads to abuse, including sterilization abuse. For example, inmates could conceivably sign a consent for sterilization believing the reward might be their early discharge or parole.

Conjugal arrangements are relatively rare in institutions; therefore, there is little need to provide access to contraceptive procedures. However, DHHS defines institution as facilities such as halfway houses where contraception options should be available. Increasing trends toward normalization, or mainstreaming, offer more opportunities for heterosexual relationships in institutions and further increase this need.

With the allowance of sterilization in institutional settings, there is admittedly a risk of later regret. But the nature of institutionalization itself causes family ruptures. When sterilized inmates are restored to society, new family situations may produce deep regret over the sterilization decision and a desire for reversal. However, institutions often provide the only tie to the health care system. When individuals leave the institution, they may not get connected to an outside system. This may result in a double denial of sterilization service—that is, both in institutions that prohibit such services and in the outside world.

A plan to resolve the legitimate needs for sterilization as expressed by some institutionalized persons is needed. Possibly a review committee such as the one discussed earlier would provide an adequate method of verifying to DHHS the actual desire of some petitioners and thereby eliminate the danger of coercive sterilizations. No citizens should be categorically denied services they desire.

CONTRACEPTIVE HYSTERECTOMY

Programs or projects to which this subpart applies shall not perform or arrange for the performance of any hysterectomy solely for the purpose of rendering an individual permanently incapable of reproducing or where, if there is more than one purpose to the procedure, the hysterectomy would not be performed but for the purpose of rendering the individual permanently incapable of reproducing.[10]

Hysterectomy is not generally considered to be an appropriate form of sterilization; it is more risky, painful, and expensive than other forms. The vast majority of the medical profession does not consider contraceptive hysterectomies to represent sound medical practice. Others hold the view that contraceptive hysterectomies should be permitted when there are medical indications that, by themselves, may not mandate a hysterectomy, but when taken together with a desire to end fertility constitute sufficient reason to choose hysterectomy as the preferred procedure.

Some recent research suggests that an increasing incidence of uterine pathology may follow tubal sterilization and require subsequent removal of the uterus.[11] Denying the option of contraceptive hysterectomy when a woman chooses sterilization could necessitate the risk and inconvenience of a second operation. In addition, some physicians contend that hysterectomies may be the method of choice when both sterilization and termination of a relatively advanced pregnancy are desired.[12]

Provision of hysterectomies to severely retarded and to physically handicapped persons may be indicated by considerations of hygiene and emotional health. A recent study concludes that women unable to cope with their own menses benefit greatly from contraceptive hysterectomy.[13]

Elective hysterectomy has become culturally patterned as a normal part of the life cycle, and an increasing number of doctors are advocating this practice. An estimated 20 percent of all hysterectomies are performed for birth control reasons, according to the executive director of the American College of Obstetricians and Gynecologists.[14]

In an era in which government assistance to the poor is rendered for almost all life needs, it appears arbitrary to take a stand contrary to wide public practice. Yet the proliferation of social services that attempt to lift the poor is a practice that often results in placing the poor in a more favored financial situation than those who work and pay the taxes that make the government largesse possible. In this setting one must ask, Should elective surgery—a contraceptive hysterectomy not medically indicated—be provided at public expense? It is the conviction of the authors that elective hysterectomy should not be financed by federal funds, but that funding should continue for all medically indicated hysterectomies. Denial of federal funds for medically justified hysterectomies may constitute discrimination against the poor. On the other hand, a person not dependent upon public assistance should not have to suffer any government interference with her arrangements for a desired contraceptive hysterectomy.

STERILIZATION CONSENT AT TIME OF EMERGENCY ABDOMINAL SURGERY

An individual may consent to be sterilized at the time of premature delivery or emergency abdominal surgery if at least 72 hours have passed after he or she gave informed consent to sterilization. In the case of premature delivery, the informed consent must have been given at least 30 days before the expected date of delivery.[15]

The intent of this regulation is to limit sterilizations of women performed during an emergency abdominal operation and to prohibit the signing of a consent form for sterilization during such a situation. If this regulation is followed, the patient would be denied a concomitant sterilization at the time of the abdominal surgery unless the consent forms had been signed more than seventy-two hours before the onset of the emergency. The person who falls short of this period of time would be compelled to return to the operating room at a later date and to be subjected to the risks, pain, and inconvenience of a second surgical procedure.

It is extremely unlikely that any significant number of people will be in the process of the thirty-day waiting period when an emergency occurs. Faced with the dilemma created by this regulation, some individuals may be tempted to sign a sterilization consent form at the time of the emergency and then attempt to postpone the abdominal surgery for seventy-two hours. This would certainly not constitute sound medical practice.

While the reasoning behind this regulation appears to be clear— namely, that such an irreversible decision not be made during the stress of a medical emergency—the findings of AVS suggest that the majority make their decisions to end childbearing long before they initiate any formal steps for surgery. Thus, the position of the federal government is totally unrealistic. The solution to the problem of sterilization during abdominal surgery lies in the assurance that the decision was not made during the time of the emergency stress.

Thus, a procedure should be devised whereby the thirty-day waiting period could be waived entirely in certain situations, allowing the escape of the double jeopardy to which some women must now expose themselves. Hence, sterilization should be permitted when the request for sterilization at the time of the emergency surgery is initiated by the patient, not by the doctor, and when witnesses will attest to the patient having made the decision for sterilization prior to the onset of the emergency.

Finally, the cost-effectivenss of combining two surgical procedures in one operation is a legitimate factor that offers a strong rationale in the minds of many patients—the price of a second anesthetic, a second operation, use of a second operating room, a second hospitalization, and a second necessity for a battery of laboratory tests. The government's strong position on the prevention of involuntary sterilization of some should not nullify the medical, economic, and emotional needs of others.

CONCLUSION

A great many of the decisions finalized in the recent federal regulations for government-funded sterilizations were dictated by political realities. No government bureaucrat wants to be held responsible for a government expenditure, especially in the social service area, that may subsequently be found to have resulted in a denial of the human rights of a citizen. This reality became abundantly clear during the public hearings conducted throughout the country at which abuses were documented. Testimony revealed the unacceptable conduct of shabby administrators and the misguiding advice of bureaucratic social workers and physicians.

In turn, the government regulations evolved from a deep public concern shared by a cross-section of citizens, from individual social worker to health commissioner and from clinician to cabinet secretary. The lengthy deliberations seem to have been thorough and deeply grounded in attempts to reach the truth. They focused on protection of citizens against involuntary sterilization early in the proceedings. Unfortunately, in its enthusiasm to respond, DHHS appears to have erred toward overprotectiveness rather than toward license of voluntary sterilization. Remembering that the regulations will be continually reviewed, it is to be hoped that the weaknesses discussed herein will be considered and acted upon and thus make this pathmaker program in medical assistance more acceptable.

NOTES TO CHAPTER 17

1. U.S. Department of Health, Education, and Welfare, "Sterilizations and Abortions," *Federal Register* 43: 52150 (November 8, 1978); 42 C.F.R. §50.203 (1980).
2. André E. Hellegers, " 'Cooling Off Period' Bad Law," *Obstetrics/Gynecology News*, October 1, 1977.
3. U.S. Department of Health, Education, and Welfare, p. 52151; 42 C.F.R. § 50.203 (a) (1980).

4. E.G. Moor, "Sequalae of Tubal Ligation, Medical and Psychological," *American Journal of Obstetrics and Gynecology* 101: 350–351 (June 1978).
5. U.S. Department of Health, Education, and Welfare, p. 52154; 42 C.F.R. §50.202 (1980).
6. Ibid., p. 52153; 42 C.F.R. §50.206 (1980).
7. P.P. Pallister and R.M. Perry, "Reflections on Marriage for the Retarded: The Case for Voluntary Sterilization," *Hospital and Community Psychiatry* 24: 173–174 (1973).
8. U.S. Department of Health, Education, and Welfare, p. 52156; 42 C.F.R. § 50.202 (1980).
9. Ibid.; 42 C.F.R. § 50.206 (1980).
10. Ibid., p. 52162; 42 C.F.R. § 50.207 (1980).
11. Michael J. Muldoon, "Gynecologic Illness After Sterilization," *British Medical Journal* 1: 84–85 (January 8, 1972).
12. Niles Newton and Enid Baron, "Reactions to Hysterectomy: Fact or Fiction?" *Primary Care: Clinics in Office Practice* 3 (December 1976).
13. Jane C. Perrin, C.R. Sands, D.E. Tinker, et al., "A Considered Approach to Sterilization of Mentally Retarded Youth," *American Journal of Diseases of Children* 130: 288–290 (March 1976).
14. Newton and Baron.
15. U.S. Department of Health, Education, and Welfare, p. 52150; 42 C.F.R. § 50.203 (1980).

18 ABORTION
Divisive U.S. Public Policy

Richard J. Kaufman, Ph.D.

Abortion has become one of the most divisive national issues in the United States since the Vietnam War. The struggle to set public policy on the question of abortion is being waged amid the complexities of the issue. Traditional abortion concerns of a medical, moral, and theological nature are presently accompanied by social, economic, political, and legal arguments. The intent of this chapter is to examine some of these major arguments as they relate to the recent anti-abortion legislation—the so-called Hyde Amendment, which has severely restricted the use of federal funds for Medicaid abortions.[1]

The Hyde Amendment is regarded by pro-abortion forces[a] as an unethical and inequitable piece of class legislation that contravenes the intent of the liberalizing 1973 U.S. Supreme Court decisions of *Roe* v. *Wade*[2] and *Doe* v. *Bolton*,[3] upholding the constitutional right of women to have an abortion. For the most part, the Hyde Amendment serves to deny the right to legal elective abortions to that group with perhaps the greatest need for them—the poor. In

---

a. Editor's Note: The so-called pro-abortion or pro-choice forces are those advocating that women should have the right to choose the continuance or the termination of a pregnancy and thereby to maintain their reproductive freedom. The pro-choice movement is being led primarily by the National Abortion Rights Action League (NARAL), a national lobbying and educational organization based in Washington, D.C., and having state affiliates throughout the country.

passing this legislation, Congress created two public policies on abortion, one for the nonpoor and one for the poor.

Supporters of the Amendment view it as ethically justifiable and a first step toward reestablishing, among all Americans, moral responsibility for the rights of the unborn child. This endorsement is generally grounded in the belief that abortion is morally impermissible. Although the issue of the morality of abortion is an exceedingly important subject, one that has been worthy of much attention, it in itself is not treated in this chapter.[4] Rather, for purposes of the following discussion, the Hyde Amendment is judged not on the basis of the ethics or morality of abortion itself, but on ethical considerations of the Amendment's development and its current impact on our society.

HISTORICAL DEVELOPMENTS OF ABORTION IN THE UNITED STATES

The first state abortion laws in the United States were passed in the early nineteenth century. By the end of the century abortion laws could be found in all of the states. Existing legislation tended to be either prohibitive or extremely restrictive. States that permitted abortions did so only in cases where evidence indicated that the continuation of a pregnancy would pose a threat to a woman's life or health.[5] During this period, abortion procedures were regarded as extremely hazardous for women, and the laws against abortion seemingly had the objective of protecting women. As late as 1858, a New Jersey judge stated that the purpose of abortion legislation was "not to prevent the procuring of abortions so much as to guard the health and life of the mother against the consequences of such attempts."[6] With therapeutic abortion mortalities running at a rate sometimes ten times higher than mortality associated with obstetric complications related to childbirth, it was little wonder that abortion in general was viewed as an offense against women.

As medical procedures became safer, a movement began for abortion law reform. Early advocates of abortion reform, such as W.J. Robinson, attempted to justify therapeutic abortions on social grounds. In 1911, Robinson addressed a need to abort certain premarital pregnancies; by 1933, his position has broadened to include the repeal of all restrictions on abortion except for those relating to the protection of the health of the woman.[7]

Despite numerous calls and considerable lobbying for repeal or reform of state laws, actual legal reform did not occur until 1967. Beginning with Colorado, thirteen states adopted less restrictive abortion statutes between 1967 and 1970. The model statute for legal reform, followed in whole or in part by these states, was provided by the American Law Institute (ALI). The ALI model law called for legalization of abortion in cases in which the "continuation of pregnancy would gravely impair the physical or mental health of the mother, or that the child would be born with grave physical or mental defect, or that the pregnancy resulted from rape, incest or other felonious intercourse."[8]

Many people felt that the ALI model did not go far enough and that the matter of abortion should rest solely on the judgment of the woman and her physician, without conditional restrictions. The American Civil Liberties Union (ACLU) proposed a model for abortion law reform that, in its simplicity, went far beyond the ALI model statute. According to the ACLU, "It is a civil right of a woman to seek to terminate a pregnancy, and of a physician to perform or refuse to perform an abortion, without threat of criminal sanctions. Abortions should be performed only by doctors, governed by the same considerations as other medical practices."[9]

In 1970, a movement for the total repeal of abortion laws led four states—Hawaii, Alaska, New York, and Washington—to adopt legislation that removed virtually all restrictions on the conditions for obtaining legal abortions.[b] This liberalized attitude on the issue was reflected in a series of nationwide Harris polls that showed that a majority of the American public believed that the abortion decision should be a private one between a woman and her physician.[10]

As the liberalizing trend among states continued, strong opposition from anti-abortion forces emerged. Between 1970 and 1973, much of the ensuing debate took place in the courts. Opponents to liberalizing abortion succeeded in several states by having nonrestrictive abortion laws declared unconstitutional. Meanwhile, citizens of states with highly restrictive abortion laws were using the courts to challenge their constitutionality. By 1971, no fewer than seventeen

---

b. In New York, the late Governor Nelson Rockefeller stood out as a staunch advocate for abortion law reform. In 1968, as he convened the first meeting of a commission he had appointed to examine and recommend changes in the state abortion law. Rockefeller is reported to have remarked, "I am not asking *whether* New York's abortion law should be changed, I am asking *how* it should be changed."

cases dealing with abortion had been referred to the U.S. Supreme Court.[11]

The Court agreed to consider the constitutional challenges presented in two cases. In *Roe* v. *Wade*, a woman claimed that the highly restrictive nineteenth century Texas statutes were unconstitutionally vague and denied her the right to personal privacy under the Constitution. In the second, *Doe* v. *Bolton*, the Court considered the conditions under the moderately restrictive 1968 Georgian statute that served to deny an abortion to an indigent mother of three who claimed she could not support another child.

Despite the advances in abortion law reform that had been occurring since 1967, few observers were prepared for the January 1973 Supreme Court rulings in these two cases.[12] The Court in essence ruled that anti-abortion laws represented an unconstitutional invasion of the fundamental right to privacy, guaranteed by the Ninth and Fourteenth Amendments. While the Court ruled that "the right of personal privacy includes the abortion decision," it also noted that "this right is not unqualified and must be considered against important state interests in regulation."[13] As such, a state could, if it chose, prohibit all abortions in the third trimester of pregnancy, except those deemed medically necessary for the life or health of the mother. In addition, a state could regulate abortions during the second trimester, but only to ensure that an abortion procedure does not imperil the health of the mother. With respect to the first trimester, the Court held that the abortion decision remained solely with the woman and her attending physician.

ABORTION POLEMICS

The Court rulings stirred political controversy by limiting the extent to which states could regulate abortions and stirred religious and moral controversy over the issue of the right to life of the unborn child. In its rulings, the Court determined that the unborn child is not a person under the Fourteenth Amendment and thus is not entitled to constitutional protection of a right to life. In taking this highly controversial position, the Court sidestepped a moral issue embraced by the Catholic Church and others—that abortion is tantamount to murder. The Court held: "We need not resolve the difficult question of when life begins. When those trained in the respective disciplines of medicine, philosophy and theology are unable to arrive at any consensus, the judiciary, at this point in the development of man's knowledge, is not in a position to speculate as to the answer."[14]

In the position assumed by the Supreme Court, two ethical principles come into direct conflict—the principle of autonomy (namely, privacy) and the principle of sanctity of human life. The Court's use of the semantic vagaries of viability, potentiality of human life, and personhood in arriving at its decision did little if anything to placate those who espouse the principle of sanctity of life.[15] However, the Court's rulings did help to crystalize many of the existing disputes inherent in the abortion issue. The confrontations among people and among principles that have followed the 1973 decisions are likely to continue for a long time. For as Veatch suggests, not all confrontations represent resolvable contradictions: "It is perfectly compatible to hold that innocent life is sacred and that individuals have the right to control their own bodies. Since neither group carries out the debate in terms of the other's fundamental principle, each appears capriciously immoral in the light of the other."[16]

One can assess the abortion issue in terms of a spectrum of contending views.[17] Those holding positions to the left of the spectrum are inclined to treat self-determination and individual rights, such as personal privacy, as absolute values. For this group, the argument is for abortion on demand. To a large extent, the requirements of this group are satisfied by the 1973 Court rulings, at least as they apply through the first two trimesters of pregnancy. As one moves toward the middle of the spectrum, the position is one that supports justifiable abortion. The conditional requirements found in the ALI model statute, in many state statutes of the late 1960s, and in the third trimester under the 1973 Court rulings reflect this middle or compromise position. As one moves further to the right of the spectrum, one assumes the position of no abortion. Although most Catholics recognize justifiable abortions in certain cases, the Church hierarchy defends the position of no abortion. The right wing also advocates state regulation and intervention in order to reduce or, ideally, eliminate the harm caused by abortion.

Catholics differ in their belief as to the precise moment at which the soul enters the physical body. While many Catholics feel that a spiritual quality begins to enter at the moment of conception, others believe that this happens at a slightly later stage of pregnancy. With the lack of consensus and the indeterminable time of this event, the only infallibly safe decision has been to offer total protection by the assertion of a right to life along the entire continuum of pregnancy. The taking of life through abortion is regarded as anathema by the Catholic Church because of the doctrine of original sin. In short, as the inheritor of original sin, the fetus is certain of eternal damnation if it should perish without benefit of baptism.[18] Beyond this, Catholic thinking is that the general practice of abortion within society will hinder man from attaining true humanity and serve eventually to undermine civilization.

As the guardian of the sanctity of life of the unborn, the Catholic Church and its right-wing following have sought to impose their value system on society at large. According to the 1973 Court rulings, a woman is allowed to choose whether or not to exercise her right to a legal abortion. The Church, however, continues its attempt to limit or eliminate this element of choice for everyone by exercising its strong political influence, by financing right-to-life groups, and by related ventures.

With an issue that is as emotionally charged and as complex as that of abortion, the line between church and state becomes easily blurred. Hence, a danger exists that Church domination over abortion policy may result in the opinion of a minority controlling the majority. In support of this contention, Swomley argues that in a secular state such as the United States, laws governing the practice of induced abortion "must have a validity apart from church doctrine or religious dogma."[19] Moreover, such laws are constitutional only inasmuch as abortion affects the public health or welfare of the people and not because a church or denomination is convinced of the appropriateness of a particular course of action.[20] There is no dearth of evidence to support the fact that the Catholic Church in this country has inspired, if not directly influenced, the ways in which existing abortion laws have been applied, as well as the development of restrictive post–*Roe* v. *Wade* abortion legislation.[21]

ADVANCES AGAINST LEGALIZED ABORTION

Following the 1973 Supreme Court decision, the right to legal abortion became available to all pregnant women in the United States, at least in theory. In actuality, however, a number of factors conspired to limit the number of abortions performed, especially for the poor. Barriers to obtaining abortions existed despite the fact that they were contrary to the intent of the Court's ruling. Thus, while abortions were nonrestrictive de jure, they were often moderately restrictive de facto in many states for certain subgroups of the population.[22]

In 1976, for example, only 21 percent of the more than 2,000 public hospitals performed any abortions. While public hospitals accounted for 26 percent of all births in the United States in 1976, they accounted for only 8 percent of the nation's abortions.[23] Despite an obvious shortage of hospitals performing abortions, Congress, bowing to right-wing pressures, passed legislation allowing hospitals, even those receiving federal funds, to refuse to perform abortions on the basis of "religious belief and moral convictions."[24]

Thus, limited hospital abortion services and geographic factors forced many women, particularly the indigent, to forego abortions or seek them outside their home states. In time, nonpoor women were able to obtain a more satisfactory level of abortion service either in one of the growing number of freestanding abortion clinics or in doctors' offices. For the poor the solution was not so easy. The default of public hospitals, the major source of health care for the poor, and an absence of affordable alternatives produced a disproportionately high level of unmet need for abortion among indigent women in this country.[25]

Inequalities in abortion services between the poor and nonpoor existed following 1973 despite the supposed availability of federal and state funds under Medicaid. Medicaid programs, implemented individually by states under federal guidelines, in theory compensate for health care inequities between the poor and nonpoor by subsidizing selected needed medical services for the poor that they otherwise could not afford and would not receive. Evidence strongly indicates that in redressing the inequalities associated with abortion, Medicaid has been highly unsuccessful. For example, in fiscal year 1977, prior to implementation of the restrictions contained in the Hyde Amendment, nearly 295,000 women obtained abortions paid for by Medicaid. This number, however, represented only about two-thirds of the estimated 427,000 Medicaid-eligible women who sought to terminate a pregnancy in that year. Thus, approximately 133,000 Medicaid-eligible women were thwarted in their efforts to obtain an abortion, "because the services were not available or accessible to them, or because the states had policies prohibiting such payments."[26]

In addition to the refusal of Medicaid support, states boldly attempted to ignore, circumvent, or reverse the intent of the Supreme Court decisions. Several states attempted to enact further restrictive abortion measures for their residents. Unsuccessful attempts were also made to modify the 1973 rulings by mandating the consent of a pregnant woman's husband[27] or of an unmarried minor's parent(s).[28] In each of these cases, the Supreme Court reconfirmed its earlier decision that the abortion choice, at least in the first trimester, remained solely that of the woman and her attending physician.

Another challenge to the Court has been mounted in the form of a constitutional amendment that would subordinate the principle of privacy to that of sanctity of life of the fetus. This strategy has received strong support from the Catholic Church, including the 1976 political pledge drive launched by the National Conference of Bishops. By the spring of 1976, there were as many as fifty bills before the U.S. House of Representatives being considered as abortion amendments to the Constitution. Two types of amendments have been sought—(1) the so-called states' rights amendments, which attempt to invest in the legislative process the power to regulate, permit, or prohibit abortion; and (2) the human life amendments, which seek to assure Fourteenth and Fifth Amendment personhood (i.e., the right to live) to the unborn and to other unwanted human beings who might be endangered by the jurisprudence of *Roe* v. *Wade.*[29]

Thus far, anti-abortion forces have not been able to gain the necessary majority in Congress to begin the process of formally reversing the 1973 Supreme Court decisions by constitutional amendment. Attempts at calling a constitutional convention to secure this change have also stalled. By far the greatest achievement of anti-abortion groups has been the Hyde Amendment, which arguably undercuts the intent of the Court at least as it applies to the poor.

THE HYDE AMENDMENT AND ITS IMPACT

The Hyde Amendment (named for its sponsor, U.S. Representative Henry Hyde, R–Illinois) restricts the use of federal Medicaid funds for abortions. As an amendment to the 1977 Labor-Health, Education, and Welfare Appropriations (Labor–HEW) Bill, the initial intent of the Hyde Amendment was to prohibit the use of U.S. Department of Health, Education, and Welfare (DHEW)^c funds for all abortions except those needed to save the life of a pregnant woman. This Amendment was enjoined from taking effect by a federal district court following a challenge from the ACLU, the Center for Constitutional Rights, Planned Parenthood of New York City, and other interested parties. The restraining order was short lived. In a series of 1977 decisions, the U.S. Supreme Court ruled that states and localities need not pay for nontherapeutic abortions for indigent women;[30] that a state could adopt a policy favoring normal childbirth over abortion and use its public funding to meet that objective;[31] and that public hospitals do not have to perform elective abortions even though they provide maternity care.[32] These decisions cleared the way for the injunction against the Hyde Amendment to be lifted.

Following months of congressional debate, during which the U.S. Senate sought to liberalize the Amendment to cover all medically necessary abortions and the U.S. House of Representatives fought to maintain the original, more restrictive language, a compromise amendment was developed. This version of the Hyde Amendment, which was found acceptable by the President, was attached to the 1978 Labor–HEW Appropriations Bill. This revised Hyde Amendment mandated that federal Medicaid funds could be used only in those instances or exceptions in which:

> (1) the life of the mother would be endangered if the fetus were carried to term; or (2) when in the opinion of two physicians "long-lasting physical health damage to the mother would result if the pregnancy were carried to term;"^{d} or (3) when the woman has been a victim of rape or incest, providing that the incident has been properly reported within 60 days of the occurrence.[33]

These categorical qualifications and restrictions represent a return to the ALI type model policies common to states in the late 1960s.

---

c. With the 1980 establishment of the U.S. Department of Education, DHEW was renamed the U.S. Department of Health and Human Services (DHHS).

d. This exception for long-lasting physical health damage to the mother was eliminated as of November 1979.

In his dissenting opinion to the Supreme Court rulings of 1977, Justice Thurgood Marshall voiced what he believed to be the significance and consequences of the Court's actions:

The impact of the regulations here [restricting public financing of abortions for the indigent] falls tragically upon those among us least able to help or defend themselves. As the Court well knows, these regulations inevitably will have the practical effect of preventing nearly all poor women from obtaining safe and legal abortions. The enactments challenged here brutally coerce poor women to bear children whom society will scorn for every day of their lives. . . . I fear that the Court's decisions will be an invitation to public officials, already under extraordinary pressure from well-financed and carefully orchestrated lobbying campaigns, to approve more such restrictions.[34]

The concerns expressed by Justice Marshall appear to have been warranted.

Enforcement of the Hyde Amendment in the summer of 1977 increased the existing high unmet need for abortions among indigent women. Abortions paid for by Medicaid have been reduced by more than 99 percent in states that have embraced the Hyde Amendment language or stricter language in their policies. About one-third of the states have exceeded the restrictions embodied in the Amendment and allowed the expenditure of state Medicaid funds only when a pregnancy endangers a woman's life. A few states have voluntarily continued to pay for Medicaid abortions that conform to the non-restrictive standards of the 1973 Court rulings. In these instances, states must pay the full cost for abortions not authorized by the Amendment. The trend has been for state legislatures to conform to the Amendment rather than have to shoulder the burden of paying for Medicaid abortions without benefit of federal assistance. If the few states that voluntarily have maintained liberal abortion policies were to follow the pattern of the majority, the estimated number of government-financed abortions for the poor would decline from the roughly 300,000 a year prior to the Hyde Amendment to fewer than 3,000 annually.[35]

Of the nearly five million Medicaid-eligible women in the United States, about half are considered at risk each year of incurring an unintended pregnancy. While women in this at risk group differ in many respects, they do share certain characteristics. They are usually young, sexually active, fertile, not pregnant or wishing to become pregnant, and poor. More than 90 percent of Medicaid-eligible women are also recipients of the federal–state public assistance program for the poor, Aid to Families with Dependent Children (AFDC).[36]

In assessing the impact of a policy such as the Hyde Amendment, one should consider whether or not welfare recipients, eligible for Medicaid, can pay for their own legal abortions once government subsidies have been eliminated.

Using data available for fiscal year 1977, one can see that the average cost of an abortion ($285) was about 18 percent higher than the average AFDC monthly payment ($241) for a typical AFDC family of a mother and two children.[37] The average cost of an abortion was roughly equivalent to an average welfare family's budget allocation for food for a three month period, for clothing for nine months, or for shelter for approximately four months. These figures suggest the very real hardship or impossibility for women on welfare to obtain a legal abortion without Medicaid or some other outside assistance. Some women, in desperation, have used their family's welfare money in order to obtain a safe, legal abortion. This was verified recently by the director of a New Jersey health center: "The fact that Medicaid recipients use their food and shelter allotments to pay for their abortions is reflected in the large number of recipients whom we serve on days welfare clients receive their monthly checks. On these days, approximately 90 percent of our patients are Medicaid recipients.[38] Abortion clinics, public and private hospitals, and charitable organizations thus far have been either unwilling or unable to provide the necessary funds or the funded services required to offset the drastic reduction of Medicaid funds.

In effect, whatever choice indigent women make in dealing with unwanted pregnancies, they are forced to place themselves and their families, if they have them, in peril of one type or another. Should these women not choose to sacrifice food, shelter, or clothing allotments, they can attempt to secure necessary funds elsewhere. This solution is distinguished by debt building and potentially dangerous health complications that can arise because of search-related delays in obtaining an abortion. If women have no means of affording safe, legal abortions, they are faced with the choices of inducing self-abortion; of seeking an illegal, less costly abortion service (usually less safe); or of carrying an unwanted pregnancy to term. Each of these choices is regarded as a contributing factor to increasing the mortality rate for these women above what it would be were they afforded the choice and means for receiving early, safe, and legal abortions.[39]

An estimated five to ninety excess deaths will result annually for women of childbearing age in the United States due to restrictions on publicly funded abortions according to a recent study.[40] These are deaths that presumably would not occur if legalized abortions were available to all women, pursuant to the 1973 Supreme Court decisions. Although specific averages or figures are not currently available, abortion-related deaths and injuries among indigent women since enforcement of the Hyde Amendment have been reported in the news media.[e]

Legalization of abortion has been associated with declines in the birthrate, in the number of out of wedlock births, in the number of newborns abandoned or put up for adoption, in abortion-related deaths and injuries, in the rates of maternal mortality and morbidity, and in the number of infant deaths.[41] Whereas nineteenth century laws prohibiting or restricting abortions served to protect the health of women, the opposite holds true late in the twentieth century. At present, a legal abortion is statistically safer than pregnancy and childbirth.[42] Thus, the rate for maternal mortality will rise as more women are forced to bear children that previously would have been aborted. In general, black women and women of racial minorities run the highest risks of maternal mortality as a result of the Hyde Amendment. Despite the disproportionate impact on minority groups, the inequity created by the Hyde Amendment is not so much a racial issue as a socioeconomic or class issue. It emerges as an issue that has separated the rich from the poor, those with power from those who have little or none.

POLITICAL AND LEGAL CONSIDERATIONS

Indigent Americans traditionally do not fare well in the political arena. The reasons for this rest in the pluralistic model of public decisionmaking. Beginning with a conflict over the selection of public options (e.g., abortions on demand, restricted abortions, or no

e. One of the more publicized abortion-related deaths was that of Rosie Jimenez—the first reported victim of an illegal abortion following enforcement of the Hyde Amendment. Supported by author Ellen Frankfort, women's rights activist Gloria Steinem and NARAL, a fund in the honor of Rosie Jimenez has been established to aid indigent women in obtaining legal abortions (*New York Times*, January 23, 1979). A legislative backlash has been associated with special funds such as this one. However inadequate they may be, their existence has been taken as justification by certain anti-abortion groups for further restricting public funding for abortion. Recent restrictions have also curtailed the use of public funds for abortions for military personnel and dependents. Abortion-related traumas are already being reported for low income military personnel affected by these restrictions (*NARAL Newsletter*, July 1979, p. 6).

abortions for all or selected subgroups of the population), various groups (such as the Catholic Church or Medicaid-eligible women) behave so as to optimize the likelihood that their preferred options will be selected. Based on their values (e.g., sanctity of life versus individual autonomy), groups differ in their goals.

Groups also differ in their capacities or power to impose their preferences on society. In a constitutional democracy such as the United States, the relative power of groups is determined by their numbers, wealth, status, education, commitment to the group's goals, and skills in effectively using these resources.[43] A postulate of pluralistic decisionmaking is that a political equilibrium is achieved by official decisionmakers balancing the claims of competing groups. Latham describes public choice in terms of a pluralist model:

> What may be called public policy is actually the equilibrium reached in the group struggle at any given moment, and it represents a balance which the contending factions or groups constantly strive to tip in their favor. . . . The legislature referees the group struggle, ratifies the victories of the successful coalition, and records the terms of the surrenders, compromises, and conquests in the form of statutes.[44]

The surrender, compromise, or conquest in the politics of abortion has been the accessibility of abortion services for the poor. Although poor women arguably have a greater need than nonpoor women for abortions,[f] as an interest group in their own behalf, they lack sufficient resources and power to defend themselves against elitist and pluralistic decisionmaking that clearly is not in their best interest. The poor historically have been regulated and controlled to help maintain national economic stability;[45] in the case of the Hyde Amendment the poor appear to have been regulated and controlled in order to maintain moral stability and to achieve a political equilibrium between left-wing and right-wing abortion factions.

The vulnerability of the poor is apparent in some of the arguments behind the Hyde Amendment. One of the major arguments for limit-

---

f. Despite high levels of contraceptive use, indigent women in the year preceding the Hyde Amendment made use of legal abortions at a rate approximately three times higher than nonpoor women. The explanation for this difference is that poor women "want somewhat fewer children than do nonpoor women (and therefore are at risk of having an unwanted pregnancy for a longer time after they have had their last wanted child)" and that poor women "are more likely than nonpoor women to experience contraceptive failure while trying to prevent an unwanted pregnancy." Contraceptive failure is associated with poverty and a correlate lack of education. The Alan Guttmacher Institute, *Abortion and the Poor: Private Morality, Public Responsibility* (New York, 1979), pp. 18–20.

ing federal spending for abortions for indigent women was because a failure to limit such public spending would involve compromising the moral integrity of the taxpayers who do not condone abortion. Since federal and state tax revenues underwrite Medicaid and since some taxpayers view abortion as murder, it has been argued that tax moneys should not pay for abortions except under the extreme situations cited in the Hyde Amendment and various state statutes. The opposing viewpoint acknowledges that some individuals will always object, on moral or other grounds, to public spending of their tax dollars. Moreover, a service or program is not ordinarily terminated due to the objections of a vocal minority.

Tax funds support penal systems that practice capital punishment. Tax funds supported defense spending that financed the war in Vietnam. Tax funds continue to support an array of medical services under Medicaid, despite the fact that Jehovah's Witnesses object to blood transfusions and Christian Scientists object to all conventional medical care.[46] In these and similar instances, the government has not intervened to inconvenience or abridge the rights of many for the sake of a few. Changes that have occurred have been the result of a clear shift in the majority opinion of Americans. Although abortion public opinion polls generally have not been specific enough to pinpoint reaction to the Hyde Amendment, they do suggest that the majority of Americans do not favor the abortion restrictions comprising it and the more limiting state statues enacted in approximately one-third of the states.[g] It would appear that the Medicaid policy change affecting the poor represents a governmental response

---

g. An August 1977 nationwide Harris poll described the restrictions under the Hyde Amendment and then asked subjects if they favored or opposed "a ban on the use of federal Medicaid funds for abortions for poor women who couldn't otherwise pay for them." Of the total, 47 percent favored the ban, 44 percent opposed it, and 9 percent were not sure. (Connie de Boer, "The Polls: Abortion," *Public Opinion Quarterly* 41: 553–564 (Winter 1977–1978). A later, 1979 Gallop poll determined that 70 percent of Americans believed that Medicaid should pay for abortions under any circumstances (23 percent) or under certain conditions (47 percent); only 28 percent fully opposed Medicaid-funded abortions. E. R. Dobell, "Abortion: The Controversy We Can't Seem to Solve," *Redbook* 153 (2): 42, 86, 91–93, 97 (June 1979). A more recent Gallop poll on the issue of abortion in general, taken in mid-1980, reports 78 percent of Americans believe abortion should be legal under all (25 percent) or certain (53 percent) circumstances. Only 18 percent oppose abortion in all situations. Despite the intensification of political efforts by anti-abortion groups, these findings suggest that support for abortion has not diminished significantly since the 1973 U.S. Supreme Court rulings. "Attitudes Toward Abortion Have Changed Little Since Mid-1970s," *The Gallup Opinion Index, Report No. 178* (June 1980), pp. 6–7.

to objections raised by the Catholic Church and other right-wing elements rather than a mandate by American taxpayers.

Whether or not the majority of Americans currently favor Hyde Amendment restrictions on Medicaid-funded abortions, these restrictions on indigent women have arguably abridged certain of their constitutional rights. The 1973 Supreme Court decision determined that the right of personal privacy, based on the Fourteenth Amendment's concept of personal liberty and restrictions upon state action, was broad enough to encompass a woman's decision whether or not to terminate her pregnancy. This right was regarded as fundamental and to be strictly protected against state infringement.[47] However, only four years later, in 1977, the Court ruled in three related cases that it was not a denial of equal protection under the Constitution to deny medical benefits to indigent women.[48] These decisions were made with full knowledge that they would have the effect of denying these women the right to exercise an established constitutional right.

The rationale behind the 1977 decision was that the government has no obligation to provide medical benefits to its citizens; therefore, it is no denial of equal protection when the denial of medical benefits also results in denial of the effective exercise of a constitutional right. In his general dissent to these cases, Supreme Court Justice Harry Blackmun noted that while the court had upheld a woman's constitutional right to abortion, it was now denying the realization and enjoyment of that right. He commented: "Implicit in the Court's holdings is the condescension that the woman may go elsewhere for her abortion. I find that disingenous and alarming, almost reminiscent of 'Let them eat cake.' "[49]

In short, as former U.S. Senator Edward Brooke (R–Massachusetts) remarked during congressional debate on Medicaid funding for abortions, "a right without access is no right at all."[50] The broader message underlying the 1977 decisions is that recipients of public assistance are not assured of the same civil liberties and individual rights as everyone else.[51]

MORAL AND ECONOMIC CONSIDERATIONS

The existence of differing abortion policies for the poor and the non-poor can be partially understood in the context of opposing theories by Max Weber[52] and Richard Tawney.[53] Weber ascribed importance and primacy to noneconomic factors such as religiocultural values as instrumental in shaping the political and economic policies of society. Tawney argued the opposite, that economic demands and requirements shape society's moral values.

According to Slaby and Tancredi, the value shifts of the 1960s and 1970s were influenced more by economic considerations (i.e., the marketplace ethic) than by religiocultural values (i.e., higher order values) and therefore are explained better by Tawney's thesis than by Weber's.[54] With respect to the liberalization of abortion policy in the United States, Slaby and Tancredi contend that the principle of sanctity of life was sacrificed because it no longer served societal needs for economic stability and development:

> When America had a growing agrarian-based economy, large families were necessary to provide manpower to farm our lands. It was therefore economically advantageous to encourage large families. By the mid-twentieth century this was no longer the case, and we now see the reverse operating. Large families are a tremendous drain on individual family and societal resources. Hence, abortion is no longer prohibited, despite the sanctity-of-life doctrine, a concept that was never really absolute in American or European history. . . . The concept of the sanctity of life was pitted against the economic exigencies of mid–twentieth century American society, and it lost.[55]

Slaby and Tancredi further observe that individual responsibility is a central concept within a society guided by a marketplace ethic. In addition to an economic need for population control, the existence of a liberal abortion policy satisfies a major demand of mid-twentieth century women—namely, that they have the individual responsibility and personal right to limit their own reproduction.[56] These responsibilities and rights presently apply to additional choices, including contraception, sexual preference, drug and alcohol consumption, and cigarette smoking. The risks associated with particular choices often involve costs that are borne by individuals (e.g., illness) and/or society (e.g., depletion of limited health resources). From time to time, when social costs are deemed too high, restrictions on certain rights may be imposed by society. Examples include imposing minimum age requirements for the purchase of alcoholic beverages or total bans on certain drugs deemed too dangerous. In such instances, some net advantage of the specific prohibition or restriction is perceived. This advantage is measurable in economic terms and/or adherence to higher order values of social justice and fairness. Usually, one or another or both ends are achieved by a specific policy decision.

In the restriction of abortions for indigent women, the net advantage is not apparent. If assessed in terms of values of social justice and fairness, the dual standard created by the Hyde Amendment appears violative and unjust. Furthermore, according to the Rawlsian theory of justice, "All social values—liberty and opportunity, income and wealth, and the bases of self-respect—are to be distributed equally unless an unequal distribution of any, or all, of these values is to everyone's advantage."[57] A denial of the liberty and opportunity of indigent women to obtain abortions is not to their advantage, nor may it be deemed advantageous to society.

The consequences of the Hyde Amendment will be costly, not only for the involved individuals, but for society in general. A rising birthrate among the poor, longer welfare rolls, and increasing rates of maternal and child mortality and morbidity constitute some of the current and anticipated social and economic costs attributable to society's indulgence of the Hyde Amendment. Estimated dollar costs to be incurred by federal and state governments due to the projected births of thousands of unwanted children to indigent women range from a conservative $75 million to more than $340 million.[58]

The reason that a net advantage for the Hyde Amendment is hard to discern is because it may not exist. The existence and nature of the Hyde Amendment suggest that its roots are Weberian in origin rather than Tawneyian. It has been spawned from judicial and legislative policymakers' responses to the religious and moral arguments of a relatively small segment of society. The result has been a policy that compares unfavorably with a more liberal position of the 1973 Supreme Court that rested more squarely on Tawneyian economic and individual rights considerations. This moral—albeit unjust—basis for the Hyde Amendment was recognized and attested to by the Carter administration. When queried about the fairness of the Amendment in denying access to safe, legal abortions only to the poor, former president of the United States, Jimmy Carter, remarked: "Well, as you know, there are many things in life that are not fair, that wealthy people can afford and poor people can't. But I don't believe that the federal government should take action to try to make these opportunities exactly equal, particularly when there is a moral factor involved."[59]

INTERPRETATIONS AND IMPLICATIONS

The "moral factor" alluded to by Carter is the principle of the sanctity of life. On the surface, at least, this principle has been the foundation for creating and implementing the unjust abortion policy for the poor. Regardless of personal conviction to this principle, the poor, as a group, have been politically, legally, and finally economically forced to adhere to it. The dubious advantages associated with the Hyde Amendment policy, as assessed in terms of social values and costs, suggest that its true worth is realized in other ways. One such way is to regard it as a means of political appeasement to the demands of right-wing groups. This appeasement is accomplished under the claims of morality and government neutrality on divisive moral issues.[h] The advantage or benefit desired as an outcome from this strategy is a reduction of right-wing pressure for further, more sweeping, change. The rights of the poor are thus sacrificed so that the middle and left-wing nonpoor can continue to indulge themselves in presumably immoral, but legal, abortions.

The underlying hypocrisy associated with the dual abortion standard created by the Hyde Amendment is further suggested by the unusualness of the Amendment itself. Anticipated high costs from its enforcement distinguish it from most legislation that directly affects the poor. Recent policy changes affecting human services and public assistance programs have reflected the growing conservatism to reduce and limit state and federal spending. This Amendment is a costly exception and suggests that political support is guided perhaps more by conscience than by pocketbook. One might argue, in addition to appeasement, that the denial of abortion rights to the poor represents an effort by judicial and legislative policymakers to ease the national conscience and expunge the collective guilt that conceiv-

---

h. A class action suit, *McRae* v. *Harris*, on behalf of all Medicaid-eligible women charged that since no clear secular purpose is achieved by the Hyde Amendment, it violates the religious freedom guarantee of the First Amendment and the equal protection guarantee of the Fifth Amendment. It was argued that the Hyde Amendment puts into law the religious dogma of the Catholic Church and ignores the right for some indigent women to exercise their own religious beliefs, which can and do include the practice of abortion (as in the case, for example, of some non-Orthodox Jews, certain Baptist groups, and certain Protestant denominations). The law suit asserted that to deny poor women funds for an abortion is a denial of religious freedom. Only if the government were to end Medicaid benefits for all pregnant women, whether or not they had abortions, would the government achieve a position of religious neutrality that did not violate First Amendment rights of indigent women.

ably stems from the liberal policy created by the 1973 Supreme Court decisions. Regardless of interpretation, the fact remains that the poor have been singled out for unusual and punitive treatment. With respect to abortion, poor Americans have been captives of the right wing for a number of years. This is a position the poor will probably occupy for some time, if not by virtue of legal and economic restraints, then by virtue of limited services and accessibility.[i]

Thus, abortion as an issue does not hold promise of being buried in the near future. The collision of the principle of the sanctity of life with that of personal autonomy (in this instance, the right of a woman to control her own body) should keep pro-abortion and anti-abortion forces locking horns for many years. This struggle will continue to be waged in the courts and legislative arenas at all levels of government. However, because of the vulnerability of the poor to moral as well as economic regulation and control, it is very probable that gains made by abortion opponents will be reflected first in yet further restrictions on the abortion rights of indigent women.[j] As such, it is expected that U.S. public policy on abortion will continue to be stamped by the inequities and moral inconsistencies that presently exist.

i. Editor's Note: At the time that this chapter was written, Medicaid financing of abortions for indigent women had resumed temporarily due to a federal district court decision holding the Hyde Amendment to be unconstitutional. This decision, based on *McRae* v. *Harris*, was appealed to the Supreme Court by the Department of Justice. In late June 1980, the Court handed down its controversial five to four decision reversing the federal district court opinion, thereby upholding the constitutionality of the Hyde Amendment. Following this ruling, Karen Mulhauser, executive director of NARAL, announced a revitalized political effort directed at elected members of Congress to reverse the Court's close, yet binding, decision. Thus, as Kaufman suggests, the status of the poor in gaining access to abortion services appears to be unchanging.

j. In an effort to obtain constitutional revisions and other legislative changes, special interest political action committees representing anti-abortion interests are pursuing a strategy of unseating legislators with liberal views on abortion and replacing them with individuals committed to a restrictive abortion stand.

As part of the Child Health Assurance Program (CHAP), intended to expand Medicaid coverage for poor children, the U.S. House of Representatives in December 1979 added an amendment—the Volkmer Amendment—that prohibits the use of Medicaid funds for abortion except to protect the life of the mother. Were such a bill to become law, this restriction would become a permanent part of the Medicaid statute, as opposed to the Hyde Amendment, which is subject to yearly evaluations as part of the annual appropriations bill for the Department of Labor-Health and Human Services. American Public Health Association, *The Nation's Health*, January 1980.

EPILOGUE

The inequity of a separate abortion policy for the poor might at least be somewhat palatable if society were responsibly meeting the needs that accompany a restrictive abortion policy. This has not been the case. Although it is reasonable to expect abortion opponents to be strong advocates for family planning, counseling services, improved sex education programs, increased welfare benefits, and expanded human service programs for pregnant women, their stand against abortion for the poor has so far not guaranteed support for these necessary alternative programs.[k]

As indigent women continue to be forced to bear children they neither want nor can afford, the moralistic shortsightedness among so-called right-to-life advocates becomes ever more apparent. The sanctity of life principle too frequently terminates with the birth of the child. The United States has yet to address adequately the health and welfare problems of children born into poverty. The Hyde Amendment unfairly mandates that the poor, because of their poverty, must bear their unwanted children, thus dooming these children to the likelihood of a life of illness, abuse, deprivation, and despair. It seems clear that the ends of justice and the interests of society would be better served by extending to the poor the same rights and the means of exercising these rights as are currently enjoyed by everyone else.

NOTES TO CHAPTER 18

1. The Departments of Labor and of Health, Education, and Welfare, and Related Agencies Appropriation Act of 1978 (Hyde Amendment), PL 95-205, § 101, 91 Stat. 1460 (December 9, 1977).
2. Roe v. Wade, 410 U.S. 113 (1973).
3. Doe v. Bolton, 410 U.S. 179 (1973).

k. Editor's Note: With pronounced support for a constitutional amendment to prohibit abortion and opposition to public support for family planning voiced by the Reagan Administration, alternative programs to decrease the need for abortion (i.e., unwanted, unplanned pregnancies) among the poor do not appear to be realistic in the early 1980s. This is further evidenced by the appointment of HHS Secretary Richard S. Schweiker and several of his key appointments that oversee public support for reproductive health programs who oppose abortion and do not strongly (if at all) back public family planning efforts.

4. For a discussion of the subject of the morality of abortion readers are referred to: Daniel Callahan, *Abortion: Law, Choice and Morality* (New York: Macmillan, 1970); Marshall Cohen, Thomas Nagel, and Thomas Scanlon, *The Rights and Wrongs of Abortion* (Princeton, NJ: Princeton University Press, 1974); John Noonan, Jr., *The Morality of Abortion: Legal and Historical Perspectives* (Cambridge, MA: Harvard University Press, 1970).
5. J. Mohr, *Abortion in America* (New York: Oxford University Press, 1978).
6. Malcolm Potts, Peter Diggory, and John Peel, *Abortion* (Cambridge: Cambridge University Press, 1977), p. 333.
7. W.J. Robinson, *The Law against Abortion* (New York: Eugenics, 1933).
8. David W. Louisell and John T. Noonan, Jr., "Constitutional Balance," in John T. Noonan, Jr., *The Morality of Abortion: Legal and Historical Perspectives* (Cambridge, MA: Harvard University Press, 1970), p. 248.
9. Potts, Diggory, and Peel, p. 336.
10. Connie de Boer, "The Polls: Abortion," *Public Opinion Quarterly* 41: 553–564 (Winter 1977–1978).
11. Potts, Diggory, and Peel, p. 344.
12. Roe v. Wade, 410 U.S. 113 (1973); Doe v. Bolton, 410 U.S. 179 (1973).
13. Roe v. Wade, 410 U.S. 155 (1973).
14. Id. at 160.
15. For a discussion of these ethical concepts, readers are referred to: Daniel Callahan, "The Sanctity of Life," in Donald Cutler, *Updating Life and Death* (Boston: Beacon Press, 1969), pp. 181–223; Norman Gillespie, "Abortion and Human Rights," *Ethics* 87: 237–243 (April 1977); Roslyn Weiss, "The Perils of Personhood," *Ethics* 89: 66–75 (October 1978).
16. Robert M. Veatch, "What about Abortions on Demand?" *Social Action* 37: 26–34 (March 1971).
17. Ralph Potter, Jr., "The Abortion Debate," in Donald Cutler, *Updating Life and Death* (Boston: The Beacon Press, 1969), pp. 85–134.
18. Potts, Diggory, and Peel, p. 7.
19. John Swomley, Jr., "Abortion and Civil Liberty," in U.S. Congress, Senate, Committee on the Judiciary, *Abortion—Part I, Hearings*, 93rd Cong., 2d sess. (Washington, D.C.: U.S. Government Printing Office, 1976), p. 673.
20. Ibid., pp. 673–685.
21. For a discussion of the position and the role of the Catholic Church on the abortion issue and other issues in American politics, readers are referred to: Mary Hanna, *Catholics and American Politics* (Cambridge, MA: Harvard University Press, 1979).
22. Institute of Medicine, *Legalized Abortion and the Public Health* (Washington, D.C.: National Academy of Sciences, May 1975), pp. 12–15.

23. The Alan Guttmacher Institute, *Abortions and the Poor: Private Morality, Public Responsibility* (New York, 1979), p. 16.
24. Barbara Allen Babcock, Ann Freedman, Eleanor Holmes Norton, and Susan Ross, *Sex Discrimination and the Law: Causes and Remedies* (Boston: Little, Brown, and Co., Inc., 1975), p. 855.
25. Ruth Roemer, "Equity in Abortion Services," *American Journal of Public Health* 68: 629–631 (July 1978).
26. The Alan Guttmacher Institute, p. 13.
27. Planned Parenthood of Central Missouri v. Danforth, 428 U.S. 52 (1976).
28. Bellotti v. Baird, 48 U.S. 132 (1976).
29. U.S. Congress, Senate, Committee on the Judiciary, *Abortion—Part 4, Hearings*, 93rd Cong., 2d sess. (Washington, D.C.: U.S. Government Printing Office, 1976), p. 106.
30. Beal v. Doe, 432 U.S. 438 (1977).
31. Maher v. Roe, 432 U.S. 464 (1977).
32. Poelker v. Doe, 432 U.S. 519 (1977).
33. "Abortions and Related Medical Services in Federally Assisted Programs of the Public Health Service," *Federal Register* 43: 4110–4185 (July 21, 1978).
34. Beal v. Doe, 432 U.S. 456 (1977).
35. The Alan Guttmacher Institute, pp. 22–25.
36. Ibid., p. 8.
37. Ibid., p. 27.
38. Ibid., p. 28.
39. Diana B. Petitti and Willard Cates, Jr., "Restricting Medicaid Funds for Abortions: Projections of Excess Mortality for Women for Childbearing Age," *American Journal of Public Health* 67: 860–862 (September 1977).
40. Ibid., p. 861.
41. "Legal Abortion in the United States: Facts and Highlights," in U.S. Congress, Senate, Committee on the Judiciary, *Abortion—Part I, Hearings*, 93rd Cong., 2d sess. (Washington, D.C.: U.S. Government Printing Office, 1976), pp. 111-123; Klaus Roghmann, "The Impact of the New York State Abortion Law," in Robert J. Haggerty, Klaus Roghmann, and Ivan Pless, *Child Health and the Community* (New York: John Wiley and Sons, 1975), pp. 210-219; The Alan Guttmacher Institute, *Provisional Estimates of Abortion Need and Services in the Year Following the 1973 Supreme Court Decisions: United States, Each State, and Metropolitan Area* (New York, 1975).
42. Willard Cates, Jr., David A. Grimes, J.C. Smith, and C. Tyler, Jr., "Legal Abortion Mortality in the United States: Epidemiologic Surveillance, 1972-1974," *Journal of the American Medical Association* 237: 452-455 (January 31, 1977).
43. Joseph Heffernan, *Introduction to Social Welfare Policy: Power, Scarcity and Common Human Needs* (Itasca, IL: F.E. Peacock, 1979), pp. 56-57.

44. Earl Latham, "The Group Basis of Politics," in Heinz Eulau, Samuel Elderszeld, and Morris Janowitz, *Political Behavior* (New York: Free Press, 1956), p. 239.

45. Frances Piven and Richard Cloward, *Regulating the Poor: The Functions of Public Welfare* (New York: Vintage Books, 1971).

46. The Alan Guttmacher Institute, *Abortions and the Poor*, p. 34.

47. Ellis Sandoz, *Conceived in Liberty: American Individual Rights Today* (Scituate, MA: Duxbury Press, 1978), p. 55.

48. Beal v. Doe, 432 U.S. 438 (1977); Maher v. Roe, 432 U.S. 464 (1977); Poelker v. Doe, 432 U.S. 519 (1977).

49. Beal v. Doe, 432 U.S. 463 (1977).

50. The Alan Guttmacher Institute, *Abortions and the Poor*, p. 39.

51. John Shattuck, "Scarce Resources and Civil Liberties," *The Center Magazine* 11:18–19 (January/February 1978).

52. Max Weber, *The Protestant Ethic and the Spirit of Capitalism* (New York: Charles Scribner's and Sons, 1958).

53. Richard Tawney, *Religion and the Rise of Capitalism: A Historical Study* (New York: Harcourt, Brace, and World, 1926).

54. Andrew Slaby and Laurence Tancredi, "The Economics of Moral Values: Policy Implications," *Journal of Health Politics, Policy and Law* 2:20–31 (Spring 1977).

55. Ibid., p. 23.

56. Barbara Sinclair Deckard, *The Women's Movement: Political, Socioeconomic, and Psychological Issues*, 2nd Ed. (New York: Harper & Row, 1979), pp. 423–424.

57. John Rawls, *A Theory of Justice* (Cambridge, MA: Belknap Press, 1971), p. 62.

58. The Alan Guttmacher Institute, *Abortions and the Poor*, p. 32.

59. Ibid., p. 35.

V RESEARCH
Benefits for Whom?

Historically, medical research and technology have contributed to major advances in medical care and to increases in the health status of the population in countless ways. However, the question, "At what cost has such progress occurred?" seldom is asked. While economic costs can be estimated, the ethical and social costs and implications of research involving human subjects are far less calculable.

Not until relatively recently, beginning with the aftermath of World War II, were international concerns voiced about unethical, and even inhumane, practices perpetrated on human subjects under the guise of sound medical research. The public disclosure of Nazi research practices led to the formulation of the Nuremberg Code in 1946. Since then, a series of successive international and domestic codes governing the professional and ethical conduct of researchers has emerged. Hence, in the past thirty-five years, public policy has dictated a course of increasing scrutiny of human subject research— medical, psychological and behavioral, and social—to protect the public from undue risk.

Public inquiry associated with the need for, the benefits and costs of, and the risks and implications of medical research has produced a multitude of difficult, unanswered questions. Do the social benefits produced by research constitute valid justification for the sacrifice of individual rights? What constitutes a policy of fairness or justice in the recruitment, selection, and use of humans for experimental purposes? Since the present generation is benefiting from the research conducted using past generations, is the current generation socially obligated to assume risks for future ones? If so, what constitutes a fair and/or a legitimate level of acceptable risk? Should research subjects be guaranteed compensation for their participation, and should greater compensation be awarded if consequences are encountered? On the other end of the spectrum, some researchers argue that emphasis on the protection of human subjects has gone too far. Many claim that government intervention through regulations designed to protect human subjects inhibits scientific progress. Others argue that such interventions constitute a violation of their rights to pursue professional careers and scientific inquiries.

Hence, these and many other major issues are being debated and considered by a variety of policy-recommending bodies, public and private institutions, and individual scientists and medical researchers. They commonly illustrate the clash between potential social good (i.e., the benefit accrued from successful experimentation to the public at large) and individual rights to be protected from undue risks and to maintain personal autonomy. Clearly conflicts arise, but efforts continually strive to reach that uneasy balance between social responsibility and individual rights. As modern research continues to test the limits of science, additional dilemmas arise that precipitate a wide range of such questions. Some even extend beyond the interest of individual human subjects into the public domain.

Earlier research, while having far-reaching impacts, appears to have posed far less dramatic implications for social change than much of today's experimentation. Although research is usually undertaken for specific therapeutic application, with some social good in mind, certain areas extend beyond commonly acceptable levels of risk, such as that which could result from cloning experimentation. Recombinant DNA research could induce uncontrollable changes in the genetic makeup of society. These are no longer issues so far removed from reality as to suggest that protective measures are unnecessary. Hence, discussion of the ethical implications of policies authorizing such research is justified. After all, examples of successful in vitro fertilization, the creation of life (i.e., General Electric's creation of oil-eating bacteria), and behavior change produced through psycho-surgery generate serious ethical and social questions.

Furthermore, coercion (to gain the participation of subjects) and covert and deceptive research precipitate even greater apprehensions. In such instances, not only may potential risks be involved, but many may not be fully aware of the implications they confront. Moreover, use of selected groups that for a variety of reasons may constitute good research populations raises other serious ethical dilemmas. Although institutionalized populations (e.g., prisoners, the aged and chronically disabled, or the mentally infirm) provide researchers with rather stable, confined groups accessible to follow-up and longitudinal study, their recruitment and use must not negate principles of beneficence, nonmaleficence, justice, and individual autonomy (e.g., voluntary informed consent and respect).

Essays raising ethical issues regarding human experimentation appear throughout earlier sections of this book. For example, in Chapter 11, Kleppick raises serious concerns with respect to the use of long-term care residents as human subjects and argues the need for administrators to protect them from unscrupulous and unwarranted research. In Chapter 16, Steele discusses similar fears regarding some genetic screening experimentation.

However, due to their significant and widespread impact, research policies and practices related to health and human experimentation warrant separate attention. This part includes three chapters that highlight the breadth of research issues of concern from a variety of perspectives.

In Chapter 19, Sanders (who as the administrative officer for ethics of the American Psychological Association is uniquely qualified to comment on this particular subject) discusses many long-standing ethical problems inherent in research using human subjects. The chapter traces the evolution of ethical principles governing psychological research in general and particularly those of a covert or deceptive nature. Sanders comments on the controversial recommendations of the National Commission for the Protection of Human Subjects of Biomedical and Behavioral Research and on several subsequent regulations promulgated by the U.S. Department of Health and Human Services. Although he carefully acknowledges possible dangers associated with covert and deceptive research and cautions about its inappropriate uses, he argues in support of such research practices on the grounds that most provide for the advancement of scientific knowledge.

A second area of conflict associated with research ethics and public policy revolves around the controversial use of children as human subjects. Pinkus and Haines (Chapter 20) examine the ethical issues, the law, and the formulation of public policy concerning children and research. More specifically, the authors concentrate on the dilemma concerning the ability and appropriateness of children to give informed consent for nontherapeutic research. Their consideration of this issue is particularly germane since children are considered as a special class by most and their rights and parental rights and responsibilities are not always in agreement. Furthermore, the authors inquire as to who should determine what constitutes fairness and competency among minors and who should decide?

In Chapter 21, Callahan analyzes the potential ethical implications and social impact of human genetic experimentation. He claims that society is generally overwhelmed by the success of medical technology and research. As a result, few ethical reservations or objections are raised by the public during or about the conduct of such research.

Genetic engineering may refer to a wide range of possible and actual scientific advances, including in vitro fertilization, cloning, and recombinant DNA research. According to Callahan, even when arguments are waged against direct intervention into the processes of procreation and reproduction or into human genetic makeup, they are generally nonpersuasive. He warns of the need to focus greater attention on the long-range social, ethical, and economic implications of policies allowing the continuation of genetic manipulations. To this end, he not only encourages the development of sound contemporary moral reasoning associated with this area of research, but strongly advocates the need to more critically examine and persuasively argue about the value of continually supporting research that potentially poses such a major impact on society and individuals.

In sum, these three chapters illustrate a tremendous range of ethical issues associated with human experimentation. They constitute only an introduction to the plethora of debates involving the use of human research subjects. However, the warnings deserve the full consideration of scientists, physicians, health administrators, and policymakers. Too little, too late may hold serious, highly undesirable results and human suffering that could be avoided.

19 ETHICAL DILEMMAS IN COVERT AND DECEPTIVE PSYCHOLOGICAL RESEARCH

Joseph R. Sanders, Ph. D.

HISTORY

Ethical problems inherent in psychological research using human participants have been identified in the professional literature for over half of psychology's one hundred year history as a science and profession.[1] However, discussion of ethical implications of covert[a] or deceptive methods in psychological research was not reported until after the American Psychological Association (APA) published its first edition of the *Ethical Standards of Psychologists* in 1953.[2] This document contained a section on "Protecting Welfare of Research Subjects" that included a statement specifying the conditions that must be met before a psychologist "is justified in misleading research subjects."[3]

Two years later, Vinacke commented that the deception of experimental subjects raises a point "which might well have major ethical importance for psychology."[4] He further stated: "The issue seems to boil down to the question of whether it is more important to avoid deceiving anyone, or, in the interests of science, to sacrifice a few people in the ultimate expectation of helping many via the knowledge gained."[5] He then proposed two kinds of research to

a. Covert research is research conducted without the prior informed consent of the person(s) involved.

deal with this issue. MacKinney responded to this proposal with a report of a survey of persons who had participated in an experiment involving deception. He concluded that at least for the particular subjects in the survey, there was very little evidence that they "were disturbed by being deceived."[6]

Published comment on the ethics of deception remained quiescent until Milgram described an experiment in which accomplices feigned pain after naive research participants supposedly administered electrical shocks to them for committing errors on an assigned task.[7] Milgram's work triggered a series of published studies and discussions on the use of covert and deceptive methods with human participants that has continued into the present.[8] From this series of publications a consensus within the psychological profession has emerged on the steps and procedures that should be taken by researchers in planning to engage in covert or deceptive research methods. The ontogenesis of this consensus was embodied in *Ethical Principles in the Conduct of Research with Human Participants* prepared by APA's Ad Hoc Committee on Ethical Standards in Psychological Research in 1973.[9] In 1977, the APA adopted the proposed ethical principles of its Ad Hoc Committee and made them part of the *Ethical Standards of Psychologists.*[10]

APA'S ETHICAL PRINCIPLES

While designed to provide ethical guidance to investigators contemplating the use of coversion or deception in an experiment involving human participants, the *Ethical Standards of Psychologists* actually created a series of dilemmas for researchers. Those segments of the standards that have created problems for investigators include:

(1) As scientists, psychologists accept the ultimate responsibility for selecting appropriate areas and methods most relevant to these areas. They plan their research in ways to minimize the possibility of their findings being misleading.[11]

(2) Psychologists recognize the boundaries of their competence and the limitations of their techniques and only . . . use techniques . . . that meet recognized standards.[12]

(3) As researchers, psychologists remain abreast of relevant federal and state regulations concerning the conduct of research with human participants or animals.[13]

(4) Psychologists respect the integrity and protect the welfare of the people and groups with whom they work. . . . Psychologists fully inform consumers as to the purpose and nature of an evaluative treatment, educational or training procedure, and they freely acknowledge that . . . participants in research have freedom of choice with regard to participation.[14]

(5) In the pursuit of research, psychologists give sponsoring agencies, host institutions, and publication channels the same respect and opportunity for giving informed consent that they accord individual research participants. They are aware of their obligation to future research workers. . . .[15]

The decision to undertake research should rest upon a considered judgment by the individual psychologist about how best to contribute to psychological science and to human welfare. Psychologists carry out their investigations with respect for the people who participate and with concern for their dignity and welfare.

In planning a study, the investigator has the responsibility to make a careful evaluation of its ethical acceptability, taking into account many principles for research with human beings. Researchers must weigh both scientific and human values to the greatest extent possible. Should the protocol suggest a compromise of any principle, investigators incur increasingly serious obligations to seek ethical advice and to observe stringent safeguards to protect the rights of the human research participants. The responsibility for the establishment and maintenance of acceptable ethical practice in research always remains with individual investigators. They are also responsible for the ethical treatment of research participants by collaborators, assistants, students, and employees—all of whom, however, incur parallel obligations.

Ethical practice requires investigators to inform participants of all features of the research that might reasonably be expected to influence willingness to participate and to explain all other aspects of the research about which participants inquire. Failure to make full disclosure imposes an additional responsibility on investigators to protect the welfare and dignity of research participants.

Openness and honesty are essential characteristics of the relationship between investigators and research subjects. When the methodological requirements of a study necessitate concealment or deception, investigators are required to insure the understanding of subjects as to reason for this action as soon as possible. Furthermore, subjects are entitled to a sufficient justification for the procedures employed.

Ethical practice requires investigators to respect the freedom of individuals to decline to participate in or withdraw from any research project. The obligation to protect this freedom requires special vigilance when investigators are in a position of power over participants (e.g., when participants are students, clients, or employees or otherwise are in a dual relationship with the investigators).

Ethically acceptable research begins with the establishment of a clear and fair agreement between investigators and research participants that clarifies the responsibilities of each. Investigators have an obligation to honor all promises and commitments included in that agreement.

Ethical investigators protect participants from physical and mental discomfort, harm, and danger. If a risk of such consequences exists, investigators are required to inform participants of that fact, secure consent before proceeding, and take all possible measures to minimize distress. A research procedure must not be used if it is likely to cause serious or lasting harm to a participant.

After the data are collected, investigators should provide participants with information about the nature of the study and remove any misconceptions that may have arisen. Where scientific or human values justify delaying or withholding information, investigators acquire a special responsibility to assure that there are no damaging consequences for participants. When research procedures result in undesirable consequences for individual participants, investigators have the responsibility to detect and remove or correct these consequences, including, where relevant, long-term aftereffects.

Given the foregoing ethical principles, investigators wishing to abide by them must decide if they can devise methods that are actually covert or deceptive and, if they can, whether such methods will be accepted by their colleagues as meeting recognized standards. If the methods of researchers are valid and meet recognized standards, they must still comply with the ethical requirement of informing their would-be research participants of the nature of the experiment. If it is determined that the use of coversion or deception is necessary to make the experiment valid, researchers must decide whether its use suggests a compromise of any principle of the *Ethical Standards*. If it does, advice should be sought from others concerning the conditions that would have to be met to properly protect all research subjects. Should debriefing procedures be used, the investigators must develop procedures that will convince participants that the use of covert or deceptive methods is justified. Finally, investigators must be satisfied that their project involves no risks that are "likely to cause serious or lasting harm to a participant."[16]

DHEW'S ETHICAL PRINCIPLES

With privately supported research, the responsibility for adherence to the *Ethical Standards of Psychologists* falls solely on the investigators. In such cases, they alone must solve the foregoing dilemmas. However, with research supported by federal moneys there is mandatory adherence to regulations established for the protection of human subjects. Federal involvement in the protection of human subjects through the regulatory mechanism using institutional review boards (IRBs) dates back to review requirements initiated by the Surgeon General of the Public Health Service (within the U.S. Department of Health, Education, and Welfare, DHEW) in 1966.[17] These requirements led to the publication of the well-known *Institutional Guide to DHEW Policy on the Protection of Human Subjects* in 1971 which established PHS requirements as DHEW policy.[18]

In May 1974, DHEW promulgated the first formal set of regulations applicable "to all Department of Health, Education, and Welfare grants and contracts supporting research, development, and related activities in which human subjects are involved."[19] Elsewhere, the regulations quote the National Research Act (PL 93-348) which provides:

> The Secretary shall by regulation require that each entity which applies for a grant or contract under this Act for any project or program which involves the conduct of biomedical or behavioral research involving human subjects submit in or with its application for such grant or contract assurances satisfactory to the Secretary that it has established (in accordance with regulations which the Secretary shall prescribe) a board (to be known as an 'Institutional Review Board') to review biomedical and behavioral research involving human subjects conducted at or sponsored by such entity in order to protect the rights of the human subjects of such research.[20]

The regulations further stipulate that "[n]o grant or contract involving human subjects at risk shall be made to an individual unless he is affiliated with or sponsored by an organization which can and does assume the responsibility for the subjects involved."[21] As subsequently amended in 1975 and 1978, these regulations governed the system of IRBs through the 1970s.

In addition to confirming the IRB protective mechanism, the National Research Act mandated the creation of the National Commission for the Protection of Human Subjects of Biomedical and Behavioral Research. The Commission was charged to undertake a wide range of investigations and studies related to the conduct of biomedical and behavioral research and to develop and submit appropriate ethical principles and guidelines for such research to the secretary of HEW.[22] Among the series of its reports, the Commission submitted *The Belmont Report: Ethical Principles and Guidelines for the Protection of Human Subjects of Research*[23] and the *Report and Recommendations: Institutional Review Boards*.[24] Largely as a result of these reports, the U.S. Department of Health and Human Services (DHHS) proposed new regulations for the protection of human subjects in 1980, received considerable comment, and issued its most recent set of final regulations in early 1981 to become effective later that year.[25]

The 1981 DHHS regulations constitute both a deregulation and decentralization of requirements. Greater responsibility is afforded local, community IRBs and a broad category of educational and social science research is exempted from mandatory IRB review (pending local IRB decisions). Since some psychological research obviously falls into this category, greater flexibility for such activity now exists and a greater responsibility to ensure the efficacy of the research and the protection of human subjects must be assumed by individual investigators.

According to the 1978 *Report and Recommendations: Institutional Review Boards* prepared by the National Commission two very important issues that must be addressed in IRB review are (1) the degree of subject risk involved with the proposed research, and (2) the assurance of informed consent. The Commission reported:

> Informed consent will be appropriately documented, unless the board determined that written consent is not necessary or appropriate because (1) the existence of signed consent forms would place subjects at risk, or (2) the research presents no more than minimal risk and involved no procedures for which written consent is normally required.[26]

According to the Commission:

> Notwithstanding the [foregoing] requirements . . . informed consent is unnecessary where the subjects' interests are determined to be adequately pro-

tected in studies of documents, records or pathological specimens and the importance of the research justifies such invasion of the subjects' privacy; or in studies of public behavior where the research presents no more than minimal risk, is unlikely to cause embarrassment, and has scientific merit.[27]

The report further acknowledges that "in some research there is concern that disclosure to subjects or providing an accurate description of certain information, such as the purpose of the research or the procedures to be used, would affect the data and the validity of the research."[28] Therefore,

> The IRB can approve withholding or altering such information provided it determines that the incomplete disclosure or deception is not likely to be harmful in and of itself or that sufficient information will be disclosed to give subjects a fair opportunity to decide whether they want to participate in the research. The IRB should also consider whether the research could be done without incomplete disclosure or deception. If the procedures involved in the study present risk of harm or discomfort, this must always be disclosed to subjects.[29]

The report continues:

> In seeking consent, information should not be withheld for the purpose of eliciting the cooperation of subjects, and investigators should always give truthful answers to questions, even if this means that a prospective subject thereby becomes unsuitable for participation. In general, where participants have been deceived in the course of research, it is desirable that they be debriefed after their participation.[30]

The National Commission further addressed similar issues in its *Belmont Report: Ethical Principles and Guidelines for the Protection of Human Subjects of Research.* This report states that:

> A special problem of consent arises [in situations in which] informing subjects of some pertinent aspect of the research is likely to impair the validity of the research. In many cases, it is sufficient to indicate to subjects that they are being invited to participate in research of which some features will not be revealed until the research is concluded. In all cases of research involving incomplete disclosure, such research is justified only if it is clear that (1) incomplete disclosure is truly necessary to accomplish the goals of the research, (2) there are no undisclosed risks to subjects that are more than minimal, and (3) there is an adequate plan for debriefing subjects, when appropriate, and for dissemination of research results to them. Information about risks should never be withheld for the purpose of eliciting the cooperation of subjects, and truthful answers should always be given to direct questions about the research. Care should be taken to distinguish cases in which disclosure would

destroy or invalidate the research from cases in which disclosure would simply inconvenience the investigator.[31]

With respect to potential risks and benefits to subjects, the Commission believes that such an assessment "requires a careful arrayal of relevant data, including, in some cases, alternative ways of obtaining the benefits sought in the research. Thus, the assessment presents both an opportunity and a responsibility to gather systematic and comprehensive information about proposed research."[32]

Only on rare occasions did the Commission conclude that quantitative techniques should be available for the scrutiny of research protocols. "However, the idea of systematic, nonarbitrary analysis of risks and benefits should be emulated insofar as possible. This ideal requires those making decisions about the justifiability of research to be thorough in the accumulation and assessment of information about all aspects of the research and to consider alternatives systematically."[33]

Investigators wishing to abide by the National Commission's recommendations, as well as by APA's *Ethical Standards*, must now decide whether incomplete disclosure or deception is in itself likely to harm their research participants. They must also determine what constitutes sufficient information to enable individuals to decide whether they want to be participants. The investigators must decide if the research could be done without incomplete disclosure or deception. Additionally, researchers must determine whether the undisclosed risks of their experiment are more than minimal. Finally, ways of weighing risks against benefits and of considering alternatives systematically must be found.

COPING WITH DILEMMAS

Many dilemmas for researchers were highlighted in the APA's *Ethical Standards of Psychologists* and the two aforementioned DHEW publications. These recent recommendations require careful consideration and adherence by the research community.

Covert Research Methods

Investigators who wish to conduct research utilizing materials about persons, such as documents, records, or pathological specimens without the knowledge of said persons, must be able to assure that such materials will remain confidential. This is consistent with the *Ethical Standards'* principle on confidentiality, which states, in part, "When data have been published without permission for identification, the psychologist assumes responsibility for adequately disguising their sources."[34]

Investigators who wish to observe public behavior of persons covertly must be able to demonstrate that their "research presents no more than minimal risk, is unlikely to cause embarrassment, and has [sufficient] scientific merit."[35] It is assumed that all other types of covert research would be considered unethical, at least from the perspective of the National Commission.

Deception Research Methods

The dilemmas associated with covert research appear relatively simple compared to those involving deception research. However, while there is very little published discussion and research evidence concerning the former, there is considerable published material on the latter.

Is the Research Actually Deceptive? Seeman studied the validity of deceptive techniques in research and concludes that the point may have been reached in which one can no longer have naive subjects, but only naive experimenters.[36] Shipley insists that deception experiments contain a logical flaw that can only be corrected through the use of an independent measure of how well participants in a particular study are deceived. He cites the Minnesota Multiphasic Personality Inventory as an example of one psychological instrument that attempts to measure the degree to which persons taking it are deceiving the examiner.[37] Seeman argues that an experiment that allows for multiple interpretations must include checks on the several possible interpretations.

Do Deception Techniques Meet Recognized Standards of Psychological Research? After comparing role playing with deception, Mixon claims that no laboratory experiment that employs deception creates a real life situation any more than one that explicitly invites the participants to play a role. He concludes that experiments using either deception or role playing are simulations of real life situations. Thus, an evaluation of both to determine the degree to which they actually elicit spontaneous and involved behavior on the part of the participants is necessary. Mixon sees the need for researchers to improve their skill in achieving such spontaneity and involvement in simulation research. Thus, in effect, he questions whether deception techniques already meet recognized standards.[38]

Do Participants in Deception Research Need to be Fully Informed About the Nature of the Research? Undergraduate students rated six published experiments involving deception and stress as either ethical or unethical. The results of their study suggests that they considered undergoing stress much more unethical than being deceived. However, they also concluded that research participants have a more positive attitude toward the use of deception when they receive enough information to convince them that they are making a significant contribution to science.[39]

Does Research Using Deception Compromise Ethical Principles? Eisner identifies a clear-cut conflict between the ethical imperative to conduct research using methods believed to be the most effective and the ethical obligation to individuals volunteering as human subjects.[40] She further states that a cost-benefit analysis cannot resolve this conflict. Furthermore, the way that the participant views the ethics of an experiment is far more important than the views of the investigator, because the participant can be hurt by the experiment more than the investigator. Eisner also argues that "demonstrating the research designs involving deception are not as good as [they are] supposed to be would, by a process of elimination, solve the ethical dilemma conclusively, provided there exist alternate methodologies with which to continue research."[41]

In her consideration of role playing, Eisner notes that replicating the results of comparable research in which deception is utilized has not been successful. She further concludes that unobtrusive measures in the field rather than the laboratory deprive research participants of both informed consent and a debriefing and thus compound the ethical problems. In addition, she suggests that psychology should "move to a very old and respected function of scientific research, that is, description and categorization, an area in which psychological data is almost non-existent."[42]

Are Debriefing Procedures Following Deception Effective? Seeman questions the assumption that explaining how and why subjects were deceived extinguishes attitudes produced in participants by an experiment. According to Seeman, "Since he will quite appropriately have lost confidence in the person's veracity, the subject may never be able to disentangle the times of truth and the times of falsity in his relationships with the experimenter."[43] Seeman further suggests classifying deception procedures as antitherapy because "[w]here the therapist helps the client to give up reality distortion as a basis for action, the experimenter in a deception study leads the subject to adopt reality distortion as a basis for action."[44]

When psychologists and students are both presented with a hypothetical experiment involving deception, a significantly larger proportion of the students judge the use of deception to be ethical.[45] On review of the psychological research literature, Holmes reports that debriefing can take the form of either dehoaxing (involving the experimenter's deception) or desensitizing (involving the subject's behavior).[46] He further concludes that:

> Dehoaxing is a viable post-experiment technique for eliminating misinformation acquired by a subject as a consequence of a deception . . . when done properly. . . . It is still each experimenter's responsibility to debrief his or her subjects as thoroughly as possible and to ascertain the effectiveness of his or her particular dehoaxing procedure before appreciable numbers of subjects participate in the experiment.[47]

By comparing subsequent performance of debriefed and nondebriefed participants, Gruder found that the debriefed participants perform significantly better on a parallel form of the previously taken intelligence tests.[48]

Is There a Possibility of Lasting Harm? Although there are relatively little published data on the effectiveness of debriefing procedures, Holmes speculates that the lack of data may actually reflect the effectiveness of post-experiment desensitization.[49] An opposite view is taken by Shipley, who concludes that there is no significant evidence in the literature showing that participants in research involving deception are not seriously harmed.[50] He adds that it is very difficult to obtain such evidence.

In their study of the ethics of social psychology in general and of deception research in particular, West and Gunn contrast the views of humanistic critics with those of the traditional experimental social psychologist. They conclude that to the former, deception experiments "can only have long-term negative effects on the participants," while for the latter, "the individual in a deception experiment experiences short-term tensions that are then reduced in some manner."[51] They express the hope that the use of empirical information in making ethical decisions will help provide a more rational basis for such decisions than the reliance solely on one's personal view of the human condition.[52]

Are There Alternatives to Deception?   Although there is some disagreement in the field, there appears to be a relatively strong positive orientation toward role playing as a viable methodological tool.[53] Krupat sees role playing as a viable alternative to deception but insists that the type of role-playing techniques used by the investigator makes a difference.[54] While those investigators who use deception must try to find out if their participants are aware, suspicious, or deceived, those who elect role playing must assess whether their participants are sufficiently in role to trust their results. In addition, Krupat cites other research that shows strong agreement among judges concerning the degree of involvement of active role players and concludes that "[t]he critical issue is not the comparability of role-playing and deception studies, but rather the validity of role-playing results."[55] Thus, while it is no panacea, role playing deserves consideration as a complementary rather than an alternative technique.

Mitchell, Kaul, and Pepinsky review the arguments and evidence for and against deception and assert that the unanswered question is how best to assure that the results of psychological experiments are generalizable to situations in everyday life. They see the question of alternative methods in social psychology as an empirical one. More importantly, however, they see public policy issues as overriding science's empirical questions. Hence, they conclude that the paramount issue is whether the psychological experiment, especially if it entails the practice of deception, constitutes a violation of human rights and dignity.[56]

SUMMARY AND CONCLUSIONS

The appropriateness of using covert methods of observation and deception in research with human participants has been debated among psychologists and in the professional literature for the past twenty-five years. The issue of when and where the use of such methods is appropriate is clarified in the set of recommendations of the National Commission and later codified in federal regulations. However, the question of when and where it is appropriate to use deception in research has not been clarified by any authoritative scientific, professional, or public group. Indeed, judging by the contradictory evidence and opinions on the subject discussed in this chapter, the issue has never been more unclear. Thus, that which follows is yet another attempt to clarify it. This attempt follows a review of both the literature on deception and the codes of ethics relevant to that literature.

One principle of ethics relevant to the dilemmas inherent in deception research admonishes psychologists to avoid dual relationships. This principle was not cited earlier because it directly concerns only those psychologists who are engaged in practice with clients and not those engaged in scientific research with human participants. However, this review on deception revealed that many investigators engaged in this type of research have indirect dual relationships with their human participants. While the primary interest of these investigators may be the advancement of science, many of their research subjects volunteer hoping to reach a personal objective through their participation and thereby threaten to create such dual relationships: such a situation poses no ethical problem for experiments that are preceded by a full and honest explanation of their true nature. In these cases, the prospective participants have enough information to enable them to decide if, in addition to the possibility of advancing science, their participation in the experiment will also help them personally. Contributing to an expectation of personal help is the fact that many experiments are conducted in settings whose primary role is the delivery of some type of human service—a school, clinic, or hospital.

According to the *Ethical Standards of Psychologists'* principle dealing with the Welfare of the Consumer, "Psychologists make every effort to avoid dual relationships with clients and/or relationships which might impair their professional judgment or increase the

risk of client exploitation."[57] Hence, as long as research that includes deception is conducted in a setting primarily devoted to the
advancement of science, it seems sufficient to present would-be participants in such research with a written or spoken statement that
succeeds in communicating the following points:

1. For the primary purpose of advancing scientific knowledge, a
    variety of research methods are used in any given institution.

2. All of these research methods are reviewed by the institution's
    IRB to determine, among other things, if they offer anything
    more than a minimal risk of harm to participants in an experi-
    ment.

3. When more than a minimal risk of harm exists in a proposed ex-
    periment, the subject will be fully and honestly informed of this
    risk before he or she is asked to participate in the experiment.

4. However, if no more than a minimal risk of harm exists in an
    experiment, the nature of that experiment may not be fully and
    honestly explained to the subject until after he or she has partici-
    pated in it. In other words, advance information about an experi-
    ment may only be withheld in experiments that offer no more
    than a minimal risk of personal harm.

5. Finally, after every experiment conducted in an institution, par-
    ticipants are always given a full and honest explanation of the
    true nature of the experiment.

If investigators wish to avoid dual relationships in settings whose
primary purpose is to provide some form of human service, they
should only conduct research that is consistent with that primary
service. Thus, two methods of helping people that have met recognized standards may be administered to research participants using a
standardized research paradigm in order to test their relative effectiveness. But research utilizing deception would not be allowed in
such settings, on the grounds that it would permit participants to
develop the false impression, from the incomplete or false explanation of the experiment given to them initially, that they would be
helped personally by their participation in it.

In summary, with respect to public policy, the use of research
involving human subjects should be restricted to those settings whose
primary purpose is clearly the advancement of scientific knowledge.

Furthermore, when research involves deception, would-be participants should be made to understand clearly that although such initially may be the case, full disclosure will occur at the end of the experiment. Finally, all potential subjects should be informed that the particular experiment was approved by the appropriate IRB and thus judged to include no more than minimal risk or harm.

NOTES TO CHAPTER 19

1. W. H. Roberts, "Behaviorism, Ethics, and Professor Weiss," *Journal of Abnormal and Social Psychology* 23: 393–396 (1928).
2. American Psychological Association, *Ethical Standards of Psychologists* (Washington, D.C., 1953).
3. Ibid., p. 12.
4. W. E. Vinacke, "Deceiving Experimental Subjects," *American Psychologist* 9: 155 (1954).
5. Ibid.
6. A. C. MacKinney, "Deceiving Experimental Subjects," *American Psychologist* 10: 133 (1955).
7. S. Milgram, "Behavioral Study of Obedience," *Journal of Abnormal and Social Psychology* 67: 371–378 (1963).
8. D. Baumrind, "Some Thoughts on Ethics of Research: After Reading Milgram's 'Behavioral Study on Obedience,' " *American Psychologist* 27: 421–423 (1964); S. Milgram, "Issues in the Study of Obedience: A Reply to Baumrind," *American Psychologist* 19: 848–852 (1964); H. C. Kelman, "The Human Use of Human Subjects: The Problem of Deception in Social Psychological Experiments," *Psychological Bulletin* 67: 11 (1967); J. Seeman, "Deception in Psychological Research," *American Psychologist* 24: 1025–1028 (1969); K. Ring, K. Wallston, and N. Corey, "Mode of Debriefing As a Factor Affecting Subject's Reaction to a Milgram-type Obedience Experiment: An Ethical Inquiry," *Representative Research in Social Psychology* 1: 67–88 (1970); R. J. Menges, "Openness and Honesty Versus Coercion and Deception in Psychological Research," *American Psychologist* 28: 1030–1034 (1973); D. L. Weisenthal, "Reweaving Deception's Tangled Web," *Canadian Psychologist* 15: 326–336 (1974); J. Forward, R. Canter, and N. Kirsch, "Role-enactment and Deception Methodologies: Alternate Paradigms?" *American Psychologist* 31: 595–604 (1976); S. G. West and S. P. Gunn, "Some Issues of Ethics and Social Psychology," *American Psychologist* 33: 30–38 (1978); J. A. Robertson, "Ten Ways to Improve IRBs: A Letter to the Secretary of DHEW," *Hastings Center Report* 9: 29–33 (1979).

9.   Ad hoc Committee on Ethical Standards in Psychological Research, *Ethical Principles in the Conduct of Research with Human Participants* (Washington, D.C.: American Psychological Association, Inc., 1973).

10.   American Psychological Association, *Ethical Standards of Psychologists* (Washington, D.C., 1977).

11.   Ibid., p. 1.

12.   Ibid., p. 2.

13.   Ibid., p. 3.

14.   Ibid., p. 4.

15.   Ibid., p. 5.

16.   Ibid., p. 7.

17.   U.S. Department of Health, Education, and Welfare, "Surgeon General's Memo to Heads of Institutions Conducting Research with Public Health Service Grants," February 8, 1966.

18.   U.S. Department of Health, Education, and Welfare, *The Institutional Guide to DHEW Policy on Protection of Human Subjects*, DHEW Publication No. NIH 72-102 (Washington, D.C.: U.S. Government Printing Office, December 2, 1972).

19.   U.S. Department of Health, Education, and Welfare, "Protection of Human Subjects," *Federal Register* 39:18917 (May 30, 1974); 45 C.F.R. § 46.101 (1980).

20.   National Research Act, PL 93-348, 88 Stat. 352-353 (July 12, 1974); 42 U.S.C. § 2891 (1974).

21.   U.S. Department of Health, Education, and Welfare, "Protection of Human Subjects," p. 18917; 45 C.F.R. § 46.102 (1980).

22.   National Research Act, 88 Stat. 348-352; 42 U.S.C. § 2891 (1974).

23.   The National Commission for the Protection of Human Subjects of Biomedical and Behavioral Research, *The Belmont Report: Ethical Principles and Guidelines for the Protection of Human Subjects of Research*, DHEW Publication No. OS 78-0012 (Washington, D.C.: U.S. Government Printing Office, September 1978).

24.   The National Commission for the Protection of Human Subjects of Biomedical and Behavioral Research, *Report and Recommendations: Institutional Review Boards*, DHEW Publication No. OS 78-0008 (Washington, D.C.: U.S. Government Printing Office, September 1978).

25.   U.S. Department of Health and Human Services, "Public Health Service Human Research Subjects," *Federal Register* 46: 8366-8392 (January 26, 1981).

26.   The National Commission, *Report and Recommendations: Institutional Review Boards*, p. 21.

27.   Ibid.

28.   Ibid., p. 26.

29.   Ibid., pp. 26-27.

30. Ibid., p. 27.
31. The National Commission, *The Belmont Report*, p. 12.
32. Ibid., p. 14.
33. Ibid., pp. 16–17.
34. American Psychological Association, *Ethical Standards of Psychologists* (1977), p. 4.
35. The National Commission, *Report and Recommendations: Institutional Review Boards*, p. 21.
36. Seeman, p. 1027.
37. T. Shipley, "Misinformed Consent: An Enigma in Modern Social Science Research," *Ethics in Science and Medicine* 4: 93–106 (1977).
38. D. Mixon, "Temporary False Belief," *Personality and Social Psychology Bulletin* 3: 479–488 (1977).
39. D.R. Glasgow, C.J. Sadowski, and S.F. Davis, "The Project Must Count: Fostering Positive Attitudes toward the Conduct of Research," *Bulletin of the Psychonomic Society* 10: 471–474.
40. M.S. Eisner, "Ethical Problems in Social Psychological Experimentation in the Laboratory," *Canadian Psychological Review* 18: 233–241 (1977).
41. Ibid., p. 236.
42. Ibid., p. 239.
43. Seeman, p. 1027.
44. Ibid., p. 1028.
45. D.S. Sullivan and T.E. Deiker, "Subject–Experimenter Perceptions of Ethical Issues in Human Research," *American Psychologist* 28: 587–591 (1973).
46. D.S. Holmes, "Debriefing after Psychological Experiments: Effectiveness of Post-deception Dehoaxing," *American Psychologist* 31: 858–867 (1976).
47. Ibid., pp. 866–867.
48. C.L. Gruder, A. Stumpfhauser, and R.S. Wyer, "Improvement in Experimental Procedures as a Result of Debriefing about Deception," *Personality and Social Psychology Bulletin* 3: 434–437 (1977).
49. Holmes, p. 864.
50. Shipley.
51. West and Gunn, p. 36.
52. Ibid., p. 37.
53. C. Hendrick, "Role-Playing as a Methodology for Social Research: A Symposium," *Personality and Social Psychology Bulletin* 3: 454 (1977).
54. E. Krupat, "A Re-assessment of Role-Playing as a Technique in Social Psychology," *Personality and Social Psychology Bulletin* 3: 498–504 (1977).
55. Ibid., p. 502.

56.   E.V. Mitchell, T.J. Kaul, and H.B. Pepinsky, "The Limited Role of Psychology in the Role-Playing Controversy," *Personality and Social Psychology Bulletin* 3: 514–518 (1977).

57.   American Psychological Association, *Ethical Standards of Psychologists*, (1977), p. 4.

20 THE RIGHTS OF CHILDREN INVOLVED IN RESEARCH

Rosa Lynn Pinkus, Ph.D.
Stephen J. Haines, M.D.

Two major issues are the subject of controversy in discussions of the rights of children who are the subjects of research. The first concerns values toward children; the second centers on various views of biomedical research. Competition among child-rearing strategies, various theories of education, and multiple philosophies of childhood are currently commonplace. According to one observer, "There is no apparent consensus about the good life for children, nor a hierarchy of ultimate values regarding their development."[1]

Likewise, biomedical research has recently met with an array of conflicting public opinions. Examining the social forces and legal philosophy behind intrusion into the field of clinical research, Curran identifies three fundamental, conflicting interests—(1) the protection of the research subject, (2) the needs of society for the fruits of clinical research, and (3) the promotion and encouragement of the medical research enterprise.[2] Curran claims, "There can be no doubt that the individual research subject is receiving the greatest legal attention at present."[3] He views this concentration on the individual as part of a more general trend in American lawmaking. Individual rights, civil rights, and consumer protection are carrying the day. "You are not alone," he advises the biomedical community and contends that no less than a legal revolution is at hand.

The ethical problems that attend medical research with human subjects are indicative of a more generalized societal trend and "rep-

421

resentative of an entire class of problems created by the impact of professionals and professional power on the general public and on public policy."[4] Whatever the source, issues of consent, therapeutic versus nontherapeutic research, individual risk versus societal benefit, the use or nonuse of children as research subjects, and the degree of organization that qualifies a procedure as an experiment are often raised when the rights of children involved in research are questioned. Given the lack of consensus in American culture regarding the role of children in general and the current deliberations about the value of biomedical research, it is not surprising that the more specific dilemmas related to research and children are in a quandry.

This chapter discusses the ethical issues, the law, and the formation of public policy concerning children and research. It concentrates on one dilemma—the need for and capacity of children to give informed consent, particularly—although not exclusively—in situations in which the research is of a nontherapeutic nature. In discussing the feasibility of allowing a child to consent to participate in medical experiments, codes from Nuremberg[5] to recent federal regulations[6] are reviewed. The use and abuse of both the law and medical ethics in deciding consent issues are outlined. The most important aspects of legal and ethical knowledge are highlighted, and suggestions are made as to when they can help or hinder decisionmaking.

Finally, the results of the authors' pilot study involving thirty-nine seven, eight, and nine year old children who agreed to answer questions about things that can make children sick or help them get better are reported. By including their insights and impressions of experiments and their willingness to participate in them, conclusions from the study add to the perplexing theoretical discussion of consent. The overall aim of the authors is to use the consent issue to provide a strategy for dealing with ethical and legal issues confronting those involved in the development of health policy.

LIMITS OF THE LAW: ITS ROLE IN DECISIONMAKING

Without access to legal counsel specifically versed in the most recent rulings regarding parental consent for involving children in research, reliance on the law can be extremely confusing. In 1969, Curran and Beecher reviewed the legal and ethical principles associated with experimentation in children and concluded that nonlegal commentators have misconstrued the law as prohibiting research in cases in which there was no direct benefit to the child.[7] They cited cases in which the courts allowed nontherapeutic research that involved the use of children. In some cases, parents were allowed to consent to procedures involving clear risk when there was neither any direct nor indirect benefit to the child, providing the child also consented. In such cases, Curran and Beecher carefully pointed to nuances of interpretation in the laws. In essence, they alerted nonlegal experts to the technicalities involved in setting legal precedent and to the dangers of basing decisions on general legal knowledge.

If legal precedent is confusing when issues of risk and benefit are discussed, it is even less effective in dealing with the question of age of consent. Technically, common law sets the age of majority at twenty-one. This arbitrary age limit is intended to "protect the minor from harm which may result from his own ignorance or rashness, and from situations where he cannot be expected to resist undue coercion or permission to give his consent."[8] Specific cases exist in which the court has favored the assent of minors, having proven that the children appreciated the nature, extent, and consequences of the invasion or medical treatment.

Reasoning that children mature intellectually and emotionally at different rates, conclusions in the social science literature suggest that the arbitrary age of majority is inappropriate as a single determining factor. Indeed, the age of consent for medical treatment has already been lowered in several states, making reliance on the law for devising national guidelines virtually impossible. When a minor is emancipated or when the court determines that a parent's consent or withholding of consent constitutes abuse, there is clear precedent for freeing the minor of the need to secure parental consent. Abiding by a more traditional interpretation, however, a recent court ruling on consent in children suggests that parental consent is necessary for a child's participation in research.[9]

Such conflicting opinions document the evolving nature of the law in American culture. Slow to adjust practice and intent, it responds to individual cases making incremental adjustments. It can take thirty to fifty years to discern clear changes in trends.[10] Moreover, judicial decisionmaking operates only when a problem has arisen and usually after the fact. Thus, until a clear rule is determined by a court of final jurisdiction, uncertainties facing actual decisionmakers persist. Furthermore, since judicial judgments are tied to facts of an individual pending case, the rulings may assume unintended characteristics.[11] Thus, while the law can offer broad guidelines with respect to practical matters, it often provides no clear basis on which researchers, parents, or physicians can rely in specific instances of consent.[12] In commenting on the integral aspects of the law and social values, Mnookin observes that "because our society presently lacks a social consensus in many areas of concern regarding consent and children in research, physicians should not expect the law to provide them with clear guidelines."[13]

PUBLIC POLICY GUIDELINES: DO THEY FILL THE GAP?

Since the law provides no immediate answer to questions involving the consent of children in research, the medical community has relied on various codes of ethics to more or less guide its activity. In reviewing these codes, it is important to understand the historical context in which they were written and also the extent to which they represent the activities of the health professions. Research on children takes place in many settings other than hospitals (e.g., in schools, state institutions, and convalescent homes). Much of this research, however, is oriented toward the behavioral or social sciences and is often inappropriately governed by medically oriented codes. There is also a variety of codes to review. Each specialty area in medicine elicits its own set of rules—some conflict, some agree. Nevertheless, the review of official guidelines provides a marker for assessing overall trends in opinion regarding research involving children. Furthermore, it exemplifies significant shifts in thought due to a changing historical circumstance.

The Nuremberg Code, which is regarded as the first modern statement of ethical conduct of research activities, is devoid of any specific mention of children. Essentially the court opinion, written at the trial of twenty-three German physicians for "war crimes and crimes against humanity," allows only "certain types of medical experiments on human beings, when kept within certain reasonably well-defined bounds."[14] These bounds are stated clearly in the ten canons of informed consent that are quite familiar to modern day researchers.[15] Taken literally, the Nuremberg Code specifically excludes children as minors who are unable to give consent. The fact that this code was written during the aftermath of Nazi atrocities should not be overlooked. Within this context, strict codes are not only understandable, but desirable. The protection of the individual, in this instance, surely takes precedence over the societal benefits of scientific knowledge.

During the post–World War II era, the United States embarked upon a health policy that stressed medical research and technological achievements in biomedicine. The National Institutes of Health (NIH) had a budget of $52 million in 1950, $430 million in 1960, and $1.6 billion in 1968. The aggregate health research commitment for 1971 was $2.5 billion.[16]

Capping a trend dating back to the 1910 Flexner reforms, medical education and medical schools themselves became dominated by an emphasis on research and science. At Harvard Medical School, the number of medical students rose from 502 in 1950 to 583 in 1970. In contrast, the number of other doctoral students in biomedicine rose from 50 to 171 during the same period. Harvard's total budget rose from $3.25 million in 1950 to $28.72 million in 1970; federal funds contributed 21 percent in 1950 and 58 percent in 1970. Forty-one percent of its 1970 budget was for research. Although these statistics are sketchy and allow room for interpretation, the overall trend is clear.[17] Between 1950 and 1970, the United States secured world acclaim as the leader in biomedical research. It is not surprising that during this period, codes of ethics for involving children in research were written, revised, and implemented. The discovery of penicillin, the isolation of the polio virus, and the creation of an effective polio vaccine provided a convincing rationale for including children in research. A healthy skepticism of the dangers that could accompany research on minors, however, which was so exquisitely brought into focus in postwar Germany, prompted regulation of this research.

The Declaration of Helsinki, drafted in 1961 and published in 1964 by the World Medical Association, did not include specific guidelines concerning children.[18] However, the 1964 code did specify that in the case of legally incompetent human beings, the consent of a legal guardian should be procured. This indirectly allows the inclusion of children in the research subject pool. The early versions of the code also furnished an important conceptual distinction between therapeutic and nontherapeutic research. This distinction was to play a significant role in future codes that did concern children since it established the precedent of allowing adults to participate in nontherapeutic research. In 1966, for example, the ethical guidelines of the American Medical Association (AMA) permitted clinical investigation "involving children in nontherapeutic situations primarily for the accumulation of scientific knowledge."[19] In such situations, a legally authorized representative was to give written consent. Logically, following the Helsinki decision, adults could consent only to nontherapeutic research for children when they could reasonably be expected to volunteer themselves as subjects in similar circumstances.

The AMA guidelines, not being representative of the broader health professions, were complemented by official guidelines issued by the U.S. Public Health Service (PHS) in 1966. The PHS guidelines stated: "Whatever the nature of the investigation, the concern for the protection of the subject and for the assurance of voluntary participation becomes most critical when the subject is not of age or competent to make adequate judgment on his own behalf."[20] This most general statement does not require benefit to the minor. In 1969, the PHS guidelines were further clarified to state: "A parent, for example, may have no authority to expose his child to risk, except for the child's own benefit."[21] Curran and Beecher cite this statement as one that promoted a misunderstanding of the law, one that was far too sweeping in its interpretation. Only very young children, they contend, may not be subjects in nontherapeutic research.[22]

Thus, the first codes dealing with children and research are quite recent in origin. They tend to be vague and have the added danger of allowing interpretation to be influenced by personal or professional advantage. Written during an era of unprecedented support for biomedical research, they provide a general approval of research using children while gently raising issues that might limit it.

While these official codes and guidelines have supported a trend toward the use of children in research—a trend that places a higher value on societal gain from such research efforts than on the benefits to individuals used in such research—a countersuspicion of possible abuses to individuals—so dramatically stated in the Nuremberg Code—surfaced during the late 1960s. The Vietnam War, the questioning of waste and duplication in federally funded research, and disagreement about health care priorities set a tone for questioning the benefits of unparalleled biomedical research. Beecher's classic work, "Ethics and Clinical Research," published in 1966, established a tone of healthy skepticism by reviewing twenty-two examples of unethical research conducted without the subjects' informed consent.[23] While admitting that "American medicine is sound, and most progress in it soundly attained," Beecher cites examples of areas that "will do great harm to medicine unless soon corrected."[24] Hesitant to criticize a profession held in such high public esteem, he nevertheless concluded that the continuation of such practices would be a great evil. The dramatic rise in ethical questioning of medical practice since Beecher's first timid step in reporting apparent abuses is well documented.

The controversial use of newly admitted mentally retarded children in Willowbrook State Hospital (Staten Island, New York) to test a vaccine for viral hepatitis in 1972 was the immediate event that led to federal regulations specifically geared to construct guidelines for research on children. In November 1973, the need for assigning responsibility for the protection of children was acknowledged by the U.S. Department of Health, Education, and Welfare (DHEW).[25] In July 1978, the federal regulations regarding children and research, a rather comprehensive policy protecting children by defining consent procedures, were finalized. They provide a mechanism for mediating the risk–benefit element of nontherapeutic research. According to the regulations, when research might expose a subject to risk without defined therapeutic benefit or other positive effect on that subject's well-being, parental or guardian consent appears to be insufficient.[26] However, an ethical review board composed of specific personnel would be consulted in these cases. Again, nonbeneficial research with appropriate safeguards was approved.

In 1974, the Declaration of Helsinki was revised. Specifically dealing with children this time, it states that "when the subject is a minor, permission from the responsible relative replaces that of the subject."[27] Again citing the distinction between therapeutic and nontherapeutic research, it allowed nontherapeutic research involving minors if the canons of informed consent were fully met. In evaluating the necessity for such research, the code clearly states that "in research on man, the interest of science and society should never take precedence over considerations related to the well-being of the subject."[28] Furthermore, "it is the duty of the doctor to remain the protector of the life and health of that person on whom biomedical research is being carried out."[29] Complex issues of paternalism aside, are there conditions in which it could prove difficult for the doctor to remain the protector? This allowance of nontherapeutic research on adults and children continued and further clarified the trend set during the 1960s.

The enactment of the National Research Act (PL 93-348) in July 1974 created the National Commission for the Protection of Human Subjects of Biomedical and Behavioral Research. The National Commission (consisting of eleven members, five of whom were medical or behavioral scientists) was to construct guidelines for research on several minority populations, including children. Under the tenets of the Act, the secretary of HEW was to publish the Commission's recommendations in the *Federal Register*, issue guidelines, and offer public explanation if the guidelines varied from the recommendations. A grace period was established, during which time interested parties were invited to comment on the proposed rules. In sorting through the data illustrating the Commission's decisionmaking process, the effect of the public response, and the actual wording of the guidelines, one has access to a variety of resources. Personal letters, published responses in the *Federal Register*, and, in this case, several articles written by individual commissioners explain how the guidelines were formulated.[30] For the most part, it was the work of the Commission that led to the July 1978 federal regulations on research involving children.

The flurry of scholarship produced by the issuance of these guidelines is instructive in itself. "At no previous time," writes Jonsen, a member of the Commission, "have so thorough and thoughtful discussions taken place regarding the ethical nature of research on children."[31] Faced with difficult and perplexing questions, there was an awareness by Commission members of the grave consequences of such research as well as the promise of new knowledge. Scholarly ethical standards were incorporated into public policy guidelines. This marked a considerably different process than allowing certain professional organizations to create individual research codes.

Considerable doubt remains about whether or not this national ethical monitoring will inhibit the progress of scientific research. Awareness of the encumbrance of the federal administrative machinery designed to protect individuals is common among physicians in the research community. Nevertheless, the current tenor of public opinion is to regulate these activities intimately. There is always an element of paradox involved in the concept of regulating freedom. In evaluating the guidelines, it is important to ask what is meant by protection of the individual and if, indeed, these guidelines do so protect. The common theme of this chapter—the child's capacity and necessity to give consent—highlights this dilemma.

In the recommendations from the National Commission on children involved in research, the term *informed consent* was not used. Rather, two terms—*assent* and *permission*—were used.[32] Previous ethical codes, most notably the Declaration of Helsinki, allowed for what was termed *proxy consent* of the parent in allowing the child to participate in research. This raised the issue of whether or not a parent could (or should) consent on behalf of the child. In therapeutic circumstances such an action was not fundamentally questioned. However, when the risk to the child was more than minimal and when the benefit was not direct, the concept of proxy consent was strongly criticized. Moreover, in cases of teenagers seeking treatment for venereal disease or guidance concerning an unwanted pregnancy, parental consent was deemed an invasion of privacy. Nevertheless, it was this concept of requiring a parent to give consent on behalf of the child that was consensually agreed upon—until quite recently.

Sensitive to the issues involved in the questioning of proxy consent, the Commission elected to deal with it by stating that when children participate in research, they are not, in fact, capable of giving legal consent. Neither can parents give legal consent because technically, they will not be subject to the risks involved. Therefore, permission is obtained from the legal guardian, while the child must give assent. Both guardians and children must be provided with a fair explanation of the proposed research and its risks and benefits commensurable with their capability to understand. Furthermore, research should not be conducted over the deliberate objection of either party. Further recommendations call for the assent to be obtained from all children seven years of age or older, although the final determination of which children must give assent remains the discretion of an institutional review board (IRB).

These guidelines for securing assent and permission also apply in cases in which children participate in nontherapeutic research. The Commission's deliberations on the issue of nontherapeutic research are reflective of concerns and caveats articulated since Nuremberg. In allowing the use of children in research that entails more than minimal risk and promises no individual benefit, three limiting conditions are stipulated. However, even with the stipulations, which clearly set guidelines for researchers, two members of the Commission declined from supporting the recommendation. This refusal further attests that concern for volunteering an individual for society's sake remains. According to one member of the Commission, "Such experimentation can be morally justified . . . only to fulfill an essential social need analogous to that involved in the drafting of youth for national military purposes. Resolution of this kind of a moral dilemma in a democracy at a minimum requires decision by society's highest political voice."[33] Nonetheless, the guidelines, do address the issue of nontherapeutic research in children with one of the stipulations for its conduct being compliance with the canons of consent as outlined by the Commission.

With the protection of the individual research subject in mind, it is instructive to trace the comments received by the secretary of HEW regarding the child's ability to assent to an experimental procedure. More than half of the comments concerning the consent guidelines referred to the stated Commission's position that children seven years of age or older are capable of giving assent. The majority of commentators opposed age seven; a few suggested the age of twelve, thirteen, or fourteen. The overriding claim was that since children mature emotionally and developmentally at different age levels, no specific age level should be set. Psychiatrists referred to the work of Piaget and others that clearly demonstrates that seven year olds have not attained the cognitive skills to make assent meaningful. Their inability to think abstractly would inhibit the assessment of the benefit to society of their participation in research. According to Solnit in his letter to the secretary, the indication is that seeking assent for all subjects seven years of age or older "not only burdens the child with a capacity and responsibility for which he does not have the developmental resources, but also places a burden on the child–parent relationship that could weaken and distort the relationship rather than to protect and/or strengthen it."[34] He speaks of "adequately preparing the child emotionally and intellectually to participate in research" and deems that this is the responsibility of individual researchers.[35]

Commission members responded to these criticisms by arguing that by assent they did not suggest that children are able to comprehend the theory of scientific investigation or to appreciate fully the risks and benefits of research. Rather, they simply meant that children can understand and should be told what participation in a research project would mean to them (e.g., in terms of time spent, activities involved, amount and nature of the discomfort that might be experienced). They contend that children of this age are familiar with the concept of helping others and generally respond positively to reasonable requests.[36] This type of point–counterpoint argument convinced the secretary to advise that assent be obtained from children seven years or older, following a full explanation based on information appropriate to the level of understanding of the children in accordance with IRB procedures. Given the lack of social consensus on this issue and the inability of the law to provide a consistent, immediate answer, on what should the IRB rely to establish such procedures?

ETHICAL THEORY: IS IT THE SALVATION?

Ramsey[37] and McCormick[38] are two strong advocates who hold conflicting moral positions regarding the participation of children in medical research. Focused mainly on research that does not hold a prospect of direct benefit for the subject, their opposing positions offer alternative approaches to the need to have children consent. Ramsey argues that such research ought to be morally prohibited, since there is no way to know what a child would or should do, from the child's perspective. Indeed, it may be that children (who are not to be treated as small adults) cannot make determinations of this sort. Therefore, since it is impossible for another person to make a valid presumption of a child's wishes in the absence of direct benefit to the child, all such research ought to be prohibited. This prohibition should extend to such apparently harmless maneuvers as weighing and measuring, for they represent transient discomfort or inconvenience called offensive touching. Ramsey does acknowledge that in some instances such research will be necessary, but then it must be recognized as sinning in an unjust world. Following this logic, proxy consent would not be ethical, and research involving children would require their assent.[39]

In contrast, McCormick argues that by society's social nature, all human beings, regardless of age, have an obligation to participate in minimal risk activities that further the general well-being. He argues that "[h]uman rights ought not to be defined before the individual is viewed as a social being, before insertion into the web of human relationships that define our very being."[40] Therefore, according to

McCormick, it is possible to presume a child's consent for participation in medical research that includes minimal risk, such as weighing or collecting urine samples. When the risk becomes more significant, this presumption is sharply limited.[41] However, the justification for proxy consent used during the past ten years in research involving children is legitimated by this ethical viewpoint.

The conflict between Ramsey and McCormick—or between the opponents or advocates of proxy consent or opponents or advocates of assent—is not resolvable on logical grounds. The difference is in basic assumptions about the nature of human existence. However, this example illustrates that ethics is a blunt instrument. With certain assumptions, it can identify appropriate courses of action. It can clarify those assumptions and thereby rule out certain alternative actions. In being concerned with violating the rules or principles that would harmonize the aims and desires of all people, ethics does not provide the fine points such as the age at which children should consent to nontherapeutic research. Rather, ethics provides the broad guidelines for deciding if and when a parent can consent for the child. Subsequently, following that decision, other disciplines, arguments, and compromises must be used to answer the specifics.[42]

The Commission's response to this uncertainty regarding proxy consent was clearly a compromise measure. Finding no philosophical stance to completely resolve the dilemma of including children in nontherapeutic research, it elected to substitute new terms (i.e., assent for consent). Thus, the door remains open for the development of new conceptual analysis. Who is to provide this analysis? Current practices suggest that this responsibility falls on IRBs. Although urging an age of assent of seven years, IRBs have the discretion to vary this according to its procedures. In addition, they may determine when and if a third party child advocate is required for consent procedures.

HOW DOES AN IRB DECIDE?

Recently, the function of an IRB, its effectiveness, and its ability to influence the ethical conduct of research at various institutions were studied.[43] The subject of much controversy in recent years, IRBs have become the sole topic of a journal intended to provide a forum for communication about the ethical aspects of research involving human subjects.[a] Because of interest in the value conflicts that they were designed to mediate and of growing concerns about the regulation of powerful professions and due to their possible adaptability to other situations, IRBs are now clearly regarded as an important social invention.

In general, IRBs are composed of at least five individuals of varying backgrounds. They include members who are able "to ascertain the acceptability of proposals in terms of institutional commitments and regulations, applicable law, standards of professional conduct and practice, and community attitudes."[44] They vary considerably in size, composition, volume of work done, number of hours devoted to such work, and type of institution they serve. For example, while the average number of members is fourteen, the range of members is from five to fifty-five, the frequency of meetings average ten per year, but range from two to fifty-one; and while the average member hours expended was 760 per year, one institution reached as high as 5,000. It seems that variety, rather than uniformity, characterizes IRBs.[45] Despite the important social function that they perform and the level of effort that their members expend, they appear to base decisions on their own past experience and specific federal regulations. In light of this, "serious efforts to improve their effectiveness" were encouraged.[46]

One area slated for improvement was the process of informed consent—particularly the communication between subjects and researchers. Decisions to elicit assent from a seven year old clearly fall within the range of communication skills. Thus, this example is used to project how an IRB might decide when and if assent should be required.

An important ethical framework for evaluating when a child is capable of assent, in addition to deciding a host of other decisions required of IRBs, is Bok's three strategies for balancing freedom of scientific investigation with minimization of risk.[47] Initially, she suggests identifying those forms of research that pose no significant risk and removing the bureaucratic impediments to free the pursuit of such inquiries. Second, she advocates identifying those investigations that recklessly endanger people and suggests forbidding these activities entirely. Establishing clear standards in these two areas will,

a. The journal, entitled *Institutional Review Boards: A Review of Human Subjects Research*, is published ten times a year by the Hastings Center, Institute of Society, Ethics, and the Life Sciences, 360 Broadway, Hastings-on-Hudson, NY 10706.

according to Bok, ease the bureaucratic burden and also keep the scientist from becoming involved in unacceptable research. Hopefully, such guidelines will minimize the third category—namely, those investigations that possess potential benefit and some risk in which reasonable people disagree about the course of action. It is this problematic third category that generates the bulk of moral and ethical disputes. Thus, according to Bok, following the best effort to minimize the size of this category, efforts must concentrate on understanding the issues in order to clarify the decisionmaking process.[48]

Although the law generally views twenty-one as the age of majority, Curran and Beecher have cited cases in which the age of consent was lowered,[49] and certain states have lowered the age of consent for medical treatment. Given these data, it appears that an upper age limit of knowledgeable minors could be identified as being capable of giving assent, when research is of a high quality, presents minimal risk, and has a good chance of success. Alternatively, a lower age limit could be established to specify when minors should not be required to give assent, because they lack sufficient skills of abstraction to appreciate the issues involved. What these upper and lower levels of assent should be, moreover, can be discerned by empiric research.

EMPIRIC TESTING: THE MISSING LINK?

Many of the specific questions that arise in implementing public policy regulations are amenable to empiric testing. For example, it should be possible to study the responses of children of various ages to hypothetical experimental situations and to glean some information about their understanding and willingness to consent for participation in research.

Fost has used a similar methodology in studying the consent process in adults.[50] Calling it a surrogate system for informed consent, he concludes that responses in his study seemed more candid and diverse than those usually gained in the real clinical setting. As a result, he suggests the use of this technique by researchers to more accurately assess consumer attitudes toward specific projects. Furthermore, this is a logical activity for the research community and could empirically validate the actions of IRBs.[51]

In order to examine the feasibility of such a validation process, the authors undertook a small study designed to elicit responses from healthy children (aged six to eleven) that might indicate their appreciation of problems related (at least hypothetically) to medical research. The authors hypothesized that the responses would relate directly to the perceived self-benefit of the child and that minor rewards (commonly perceived as beneficial to children) would easily induce participation in children who were initially reluctant.

A questionnaire[b] was administered that posed four hypothetical situations. Each question indicated that there would be temporary discomfort but one mentioned possible self-benefit, one mentioned the possibility of worsening illness, one stressed the potential benefit to others, and one specifically used the word experiment to detect reaction to that word. In all instances, any child who refused to participate in the hypothetical research project was offered a series of inducements in an attempt to measure the strength of his or her convictions.

The questionnaire was administered to children in a private open school that emphasizes independent decisionmaking by its students. The school administration was highly receptive to participation in the study. Hence, the children in the study group constituted a highly select group both economically and intellectually and were expected to be more than usually receptive to the proposed research.

An attempt was undertaken to also include a group of public school children from a less affluent, working class neighborhood; this effort was unsuccessful because the administration of the public school refused permission. Essentially, its position was that children of this age are so incapable of rendering a decision of the type required by this questionnaire that the study was preposterous. Hence, the results of this study are not representative of all children's response to these questions but are only an example of the feasibility of attacking these issues in an empiric fashion—that is, gathering data to allow appropriate actions to be taken.

Generally, the children seemed to perceive the main thrust of each question and responded as expected. Where self-advantage was emphasized they overwhelmingly agreed to participate, citing self-advantage as the reason. Where possible benefit for others was mentioned, there was general agreement with participation citing altruistic motivation. When risk was explained, cooperation was

b. For a copy of the questionnaire and the raw data collected, contact Rosa Lynn Pinkus, Ph.D., Department of Neurological Surgery, Presbyterian-University Hospital, Pittsburgh, PA 15261.

generally refused. When the strength of convictions were tested, the children were consistently resistant to the offers of various inducements. The word "experiment" appeared to generate confusion and produced no consistent responses. No clear age trends were observed.

A few select responses to the questionnaire provide some indication of the wisdom offered by the young respondents. One seven year old female consistently refused to participate in the proposed experiments. She got allergy shots every week and has had them for so long that she did not want any more. When asked whether she would agree to participate if her parents said so, she replied, "You should make the decision because it is happening to you." Two children (one was seven and the other was eight), both unwilling to participate themselves, offered alternative suggestions: "Do it on a grown-up; kids are too sensitive" and "I'm not falling for it because it could be dangerous—do it on a mouse." Another seven year old was concerned "because they usually don't wipe the blood away."

Not all of the respondents were particularly perceptive. Many answered simply, "I don't know." Others offered insight into their priorities. When asked to participate in a test that might make her sick, a seven year old girl replied: "I'd take a chance—to get away from school." Others, while not liking the shot and initially replying negatively to a request to participate, changed their minds when offered ice cream simply because they "liked it." Several children consistently refusing to participate, indicated that they would for $100.

Studies such as this pilot one reported by the authors are fraught with difficulties. Sampling variation, interviewer bias, and emotional impact of the hospital setting all conspire to make the gathering of widely applicable data difficult. However, even in this highly select group of children, a clear ability to identify a single ethical issue is seen. At the same time, the findings suggest that by wording the question in a way that makes a single issue predominate, it is possible to manipulate the responses of children. That which remains unclear is the ability of children to weigh risk–benefit ratios and to reach rational decisions. This is not surprising, since this is a very difficult area for adults, but the degree of pliability of the responses implies that regulations must specifically state how much risk must be emphasized in the process of obtaining assent from children.

From the authors' limited experience with this pilot study, it is concluded that given the present level of moral and ethical sophistication, such studies will not fully resolve conflicts on moral and ethical issues. However, studies can be constructed to gather data to assist in answering specific questions that arise in the attempt to operationally define rules for ethical conduct. They can also attempt to validate some of the assumptions that underlie specific ethical positions. In short, public policies should be based on facts verified by the same rigorous procedures required for the investigations that they are attempting to regulate.

CONCLUSION

The current public atmosphere of vigorous legal protection of individual rights has generated controversy over the appropriate role of nontherapeutic research in children. In this regard, the law is of greatest value in defining general guidelines for behavior and resolving individual conflicts after the fact, but it does not significantly contribute to ongoing individual decisionmaking.

Public policy has attempted to provide more definite guidelines, but has left many specific questions to the discretion of IRBs. Ethical theory again provides only general guidelines. IRBs appear to make their decisions based on past experience when federal guidelines are imprecise. Thus, when confronted with specific questions in implementing general guidelines in a particular case, submitting proposed answers to empiric testing, rather than relying on past experience and personal intuition, appears to be the most rational and scientifically sound approach.

NOTES TO CHAPTER 20

1. R.H. Mnookin, "Children's Rights: Legal and Ethical Dilemmas," *The Pharos* 41: 2 (April 1978).
2. William J. Curran, "Current Legal Issues in Clinical Investigation with Particular Attention to the Balance Between the Rights of an Individual and the Needs of Society," in Stanley Joel Reiser, Arthur J. Dyck, and William J. Curran, *Ethics in Medicine: Historical Perspectives and Contemporary Concerns* (Cambridge, MA: The MIT Press, 1977), p. 301.
3. Ibid.
4. Bernard Barber, "The Ethics of Experimentation with Human Subjects," *Scientific American* 234: 31 (February 1976).

5. "The Nuremberg Code," *Trials of War Criminals Before the Nurenberg Military Tribunals under Control Council Law No. 10, Vol. 2* (Washington, D.C.: U.S. Government Printing Office, 1949), pp. 181–182.

6. U.S. Department of Health, Education, and Welfare, "Protection of Human Subjects: Research Involving Children," *Federal Register* 43: 31786–31794 (July 21, 1978).

7. William J. Curran and Henry K. Beecher, "Experimentation in Children: A Reexamination of Legal Ethical Principles," *Journal of the American Medical Association* 210: 77–78 (October 6, 1969).

8. Ibid., p. 77.

9. National Commission for the Protection of Human Subjects of Biomedical and Behavioral Research, *Report and Recommendations: Research Involving Children*, DHEW Publication No. (OS) 77–0004 (Washington, D.C.: U.S. Government Printing Office, September 1977), pp. 83–84.

10. S. Fine, *Laissiez Faire and the General Welfare State: A Study of Conflict in American Thought, 1865–1901* (Ann Arbor: The University of Michigan Press, 1967), pp. 352–372.

11. Alexander M. Capron, "Legal Definition of Death," in Julius Korern, *Brain Death: Interrelated Medical and Social Issues* (New York: The New York Academy of Sciences, 1978), pp. 349–362.

12. Having reviewed the literature regarding legal and ethical aspects of research involving children, the authors encourage any perplexed readers to see the Curran and Beecher paper, "Experimentation in Children," (Note No. 7 above). Their discussion contains suggestions for standards involving research and children that are extremely helpful conceptually and factually.

13. Mnookin, p. 7.

14. "The Nuremberg Code," p. 181.

15. Ibid., p. 182.

16. R.W. Wentz, *Readings on Ethical and Social Issues in Biomedicine* (Englewood Cliffs, N.J.: Prentice–Hall, Inc., 1973), pp. 1–12.

17. Ibid.

18. World Medical Association, *Declaration of Helsinki: Recommendations Guiding Medical Doctors in Biomedical Research Involving Human Subjects* (Helsinki, 1964; revised, Tokyo, 1975), in Reiser, Dyck, and Curran, *Ethics in Medicine*, pp. 328–329.

19. Curran and Beecher, p. 80.

20. Ibid.

21. Ibid.

22. Ibid.

23. Henry K. Beecher, "Ethics and Clinical Research," *New England Journal of Medicine* 274: 1354–1360 (1966).

24. Ibid., p. 1354.

25. U.S. Department of Health, Education, and Welfare, "Protection of Human Subjects, Policies and Procedures," *Federal Register* 39: 31742 (November 16, 1973).

26. U.S. Department of Health, Education, and Welfare, "Protection of Human Subjects: Research Involving Children."

27. World Medical Association, p. 329.

28. Ibid.

29. Ibid.

30. Kenneth J. Ryan, Letter to Secretary Califano (personal correspondence, 1978); Albert J. Solnit, Letter to Secretary Califano (personal correspondence, September 18, 1978); Robert J. Levine, "Research Involving Children: The National Commission's Report," *Clinical Research* 26: 61–66 (1978); James J. McCartney, "Research on Children: National Commission Says 'Yes, If ...,' " *Hastings Center Report* 8: 26–31 (October 1978); Albert R. Jonsen, "Research Involving Children: Recommendations of the National Commission for the Protection of Human Subjects of Biomedical and Behavioral Research," *Pediatrics* 62: 131–136 (1978).

31. Jonsen, p. 136.

32. McCartney, p. 27.

33. Jonsen, p. 135.

34. Solnit, p. 2.

35. Ibid.

36. Ryan.

37. Paul Ramsey, "The Enforcement of Morals: Non–Therapeutic Research on Children," *Hastings Center Report* 6: 21–30 (August 1976).

38. Richard A. McCormick, "Experimentation in Children: Sharing in Sociality," *Hastings Center Report* 6: 41–46 (December 1976).

39. Ramsey.

40. McCormick, p. 42.

41. Ibid.

42. K. Danner Clouser, "Medical Ethics: Some Uses, Abuses, and Limitations," *New England Journal of Medicine* 293: 384–387 (August 21, 1975).

43. Bradford H. Gray, Robert A. Cook, and Arnold S. Tannenbaum, "Research Involving Human Subjects: The Performance of Institutional Review Boards," *Science* 201: 1094–1101 (September 22, 1978); Robert M. Veatch, "The National Commission on IRBs: An Evolutionary Approach," *Hastings Center Report* 9: 22–28 (February 1979).

44. National Commission for the Protection of Human Subjects of Biomedical and Behavioral Research, *Report and Recommendations: Institutional Review Boards*, DHEW Publication No. (OS) 78–0008 (Washington, D.C.: U.S. Government Printing Office, September 1978), pp. 55–89.

45. Gray, Cook, and Tannenbaum.
46. Ibid., p. 1101.
47. Sissela Bok, "Freedom and Risk," *Daedalus* 107: 115–127 (1978).
48. Ibid.
49. Curran and Beecher.
50. N. Frost, "A Surrogate System for Informed Consent," *Journal of the American Medical Association* 233: 800–803 (August 18, 1975).
51. Ibid.

21 ARGUING THE MORALITY OF GENETIC ENGINEERING

Daniel Callahan, Ph. D.

Of all the issues to emerge from biomedical research since the Second World War, that of genetic engineering has taken on a special symbolic significance. The term has never had a strict technical meaning; indeed, many scientists dislike it intensely. Loosely speaking, it has been used to refer to a wide range of possible and actual scientific breakthroughs—in vitro fertilization and cloning (which belong to the domain of reproductive biology), genetic manipulation and recombinant DNA (where the term engineering is more appropriate), and the development of new forms of human life (which is genetic engineering carried to the extreme of science fiction). Prenatal diagnosis and mass genetic screening have also often been included on the roster. Despite the broadness of the term, however, it does serve well enough to describe that aspect of the biological revolution that has elicited the most severe chills for some and thrills for others—a direct intervention into either the processes of procreation and reproduction or into the human genetic makeup.

It is much too early to pass any full historical judgment on the moral debate about genetic engineering. Nonetheless, two conclusions seem so far to be almost inescapable. The first is that both the scientific community and the general public are more prepared than

An earlier, shorter version of this chapter appeared under the title "The Moral Career of Genetic Engineering," *Hastings Center Report* 9: 9, 21 (April 1979).

ever to go ahead with it. If there ever was a technological backlash in this country, it has been a fitful and essentially literary movement, having little impact on the mainstream of scientific and technological research. To be sure, there have been commissions, regulations, hearings, and acrimonious debate; and they have probably slowed the momentum. But if one tries to find concrete examples of possible lines of research that have been stopped and remain so, hardly a single example could be identified. The only two possible exceptions are some forms of recombinant DNA research still banned by U.S. Department of Health and Human Services (DHHS) regulations (which seem destined not to last long in any case) and the static state of cloning research (which probably reflects lack of scientific interest rather than the force of public opposition).

Moreover, whenever there has been a scientific breakthrough, the general reaction has been one of wondrous excitement—in the scientific no less than the public media. Ethical reservations or objections voiced prior to the breakthrough have been swept away with an astonishing rapidity once the actual events took place. In the late 1960s and early 1970s, there was both a scientific and a public outcry against the reported efforts to develop in vitro fertilization (i.e., fertilization, or conception, that occurs outside of a woman's body); a number of articles were published that listed a variety of moral objections to it. Given that negative response, some might confidently have predicted that in vitro fertilization research would not go forward and, if it did, that it would receive little if any support. Little was heard about the matter for over five years. But the research was—quietly—going forward, and when Louise Brown was born in July 1978, the reaction was one of almost unbridled enthusiasm. The combination of a healthy baby, overjoyed parents, and the successful achievement of a difficult technological feat easily triumphed over moral reservations. The seductive charm of scientific prestidigitation had captivated the public once again.

A second and, in the author's opinion, equally inescapable conclusion is that those opposed to genetic engineering have not been able to mount generally persuasive arguments. A distinction is in order here, however, between a good argument and a generally persuasive argument. The latter, in addition to having a logical consistency, has a powerful emotional attractiveness—one sufficient to induce people to act or not act.

The key to the difference among the kinds of arguments lies in the cultural power of their premises. Many of the most articulate opponents of genetic engineering make use of moral premises and modes of moral reasoning that no longer carry very much cultural weight.[a] Some argue from a conservative theological point of view. Such a perspective does not carry a very strong weight in the scientific or intellectual community regardless of the force it may still retain in the general American culture.

Other skeptics about the morality of genetic engineering are prone to return to an analysis of nature, some by a recourse to classical sources in Plato and Aristotle and others by a return to natural law theory. While these modes of moral analysis still have their adherents, they are considerably removed from the philosophical and scientific mainstream. Although some can both understand and respond with pleasure to these modes of reasoning—if only because they were part of their intellectual training—most contemporary intellectuals cannot. It is not so much that their arguments are contended with and then rejected; instead, it is that these modes of argumentation are usually not at all understood and are thus bypassed. Their great strength is that they stem from long-established traditions, have behind them centuries of elaboration, and have built within them a broad sense of the human community and of the human good. Yet perversely, it seems as if what ought to be the strongest grounds of support for them are precisely those that are held against them. They are viewed to be anachronistic and long discredited. Even when hesitancies and reservations are expressed that do not explicitly use the language either of religion or of nature, there is a strong tendency among many to detect an implicit bias in that direction and therefore to dismiss worries out of hand because that appears to be their source. Some of the most articulate doubters about the wisdom of recombinant DNA research were accused of harboring religious views (of an unspecified kind)—a charge thought sufficient, without further elaboration, to locate the source of their errors.

Yet, if a still strong bias toward scientific advancement and a strong cultural resistance to forms of moral argumentation that draw upon older premises and ways of looking at the world help to explain much of the reaction to moral questions of genetic engineering, then there is still a third, and possibly even more powerful, cultural force operating. For purposes of discussion, albeit a crude and imprecise name, this third force may be called a civil liberties ethic. In such an

---

a. Cultural weight is not equivalent to intellectual or philosophical weight.

444 RESEARCH: BENEFITS FOR WHOM?

ethic, one can find moral premises that appear culturally persuasive in our society and a language with which a large number of people, particularly in the scientific and legislative communities, feel particularly comfortable.

Within this so-called civil liberties ethic, there are five moral premises that can be discerned. It is worth noting that while some of them have received a great deal of attention on the part of moral philosophers and moral theologians, others represent a way of talking about morality that has not been common to academic moral discourse. Grouped together, however, they have been decisive in removing most serious moral obstacles to the development of genetic engineering and have by and large been equally decisive in providing a way of resolving most disputes—and resolving them in one direction only, toward that of greater permissiveness.

The first principle is that of individual liberty, encompassing not only a right to be left alone, but also a right to seek that which one desires if there is no clearly demonstrable harm to others. When this principle is invoked—whether as an argument for the rights of individuals to make use of in vitro fertilization or prenatal diagnosis or for the right of scientists to pursue recombinant DNA research—the burden of proof almost automatically falls on those who would claim that an exercise of individual liberty will pose harm to others. In other words, if I want to stand in the way of your doing what you want to do, then it is up to me either to prove that you are doing direct harm to me or that you are doing direct harm to some third party for whom we all ought to have a responsibility.

The second is the principle of risk–benefit analysis. In matters of uncertainty, risks and benefits are to be compared and moral actions determined by the outcomes of the equation. Technically, of course, risk–benefit analysis in its historical development is supposed to be only a value-free methodology. However, it has increasingly come to have the status of a moral principle in that all proposed actions ought to be judged in terms of their comparative risks and benefits. This means that an essentially consequentialist mode of moral reasoning has come to be built into the principle; morality is determined by the outcomes, or consequences, of choices. Moreover, this principle relates closely to the first principle in an important respect—the burden of proof is normally placed on those who argue from the risk side. They must prove, in the face of those who would pursue benefits, that risks will outweigh benefits. The normal bias is in favor of pursuing benefits—especially when particular individuals urge that the benefits they seek are for their own welfare or for the welfare of others. The bias in favor of seeking benefits has been a powerful impetus to researchers in the case of in vitro fertilization and recombinant DNA. In both cases, it has been up to those who allege risk to prove their point and to prove it with a degree of precision not demanded of those who envision benefits.

The third principle is that it is always better to attempt to do good than to try to avoid harm. Put more strongly, a failure to pursue the good (i.e., benefits) is taken to be a form of doing harm or seen as a sin of omission. Hence, the traditional principle of medical ethics—do no harm—is now viewed, contrary to its original meaning, to be a positive mandate to attempt to do good. Thus, many have argued that it would be a moral failure of the first order not to pursue recombinant DNA research, an omission that would deny a number of potential goods to future generations.

The fourth principle is that it is irresponsible not to take advantage of the new biomedical technologies. If a technology exists, and if it promises some benefits to someone, then it ought to be employed. The development of prenatal diagnosis would serve as a good example of such a situation. A decade ago, when prenatal diagnosis was still in its infancy, it was contended that the research should proceed in order to provide a wider range of options to those bearing children—the option of having foreknowledge of whether a fetus was defective and, with that knowledge in hand, the possibility of taking action to avoid giving birth to a defective child. It was strongly contended that use of the technology would be voluntary only, with no social pressure on people one way or the other. Yet as the technology has developed and has proved to be safe, the original idea of presenting new choices only has weakened considerably. There is now exceedingly strong social pressure on women to avail themselves of prenatal diagnosis; it is increasingly suggested that it would be morally irresponsible for them not to do so. Not surprisingly, the widespread efforts to educate women about the advantages and availability of prenatal diagnosis have also had the effect of, if anything, inducing an even greater anxiety about the dangers of bearing defective children than was the case in the past.

The fifth principle is that for public policy purposes, compromise solutions should always be sought, rather than solutions that decisively support one moral side or the other in public debates. Or perhaps put more accurately, the most inevitable effect of debates on genetic engineering and public policy is that of insuring middle ground solutions—namely, solutions that put aside the more extreme views and that find a way of encompassing the widest, not the narrowest, range of positions. Thus, it was hardly a surprise that the National Institutes of Health guidelines on recombinant DNA suggested a middle ground between those who felt that research should be halted altogether and those who denied there was any problem whatsoever. The compromise took the form of a set of regulations forcing caution and care—a prudent enough solution, but one that inevitably satisfied neither of the two extreme parties and at the same time allowed research to continue.

It is beyond the scope of this chapter to attempt a specific critique of each of the five cited principles. Nonetheless, it is worth noting the kind of policy bias they produce when taken together and how some of them very systematically overturn more well-established moral principles. The primary weakness of the first principle is that it fails to allow the posing of larger questions about the good of the human community or society as a whole. It focuses only on the good of individuals; at best, the community is viewed only in terms of potential harms to that community. Its working assumption is that the good of individuals, and in particular the maximization of the liberty of individuals, is tantamount to the good of the community as a whole—a very strong, classically liberal bias.

The major shortcoming of the second principle is that by requiring that all possibilities be put on a balance scale of risks and benefits, it forces an ignoring of that very strong moral tradition that would argue that some acts ought not to be conducted regardless of beneficial consequences. Risk–benefit analysis systematically excludes that moral option, and inevitably favors a utilitarian bias toward the greatest good of the greatest number. In principle, of course, risk–benefit analysis is supposed to encompass strongly held social and moral values. But in practice it is a technique that has proved very poor at quantifying moral values, and thus its tendency is simply to omit them from the equation altogether. Risk–benefit analysts deny that such omissions should occur, but it is extraordinarily difficult to find cases in which moral values have been built into risk–benefit analyses.

The main shortcoming of the third principle is that it takes a very firm and well-established principle—do no harm—and turns that principle on its head. For reasons rarely made clear, the assumption is that since scientific research has led to progress in the past and since it is possible to envisage benefits from present research, it would be a moral failure not to proceed apace. Thus, not acting becomes a form of doing harm, and the burden of proof is placed on those who express doubts and skepticism about the pursuit of benefits. It is further assumed that the greatest good of the greatest number always requires trying to do away with evil in the world, whether it be illness or some other things harmful to human beings.

The obvious shortcoming of the fourth principle is that it systematically overthrows the very premise upon which new technologies were developed in the first place, that of providing people with a wider range of choices. Those who hold this principle fail to realize the force of the technological imperative: New technologies tend in the long run to eliminate, not increase, choices. The weakness of the fifth principle is that it forces solutions that systematically exclude those viewpoints not amenable to compromise. Effective public policy is not that policy that reflects the truth of the human condition, but that policy with which most people will find it possible to live.

The above arguments are not meant to imply that all of those principles are wrong. The great difficulty is that each contains a very powerful grain of truth. Surely one ought to respect individual liberty, and just as surely one ought to try to make some comparison of risks and benefits before one acts. Moreover, seeking to reduce illness and death is surely a worthy enough goal, just as in many cases it would be irresponsible for people not to take advantage of medical technologies (e.g., parents ought to take advantage of immunization programs for their children). In a democratic society, policies should be developed that not only try to promote the common good, but that also represent a way in which people can live in some peace together.

The major point is that when these principles are employed together (as they normally are), they create an enormous bias in the direction of technological advancement and development. They place a heavy burden of proof upon those skeptical of pursuing new benefits and force those who perceive possible harms to provide far more solid evidence than those who perceive possible benefits. Furthermore, since none of the principles contain within them any way of determining what is actually good for individuals—much less the community as a whole—they have a very strong tendency to push all moral arguments based on deeper notions of the human good to one side.

The most important characteristic of those traditions cited earlier as no longer carrying important cultural weight was that they sought to discover that which is inherently good for human beings. In many ways, to be sure, we are all beneficiaries of the more recent tradition expressed by the five principles—a tradition that is highly resistant to totalitarian governments and no less resistant to the imposition of the values of one group on other groups.

Nonetheless, the price to be paid for that gain is an extreme moral thinness. In what does the nature of human happiness consist? What is the most appropriate and valuable direction that science as a whole should take? What are the best ends to which human freedom ought to be directed? These are critical questions, but none of the five principles described encourages the asking of such questions, none has any effective means of helping us to find answers to such questions. Yet unless at least some tentative answers to these larger questions can be found, there will be absolutely no way of putting the ever-increasing number of specific questions about genetic engineering into any wider moral context. Each new scientific development will simply be treated in isolation from all others. Furthermore, aggregating the principles will guarantee that almost any conceivable line of research will advance—if only because every conceivable line of research is likely to benefit someone, if only the researchers themselves.

In the instance of most other nongenetic technologies, such as the automobile, the widespread use of chemicals, or the artificial respirator, historical experience has tempered much of the early enthusiasm. However, all of the developments in genetic engineering are very recent, and there has been no time to measure their long-term impact. Given that which is known about other, older technologies, one might wonder why the built-in skepticism now applied to them has never been brought to the alleged benefits of the developments in genetic engineering. One should now be able to see how the use of the five principles cited above has worked in other technological areas and then question whether they are likely to be any more effective in the area of genetic engineering.

The present excessive economic dependence upon the automobile has its historical roots in the premise that individuals ought to have a choice about their mode of transportation. No one could have proved in the early days of the automobile that that would turn out to be a partially mistaken premise. Only now can one acknowledge that the cumulative impact of the automobile has created enormous problems for society—problems that threaten the common good—however difficult it would be to prove that any one individual's automobile works direct harm on any other individual. The development of nuclear energy proceeded on the assumption that the potential benefits far outweighed the risks; it is only now that many are beginning to see that the overall risks in developing nuclear energy may be greater than the potential good that might be done by any given single nuclear power plant.

As pessimistic as the tone of these comments, I am not opposed to the development of genetic engineering in many cases. There have been some important gains in the development of prenatal diagnosis, and the emergence of in vitro fertilization will make it possible for many women for whom that option would otherwise have been closed forever to bear children. However, it is instead the cumulative impact of the contemporary form of moral reasoning that is of greatest concern. It provides very few decisive means of stopping any technology; it forces a narrow rather than a broad view of human welfare; and it systematically excludes viewpoints that might provide a deeper mode of moral analysis. That may be an important moral loss.

ABBREVIATIONS

ACHA	American College Health Association
ACLU	American Civil Liberties Union
AFDC	Aid to Families with Dependent Children
AHA	American Hospital Association
AHPA	American Health Planning Association
AICP	American Institute of Certified Planners
ALI	American Law Institute
AMA	American Medical Association
AMRA	American Medical Record Association
ANA	American Nurses Association
APA	American Psychological Association
	American Psychiatric Association
AVS	Association for Voluntary Sterilization
BC/BS	Blue Cross/Blue Shield (the Blues)
CIA	Central Intelligence Agency
CON	Certificate of Need
D	Democrat
DHEW	U.S. Department of Health, Education, and Welfare
DHHS	U.S. Department of Health and Human Services
DNA	Deoxyribonucleic Acid (Double Helix)
FBI	Federal Bureau of Investigation
FOIA	Freedom of Information Act

451

GNP	Gross National Product
HMO	Health Maintenance Organization
HSA	Health Systems Agency
IRB	Institutional Review Board
JCAH	Joint Commission on Accreditation of Hospitals
NARAL	National Abortion Rights Action League
NHI	National Health Insurance
NHS	National Health Service
NIH	National Institutes of Health
PCMS	Patient Care Management Systems
PHS	U.S. Public Health Service
PL	Public Law
PROMIS	Problem Oriented Medical Information System
PSRO	Professional Standards Review Organization
R	Republican
TSD	Tay Sach's Disease
UNH	University of New Hampshire
UR	Utilization Review
US	United States
USSR	Union Soviet Socialist Republic
v.	versus
WPPHC	Western Pennsylvania Public Health Council, Inc.
ZPG	Zero Population Growth, Inc.

INDEX

Abortion, 304, 306-307, 313-314, 320, 339, 375-394
  therapeutic, 348, 349, 351, 353, 355. *See also* Laws and legal doctrine
Advocates, patient, 272, 367, 432
  college health services as, 239
  long-term care administrators as, 250, 253-254, 255, 256-257
Age and aging, 247, 252-253, 255, 296, 318. *See also* Elderly
Agencies, 68, 69-70, 143, 163-164, 174
Aggregate data, 229-231
Aggregate health, 57-59, 68-69, 71
Aid to Families with Dependent Children, 384-385
Alienation, health consequences of, 102
American Association for Hospital Consultants, 80
American Civil Liberties Union, 284, 377, 383
  The Rights of Hospital Patients, 5
American College Health Association, 224, 225, 227, 230, 237
American College of Hospital Administrators, 80

American College of Obstetricians and Gynecologists, 370
American Health Planning Association, 80, 82
American Hospital Association, 5, 154, 165
American Institute of Certified Planners, 80-82
American Law Institute, 377, 379, 383
American Medical Association
  Principles of Medical Ethics, 5, 160-161, 165, 221-222, 223, 426
American Medical Record Association, 154n, 156
  "The Confidentiality of Medical Information," 156
American Psychiatric Association, 224
American Psychological Association, 401, 403, 404-405
Amniocentesis, 346
Anarchy, State, and Utopia (Nozick), 55, 56
Annas, G., 345
Antenatal diagnosis, 348, 349, 351, 355, 445
Antinatalism, 327, 328

453

456   INDEX

Crisis therapy, 291
Cultural weight of arguments,
442–444, 448
Curran, William J., 226, 232, 421,
422–423, 426, 434
Curreri, Anthony, 188

Daly, Herman, 115, 116
Dangerousness to others, 274–276,
279
Dangerousness to self, 277–278, 289
Death and dying, 11–12
and decisionmaking, 37–39
and proxy decisionmaking, 212–213
Death of Ivan Illich, The (Tolstoy),
183
Debriefing, 406–407, 409, 412, 413,
415, 416, 417
Decent minimum principle, 10
Deception in research, 403–404, 405,
406, 409–410, 411-417
Decisionmaking, health care, 49,
74–79, 321, 350
class bias in, 101–102
and government intervention, 305
medical ethic principles used in, 16
in physician–patient relationship,
111, 113, 114, 116, 136–140,
141–143, 146–147, 365, 368,
371–372. *See also* Physician or
provider–patient relationship,
decisional authority in
by proxy, 211–213, 367–368
See also Informed consent; Policymaking, public
Dehoaxing, 413
Deinstitutionalization, 262
de la Cruz, F., 345
Demand for health care, 30–32,
317–318
Demand side regulation, 122, 127,
128–132
Deontological approach to ethics, 25,
26, 304
Deprofessionalization, 109, 112
Dershowitz, A.M., 289
Desai, Prime Minister, 146
Desensitization, 413
Desires and needs, 63–64
Deviance, definition of, 296–297
Diagnosis, psychiatric, 280, 289, 290,
291–292, 298

Dignity, 251, 252–253
Disclosure
of medical records. *See* Medical
records
standards of. *See* Information
Discriminatory regulations, 363, 365,
367, 369, 370
and abortion, 375–376, 381–382,
384–386, 389, 391–394
Dix, Dorothea, 262
Doe v. *Bolton*, 375, 378
Donaldson, Kenneth, 263
Dual relationships, 415–416
Due process, 273, 276, 289
Dyck, Arthur, 321

Eagleton, Senator Thomas, 165,
261–262
Eastman, David, 18
Economics
conservative, 107–108
liberal, 109–110
and medical ethics, 19–20
Economic stability
and capitalism, 96, 109, 112–113
desire for, 387, 390
and health status, 96–97, 112–113
Economic system
effect on health policy, 50, 93,
113–114, 115
and health status, 93–107, 111–113
and moral values, 390
Education, 103–104, 339, 350
in medical ethics, 77–79, 157
Efficiency
and equity, 64, 68–69, 71
as organizational goal, 250
in psychiatry, 292–293, 295, 298
Egalitarianism, 10, 41
and distribution of health care,
61–67, 89
and public health policy, 67–72,
114–117
Eisenhower, President Dwight D., 309
Eisner, M.S., 412
Elbing, J. and C., 251
Elderly
health care for, 318
mental health care needs of, 292,
294, 296
population increase in, 316–317

458   INDEX

Goldman, Marshall, 105
Government intervention, 109–110,
    113, 143, 146, 305. See also
    Regulation, government
Great Britain, 103
Grossman, Michael, 103
Gunn, S.P., 413–414
Gustafsone, J.M., 345

Harvard Medical School, 425
Hayden, Trudy, 161, 162
Health education, 136–144, 146, 147
Health ethics, 5–6
Health insurance, 122, 128–132
Health Maintenance Organizations,
    69, 129–130
Health planners, 50, 77, 79–82
Health status and health
    and behavior, 141–143, 146–147
    and the economic system, 93–107,
    111–113, 116
    and the environment, 105–107, 141
    as a value, 246
Health Systems Agencies, 69, 123,
    124
Hearings, commitment, 269, 270,
    271, 273, 275, 276, 277, 280
Hellegers, André R., 88, 363
Helsinki Declaration
    of 1961, 35, 425–426
    of 1974, 35, 427
Herbert, Victor, 257
Hill–Burton era, 85
Hill–Burton Hospital Construction
    and Survey Act, 54, 77
Hiller, Marc D., 18
Hilton, Bruce, et al., 345
Hippocratic Oath, 5, 11
    individualistic bias of, 56
    and patient privacy, 157, 160, 221,
    223
    and truth telling, 185, 190
Hollingshead, A.B., 293
Holmes, D.S., 413
Holmes, Oliver Wendell, 184
Hospital(s), 214, 246
    abortion services in, 381, 383
    administrators of, 126
    cost containment and, 123–132
    and medical records, 154–159,
    164–171, 172, 175, 178
    state mental, 293–294

Hospital bed allocation model, 85
Hospitalization, 127, 293–294, 296
Human Experimentation.
    See Research subjects
Hume, David, 26
Hyde Amendment, 375–376,
    382–386, 387–389, 391–394
Hyde, Representative Henry, 382
Hypothyroidism, 346n.b
Hysterectomy, contraceptive,
    369–370

Illich, Ivan, 112
    Medical Nemesis, 108–109
Immigration, 310, 312, 337–339,
    341
Incentives, 331–332
Individual rights, 55–56, 220–221,
    304, 362, 379, 389, 421
    and egalitarianism, 64–66
    principle of, 108. See also
    Entitlement principle
    v. social benefits, 40–41, 229–230,
    299–300, 353, 390, 391,
    399–400, 431–432
Industrialization, 105, 112
Inequalities, social and economic
    and health care distribution,
    98–100, 101–102, 113–114,
    293–294
    and health status, 99–100, 102,
    103–104, 106–107, 112–113, 116
    and Rawlsian theory, 60–61, 89.
    See also Rawls, John and Rawl-
    sian theory
Information
    disclosure of, in psychiatric inter-
    views, 289–290
    disclosure of, to research subjects,
    405–406. See also Deception in
    research
    gathering of, and privacy, 163–164,
    172–173, 174, 177, 226, 228,
    229–231
    and policymaking, 136–138,
    Fig. 6–1, 143, 146
    and truth telling, 186
Informed consent, 5, 151, 197–215,
    285–286
    and competency, 38–39, 199,
    208–209, 234–235, 254, 367–368

460   INDEX

and the economic system, 93,
98–102, 113–114
in egalitarian thinking, 61–72, 89
in liberal thinking, 109, 113–114
by market forces, 127–128, 132
models for the, 55–62, 89
in psychiatric care, 293–296
Respect, 251–252
Responsibility, personal, 390
Ricardo, David, 107–108
Rights, 221. *See also* Individual rights;
Patients' rights
Rights and Rules (UNH), 239
Rights of Hospital Patients, The
(ACLU), 5
Rights of the unborn child, 376
Right to health care, 10, 48, 53–72
Right to life. *See* Sanctity of life
theory
Right to truth, patients', 187
Risk(s)
age as, 253
analysis of, 58–59, 145–146
and decisionmaking, 135, 145–146
disclosure of, in informed consent,
200, 204, 205, 211, 406,
408–410, 416, 417
disclosure of, to research subjects,
406, 408–410
to research subjects, 423, 427, 429,
432, 433–434, 435–436
voluntary, 65
Risk–benefit ratios, 145–146, 269,
435–436, 444–445, 446
Robbins, R., 345
Robinson, W.J., 376
Rockefeller, Governor Nelson, 377n
Roe v. *Wade*, 375, 378, 382
*Role of Medicine: Dream, Mirage or
Nemesis, The* (McKeown), 95
Role-playing, 411–412, 414
Roles, women's access to, 329, 330,
333, 334, 341–342
Rosenthal, Gerald, 110, 111
Roth, Loren H., 229, 275
Rule, James, et al.: *The Politics of
Privacy*, 159

Sade, Robert, 56, 60
Safeguarded paternalism, 278
*Saikewicz Superintendent of Belcher-
town State School* v., 212
Salkever, David S., 99, 124

Samp, Robert, 188
Samuelson, Paul, 109
Sanctity of life theory, 38, 304,
379–380, 382, 390, 392–393,
394
Sanger, Margaret, 333–334
Schizophrenia, 297
Schizophrenogenic mother, 297
Schloendorff v. *New York Hospital*,
160
Schweiker, Richard S., 394
Scientific reasoning, 86–87
Scientific tradition, 83, 84–85
Seavey, John W., 18
Security and survival, 320, 321
Seeman, J., 411, 413
Segregation of dangerous patients,
275
Self-care, 108–109, 111–112,
115–116, 140, 141
Self-determination. *See* Autonomy
Self-help, 298
Self-incrimination and involuntary
commitment, 289
Seskin, Eugene, 106
Severity of mental illness and distri-
bution of care, 294
Sex education, 339
Shaw, A., 13
Shipley, T., 411, 413
Sickle cell disease, 346, 347–348,
350–351
screening for, 353–355, 358
Sickle Cell Foundation, 354
Slaby, Andrew E., 236, 390
Smith, Adam, 107–108
Social benefits v. individual rights,
40–41, 229–230, 299–300, 353,
390, 391, 399–400, 431–432
Social costs, 121, 124–125, 132, 133,
390, 391
of deception, 189–190
Social need for behavioral control,
299–300
Social pressures, 328–330, 333–334
Social reform tradition in health plan-
ning, 83–84
Social Security Administration, 159
Socioeconomic status, 99, 292, 350
Solnit, Albert J., 430
Sonography, 346n.c
Soviet Union, abuse of psychiatry in,
296

466   INDEX

ABOUT THE EDITOR

Marc D. Hiller is an assistant professor in the Health Administration and Planning Program in the School of Health Studies at the University of New Hampshire (UNH). Before coming to UNH in early 1979, he was on the faculty of the Long Term Care Unit of the Department of Health Services Administration of the Graduate School of Public Health at the University of Pittsburgh, where he also served on its Committee on Research Involving Human Volunteers and on the University Health Center of Pittsburgh's Task Force on Human Values.

Maintaining an interdisciplinary public health orientation, Dr. Hiller is deeply involved in public policy issues and decisionmaking related to ethics and health care. His publications and other academic activities reflect a wide range of scholarly interests in health policy and planning. Among his responsibilities since joining the UNH faculty, he teaches courses in medical ethics, and the law, health planning, and health care systems. He chairs the University's Health Services Advisory Committee and serves on the UNH Institutional Review Board for the Protection of Human Subjects. Dr. Hiller is engaged in health affairs at the local, state, and national levels and serves in many capacities in numerous professional associations.

467

LIST OF CONTRIBUTORS

Ralph L. Andreano, Ph.D.
Chairman and Professor
Department of Economics
University of Wisconsin
Madison, WI

Vivian Beyda, M.P.H.
Doctoral Candidate
Department of Health Services
  Administration
Graduate School of Public
  Health
University of Pittsburgh
Pittsburgh, PA

Daniel Callahan, Ph.D.
Director
The Hastings Center
Institute of Society, Ethics, and
  the Life Sciences
Hastings-on-Hudson, NY

Betty L. Gonzales, R.N.
Deputy Director of National
  Programs
Association for Voluntary
  Sterilization, Inc.
New York, NY

Lawrence W. Green, Dr.P.H.
Director
Office of Health Information,
  Health Promotion, and Physical
  Fitness and Sports Medicine
Public Health Service
U.S. Department of Health and
  Human Services
Washington, D.C.

Ronald M. Green, Ph.D.
Associate Professor, Ethics
Department of Religion
Dartmouth College
Hanover, NH

Stephen J. Haines, M.D.
Chief Resident
Department of Neurological
  Surgery
School of Medicine
University of Pittsburgh
Pittsburgh, PA

Marc D. Hiller, Dr.P.H.
Assistant Professor
Health Administration and
  Planning Program
School of Health Studies
University of New Hampshire
Durham, NH

Richard J. Kaufman, Ph.D.
Assistant Professor
Department of Social Services
University of New Hampshire
Durham, NH

Annabelle L. Kleppick, Ph.D.
Director and Research Associate
  Professor
Long Term Care Unit
Department of Health Services
  Administration
Graduate School of Public Health
University of Pittsburgh
Pittsburgh, PA

Michael E. Kraft, Ph.D.
Associate Professor of Political
  Science and Public and
  Environmental Administration
University of Wisconsin at
  Green Bay
Green Bay, WI

Alan Meisel, J.D.
Associate Professor of Law
  and Psychiatry
School of Law and
School of Medicine
University of Pittsburgh
Pittsburgh, PA

Joseph C. Morreale, Ph.D.
Associate Professor of Economics
  and Director
Community, Health, Regional, and
  Environmental Studies Program
Bard College
Annandale-on-Hudson, NY

Basil J.F. Mott, Ph.D.
Dean
School of Health Studies
University of New Hampshire
Durham, NH

Deborah Oakley, Ph.D.
Assistant Professor of Nursing
School of Nursing
The University of Michigan
Ann Arbor, MI

Michael J. O'Sullivan, Dr.P.H.
Assistant Professor
Health Administration and
  Planning Program
School of Health Studies
University of New Hampshire
Durham, NH

Rosa Lynn Pinkus, Ph.D.
Assistant Professor of
  Neurosurgery
Department of Neurological
  Surgery
School of Medicine
University of Pittsburgh
Pittsburgh, PA

Loren H. Roth, M.D., M.P.H.
Director, Law and Psychiatry
  Program
Western Psychiatric Institute
  and Clinic
and
Associate Professor of Psychiatry
Department of Psychiatry
School of Medicine
University of Pittsburgh
Pittsburgh, PA

Joseph R. Sanders, Ph.D.
Administrative Officer for Ethics
American Psychological Association
Washington, D.C.

Robert W. Sansoucie, M.Div.
United Church of Christ
and
Lecturer
American Business Institute
New York, NY

Andrew E. Slaby, M.D., Ph.D.,
   M.P.H.
Psychiatrist-in-Chief
Rhode Island Hospital
and
Professor of Psychiatry and Human
   Behavior
Brown University
Providence, RI

Mark W. Steele, M.D.
Director, Division of Medical
   Genetics
Children's Hospital of Pittsburgh
and
Associate Professor of Pediatrics
Department of Pediatrics
School of Medicine
University of Pittsburgh
Pittsburgh, PA

Laurence R. Tancredi, M.D., J.D.
Associate Professor of Law and
   Psychiatry
School of Medicine and
School of Law
New York University
New York, NY

Robert M. Veatch, Ph.D.
Professor of Medical Ethics
The Joseph and Rose Kennedy
   Institute of Ethics
Georgetown University
Washington, D.C.

Harold R. Wilde, Ph.D.
Special Assistant
University of Wisconsin System
Commissioner of Insurance (former)
State of Wisconsin
Madison, WI